Ebenezer Mission Station, 1863–1873
THE DIARY OF MISSIONARIES
ADOLF AND POLLY HARTMANN

Aboriginal History Incorporated
Aboriginal History Inc. is a part of the Australian Centre for Indigenous History, Research School of Social Sciences, The Australian National University, and gratefully acknowledges the support of the School of History and the National Centre for Indigenous Studies, The Australian National University. Aboriginal History Inc. is administered by an Editorial Board which is responsible for all unsigned material. Views and opinions expressed by the author are not necessarily shared by Board members.

Contacting Aboriginal History
All correspondence should be addressed to the Editors, Aboriginal History Inc., ACIH, School of History, Research School of Social Sciences, ANU RSSS Building, The Australian National University, Canberra ACT 2600, or aboriginalhistoryinc@gmail.com.

WARNING: Readers are notified that this publication may contain names or images of deceased persons.

Ebenezer Mission Station, 1863–1873

THE DIARY OF MISSIONARIES
ADOLF AND POLLY HARTMANN

EDITED BY
FELICITY JENSZ

ANU PRESS

Published by ANU Press and Aboriginal History Inc.
The Australian National University
Canberra ACT 2600, Australia
Email: anupress@anu.edu.au

Available to download for free at press.anu.edu.au

ISBN (print): 9781760465674
ISBN (online): 9781760465681

WorldCat (print): 1381112514
WorldCat (online): 1381113757

DOI: 10.22459/EMS.2023

This title is published under a Creative Commons Attribution-NonCommercial-NoDerivatives 4.0 International (CC BY-NC-ND 4.0) licence.

The full licence terms are available at creativecommons.org/licenses/by-nc-nd/4.0/legalcode

Cover design and layout by ANU Press. Cover image: View of Ebenezer, Victoria, c. 1862 (TS Bd.21.097.b, Unitätsarchiv; Herrnhut).

This book is published under the aegis of the Aboriginal History editorial board of ANU Press.

This edition © 2023 ANU Press and Aboriginal History Inc.

Contents

Foreword	vii
Acknowledgements	ix
List of figures	xi
Abbreviations and notes	xiii
Introduction	1
Timeline of diary	49
Adolf and Mary (known as Polly) Hartmann's Diary, 1863–1873	51
Selected bibliography	285
Index	297

Foreword

My name is Aunty Hazel McDonald. I am a Wotjobaluk elder. My ties to the Ebenezer mission are through my family. My family are the Marks family, who lived on the reserve at Antwerp with other families, such as the Harrisons, the Kennedys.

Growing up, we were always told about Ebenezer mission. Told that missionaries were not doing any good for anyone. They had our people on the mission, making them into Christians and taking them at some age away from their families. We were told a lot on the Aboriginal side of things, but not what really happened at Ebenezer. So, I have enjoyed reading this diary and it has really opened my eyes to what actually was done and what was achieved at the Ebenezer mission. It opened my eyes that they, the female missionaries, were teaching the young girls and women on the mission to do sewing and domestic life in their way. Well, it was probably better for them to learn that for today's society. The world was changing. These people probably looked at it and thought, we'll teach them this. When everything was said and done, and the boards were gone and people could actually live properly, they would have to have those skills, and these are with them today. These skills were passed on to the children and the other women. I was really interested in reading about Polly. She was only a young bride sent out to this harsh place and the heat really knocked her to the ground. A bit different from England's weather. I feel sorry for her, because it would have been hard for her, away from her people and her parents, going off with her husband, not really knowing anyone. She put up with all those changes in her life so quick, and the miscarriages, that all took a toll on her. It is a shame she got sick. I would say she was a good woman. She still continued her duties out there as a missionary, but it still affected her whole life, until it got too much for her.

EBENEZER MISSION STATION, 1863–1873

A lot of the Aboriginal people were mission-managed. They didn't go back to their tribes. Lots of these people lost contact with their family, because as the years went on they were given only one name, they didn't have their tribal name. They had one English name, they didn't have surnames. It is sad that they went like that, because if you can be a Christian, you can be Christianised, but you can still go back to your family. You've still got your family, but it wasn't so like that at the mission. They didn't go back. From an Aboriginal perspective, I don't think that I would have liked to do that, being mission-managed by someone and not seeing my mum, my dad or my siblings; it would be horrifying if it happened to me. But I suppose the converted people believed they were there for the good. Everyone can believe in what they want, the missionaries were there for a reason, to convert all these black people to be Christians and therefore walk forward into the white world. But even the 'heathens' back then, they also walked through to the white world. So it all panned out just the same.

Reading this diary has portrayed to me a picture of the lives among those buildings out there on the Ebenezer mission. They all worked so hard together in the harsh conditions of the hot heat of summer and the cold winter to achieve something. All that would not have been achieved unless people were working together. Yes, you have the white Moravian missionaries telling the Aborigines what to do, but that is giving him a skill as well. Go forward to do what he needs to do. This diary of Ebenezer is a good read. Sometimes I just go back and have another read and see what is in there.

Acknowledgements

This diary project has evolved over time, with the COVID-19 pandemic and resulting forced home-office period providing the opportunity to annotate the diary. That said, the annotations have no claim on completeness, nor has the diary been checked rigorously for veracity. There will be omissions and contradictory claims in the diary, as is the nature of personal writings penned from a particular perspective.

This project was funded by the Deutsche Forschungsgemeinschaft (DFG, German Research Foundation) Excellence Strategy EXC 2060, 'Religion and Politics. Dynamics of Tradition and Innovation' (390726036). I am grateful to the Cluster of Excellence for Religion and Politics at the University of Münster, Germany, for the opportunity to work on this diary and for the provision of funding needed to travel to various archives. Funds were also provided to employ student research assistants, with Antonia Schweim deserving special mention. This work has been helped by many interested and interesting people. Particular thanks are extended to Aunty Hazel McDonald and her daughter Robyn Lauricelle, who chatted with me over cups of coffee about the diary and more; Dale Conway at the Dimboola and District Historical Society Archive for providing me with material and ideas; Ann Jensz for her interest, help and so much else; Ted Ryan for sharing his research with me; archivists at the various Moravian archives around the world, including Paul Peucker, Thomas McCullough and the former assistant archivist Lanie Yaswinski at the Moravian Archives in Bethlehem, Pennsylvania, in the United States of America; Olaf Nippe at the Unitätsarchiv in Herrnhut, Germany; Lorraine Parsons at the Moravian Church Archive and Library in London, England, and the late Robin Hutton at the Moravian Archives in Fulneck, England. My thanks is also extended to ANU Press, my editor Rani Kerin, the two thoughtful reviewers, and all involved in helping transform this diary from a handwritten, paper-based nineteenth-century document stored in an archive in the United States to an online book widely accessible to interested readers.

List of figures

Figure 1: 'Mission der Brüder Unität in Australien'. Karte von Victoria, Neu Südwales, Südaustralien und südlichem Queensland mit Angabe der Missionsstationen der Brüdergemeine, mit Angabe der Reiserouten von Spiesecke [sic], Walder, Kramer und Meissel. 13

Figure 2: Portrait of unnamed child, n.d. 17

Figure 3: Portrait of Adolf Hartmann, n.d. 21

Figure 4: Portrait of Adolf Hartmann from his wedding day in England, 29 December 1863. 22

Figure 5: Portrait of Mary 'Polly' Hartmann, née Hines, from her wedding day in England, 29 December 1863. 23

Figure 6: Portrait of Steward and wife, Susan, n.d. 25

Figure 7: Detail (3 May) from the diary of Adolf (JAH) Hartmann, 1863–1873. 29

Figure 8: Portrait of Mary 'Polly' Hartmann, née Hines, and Eleanor (Nelly) Hartmann, in Australia, c. 1870. 30

Figure 9: Portrait of Mary 'Polly' Hartmann, née Hines, and Heinrich (Henry) J Hartmann, in Australia, c. 1870. 31

Figure 10: Portrait of Philip Pepper with his wife Rebecca and her niece Rosa, n.d. 41

Note: The names used in the image captions follow the information provided by the various archives; however, it is possible that they are incorrect and ascribe the wrong names to people.

Abbreviations and notes

BPA	Board for the Protection of the Aborigines in the Colony of Victoria
Br.	Brother (term for a male member of the Moravian Church)
DDHS	Dimboola and District Historical Society Archive
MAB	Moravian Archives Bethlehem, Pennsylvania, USA
PEC	North American Provincial Elders Conference
PMD	Protocoll des Missionsdepartement (Minutes of the Mission Department, Herrnhut)
PP HJAH	Personal Papers of John Adolphus Hieronymus Hartmann held at the Moravian Archives Bethlehem, Pennsylvania, USA
Rev.	Reverend
S./Sp.	Friedrich Spieseke, the other Moravian missionary at Ebenezer during the Hartmanns' stay
Sr.	Sister (term for a female member of the Moravian Church)
UA	Unitätsarchiv (Moravian Archives), Herrnhut, Germany
UEC	Unity Elders Conference (the committee that was responsible for making decisions between the general synods of the Moravian Church)

Notes

Most of the original diary entries begin with a symbol indicating the day of the week on which the entry was made. Here, in place of a symbol, the day has been inserted in square brackets at the beginning of the entry.

Square brackets [ ] have also been used to indicate that I have added to the text to make it more readable.

EBENEZER MISSION STATION, 1863–1873

This is a true copy, which means that all the editing marks, crossing out, insertions and the like have been kept, along with the inconsistencies in spelling and grammar.

Diary entries written or partly written by Polly/Mary are indicated by an asterisk (*). Her entries are further indicated by a different font.

Introduction

Background and content of the diary

In April 1864, a newly married couple—Adolf and Polly Hartmann (also Hartman)—arrived in Melbourne, Australia. He was a son of missionaries, born in Suriname and raised in the German-speaking Kingdom of Saxony, and had worked for a number of years as a teacher in Saxony and at a school in England. She was the daughter of a minister, raised in England, and had subsequently trained as a teacher and worked in England and Prussia. They both belonged to a religious group called the Moravian Church, which is how they knew of each other. It was also the church that sent this newly married couple to Australia to work as Christian missionaries among Indigenous people. Adolf and Polly Hartmann were sent to Wotjobaluk country, where, in 1859, Moravian missionaries had established the Ebenezer mission station in the north-west of what was known as the Colony of Victoria. The lives of this couple among the residents of the mission station, the district and the colony are described in the following diary. Each page of the diary was dedicated to a calendar day of the year, with multiple years entered on each page. Not every day of every year was recorded, but what was recorded—from the period before the couple left England and over their eight-year stay in colonial Victoria, and throughout their time as missionaries in Canada among the Lenni Lenape—provides a fascinating insight into daily interactions and the ups and downs of mission life. The diary includes entries from 1863, before the Hartmanns arrived in Australia, and entries for 1873, when they were missionaries in Canada. Most of the entries in this diary concern themselves with the Hartmanns' time in Australia—specifically, at the Ebenezer mission station, in the Wimmera district of the Colony of Victoria—from their arrival on 7 May 1864 to their departure on 9 March 1872.

The mission was on traditional Wotjobaluk country where the Wergaia language was spoken. By 1864, Aboriginal people were not able to move as freely across land due to the increased settler colonists in the area. The mission become a space where some people chose to reside, and some people chose to listen more intently to the stories the Hartmanns and other missionaries told. Many others chose not to.

Adolf, whose full name was John Adolphus Jerome Hieronymus Hartmann, wrote in some detail about the period before his marriage to Mary Hines, affectionately known as Polly, and the preparations that they made together before sailing from England to Australia in early 1864. Their time in Australia was cut short due to Polly's poor health. On 9 March 1872, they travelled back to England, leaving Melbourne on the ship *Agamemnon*.[1] There they remained for a nine-month period, after which they were sent as missionaries among the Lenni Lenape (also known as the Delaware) at New Fairfield in Canada, for which a number of diary entries exist for 1873.[2] This diary thus includes observations from England, Germany, Australia and Canada, providing a transnational account of mission work in the third quarter of the nineteenth century, in a period just prior to British high imperialism. The originals of this diary sit in the archives of the Moravian Church in Bethlehem, Pennsylvania, in the United States of America, along with letterbooks, notebooks, letters, photographs and other memorabilia from the couple and their epistolic network.[3] This final resting place for the diary is a half a world away from the events it describes. It was placed there in 1979, after the death of a granddaughter of Adolf and Polly Hartmann. By this time, the diary was over a century old, having recorded a period of cultural interaction and change between settlers and Aboriginal Australians in the western part of the Colony of Victoria in the 1860s.

---

1   *The Periodical Accounts relating to the Missions of the Church of the United Brethren Established among the Heathen* (hereafter *Periodical Accounts*) vol. 28 (1871): 280.
2   For the early history of the New Fairfield mission see: Amy C Schutt, *Peoples of the River Valleys: The Odyssey of the Delaware Indians* (Philadelphia: University of Pennsylvania Press, 2007).
3   I acknowledge the Moravian Archives Bethlehem, Pennsylvania, USA [MAB] for permission to publish this diary. The diary has the following archival reference: MAB, Personal Papers [PP], John Adolphus Hieronymus Hartmann [HJAH], 9, Diary written by Adolf Hartmann 1863–1873. See also the catalogue entry: www.moravianchurcharchives.findbuch.net/php/main.php?ar_id=3687#5050204 84a4148. Henceforth, the dates preceded by 'Ref' correspond to dates in the diary with this archival signature.

The inhabitants of the Ebenezer mission are described in the diary as having control over some aspects of their lives, moving in and out of the sphere of influence of the missionaries, yet at times restricted to the boundaries of the mission. In the 1840s, the first squatters started moving into Wotjobaluk country, where the mission was located, bringing with them disease, sheep and guns.[4] Over a short amount of time, the landscape was transformed into squatting runs with thousands of heads of cattle and hundreds of thousands of sheep, with this transformation the backdrop to Aboriginal–settler violence.[5] Indigenous men were commonly engaged in shearing the squatters' sheep. The shearing period was also one of increased sexual contact between white males and Indigenous women, with reports indicating that not all of these sexual encounters were mutually consensual.[6] The influx of strangers into Wotjobaluk country also brought opportunities for friendly cross-cultural interactions between Indigenous peoples and European settlers as well as Chinese shepherds. Other diaries from the period indicate that there were occasions where people from various cultural groups worked together, sharing resources over large distances.[7] From the late 1850s, Moravian missionaries also settled in Wotjobaluk country, bringing with them Bibles, and later guns to hunt. They also procured sheep to farm with the labour of mission inhabitants. The formalised administration by Europeans of the broader local area around the mission was established in 1862 with the Horsham District Roads Board. Through the local government *Electoral Act 1863*, the Wimmera Shire was established in March 1864.[8] A settlement called Nine Creeks was established around the same time, formally surveyed in 1862, and called Dimboola (although the term Nine Creeks was used throughout the 1860s). Nine Creeks was a location for purchasing supplies as well as the site of a public house, against which the missionaries had protested unsuccessfully.[9] The number of Aboriginal people on the Ebenezer mission fluctuated. In 1864, there were 32 people on average living on

---

4   See Anne Longmire, *Nine Creeks to Albacutya: A History of the Shire of Dimboola* (North Melbourne: Hargreen Publishing Company, 1985).
5   Phil Taylor, *Karkarooc: Mallee Shire History, 1896–1995* (Yarriambiack Shire Council: Warracknabeal, 1996), 20–22.
6   Missions-Blatt aus der Brüdergemeine (hereafter *Missionsblatt*) 3, (1864): 64.
7   The Dimboola and District Historical Society Archive (DDHS), The Lorquon Diary of Hugh Campbell, 19 October 1863 to 27 February 1864, copy of the diary supplied by Mr MDN Campbell, a descendant of Hugh Campbell.
8   Longmire, *Nine Creeks to Albacutya*.
9   See: Melbourne Association in Aid of the Moravian Mission, *Further Facts relating to the Moravian Mission Read in Connection with the Report of the Committee at the Annual Meeting of the Melbourne Association in Aid of the Moravian Mission* (hereafter *Further Facts*), *Third Paper* (Melbourne: WM Goodhugh & Co, 1862), 8.

the mission.[10] By 1872, the year the Hartmanns left Australia, the average monthly attendance fluctuated between 42 (June) and 89 (December).[11] Not all people living on the mission are mentioned in detail in the diary. There are some 150 names of people mentioned in the diary; many, like a man called Davy, are only mentioned once.[12] Some, such as Timothy (formerly Tallyho, alternatively Taliho, before his Christian baptism), are frequently mentioned—in his case almost 50 times. Phillip (formerly known as Charley Charley) is mentioned over 80 times. The frequency of names in the diary in some way reflects the close interaction between residents of the mission, and indeed, there were a core number of couples who were important, in the missionaries' minds, to the stability of the mission. Many of these people formed married couples; however, the term 'married' is itself an indication that the diary was written in a time of cultural flux, as the term referred to stable couples, not necessarily people who had married under church or colonial laws.

There is no doubt that Adolf and Polly, along with another missionary couple, Friedrich Wilhelm and Christiane Johanna Spieseke[13] (née Fricke), were strict in their control over Indigenous residents of the mission and tried to instil Christian moral codes among the residents. The diary also demonstrates, however, that there were moments of laughter, shared grief, community, advocacy and reciprocal learning. Among these were also the mundane daily chores of the mission. The diary thus brings to light the regular and routine (as well as the extraordinary) events on the mission station in a way that official reports, formal letters and overviews of the work cannot. It is not complete, there are dates missing, notably from late 1870, when Polly suffered a miscarriage, until the resumption of the diary in Canada in 1873. On some days, there were no entries at all. Some entries do not provide important details, such as baptismal names, which are important for the forward tracking of individuals. It is very settler-centric in its descriptions, and does not attempt to engage with Aboriginal people's concerns that do not reflect the worldview of the missionaries. Yet, the diary does include information, albeit obliquely, about Aboriginal people's experiences. It records emotions such as grief, joy and anger and reports

---

10 See: *Fourth Report of the Central Board Appointed to Watch Over the Interests of the Aborigines in the Colony of Victoria*, no. 19 (Melbourne: John Ferres, Government Printer, 1864), 7 (reports in this series hereafter referred to as, e.g., *First BPA Report*).
11 *Eighth Annual BPA Report*, 18.
12 Ref: 16 November 1865.
13 'Spieseke' was at times written 'Speiseke'—for example, in official reports of the Board for the Protection of the Aborigines in Colonial Victoria (BPA).

declarations of community, ownership and defiance. There are descriptions of how Aboriginal people engaged with as well as evaded missionary discipline and control. Through the recording of names of people moving in and around the mission and to stations and places beyond the reach of the missionaries, the diary demonstrates the connections that Aboriginal people maintained to people and places after the incursion of settler colonists. Taken as a whole, the approximately 1,000 entries of the diary provide rich insight into the daily lives of missionaries and Indigenous inhabitants of the mission, as well as the broader district and colonial settings and changes over time, albeit from one particular perspective.

This diary is not just a recording of a local context; it records events in four locations spread over three continents, and demonstrates the entangled nature of missionary work as well as its global reach. Within the historiography of the British Empire, a recent strand of scholarship highlights the interconnectedness of colonial spaces to ideas, knowledge and people beyond the limits of a particular colonial space. Within this 'global turn', scholars such as Tony Ballantyne have been influential in describing empire in terms of 'webs' that connected Britain and its colonies as well as connecting the colonies with each other.[14] This is an important insight, which has been taken up by scholars of mission history such as Rebekka Habermas, who focuses upon the global reach of missionaries, describing them as one of the most connected professions in the nineteenth century.[15] Thus, in framing this diary as a reflection of an entangled, global history, this introduction points to ways in which the diary can be read on various levels: from the microcosmos of the station, to the meso-layer of colonial politics, to the global interactions of Christian humanitarian and philanthropic influences that deemed Indigenous Australians as in need of saving from the vices of 'civilisation'.

On the local level, there has been sustained community attention on the mission and its history, albeit with various levels of intensity. Since 2000, the Ebenezer mission station has received increased academic attention, with a focus on the archaeology of the site and the entangled worlds of European missionaries and Indigenous peoples, as well as the tensions between

---

14 See for example: Tony Ballantyne, 'The Changing Shape of the Modern British Empire and its Historiography', *Historical Journal* 53, no. 2 (2010): 429–52, doi.org/10.1017/S0018246X10000117.
15 Rebekka Habermas, 'Mission im 19. Jahrhundert. Globale Netze des Religiösen', *Historische Zeitschrift* 56 (2008): 62979, doi.org/10.1524/hzhz.2008.0056, here page 641.

German missionaries and the British colonial state.[16] This is in line with the increased interest in uncovering more nuanced histories of missions, beyond that of the often self-congratulatory mission histories written by religious groups.[17] Much of the written material that has been used in writing the history of the Ebenezer mission has been official documentation, either English-language reports or German official correspondence. The Hartmanns' diary sheds a further perspective on the mission, that being of daily encounters between inhabitants, both Indigenous and European, and visitors in and beyond the space. It is unique insofar as it provides a view of the life of the mission that lingers over an eight-year period and provides layers of detail that create a complex image, beyond any of the few extant written impressions of the mission from short-term visitors. Unlike the other Moravian-run mission in the colony, Ramahyuck, which was located near Sale and received significant public attention partly due to its closer proximity to Melbourne, Ebenezer received very few high-profile visitors. Thus, there are limited external reports on the state of the mission beyond those provided to the Board for the Protection of the Aborigines in the Colony of Victoria (BPA, previously the Central Board Appointed to Watch Over the Interests of the Aborigines in the Colony of Victoria). The uniqueness of the source provides a rare insight into the operations at Ebenezer and into the networks that the mission was part of that reached beyond the geographical site of the mission. In this vein, the diary is similar to the personal papers of Ellie Hagenauer Le Souëf, the daughter of a Moravian missionary at the contemporary Ramahyuck mission in Gippsland, Friedrich Hagenauer, as it offers material to help reconstruct a more nuanced

---

16   See: Felicity Jensz, *German Moravian Missionaries in the British Colony of Victoria, Australia, 1848–1908: Influential Strangers* (Leiden: Brill, 2010), doi.org/10.1163/ej.9789004179219.i-274; Robert Kenny, *The Lamb Enters the Dreaming: Nathanael Pepper and the Ruptured World* (Melbourne: Scribe, 2007); Jane Lydon, *Fantastic Dreaming: The Archaeology of an Aboriginal Mission* (Lanham, Maryland: Altamira Press, 2009).

17   See for example: Bain Attwood, *The Making of the Aborigines* (Sydney: Allen & Unwin, 1989); Amanda Barry, Joanna Cruickshank and Andrew Brown-May (eds), *Evangelists of Empire? Missionaries in Colonial History* (Melbourne: University of Melbourne eScholarship Research Centre, 2008); Peter Sherlock, 'Missions, Colonialism and the Politics of Agency' in Barry, Cruickshank and Brown-May, *Evangelists of Empire?*, 12–20; Peggy Brock, *Outback Ghettos: A History of Aboriginal Institutionalisation and Survival* (Cambridge: Cambridge University Press, 1993); Peggy Brock (ed.), *Indigenous Peoples and Religious Change* (Leiden: Brill, 2005), doi.org/10.1163/9789047405559; Christine Choo, *Mission Girls: Aboriginal Women on Catholic Missions in the Kimberley, Western Australia, 1900–1950* (Perth: University of Western Australia Press, 2001); Norman Etherington, 'Missions and Empire', in *Oxford History of the British Empire. Vol. V: Historiography*, ed. R Winks, 303–14 (Oxford: Oxford University Press, 1999); Tony Swain and Deborah Bird Rose, *Aboriginal Australians and Christian Missions: Ethnographic and Historical Studies* (Adelaide: Australian Association for the Study of Religions, 1988); Laura Rademaker, *Found in Translation: Many Meanings on a North Australian Mission* (Honolulu: University of Hawai'i Press, 2018), doi.org/10.1515/9780824873585.

image of the daily experiences on a mission station.[18] The purpose of this introduction and of the annotations in the diary is to provide some context to the events portrayed, in order that the diary, which had been left so long in an archive in North America, might be made openly available to scholars and to descendants of those who lived on mission stations in the mid-nineteenth century. The annotations are not exhaustive and, as they rely primarily on texts produced by missionaries and their supporters, are biased towards settler-colonial readings of the mission's history and inevitably contain mistakes or half-truths. It is hoped that this diary will encourage people to engage in further research and to rectify in their own scholarship some of the errors and omissions in this text. As a snapshot into a period of the mission, the diary does not include the complex relationship between people beyond the period it documents, nor is it complete in its description of the people or events on or surrounding the mission. These silences, gaps and omissions are evidence of the asymmetrical power relations on the mission, of the selective recording of events to suit European agendas, and of the privileging of some ways of knowing over others.

The annotations are primarily drawn from printed and handwritten Moravian and government sources such as the English-language Moravian periodical, *Periodical Accounts;*[19] the BPA annual reports; the reports from the Victorian Association in Aid of the Moravian Mission; the handwritten minutes from the *Unitätsältestenkonferenz* (Unity Elders Conference, UEC), a Moravian committee in Germany which made decisions for the Australian province; the handwritten minutes of the Moravian Mission Board in Germany; some further handwritten material from the Hartmann collection at the Moravian Archives in Bethlehem, Pennsylvania; material from the Moravian archives in Fulneck, England; and other contemporaneous reports and books. The Hartmanns produced many hundreds of pages of texts, mostly in the form of letters, which still need to be systematically analysed and are thus only partly included in this diary project. The annotations have no claim on completeness, nor

---

18   Joanna Cruickshank and Patricia Grimshaw have made varied use of Ellie Hagenauer Le Souëf's papers, held in the Le Souëf Family Papers, MN 1391 at the JS Battye Library in Western Australia. See: Joanna Cruickshank and Patricia Grimshaw, *White Women, Aboriginal Missions and Australian Settler Governments: Maternal Contradictions* (Leiden: Brill, 2019), doi.org/10.1163/9789004397019. See also Friedrich Hagenauer's papers in the National Library of Australia in Canberra: NLA MS 3343.
19   The *Periodical Accounts* are freely available via the Memorial University of Newfoundland Digital Archives Initiative (collections:mun.ca/cdm/search/collection/cns_permorv). The volumes cover multiple years: for example, volume 25 covers the years 1863–66. In the footnotes, the first year is given, not the full timeframe—for example, *Periodical Accounts* 25 (1863).

has the diary been checked rigorously for veracity. It stands as a document created in the third quarter of the nineteenth century by two individuals who were sent at the behest of a missionary organisation from Europe to Australia with the aim of converting Indigenous Australians to the Christian religion. The Hartmanns only recorded what they deemed important, not necessarily what might be retrospectively considered important for tracing family histories or community connections. No attempt has been made here to ascribe people into language groups, clans or 'tribes', except where the literature is unambiguous. The diary and contemporaneous reports used here to annotate the diary do not allow for such reconstructions, nor is it the intent of the annotations to do so. The following section will provide an overview of the global Moravian Church before describing briefly the mission landscape in colonial Victoria, and then finally describing the structure of the diary and its peculiarities.

The global Moravian Church

The Church that Adolf and Polly Hartmann belonged to, the Moravian Church, had its roots in eighteenth-century German pietism. This evangelical Christian Church was established, or renewed, in 1725 by Count von Zinzendorf in Lower Saxony (current-day Germany), drawing on a group of religious enthusiasts including some who claimed to be traditional followers of the fourteenth-century Bohemian martyr and reformer Jan Hus.[20] In German, the church is known under various names (*Brüder-Unität*, *Unitas Fratrum*, *Herrnhuter*), whereas in English it is predominantly known as the Moravian Church, due to the historical connection to the followers of Jan Hus.[21] Zinzendorf, an aristocrat, was connected and related to the courts of Europe, particularly the Danish court, where, in his early years, he met some converted slaves from the Danish Caribbean. In 1732, the Moravian Church sent out the first two missionaries to try to convert African slaves to Christianity on the Danish Caribbean island of St. Thomas. Further mission fields were established in places such as Greenland, Suriname,

---

20   J Taylor Hamilton, *A History of the Church Known as the Moravian Church, or the Unitas Fratrum, or the Unity of the Brethren, during the Eighteenth and Nineteenth Centuries* (Bethlehem, Pennsylvania: Times Publishing Company, 1900); Colin Podmore, 'Zinzendorf and the English Moravians', *Journal of Moravian History* 3 (Fall 2007): 31–50, doi.org/10.2307/41179832; JCS Mason, *The Moravian Church and the Missionary Awakening in England, 1760–1800* (Suffolk: The Boydell Press for The Royal Historical Society, 2001).

21   Colin Podmore, *The Moravian Church in England, 1728–1760* (Oxford: Clarendon Press, 1998), doi.org/10.1093/acprof:oso/9780198207252.001.0001.

North America, South Africa, Ghana, Labrador, Ethiopia, Jamaica, India, Ceylon (current Sri Lanka), Nicaragua, West Tibet, Palestine and Alaska. By the mid-nineteenth century, there were Moravian missions spread across the globe in Dutch, Danish and British colonies, with their missionary work inspiring other evangelical groups as well as being considered a benchmark of what good mission practice was. The Moravians were at the forefront of the pietist missionary movement of the early eighteenth century and of the evangelical revival of the late eighteenth century, movements which saw various missionary bodies being established and sending out missionaries to convert Indigenous and enslaved peoples to Christianity, in the belief that Christianity encompassed the highest morals of any religion.

European settlements of Moravians were also spread over the globe, in Germany, the United States, Britain and Australia (at Bethel in South Australia).[22] In the mid-nineteenth century, the worldwide Moravian community was fewer than 20,000 people of European descent, with some 77,500 new Christians in the various mission fields,[23] with many other non-converted local peoples attached to the missions in some form. The geographical distance between church members was countered by a strong sense of community fostered by a focus upon common music and religious practices. Peter Vogt has described these transportable communal practices as a means of Moravians being 'everywhere at home'.[24] The multilingual, international community was further connected through epistolic networks and periodicals, and through people moving between locations.[25]

By the mid-nineteenth century, the Moravian Church was looking to extend its missionary work, with three new 'fields' being established in Australia, Nicaragua and West Tibet. At this time, the secretary of the Moravian Church in London was the brother of Charles Joseph La Trobe, the first governor

---

22 There is no recent overview of the Moravian mission in English. For a German account see: Hartmut Beck, *Brüder in vielen Völkern: 250 Jahre Mission der Brüdergemeine* (Erlangen: Verlag der Ev. -Luth. Mission, 1981). For an antiquated English version see: J Taylor Hamilton, *A History of the Missions of the Moravian Church during the Eighteenth and Nineteenth Centuries* (Bethlehem, Pennsylvania: Times Publishing Company, 1901) (available via Google Books). For more on the Moravians in Bethel, South Australia, see: Felicity Jensz, 'Religious Migration and Political Upheaval: German Moravians at Bethel in South Australia, 1851–1907', *Australian Journal of Politics & History* 56, no. 3 (2010): 351–65, doi.org/10.1111/j.1467-8497.2010.01558.x.
23 'Table, Containing the Numerical Result of the Missionary Labours of the Church of the United Brethren, about the Beginning of the Year 1861', *Periodical Accounts* 24 (1861): xxvii–xxx.
24 Peter Vogt, '"Everywhere at Home": The Eighteenth-Century Moravian Movement as a Transatlantic Religious Community', *Journal of Moravian History*, no. 1 (2006): 7–29.
25 Gisela Mettele, *Weltbürgertum oder Gottesreich: Die Herrnhuter Brüdergemeine als globale Gemeinschaft 1727–1857* (Göttingen: Vandenhoeck & Ruprecht, 2009).

of the Colony of Victoria. This family connection provided support for the first Moravian mission in Australia, at Lake Boga, on Wemba Wemba land. Initially two male Moravian missionaries were sent there in late 1849. They began their work at Lake Boga, south-east of Swan Hill, in 1851. Andreas Friedrich Christian Täger and Friedrich Wilhelm Spieseke were joined by a third missionary, Paul Hansen, in 1854. By 1856, the mission was abandoned, with the blame being placed on gold-seekers trespassing on to the mission station. The missionaries complained that the neighbouring settlers were slanderous towards them in order to hinder Aboriginal people from settling on the mission, and to ensure that Aboriginal people's labour was available to settlers and not to the missionaries. The missionaries erected a fence around the mission reserve; however, as it enclosed a thoroughfare the fence was constantly pulled down by travellers, who, according to the missionaries, often 'annoyed the natives'.[26] Täger went to Melbourne to complain to the governor of the colony, but he received no support. In 1856, the three missionaries left the mission and returned to Europe without permission from the Moravian Church.[27]

Once back in Europe, Täger received most of the blame for the insolence of returning without permission. The Church looked to re-establish a mission with the support of the governor of the Colony of Victoria, Sir Henry Barkly, who suggested the Wimmera district as a location.[28] Spieseke was considered a suitable candidate as he already had experience in Australia and had acquired some of the language spoken by the Wemba Wemba. He was accompanied by Friedrich August Hagenauer, who would subsequently travel to Gippsland to establish the Ramahyuck mission station in 1862 as a collaboration between the Moravian Church and the Presbyterian Church. Once arriving in 1858, the missionaries met with supporters in Melbourne and learned that there were three sites that the government had reserved for a potential mission station from which they could choose.[29] One of these sites was close to the squatting run of Horatio Ellerman, who was described as a friend of the bishop of Melbourne.[30] The land was in the north-west of the colony in Wotjobaluk country. The missionaries initially lived with Ellerman from 20 December 1858 and travelled daily from his place to where the mission would be built. On 2 May 1859, they moved

---

26 *Periodical Accounts* 22 (1856), 203.
27 See: Jensz, *German Moravian Missionaries*.
28 *Periodical Accounts* 22 (1856), 361.
29 *Periodical Accounts* 22 (1856), 522.
30 *Periodical Accounts* 22 (1856), 522.

to the hut built for them on the land that became the mission station.³¹ Moravian reports suggest that the 'mysterious beginning' of the Ebenezer mission was on the first anniversary of the mission, 2 May 1860. On that evening Hagenauer read to a number of boys preparing for baptism a pamphlet written by the Rev. Chase, about a little Aboriginal boy who he took back to England with him. The boy, known as Willie Wimmera, was, according to Moravian reports, known by local men as Jim Crow. Among those listening to the story was Pepper, who became the first convert of the mission. He was baptised on 12 August 1860, taking the name Nathaniel (also Nathaneal).³²

The Ebenezer mission station, known also as Lake Hindmarsh station, due to its proximity to the lake of the same name, had been running for some five years when the Hartmanns arrived in early 1864. This mission was under the purview of the Moravian Church in Germany, through the Mission Department and also through the UEC, the committee responsible for making decisions between the general synods of the church. Ebenezer was initially run by Spieseke and Friedrich Hagenauer. After the 'success' of Nathaniel's baptism, interest in supporting the Moravian mission increased among other religious groups in the colony, including the Anglicans, Presbyterians and Lutherans. The Presbyterians provided funding for a second Moravian-run mission, Ramahyuck, which was established at Lake Wellington in Gippsland in 1862.³³ These two Moravian stations were among a number of mission and government stations in operation during the time the Hartmanns were in Australia.

Adolf and Polly Hartmann took over the position left by Job Francis's departure from Moravian mission work at Ebenezer. As a single man among two married couples (the Spiesekes and the Hagenauers), Francis had found working at the mission difficult. He had been given the task of working with the young and running the school, with his work beginning in November 1861. In July 1862, after Hagenauer had left for Ramahyuck, Francis wrote to the UEC in Herrnhut asking for a wife, and provided the name of a potential partner. He suggested that his work among Aboriginal women was not possible without being married. Ultimately, he left the service of the Moravian Church having married a non-Moravian woman,

---

31   Melbourne Association in Aid of the Moravian Mission, *Facts relating to the Moravian Mission, First Paper*, (Melbourne: WM Goodhugh & Co, 1860), 4.
32   See also: *Further Facts, Second Paper*, 4–5. See also: Kenny, *The Lamb Enters the Dreaming*.
33   For more on Ramahyuck see: Attwood, *The Making of the Aborigines*.

although he remained in contact with the UEC in Germany.[34] With Francis gone, the Ebenezer mission had only one missionary couple, which was not enough for all the work they intended to do. On 13 August 1863, Adolf Hartmann received his call to be a missionary in Australia. He left England in January 1864, landed in Australia in mid-April, and finally arrived at Ebenezer on 7 May, at two o'clock in the afternoon, just under seven months after having received his call, with a new wife and a new occupation. Spieseke remained the primary missionary to correspond with the German Moravian committees; however, Hartmann also sent letters to the Moravian administration informing them of the work, especially of the progress of the school, which he was in charge of and which drew upon his previous occupation in England. He was required to undertake an examination for the Board of Education, which was established in 1862.[35] However, as he was an ordained minister he was not eligible to become a government-paid schoolteacher.[36]

At around the same time as the Hartmanns were preparing to come to Australia, four other Moravian missionaries were similarly preparing to establish a mission in the Australian interior, as part of the European settlers' and Australian colonial government's response to the failed Robert O'Hara Burke and William John Wills Expedition of 1860–61. By early 1864, the four missionaries Heinrich Walder, Carl Wilhelm Kramer, Wilhelm Julius Kühne and Gottlieb Meissel met with the UEC and the Missions department, receiving their instructions for their proposed mission in the interior of Australia. Their arrival in Australia was greatly anticipated, particularly by Hagenauer in Gippsland, who knew two of the four personally.[37]

---

34 Unitäsarchiv Herrnhut, Germany (UA), Unity Elders Conference (UEC) Minutes, 24 July 1862, #15, 52; 4 August 1863, #13, 98; 9 November 1867, #14, 156.
35 See: UA, UEC Minutes, 2 March 1867, #8, 220.
36 See: UA, UEC Minutes, 9 January 1868, #5, 28.
37 It does not state which ones he knew. UA, UAC Minutes, 31 May 1864, #12, 236.

Figure 1: 'Mission der Brüder Unität in Australien'. Karte von Victoria, Neu Südwales, Südaustralien und südlichem Queensland mit Angabe der Missionsstationen der Brüdergemeine, mit Angabe der Reiserouten von Spiesecke [sic], Walder, Kramer und Meissel.

[English Translation: Mission of the Brethren Unity in Australia. Map of Victoria, New South Wales, South Australia and southern Queensland, showing the mission stations of the Brethren Unity, indicating the itineraries from Spieseke, Walder, Kramer and Meissel.]

Source: Unitätsarchiv (UA), Herrnhut, Germany, Landkarte, TS.Mp.272.7.

EBENEZER MISSION STATION, 1863–1873

The Victorian Association in Aid of the Moravian Mission (formerly Melbourne Association) was responsible for deciding where and when to send the four missionaries into the interior. After arriving in Australia, Meissel and Walder travelled to Ebenezer late in 1864, with there being many references to these two men in the diary. Kramer went to Ramahyuck. During the same period, Kühn was at Kadina on the York Peninsula with the Congregationalist William Wilson.[38] All were waiting for the drought to break in the interior. Meissel and Walder left Ebenezer on 1 April 1865 with Daniel, an Indigenous man who was previously known as Young Boney (sometimes written Bony) and who, according to Moravian reports, desired to evangelise among Indigenous people of the interior. Boney was baptised on 6 December 1863 on the same day as his brother, Talliho (Tallyho), who took the name Timothy. However, Daniel died in Adelaide before he could travel further. Ultimately, three Moravian missionaries travelled to the interior. Kühn stayed at Kadina and later married an English woman. The three others established a mission near Lake Hope called Kopperamana. The mission faced many difficulties. Polly referred to some of these in the diary, stating:

> Heard to day [sic] of the compulsory flight of the Brethren from Kopperamana their station; they took refuge with the Lutheran Missionaries at Kilalpanina. They had a narrow escape of their lives, as they heard afterwards that the blacks intended to shoot them on the very day they escaped. About a thousand were collected in the neighbourhood. Their watchword was 'Down with the whites'.[39]

Finally, at the end of 1868 it was increasingly certain that the mission would be closed.[40] Walder was subsequently sent to Jamaica and Meissel to Suriname.[41] Kramer stayed in Australia, helping Hagenauer in Ramahyuck.[42] Not long after the closure of the mission at Lake Kopperamana, the Hartmanns returned to England. Their positions were filled in early 1872 by Johann Heinrich Stähle and his wife Marie Magdalene, who died in childbirth in October of that year. Stähle departed the mission shortly after. With a further change in personnel, the Moravian missions continued into the early twentieth century. Yet the increasing draconian legal measures

---

38 UA, UEC Minutes, 2 June 1866, #10, 257.
39 Ref: 27 April 1867.
40 Jensz, *German Moravian Missionaries*.
41 UA, UEC Minutes, 7 January 1869, #10, 22.
42 Sister Emilie Beyer accepted the call to become Kramer's wife and travel to Australia in 1868. UA, UEC Minutes, 15 May 1868, #8, 156; UA, UEC Minutes, 2 June 1868, #2, 185.

enacted against Aboriginal people, such as the *Aborigines Protection Act 1869* (Vic) and the so-called Half-Caste Act of 1886, regulated the lives of Aboriginal Australians and legislated who was entitled to be considered an Aboriginal person, and with that, who was allowed to live on the site of the mission. This legislation reduced the numbers of people legally allowed to reside on the mission, resulting in the closure of Ebenezer. The Ebenezer mission land was opened up to selection in October 1904. With the closing of the mission the inhabitants moved to other reserves or locations. In 1908, the Ramahyuck mission was also closed. In North Queensland, Moravians established missions, such as Mapoon, in collaboration with the Presbyterians from the late nineteenth century. However, these missions were given over to the Presbyterians at the outbreak of World War I, bringing the Moravian mission presence in Australia to an end.[43]

Other reserves and missions in colonial Victoria

In the 1860s, there were numerous sites where Indigenous people were encouraged to settle, both as a means to 'civilise' people through sedentary lifestyles and as a way of facilitating settler-colonial access to land. At Coranderrk, near the junction of Coranderrk Creek and the Yarra River, a government reserve was run by Mr and Mrs John Green.[44] Other stations included the Yelta mission station on the Murray River, run by Thomas Hill Goodwin, and the Lake Tyers mission station in Gippsland, run by the Church of England under the supervision of John Bulmer. On the Lower Murray, at Tyntyndyer, Peter Beveridge supplied government rations to the local Indigenous people. Numerous other depots scattered around the state provided supplies to Indigenous peoples.[45] The increased number of missions and mission attempts, both in the colony of Victoria and elsewhere

---

43 Regina Ganter, 'Letters from Mapoon: Colonising Aboriginal Gender', *Australian Historical Studies* 29, no. 113 (1999): 267–85, doi.org/10.1080/10314619908596102; John Harris, *One Blood. 200 Years of Aboriginal Encounter with Christianity: A Story of Hope* (Sutherland: Albatross, 1990).
44 For more on Coranderrk see: Diane Barwick, *Rebellion at Coranderrk*, Aboriginal History Monograph 5 (Department of History, ANU: Canberra, 1998).
45 For more on mission stations in Victoria see: Harris, *One Blood*. See also: Attwood, *The Making of the Aborigines*; Richard Broome, *Aboriginal Victorians: A History Since 1800* (Crows Nest: Allen & Unwin, 2005); Claire McLisky, Lynette Russell and Leigh Boucher, 'Managing Mission Life, 1869–1886', in *Settler Colonial Governance in Nineteenth-Century Victoria*, ed. Leigh Boucher and Lynette Russell, 117–38 (Canberra: ANU Press, 2015), doi.org/10.22459/SCGNCV.04.2015.05.

in Australia, was a reflection of humanitarian concern for Indigenous people and their spiritual state as well as an indication of the growing control over the lives of Indigenous peoples.

In addition to the reserves and missions in operation in the 1860s, honorary correspondents aided the Central Board Appointed to Watch Over the Interests of the Aborigines in the Colony of Victoria. The police ensured that regulations, such as the ban on selling intoxicating liquors to Aboriginal people, were upheld.[46] The consumption of intoxicating liquors by Indigenous people had been a concern to the board since its inception, as liquor was considered to be detrimental to the health of Aboriginal people. As the Hartmann diary records, alcohol was not tolerated on the mission. Port wine was, however, commonly used as a medicinal treatment for fever on other stations.[47]

In 1864, there were some 40 or so stations where government supplies were distributed to Aboriginal people, where supplies such as foodstuffs and clothing, including flour, tea, sugar, tobacco, rice, oatmeal, soap, blankets, serge shirts, twill shirts, trousers, boys' jumpers, dresses, chemises, petticoats, tomahawks, and pint and quart pots were provided. The clothing remained the property of the government, with a particular pattern of brown and yellow stripes being implemented in 1864, the year the Hartmanns arrived in Australia, so that these blankets could be identified as government property, with anyone in possession of them, other than Aboriginal people, liable to fines.[48] Some of these local guardians were supporters of the mission—for example, Charles Wilson of Walmer, near Horsham, who is often mentioned in the diary.[49] The motivation of the supporters of the mission—be they humanitarian, philanthropic or self-serving—are not mentioned in the diary; indeed the diary describes actions rather than inner states or reflections.

---

46   Leigh Boucher, 'The 1869 *Aborigines Protection Act*: Vernacular Ethnography and the Governance of Aboriginal Subjects', in Boucher and Russell, *Settler Colonial Governance*, 73.
47   See for example: *Seventh BPA Report*, 11.
48   See: *Fourth BPA Report*.
49   Walmer was not the only squatting run Charles Wilson held, with Tulganny, Green Hills, Longerenong and several other runs listed under the Wilson Brothers. See: Anonymous, *The Squatters' Directory, Road Guide, and Key to the Squatting Map of Victoria* (Blundell & Ford: Melbourne, 1865), trove.nla.gov.au/version/264832355, 45.

Figure 2: Portrait of unnamed child, n.d.
Source: MAB, PP Edmund de Schweinitz (SchwED), 'Scrap Book of Pictures relating to the Unitas Fratrum. Begun in Philadelphia in 1854' (n.d., Volume B), compiled by Edmund de Schweinitz, page 99.[50]

---

50 Please note: the names used in the image captions follow the information provided by the various archives; however, it is possible that they are incorrect and ascribe the wrong names to people.

EBENEZER MISSION STATION, 1863–1873

As a mission reserve in the Colony of Victoria, the Ebenezer mission station was under the supervision of the Central Board Appointed to Watch Over the Interests of the Aborigines in the Colony of Victoria established in 1860. In 1869, the name of the Central Board was changed through the *Aboriginal Protection Act 1869* (Vic) to the Board for the Protection of the Aborigines in the Colony of Victoria (BPA). The change in name was one piece of external evidence of the increased control over the lives of Indigenous people and the patronising and infantilising nature of the board. The BPA sought to have all Aboriginal people under their direct control. To facilitate this, they supported the notion of moving children on to mission stations and reserves, particularly Coranderrk, for schooling and general education away from the perceived 'bad' influence of the children's families. Older people were provided with food, clothing and medical attention—however, this was little consolation given what was taken from them in return. The BPA considered Aboriginal people capable of being 'civilized' and 'equal to the performance of the duties which civilization imposes'.[51] In the nineteenth century, 'civilisation' included the notions of Christian morals, and thus religious instruction was considered an indispensable aspect of the civilising mission. People were expected to work for their keep and expected to assimilate into the settler-colonial society, lessening the financial strain on the colonial government for supporting Aboriginal people.

In the early 1860s, Aboriginal people on the missions and stations could move about, relatively unhindered. Other contemporaneous diaries suggest that Aboriginal people moved over large distances, mixed with Chinese shepherds and worked as message bearers for local squatters.[52] However, this ability to move freely among whom they pleased was being curtailed as land was being increasingly claimed by settlers. In August 1867, Spieseke went to Melbourne to discuss some points in relation to the mission, including an application for more land, the stopping of government rations at neighbouring stations, and ways to obtain more power to keep children on the mission and to educate them.[53] The control over children would be enshrined into law in the *Aboriginal Protection Act 1869*, which provided for the 'Management and Protection of the Aboriginal Natives of Victoria'. This Act gave powers to the governor to decide upon where individual Aboriginal people or 'tribes' were allowed to reside, to prescribe the terms

---

51   *Seventh BPA Report*, 3.
52   DDHS, The Lorquon Diary of Hugh Campbell.
53   Ref: 24 August 1867.

INTRODUCTION

of employment contracts between Europeans and Aboriginal people, and to regulate 'the care, custody and education of the children of Aborigines'.[54] The 1869 Act was not mentioned in the Hartmann diary—indeed there are comparatively few mentions of government acts, boards or interference. Yet in other letters to his parents-in-law he mentioned the Act, hoping that it would be passed soon for it would help for 'the better management of the Aborigines'.[55] Increasingly, from the introduction of the 1869 Act, missions became total institutions, where Aboriginal people lived and were instructed; in exchange, they contributed to the running of the mission and its agricultural and industrial needs. The particular form of settler colonialism seen in colonial Australia was, as Pat Grimshaw and Elizabeth Nelson have noted, harsher on Indigenous peoples than seen contemporaneously in places such as Hawai'i or New Zealand, leading to intense control over the lives of Indigenous peoples by the end of the twentieth century.[56] In the period that this diary covers, governmental control was not yet as strict as it would be in the later period. Moreover, it was a period in which the size of the mission was expanding, in terms of land and inhabitants.

The Hartmanns

Before coming to Australia, Johannes Adolf and Mary/Polly (née Hines) Hartmann had both moved countries at the behest of the Moravian Church. Adolf, as he was commonly called, was born in Suriname in October 1831. As a five-year-old child, he was sent to Saxony (now part of Germany) by his parents to be educated at the mission school at Kleinwelka, and to be close to Herrnhut, the global centre of the Moravian Church. As with many missionary children in the nineteenth century, both Moravian and other denominations, Adolf would never see his parents again. As a young man, he taught at the Moravian boys' school in Neuwied, and subsequently he was called to work at the Moravian boys' school in Fulneck, England, where the Moravians had had a presence since the early eighteenth century. In his position as schoolteacher he was remembered as a science teacher, who

---

54   Boucher, 'The 1869 *Aborigines Protection Act*'.
55   MAB, PP HJAH, 3, Letters, written by Adolph and Mary Hartmann to their parents and siblings (1864–1871), Adolf Hartmann to Hines family, Ebenezer, 6 October 1869.
56   Patricia Grimshaw and Elizabeth Nelson, 'Empire, "the Civilising Mission" and Indigenous Christian Women in Colonial Victoria', *Australian Feminist Studies* 16, no. 36 (2001): 295–309, doi.org/10.1080/08164640120097534.

inspired many boys with this mechanical inventions.[57] During his time at Fulneck, aside from his duties teaching, he trained for the Moravian ministry. In September 1863, Adolf was invited by Levin Reichel, a member of the Moravian's mission board, to take a trip to Herrnhut. After receiving a positive response from Mary (Polly) to the proposal of marriage, and also after meeting her, he left England for Germany in November 1863, arriving in Herrnhut on 12 November. His time there was spent in administrative duties as well as visiting family members, such as his sister Caroline, and friends. He married the 25-year-old Mary, whom he affectionately called Polly, in December 1863.

Polly was born on 26 November 1838 into a Moravian family in Carlton in Lindrick, Nottinghamshire, England. Her father was the principal of the boys' school there. She was one of six children. She followed her father's profession as an educator, beginning as an assistant teacher in the girls' school at Carlton, and further training at a special training institute for teachers. She had taught for some eight years at Moravian girls' schools in both Fulneck, England, and Gnadenfrei, Silesia, Prussia (current-day Piława Górna, Poland). It was while she was in Gnadenfrei that the call came from the Church for her to marry Adolf and for them to become missionaries in Australia. It was common practice during this period for the Moravian church administration to call people to many of the mission fields across the globe through casting lots, and also common practice to marry within the church. Indeed, to marry outside the church meant exclusion from the church, as was the case with Adolf's sister Caroline.[58]

---

57 *Fulneck School Magazine*, 1889, 19–20. From a photocopy provided by Robin Hutton at the Moravian Archives in Fulneck, England.
58 Ref: 10 January 1869.

Figure 3: Portrait of Adolf Hartmann, n.d.
Source: MAB, PhotPortraits H.080.

Figure 4: Portrait of Adolf Hartmann from his wedding day in England, 29 December 1863.
Source: MAB, PhotPortraits H.078.

Figure 5: Portrait of Mary 'Polly' Hartmann, née Hines, from her wedding day in England, 29 December 1863.
Source: MAB, PhotPortraits H.087.

In the diary, Adolf Hartmann notes some of the items that he purchased for his position in Australia, including clothing in Manchester, and in London tools, lamps and a gun.[59] He found the funds available to him to purchase equipment to be too meagre, complaining to the Mission Department in December 1863 that woollen garments were expensive, as were other textiles. The Mission Department was, however, not willing to provide more funding, suggesting that the £42[60] was appropriate.[61] The money that he requested for a harmonium was expected to come from donations, including some funds from the Sisters in Königsfelder, a Moravian community in the Black Forest (established 1807). Eighteen months later, the Mission Department was planning to establish a new mission in the interior of Australia and calculated that the four missionaries would need some £600 for their collective equipment needs.[62]

The Hartmanns left England at the beginning of 1864 on the ship the *Norfolk*. They arrived in Melbourne on 15 April 1864, after three months at sea. The diary does not record the ship voyage out. This is in contrast to shipboard journals of the period, which only describe the journey out, for the act of recording helped transcend the two worlds and two lives; the past and a future, better life in Australia. Scholars have described the voyage out as a transformative period in which individuals were confronted with anxieties, sickness and boredom, and in writing down these details the authors constructed the voyage experience.[63] Although not written in the diary presented here, Polly wrote in diary form to her parents of the voyage out. It included descriptions of animals, the passing of a convict ship, descriptions of her fellow passengers and a description of their daily routines.[64] Some of this material was also written down in a separate notebook.[65] This separate notebook is often referred to in the diaries; however, often the pages in the small notebook that the large diary refers to are ripped out, leaving it unclear as to what was being referred to, or why these pages are missing.

---

59   Ref: 17 December 1863 and 16 January 1864.
60   In 1860, £42 was equal to 210 days of earnings for a skilled tradesman. Conversion undertaken with The National Archives, UK, *Currency converter: 1270–2017*, accessed 2 March 2020, www.nationalarchives.gov.uk/currency-converter/.
61   UA, Protocoll des Missionsdepartement [PMD], 1861–66, 22 December 1863, #1.
62   UA, PMD, 1861–66, 7 June 1865, #7.
63   Tamson Pietsch, 'Bodies at Sea: Travelling to Australia in the Age of Sail', *Journal of Global History* 11, no. 2 (2016): 209–28, doi.org/10.1017/S1740022816000061. See also: Andrew Hassam, *Sailing to Australia: Shipboard Diaries by Nineteenth-Century British Emigrants* (Melbourne: Melbourne University Press, 1994).
64   MAB PP HJAH, 3, Letters, Polly Hartmann to Hines family and friends, Melbourne, April 1864.
65   MAB, PP HJAH, 10, Diary written by Adolph Hartmann, including diary of voyage to Australia (1864–1870), loose-leaf.

Figure 6: Portrait of Steward and wife, Susan, n.d.
Source: MAB, PP SchwED, 'Scrap Book of Pictures relating to the Unitas Fratrum. Begun in Philadelphia in 1854' (n.d., Volume B), compiled by Edmund de Schweinitz, page 99.

For the Hartmanns, religion was a focus of their identity and already, on the voyage from England to Australia, they were conscious of finding respectable company among an appropriately religious group. Their main company consisted of two clergymen and their wives, two sisters of the clergymen, and a young gentleman, who was the nephew of a known clergyman in London.[66] Upon disembarking in Melbourne, the first people that the Hartmanns visited were religious supporters of the mission, including Anglicans and German Lutherans.[67] Within the first month of the Hartmanns' arrival (see entry for 8 May 1864), there was a triple baptism of Charley Charley, who was Nathanael's brother, Charley's wife Jessie (also written Jessy), and Liberty. Charley Charley took on the name Phillip, Jessie took the name Rebecca and Liberty the name Matthew. In the afternoon of that same day, Phillip and Rebecca were married by the Presbyterian Rev. Simpson of Horsham, who had also baptised the three.

Baptisms, births and deaths were recorded (but not always with names) in the diary, following the religious motivations of the Hartmanns. Particularly, 'happy deaths'—deaths of people who had been open to the Christian message, or baptised—were deemed to be bright points in the life of the mission.[68] Yet the number of deaths also reflects the compromised health of Indigenous peoples due to introduction of foreign diseases and the ineffectiveness of known medicine to treat these diseases.

The Hartmanns arrived at Ebenezer on 7 May 1864. They were reported to be 'agreeably surprised' by the state of the mission.[69] Adolf wrote back to Germany: 'Our first impressions of Ebenezer and its inhabitants were decidedly favourable.'[70] Such comments from Moravian missionaries arriving in Australia were common, suggesting that the information that they had read in missionary periodicals about Aboriginal people in Australia portrayed a less positive image than reality, possibly to entice people to support the mission. Indeed, Adolf had heard prior to arriving in Australia that Aboriginal people were ugly and dumb, and was pleasantly surprised when this was not the case.[71] When they arrived, the mission had been running for a number of years: young men and boys resided in a large house, girls in a little room attached to the missionaries' house. Another four log huts were on the station. The school was small, but some people had already learned to read and write. There were

---

66 MAB, PP HJAH, 3, Letters, M Hartmann to Hines family and friends, April 1864.
67 MAB, PP HJAH, 3, Letters, M Hartmann to Hines family, May 1864.
68 See: *Periodical Accounts* 26 (1866), 27.
69 *Further Facts, Fifth Paper*, 4.
70 *Periodical Accounts* 25 (1863), 234.
71 *Missionsblatt* 9 (1864), 171.

still many people around, including many who lived at Lake Hindmarsh, who were not under the influence of the missionaries and 'wander[ed] about continually'.[72] Adolf and Polly took over the responsibilities of schooling, with Adolf starting a school for the men,[73] and Polly commencing a knitting school with Mrs Spieseke for the women and girls.[74] The attendance at the school varied greatly, with frequent breaks when the men and boys went off to work at neighbouring stations. As an experienced schoolteacher, Adolf spent much time with people, yet his classes were difficult, as he reported that many of the older people did not have a good command of the English language, which made school lessons challenging. The old people, he stated, 'always converse in their language'.[75] In 1862, the *Victorian Common Schools Act* (1862) was passed; it remained in force until the *Education Act 1872* (Vic), which provided for the compulsory education of all children in the colony.[76] For the Ebenezer mission, the 1862 Act brought with it some difficulties: the school could not receive any government support, for the Act stated that schools needed to have at least 20 pupils on the roll and school must be held for four hours a day, two consecutive hours in the morning and two consecutive hours in the afternoon. As Adolf was ordained, he was not eligible to become a government-supported teacher. The Ebenezer school, given its shortened hours and the fluctuating pupil numbers, could not meet the Act's requirements for support.[77]

Within a fortnight of the Hartmanns arriving at the mission, the presiding missionary couple, Friedrich and Christiane Spieseke, took six weeks' leave in order to travel to Portland to search for potential mission sites (their itinerary can be seen on the map in Figure 1). With the Spiesekes absent, Polly and Adolf were immediately thrown into the supervision of, and work on, the mission station.[78] Once settled at Ebenezer, the Hartmanns continued to surround themselves with religiously likeminded people, with Polly finding female companions among the wives of nearby squatters, and Adolf doing the same among the menfolk. Although they were constantly in the company of Indigenous peoples, they did not seem to form close emotional relationships with them; rather they maintained such relationships with fellow settler-

---

72 *Fourth BPA Report*, 6–7.
73 Ref: 11 May 1864.
74 Ref: 18 Feb 1867.
75 *Periodical Accounts* 25 (1863), 466.
76 Leslie J Blake, *Vision and Realisation: A Centenary History of State Education in Victoria, vol. 2* (Melbourne: Education Department Victoria, 1973); Catherine Byrne, '"Free, Compulsory and (Not) Secular": The Failed Idea in Australian Education', *Journal of Religious History* 37, no. 1 (2013): 20–38, doi.org/10.1111/j.1467-9809.2011.01163.x.
77 UA, UEC Minutes, 9 January 1868, # 5, 28.
78 MAB, PP HJAH, 3, Letters, M Hartmann to Hines parents, 13 December 1864.

colonists. As Polly wrote to her parents, 'we are not altogether shut out of society' for they often received guests and made visits to other stations.[79] One of her closest companions and friends was Mrs Ellerman, wife of the neighbouring squatter and later Presbyterian clergyman the Rev. Horatio Ellerman, who was an honorary corresponding member of the BPA.[80] Ellerman features prominently in the diary as a supporter of the mission, which contrasted to his earlier position towards Indigenous people, which was much more hostile, even violent.[81] Other honorary correspondents of the BPA formed part of the Hartmann's religious colonial circles, such as Mr Charles Wilson and his wife, who lived at Walmer, near Horsham, and who presented the mission with gifts of stock. The Hartmanns visited Horsham, which was 50 kilometres away, on numerous occasions as it was a significant location for the missionaries to raise support for the mission. The Hartmanns also maintained friendships with the Scotts of Warracknabeal, some 40 kilometres from the mission. It was on a tour to that station in December 1864 that they met many people, such as Kitty, Neptune, Napoleon and Hearty, who would have connection to the mission station in the following years.[82]

The diary allows for an insight into the lives of both Adolf and Polly, with one of peculiarities of the diary being the appearance of two voices, sometimes discerned as two handwritings—they have been marked in this version of the diary in different typefaces and an asterisk at the dates where Polly has written at least part of the entry. Both Adolf and Polly write in the first person, with Polly sometimes writing in the third-person singular. The first-person voice of Polly provides insight into the everyday interactions that female missionaries had with Indigenous women as well as settler colonists on the mission station. The perspective of female missionaries has, until recently, been relatively overlooked. However, the literature, both internationally and in Australia, has increasingly examined the formative roles that white women played on mission stations.[83] Rather than passive actors, women often took significant roles in missions, creating relationships between women, organising Indigenous girls to work in the domestic sphere of missions, and training people to 'be like them'. Polly was engaged in all of these activities.

---

79 MAB, PP HJAH, 3, Letters, M Hartmann to Hines parents, 6 July 1864.
80 Ref: 10 January 1865.
81 Jensz, *German Moravian Missionaries*.
82 MAB, PP HJAH, 3, Letters, M Hartmann to Hines family, 15 December 1864.
83 See the overview in: Cruickshank and Grimshaw, *White Women*. See also: Regina Ganter and Patricia Grimshaw, 'Introduction: Reading the Lives of White Mission Women', *Journal of Australian Studies* 39, no. 1 (2015): 1–6, doi.org/10.1080/14443058.2014.1001308; Hilary M Carey, 'Companions in the Wilderness? Missionary Wives in Colonial Australia, 1788–1900', *Journal of Religious History* 19, no. 2 (1995): 227–48, doi.org/10.1111/j.1467-9809.1995.tb00257.x; Dagmar Konrad, *Missionsbräute: Pietistinnen des 19. Jahrhunderts in der Basler Mission* (Münster/New York/München/Berlin: Waxmann, 2001).

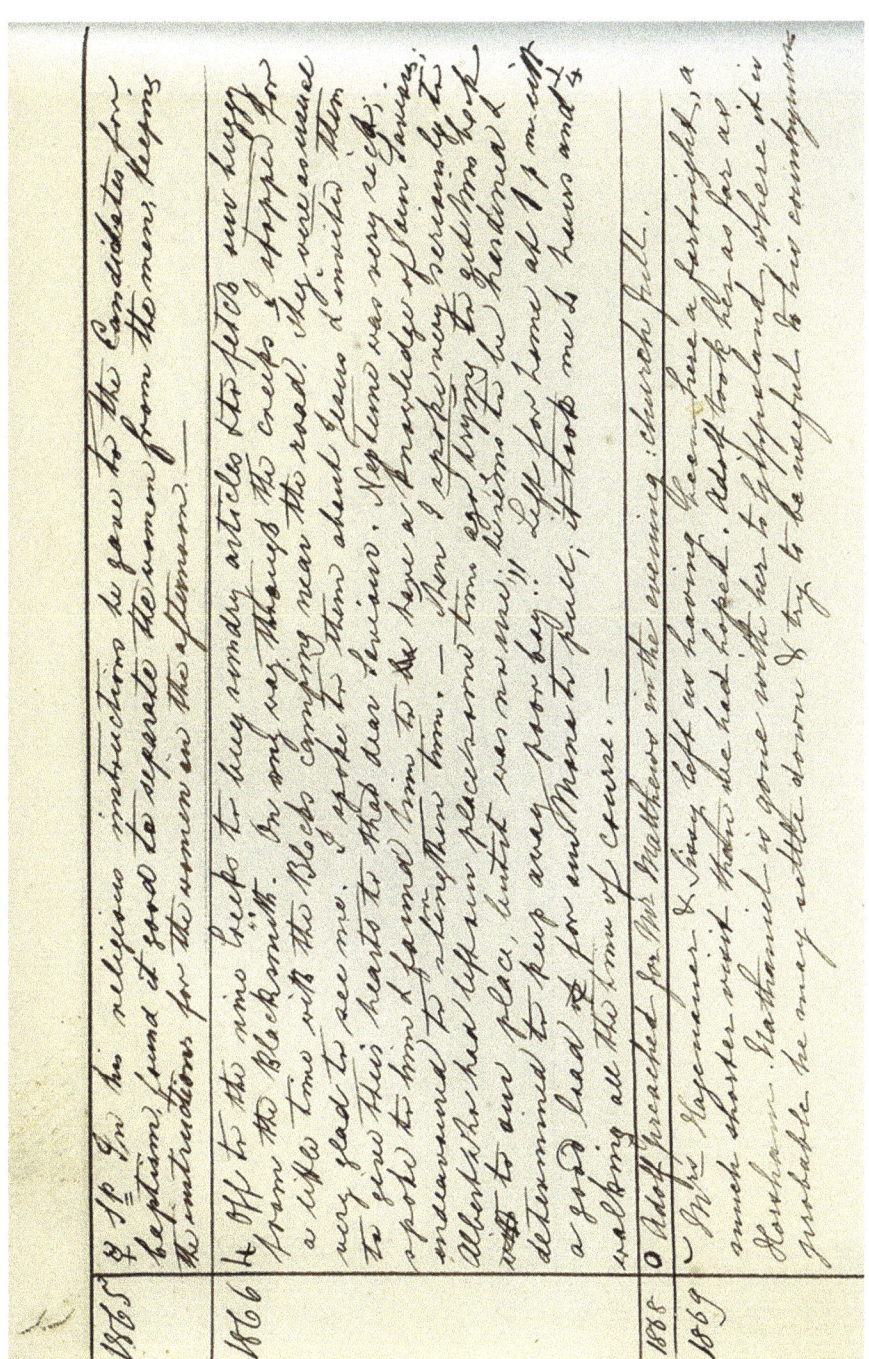

Figure 7: Detail (3 May) from the diary of Adolf (JAH) Hartmann, 1863–1873.
Source: Moravian Archives Bethlehem, Pennsylvania, USA (MAB), Personal Papers (PP), John Adolphus Hieronymus Hartmann (HJAH), 9, Diary, written by Adolf Hartmann 1863–1873.

Figure 8: Portrait of Mary 'Polly' Hartmann, née Hines, and Eleanor (Nelly) Hartmann, in Australia, c. 1870.
Source: MAB, PhotPortraits H.069.

Figure 9: Portrait of Mary 'Polly' Hartmann, née Hines, and Heinrich (Henry) J Hartmann, in Australia, c. 1870.
Source: MAB, PhotPortraits H.074.

Initially, as at Lake Boga, Aboriginal women did not engage with the two European missionaries. As this slowly changed, the missionaries and the mission direction saw the need for wives to be sent to Australia to help spread the Christian message among females. Thus, when Ebenezer was established, wives were quickly sent out to work as missionaries among Aboriginal women. Although male missionaries wrote substantially more than females, many Moravian women left records of their time in foreign mission fields. Some, like Adolf's sister Maria Heyde in Tibet, wrote detailed diaries, which have since been transcribed and published.[84] Some, such as Sister Hahn at the Ramahyuck mission from 1876, had their writings published in periodicals such as the *Periodical Accounts*.[85] The writings of female missionaries allow us to uncover the lives of Indigenous, settler-colonist and missionary women in a way that male voices do not. Within the historiography of women on missions in Australia, Patricia Grimshaw's work is pioneering in uncovering the lives of both Indigenous and European women.[86] Her work, both as a single author and with others, has demonstrated the integral role that women had in establishing and contesting gender roles. Grimshaw's work reminds us of the necessity of engaging with female narratives on mission stations, reflecting their provision of insights parallel to those of 'official' reports, as well as their more intimate engagement with women and children in comparison with typical male missionaries. Diaries such as this one provide an insight into female settler colonists' reactions to Indigenous women, and to the broader settler-colonial structures. Within the Moravian Church, married missionaries were the norm in the nineteenth century. Husbands predominantly had the main responsibility for official correspondence, leaving their wives' writings in the private sphere and out of the archives. The Hartmann diary goes also some way into describing how European women saw their positions within the structures of a mission, and the variability and vulnerability of these roles. It indicates the gender expectations, both on Adolf as provider, husband, builder, famer, religious leader and father figure, and also on Polly as wife, mother, teacher and missionary to Indigenous women. As with the vast majority of missionary sources,[87] there are limitations here

---

84 Frank Seelinger, *Maria Elisabeth Heyde–Versuch einer biographischen Annäherung auf Grundlage der Tagebuchnotizen für die Jahre 1862 bis 1870, inklusiv Transkription* (Ulm: Technische Hochschule Wildau, 2005), opus4.kobv.de/opus4-th-wildau/frontdoor/index/index/docId/18.
85 *Periodical Accounts* 30 (1876), 10–11.
86 See for example: Patricia Grimshaw, 'Rethinking Approaches to Women in Missions: The Case of Colonial Australia', *History Australia* 8, no. 3 (2011): 7–24, doi.org/10.1080/14490854.2011.11668386.
87 David Arnold and Robert Bickers, 'Introduction', in *Missionary Encounters: Sources and Issues*, ed. Robert A Bickers and Rosemary Seton, (Surry: Curzon Press, 1996), 1-10.

insofar as the diary provides little insight into the experiences or thoughts of Indigenous people beyond her narrow descriptions. Instead, they provide insight into the daily life of a European woman on an Aboriginal mission in the nineteenth century, notions of 'respectable whiteness', and how pity was utilised, as well as throwing light on her understanding of her place within the different communities in which she was enmeshed.

Polly's first emotional response towards female Aboriginal Australians was one of pity, as they were deemed to have only a limited cognitive ability, viz:

> Sometimes I feel very sad about the poor old lubras [Indigenous women]. They are so entirely ignorant seeming to understand very little English, & even when spoken to in their own language, can take in so very little.[88]

From this position of pity she endeavoured to undertake activities that would engage the women and provide her with opportunities to contribute to the industry and community of the mission, such as manual labour: using Indigenous women to wash the missionaries' clothing and to keep the mission buildings neat and tidy.[89] Polly's pity can be understood as an emotion used to reproduce colonial categories, particularly that of portraying non-Europeans as in need of 'raising', whether in social, cultural, religious or intellectual terms, effectively homogenising the non-European 'other' into a singular object of pity, as opposed to individual subjects of compassion.[90] She was mostly disappointed at the lackadaisical response to her proselytizing, noting in her diary that 'while baking in the kitchen [I] had a long talk with Mary alone. I am not without hopes of her, although like the rest, she appears very indifferent.'[91] Yet, such disappointments were considered an important aspect of the missionary experience: 'If that were not the case, we might get proud & self-sufficient: but by them we are repeatedly reminded of our dependence on our Master.'[92] These quotes indicate Polly's ambivalence and displacement in her role as missionary wife. She was unsure if her efforts had any effect, with her faith being both the regulator and the driver of her emotional response to these disappointments.

---

88   Ref: 24 May 1864.
89   MAB, PP HJAH, 3, Letters, M Hartmann to Hines parents, 6 July 1864.
90   Marianne Gullestad, *Picturing Pity: Pitfalls and Pleasures in a Cross-Cultural Communication; Image and Word in a North Cameroon Mission* (New York: Berghahn Books, 2007), 22.
91   Ref: 10 June 1864.
92   MAB, PP HJAH, 3, Letters, M Hartmann to Hines parents, 13 December 1864.

Within the local religious community of the mission station, Polly clearly saw herself in a position of religious, moral and cultural superiority over the Indigenous inhabitants of the mission. She did, nevertheless, build reciprocal relationships with numerous Indigenous women through gift-giving and knowledge exchange. She, along with Adolf, was a willing pupil in Indigenous language acquisition. In a letter to her parents in mid-1864 she wrote:

> We are doing our best at the blacks language, but at the present we do not find much time for it. It is very peculiar. A great many of the words begin with a sound which is represented best by our ty as tyah – ground. tyahb mouth. tyally – news. But more words still begin with ny as nyettuek – piece. nyouwy - sun – nyallo spring. Now these are not pronounced as our ty in tyrant or ny in many: but the y is has the sound of our y in yard, & the t or n is pronounced before it.
>
> I am sure we shall find it very useful, especially for the old people. Many of the wandering blacks do not understand good English, but feel have to be spoken to in a peculiar English of their own. For instance:- 'Big one fellow, him very poor, him very wicked, plenty time him hear about big Master Jesus, but him no come to him. Big one fellow little while here, then pull away along o' bush, no think any more about good master Jesus.' But I made a mistake: they call a 'little while' – 'pickaninny time'. They call all their children 'pickaninny' even when grown up to men & women. Nathaniel's mother always calls him her pickanninny.[93]

Polly also took basket-weaving lessons from Mary and other Aboriginal women.[94] Yet, despite reporting at times upon the 'pleasant time' that she had had with Indigenous women,[95] she does not provide any information in her correspondence to suggest intimate friendships with any Indigenous women. When she did describe Aboriginal people in a letter, at the request of her father, her descriptions were commonly of a proto-ethnographical nature rather than of descriptions of emotionally reciprocal relationships,[96] mirroring the emotional distance evident in the creation of a 'respectable

---

93   MAB, PP HJAH, 3, Letters, Adolf and Polly [Mary] Hartmann to Hines parents, 6 July 1864 (Polly's writing).
94   Ref: 25 July 1866; 30 July 1867.
95   Ref: 3 December 1864.
96   See for example: MAB, PP HJAH, 3, Letters, M Hartmann to Hines family, 13 February 1866.

whiteness' on other missions in colonial Victoria.[97] She was present at intimate events within the lives of Indigenous women, such as birthing; however, she did not have any Indigenous women present when she herself gave birth to their two children Eleanor (Nelly, born December 1865) and Henry (born November 1868),[98] further indicating an unequal relationship between her and other women on the mission.

As the second missionary at Ebenezer, Adolf was not initially on equal status with Spieseke and there are moments of tension in the diary. For example, in 1869, during a period when Spieseke's eyes were particularly bad and Adolf had to take up the slack, he wrote to his parents-in-law that he found that he much to do, but as he was not the manager of the station, he did not have the freedom to decide things which Spieseke could do on his own.[99] He did, however, have some freedom in his work as a teacher as well as a handyman around the mission, building a windmill in 1865 to better irrigate the flower and vegetable gardens. Indeed, the diary documents lots of building on the mission, including huts for the inhabitants of the mission. For example, in February 1865 there was considerable work done on Matthew's hut. In later years, after the Hartmanns had left the station, there would be much discussion about the providence of these huts, as the people who built them assumed that they could pass them on to their families, whereas the missionaries believed that the huts remained property of the government.[100] Adolf also contributed to ethnographical studies, providing material for Robert Brough Smyth's 1878 *The Aborigines of Victoria*, including stories, linguistic material and physical measurements of the inhabitants of the stations.[101] This work for Smyth's book is not mentioned in the diary.

---

97 Joanna Cruickshank, '"A Most Lowering Thing for a Lady": Aspiring to Respectable Whiteness on Ramahyuck Mission, 1885–1900', in *Creating White Australia*, ed. Claire McLisky and Jane Carey (Sydney: Sydney University Press, 2009), 65–78, doi.org/10.30722/sup.9781920899424.
98 Ref: 11 December 1865; 5 January 1868.
99 MAB, PP HJAH, 3, Letters, Adolf Hartmann to Hines family, 6 October 1869.
100 Rose Kennedy, for example, wrote to the BPA in 1884 enquiring as to the ownership of a hut, which her deceased uncle and aunt has left to her in their will, yet which the missionary Kramer had given to Albert Coombs as his residence. Rose Kennedy did not receive ownership of the hut and subsequently lived in a tent in Dimboola. See: Elizabeth Nelson, Sandra Smith and Patricia Grimshaw (eds), *Letters from Aboriginal Women of Victoria, 1867–1926* (Melbourne: The University of Melbourne, History Department, 2002), 124–25.
101 Robert Brough Smyth, *The Aborigines of Victoria: With Notes relating to the Habits of the Natives of Other Parts of Australia and Tasmania. Compiled from Various Sources for the Government of Victoria, vol. II* (Melbourne: John Ferres, Government Printer, 1878).

EBENEZER MISSION STATION, 1863–1873

Adolf was a keen photographer, dedicating much free time to it. He received a camera from the boys at Fulneck School in October 1863 as a farewell present.[102] As photography was a relatively new activity for the period, he spent much of his free time experimenting with chemicals and exposure and building a darkroom, as the diary records. Already in 1864, in the months after his arrival at Ebenezer, he wrote to Germany saying that he hoped to be able to supply the church with some images of the Aboriginal people of the mission.[103] Profits from the sales of the photographs were earmarked for the purchase of more chemicals for further photography. When he was back in England in 1872, he used the images to illustrate his lectures on his Australian mission work, and sold copies to interested people.[104] His list of photographs for sale from that notebook reflected his interest in the people of the mission, as many individuals were photographed. These included Philip, Rebecca, Rosa, Sarah, Albert, Ida, Davy, Elizabeth, Henry, Diana, Jackson Steward, Susan Steward, Jing Stewart, Charley, Jenny (old), Thomas, and King Peter. The existence or whereabouts of these images is not currently known.

Adolf's interest in documenting his surroundings was common among Moravian missionaries, with many other men being competent illustrators and, later in the nineteenth century, photographers. By the turn of the century, many of the Moravian mission fields had been photographed, with Adolf's images from Australia being some of the earlier photographs originating from Moravian mission fields worldwide.[105] Adolf continued taking photographs following his time in Australia. In 1884, Adolf, who by this time was residing with Polly and their two children as a missionary in Canada, was asked to undertake a missionary journey to Alaska, where the Moravians were contemplating establishing a new mission to the Inuit. During this tour, he took many photographs, which were published in a series and sent to museums such as the Smithsonian and published in contemporaneous American governmental reports.[106]

---

102 Ref: 24 October 1863.
103 *Periodical Accounts* 25 (1863), 289.
104 MAB, PP JHAH, 21, Notebook, Personal notebook of Adolf Hartmann (1872).
105 Rüdiger Kröger, *Bilder aus der Herrnhuter Mission. Fotografien des 19. Jahrhunderts aus den Sammlungen des Unitätsarchivs* (Herrnhut: Comenius-Buchhandlung GmbH, 2008).
106 See: Sheldon Jackson, *Report on Education in Alaska: With Maps and Illustrations* (Washington: Department of the Interior/Government Printing Office, 1886).

Polly's health, like that of many other missionary wives around the globe, affected her work.[107] Her time at Ebenezer was prematurely ended due to her own poor health, or, in her words, her 'nervous weakness'.[108] By mid-1871, Polly's health was deemed so bad that Adolf asked the UEC if they could be transferred to somewhere other than Australia. A transfer to Gippsland was not under consideration, as Hagenauer did not think Adolf talented enough to take over Kramer's work in the school, nor did Sister Hagenauer have the capacity to look after sickly Polly.[109] Polly was unable to work in the girls' school.[110] Her 'nervous weakness' hints at a mental breakdown; however, the reason behind it was never clearly stated, although as it corresponded with her second miscarriage, this could have been a contributing factor.[111] As Polly's health was so poor, Adolf, with a heavy heart, requested to be removed to a colder climate.[112] Other missionaries in Victoria and even her family in London involved themselves in trying to expedite the process, demonstrating how colonial and family networks rallied to help her.[113] Poignantly there is little evidence in Polly's personal correspondence to suggest what she thought about her removal from Ebenezer; rather, in her letters to her family around this time she focuses upon her corporeal state rather than any thoughts of pending geographical dislocation.

The Hartmanns were allowed to return to England and in their place Johann Heinrich Stähle was called, through a drawn lot, to mission work at Ebenezer.[114] On the day they left Ebenezer, 9 March 1872, Adolf reported that some 120 Aboriginal people came to send them off, with many turning up especially for the occasion and with many tears of farewell.[115] Interestingly, their departure from Ebenezer after some eight years is not recorded in the diary. After arriving in England, there was discussion of sending the Hartmanns to Jamaica, however, given the inability for Polly to deal with the Australian climate, this discussion did not progress further.[116] A couple of months later, at the beginning of 1873, the North American Provincial

---

107 Alison Longworth, '"Was It Worthwhile?" An Historical Analysis of Five Women Missionaries and Their Encounters with the Nyungar People of South-West Australia' (PhD thesis, Murdoch University, 2005).
108 MAB, PP HJAH, 3, Letters, M Hartmann to Dan Hines, 9 August 1870.
109 UA, UEC Minutes, 21 September 1871, #5, 211–12.
110 MAB, PP HJAH, 3, Letters, M Hartmann to Hines family, 3 November 1870.
111 Felicity Jensz, 'Miscarriage and Coping in the Mid-Nineteenth Century: Private Notes from Distant Places'. *Gender & History* 32, no. 2 (2020): 270–85, doi.org/10.1111/1468-0424.12478.
112 UA, PMD, 20 September 1871, #1.
113 UA, PMD, 7 February 1872, #6; UA, PMD, 8 February 1871, # 2; UA, PMD, 15 March 1871, #2.
114 UA, UEC Minutes, 30 September 1871, #8, 228; UA, UEC Minutes, 12 October 1871, #8, 33.
115 *Missionsblatt* No. 6 (1872), 140.
116 UA, UEC Minutes, 14 December 1872, #2, 221–22.

Elders Conference sent a telegraph to the UEC in Herrnhut stating their agreement that the Hartmanns should be called to the Moravian mission in New Fairfield, Canada to work among the Delaware Indians.[117] By 1 May 1873, the Hartmanns were on their way to Canada, having spent some time in Herrnhut before their departure to North America.[118] There is also a glimpse in the diary of their time in New Fairfield, with diary entries from 1873. These entries have not been annotated here, as the focus is on Adolf and Polly Hartmann's period in Australia.

Topics in the diary

One significant issue running through the diary is land. Ebenezer was one of the smaller reserves in terms of land, with 1,897 acres reserved for the mission in September 1861.[119] From 1867, Spieseke communicated frequently with the BPA requesting more land to be added to the mission reserve.[120] The land was deemed too dry for effective cultivation, with a focus placed instead upon sheep farming, with lamb and mutton being part of the diet. The diary notes that individual Aboriginal men, such as Philip Pepper, Stewart [Wirremande Steward] and Matthew, also wrote to the board.[121] The discussion about the extension of the land for the mission was not settled immediately after Spieseke's visit to Melbourne in August 1867. He returned to Ebenezer on 11 October, bringing word that the Central Board was looking into the possibility of securing 12,000 acres for an Aboriginal reserve.[122] Spieseke, as many other missionaries of the time, believed in the dignity of labour. In a letter from October 1866 published in the London Moravian *Periodical Accounts*, Spieseke lamented that many Indigenous people had to rely upon charity to survive as they had no land to cultivate, nor access to land upon which to hunt.[123] The UEC in Germany was concerned about the reactions of the neighbouring squatters if the mission reserve was increased by too much land, believing that too much land could bring the mission into disrepute.[124] Nevertheless, the quest for more land

---

117 UA, UEC Minutes, 9 January 1873, #15, 23.
118 UA, UEC Minutes, 1 May 1873, #15, 144.
119 *Fourth BPA Report*, 17.
120 Ref: 11 October 1867. See also: MAB, PP HJAH, 1, Letterbook, containing copies of letters written by Adolf Hartmann mostly to Australian officials (1868–1871), A Hartmann to Central Board for the Protection of the Aborigines, 5 October 1869.
121 Ref: 22 November 1869; 6 January 1870.
122 Ref: 11 October 1867.
123 See: *Periodical Accounts* 26 (1866), 195.
124 UA, UEC Minutes, 9 January 1868, #5, 28.

continued. John Green, the inspector for the Central Board, reported of his visit to Ebenezer in November 1868 that he believed that if the station was to be increased by four times its size it would be able to support all the Aboriginal people of the Wimmera. He also recommended that more sheep be kept, with the wool sold to support the purchasing of goods.[125]

In November 1869, a further request was made for more land. This time it came from Aboriginal men on the mission, who wrote letters to the Legislative Assembly of Victoria 'asking for a grant of land to enable the Blacks to have about 4000 sheep'. Among the letter-writers were Wirremande Jackson Steward (written in the diary as Stuart, Stewart and Steward), Philip and Matthew. Adolf wrote a general petition, which was copied by Albert and signed by a number of other mission residents. According to Adolf, the local squatters were very much against the movement, and he was concerned that if the people continued their push for more land that more opposition could arise.[126] The missionaries believed that only through access to land for farming would Aboriginal people be able to earn their own living and become 'civilised' through hard manual labour.[127] Moreover, the Central Board replied to the letter 'disapproving of the action taken in the matter'.[128] The application for more land was pursued, however, according to a letter written by Adolf to the Moravian Board and printed in the *Periodical Accounts*:

> A friend informed us, as the opinion of several influential gentlemen in Melbourne, that if the grant of additional land were made, Ebenezer would cease to be a mission-station, and come under the control of the Government. On hearing this, the natives at once decided to withdraw their application, giving as a reason, that it would create enmity to our work here. The letter to this effect was sent in to the Board, and we had all concluded that there was an end of the whole matter, when a letter arrived, addressed to 'Mr. Wirremonde Stewart and others,' from the Assistant Commissioner of Lands and Survey.[129]

---

125 *Sixth BPA Report*, 9–10.
126 *Periodical Accounts* 27(1868), 409.
127 Ref: 22 November 1869. See also discussion of this petition and further letters to the Board of Land and Works particularly in files in Public Records Office (Victoria): PROV, VPRS 242, as cited in: Edward Ryan, 'Wergaia Worlds: A Study of Indigenous/European Cultural Contact in the Mallee Region of North-west Victoria, 1870–1910' (Honours thesis, Department of History, La Trobe University, 1999), 29–33.
128 *Periodical Accounts* 27 (1868), 409.
129 *Periodical Accounts* 27 (1868), 409.

This incident was also described in the diary in 1870, when Adolf reported the following:

> A letter arrived, addressed to Wirremande Steward, from the office of lands & works stating contrary to our expectation that sufficient land should be added so as to carry 3,000 sheep.[130]

In March 1870, an additional 1,710 acres was added to the 1,897 acres already gazetted in September 1861, almost doubling the reserve, but stopping far short of the 12,000 acres which Spieseke spoke about in 1867.[131] In the *Periodical Accounts*, Adolf attributed the granting of addition land, despite the withdrawal of the application, to divine intervention.[132] The hope associated with the increase of acreage of the mission was that it would be self-supporting and that the men and women would be able to grow and farm their own food, plus be able to sell the wool from the sheep. Sheep were an important source of both income as well as food for the mission. In 1865, for example, 2,000 pounds of wool were shorn, with many Aboriginal people involved in the wool washing and men in the shearing. Another 400 pounds of skins were produced in that year.[133] Farming sheep was one way for the mission to earn money and go a way towards supporting itself. The Central Board and later the BPA hoped that all missions and reserves would sooner, rather than later, become self-sufficient, in order to reduce costs to public funds as well as help Aboriginal people on their way to becoming 'civilized'. Although Aboriginal people were collectively considered worthy of land grants, individual requests were refused. For example, in early 1871, Steward from the Ebenezer mission requested a local guardian, Mr Gummow, to apply for land to run sheep on; however, his request was refused as Gummow decided that Steward was 'better off where he [was]'.[134] In early 1878 he was finally successful in realising his plan for land to farm himself.[135] While the diary thus offers insights into the request for land and the main petitions, it does not describe all the petitions or letters sent by Indigenous people requesting more land, as more petitions survive in the public records office than are recorded in the diary.[136]

---

130 Ref: 9 March 1870.
131 *Eighth BPA Report*, Appendix XII, 27; Ref: 22 November 1869. See also: *Periodical Accounts* 27 (1868), 408.
132 *Periodical Accounts* 27 (1868), 410.
133 *Periodical Accounts* 26 (1866), 28.
134 *Seventh BPA Report*, 20.
135 *Periodical Accounts* 30 (1876), 494–95.
136 Edward Ryan notes, among others, the following files of interest for land claims: PROV, VPRS 242, 22/5/1871; PROV, VPRS 242, 21/10/1871 and PROV, VPRS 242, 16/7/1872. See: Ryan, 'Wegaia Worlds', 28–35.

Figure 10: Portrait of Philip Pepper with his wife Rebecca and her niece Rosa, n.d.
Source: MAB, PP SchwED, 'Scrap Book of Pictures relating to the Unitas Fratrum. Begun in Philadelphia in 1854' (n.d., Volume B), compiled by Edmund de Schweinitz, page 99.

Besides land, the diary also highlights the ways in which Indigenous labour was used, both on and off the mission. Jacky (later Stephen) and Makenzie told Adolf that 'they liked to be at our place but they had to go to Mr Ellerman to drive in some cattle, but they would soon be here again'.[137] Jacky's labour was used not only by Mr Ellerman; the missionaries also took advantage of it, engaging him with other men to cut bark for the missionaries' house.[138] Some squatters, such as Mr Archibald, from beyond Lake Hindmarsh, arrived at the mission in September 1866 asking for an Indigenous labourer for a fortnight. Adolf reported that 'he got James, who was very glad for the opportunity'.[139] Such comments suggest that there was an amount of reciprocal advantage for people in being hired out, although other comments in the diary suggest that settler colonists were not fair in their terms. This may have been the case when Philip and Stephen were hired to build a fence for Mr Fleming over a period of eight weeks in 1867.[140] Adolf recorded in the diary that he spoke to Fleming about the payment, suggesting that the framework of remuneration was not clear.[141] Indigenous people's labour was also used to raise sheep with the profits going to support the mission, and individuals. Not only Indigenous men, but also women were engaged in the economics of the mission station. Women were used as housemaids for the missionaries as well as cooks. No clear indication is made in the diary as to if and what these women were paid, or what they thought of this labour.

Besides physical labour, Indigenous people also worked in a religious capacity for the mission. Nathanael Pepper and his brother Phillip were considered important spiritual workers for the mission, holding religious meetings and speaking to people about Christianity. Spieseke thought so much of their work that he requested the UEC pay both men a small wage as spiritual workers; however, the UEC refused, saying a wage was not justified with such a small congregation.[142] The men did, however, receive a wage by September 1865, when both Nathanael and Philip were paid a salary of £12 for their work as missionary assistants, with the funds supplied by Mr Simpson, the Presbyterian minister in Horsham.[143] The payment of the funds by another denomination demonstrates ecumenical collaboration

---

137 Ref: 23 May 1864.
138 Ref: 7 June 1866.
139 Ref: 27 September 1866.
140 Ref: 10 September 1867.
141 Ref: 11 September 1867.
142 UA, UEC Minutes, 12 December 1865, #12, 262.
143 See: *Periodical Accounts* 26 (1866), 28.

in the conversion of Australian Aboriginal people to Christianity, with such collaboration occurring at various other Aboriginal missions in Australia. Nevertheless, such collaboration was not always smooth. In 1866, Spieseke reported to the UEC that the Assembly of the Presbyterian Church had voted to pay the two men, Phillip and Nathanael, to be evangelists under the auspice of the Presbyterians in the Wimmera. Although the Presbyterians had done much for the Moravian mission at Ramahyuck, working together with the Moravians to establish the mission, Spieseke considered the Victorian Association in Melbourne to have done more for Ebenezer, and indeed this association provided substantial funding and political support. The UEC were concerned, for their part, that if the Presbyterians paid for the two men, then this would constitute too much interference into Moravian Church policies and may send a signal to others that a connection to the missionaries would be rewarded with money or status, rather than undertaken out of conviction. Phillip and Nathanael, the UEC noted, should be kept in the dark about what was discussed about them lest they became inflated with their importance.[144] Thus in both physical and religious working roles, Indigenous people were deemed in need of training to reach the full potential of their relegated positions.

A further topic that runs through the diary is the collection of children from locations further afield to raise on the mission, despite the children having parents. During the period that the Hartmanns were in Australia, there was a concerted effort by the Moravians, other religious people and the government to remove Aboriginal children to mission stations or government reserves so that the children could be educated by the Central Board and later the BPA. The focus went beyond those children considered abandoned or orphaned, and was applied to all Aboriginal and 'half-caste' children. In the Central Board's report of 1864 there was a hint that the board wished to push for a government Act to be passed to 'authorise the removal of half-caste girls and orphans against the wishes of those persons who may have assumed charge of them', with the reasoning being that these children were particularly in peril.[145] In this respect, Coranderrk was the most important reserve in the collection of children, with John Green, the manager, making three trips to Ebenezer during the Hartmann's residence to inspect the mission and to discuss many aspects of the government's Aboriginal policies.[146] The numerous attempts to 'gain' children for the

---

144 UA, UEC Minutes, 26 April 1866, #3, 110–16.
145 *Fourth BPA Report*, 10.
146 Ref: 29 October 1864; 23 November 1866; 30 October 1868.

Ebenezer mission were undertaken both by the European missionaries and by the Indigenous men on the mission. Phillip (formerly Charley Charley), for example, went on numerous missionary journeys to bring back children. Steward 'collected' his younger half-sister and some other children for the mission station.[147] Some of the journeys which the Hartmanns or Spiesekes made were under the auspices of the government. Spieseke, for example, went on a journey to the west in July 1867.[148] Not all of these journeys were noted in the Hartmann diary—such as a trip in January 1869 from which two young girls were brought to the mission. Neither their names nor their circumstances nor their locations were recorded.[149] At times, settler-colonists requested that the mission take in so-called 'half-caste' children.[150] During the time the Hartmanns were at Ebenezer, a focused attempt to gain children for the mission was undertaken; however, this backfired in some ways, as the parents and guardians not infrequently came to retrieve their children, to the dismay of the missionaries. In late 1868, Green suggested in the annual report that Hartmann be 'instructed to try and collet all the children as far up as Carr's Plains', and if this was not possible, that the children be sent to Coranderrk.[151] Hartmann had already travelled to Carr's Plains in early December 1866 to entice people to come back to the mission, which indicates that Green's plans were not unique, but rather part of an ongoing and broader strategy undertaken to centralise the protection of Aboriginal people on the missions and reserves, particularly the younger people. By July 1870, the missionaries had collected 20 children to live at the mission; however, the circumstances of them coming, and their parents' reactions, were not always noted in the diary.[152] By the end of the following year, Spieseke noted, following a journey to Pleasant Creek, from which he had brought back a boy and three girls, that the total number of children on the mission was 34. In Spieseke's words, the children were 'almost all destitute orphans'.[153] His comments reflect his limited, rather than expanded, understanding of family networks. The reaction of the children to the displacement from their parents is, however, rarely recounted beyond curt descriptions of emotional outbreaks.

---

147 *Missionsblatt* 2 (1870), 48.
148 UA, UEC Minutes, 14 September 1867, #15, 245.
149 UA, UEC Minutes, 20 April 1869, #12, 76.
150 *Missionsblatt* 9 (1870), 222.
151 *Sixth BPA Report* 9–10.
152 MAB, PP HJAH, 3, Letters, Adolf to Hines family, Ebenezer, 12 July 1870.
153 *Periodical Accounts* 28 (1871), 279–80.

INTRODUCTION

Structure of the diary

The original diary is structured so that a double opened physical page of the diary is dedicated to a day of the year, with multiple years corresponding to the day recorded on each page. Generally, the diary entries are written on the left-hand side of the open page, with the right-hand side of the double page mostly left blank, presumably in the expectation that it too one day would be filled. At times there are no entries at all for a specific day; these blank pages, I suggest, exemplify the silences that this diary encapsulates. These blank pages and silences are demonstrative of the selective and subjective nature of recording and the inability of some voices and events to be captured in text. For these reasons, the structure of the original diary is kept here to remain true to the original format, as well as to allow readers to more easily compare years and to cross-reference individuals from the extensive index. Moreover, within the Moravian Church, as in many other religious groups, specific dates are imbued with importance, referencing moments of importance to the religious community that could be celebrated and commemorated over time and distance. As such, the structuring of the diary with multiple years per calendar day reflects the internal logic of religious organisations that hoped to convert people to Christianity, as it was often only with hindsight that the beginning of the conversion process was evident. Thus, it was important for Moravian missionaries to write of events that might be later seen as the beginnings of conversions, so as to know what could be done to stimulate further conversion.

The diary begins on 14 August 1863, although at the beginning of the diary it is stated that 'this diary was commenced in Fulneck on Friday the 24th of July'. There are earlier entries, such as 25 March 1796, which was the birthday of Adolf's father, Johann Gottlieb Hartmann. The actual diary was begun by Adolf, who in the first entries wrote about his preparations for his time in Australia and his journey back to Herrnhut, Germany, where he received information about his future work as a missionary. Polly started writing from late May 1864, once they had reached Australia. She did not write as frequently as Adolf; however, there are many entries in her hand. The Moravians, like many other religious groups, called members of their religious community Brother and Sister, abbreviated to B^r and S^{is}. This was not, however, always the case in Hartmann's diary, as Friedrich Wilhelm Spieseke, the other Moravian missionary at the Ebenezer mission station, was at times referred to as Mr. S, or even just S.

EBENEZER MISSION STATION, 1863–1873

The core dates of the diary are from 1863 to 1873. From comments in the diary, we can ascertain that the diary was not always written up each day. For example, a diary entry on 29 February 1865 is annotated: '(This should be on the 1st of March.)' The following table gives the number of entries per year, demonstrating that 1865, with 270 entries, was the most recorded year. It was also the first full calendar year that the couple spent at the Ebenezer mission. Alternatively, 1870, the year in which Polly miscarried for the second time, has only 11 entries, and 1871, the year in which the Hartmanns were still in Ebenezer, has no entries at all. In this version of the diary, I have added excerpts of a letter in diary form from 1870, in which Polly describes events to her family. I have indicated where these are letter excerpts rather than diary entries. They are not counted in the following table under 1870.

Table 1: Number of entries in the Hartmanns' diary per year.

Year	Number of diary entries
1863	30
1864	207
1865	270
1866	179
1867	144
1868	67
1869	61
1870	11
1873	19

Source: Author's summary.

Most of the Aboriginal people mentioned in the diary were only mentioned by first names—mostly European. As with many other governmental reports from the period, surnames were not uniformly used for Aboriginal people during the 1860s. However, from the 1870s, there was an increase in administration and surveillance, and more surnames were recorded in official documentation. For example, Matthew, formerly known as Liberty, did not have a family name recorded in the diary. However, other sources from the missionaries note that he was called Matthew Elliott.[154] Individuals often had multiple names in the diary, with European pre-baptismal names being replaced with new European names taken on at baptism. Charley

---

154 See also: *Further Facts, Fifth Paper*, 6.

Charley became Philip, Kitty became Amelia, Dick-a-Dick became Paul and Jessie became Rebecca, to name just a few. Also, non-European names were spelt in various ways. Thus, we have the name George Bupbup (seen on Ref: 26 February 1865), Booppoop (Ref: 22 May 1864), Boop-poop (Ref: 29 May 1864), Bopoop (Ref: 9 July 1864) and Bubbud (Ref: 11 July 1864), as well as George, all presumably for the same boy. He was the son of Judy, and the brother of Kitty. The various iterations of his name demonstrate that there was no standard orthography for names.

There are also multiple people noted in the diary with the same name. For example, the names Peter, Mary, Nancy, and Susan refer to multiple people. Where able I have tried to differentiate, although this is not always possible. Besides names, the diary has many other irregularities in spelling. Nhill, for example, is spelt Niel, Nhel and Nhill, with only the initial alternative spelling receiving a footnote indicating the current correct spelling. Moreover, I have opted not to use '*sic*' in the diary itself; where one would normally use it to indicate that a word or phrase may appear incorrect, I have left the original spelling and grammar. Additionally, I have left the original mark-up of the diary, including underlines and superscript, to demonstrate the rawness of the diary. I have not opted to provide a 'clean' copy of the diary—that is, I have left the original diary with all of its grammatical and orthographical inconsistencies, to provide a sense of closeness to the original text. This includes indicating where words were later squeezed into the text, through providing them in this version as superscript, as well as the underlining that indicates passages important to the writer. Through doing so, I hoped to provide a sense of immediateness to the situation in which the diary was created: often written in short busts, quite often after an incident of heightened emotions, or at the end of a mundane day when spirits were low. Although Adolf spoke German, the majority of the diary is in English, the Hartmanns' common language. When there are passages in German, I have given the translations in the footnotes. The diary is peppered with Biblical references, which can be found in the King James Version (of 1611), the English-language Bible most commonly used at the time.

The diary reflects the language used in the mid-nineteenth century, some of which is deemed inappropriate in contemporary times. The paternalist tone of the missionaries is reflected in Polly and Adolf referring to people living on the station as 'our blacks', or 'blacks'. I have left these references without commenting on them. To help the reader track the individuals there is an extensive index with people listed alphabetically, with the entries for each person ordered chronologically by year, diverging from the structure of the diary. The first time a person appears in the pages of the diary from January to December (and not the first actual entry of a person), a longer biographical account is given of them, which includes information drawn from contemporaneous printed government and religious sources as well as the German handwritten minutes of two Moravian administrative bodies. These notes are neither extensive nor even, given that for some people more material was preserved in government documentation and missionary reports than for others. A final point to help the reader navigate the diary is the cross-referencing within the annotations: this is indicated by 'Ref:' and then the date to which more information can be found, either in the text or in the footnotes.

The informal note-based entries of the diary suggest that it was not designed for prosperity but was, rather, more of a mnemonic for later letterwriting. For example, Polly wrote a letter to her parents in May 1864 using almost the same words as in her diary entries from 22 May until 14 June 1864. The entry for Tuesday 14 June 1864 relates the incident when Paddy wished to take his daughter Emma away. In the continuation of her letter for Wednesday 15 June 1864, Polly continues the story of Emma, a story that is not included in the diary. It reads: 'Emma went this morning. We hope to get her back soon …'[155] Such expressions of hope for young children to be raised on the mission were expressions of optimism for the Christian future of the station. The continuation of the story of Emma outside of the pages of the diary also reflects the limitations of the diary in terms of what it contains, as well as the specific Christian perspective of the missionaries. Nonetheless, it must be emphasised as to how much detail the diary does contain, which provides a fascinating insight into daily interactions and the ups and downs of mission life. Through this publication, the diary is available for the first time to broader audience beyond that of the Hartmanns and their religious network, providing rich, detailed insights into the daily operation and broader community of an Aboriginal mission station in the nineteenth century. There are many silences and omissions in this diary; however, it is hoped that it will provide impetus for further historical research and exploration.

---

155 MAB, PP HJAH, 3, Letters, A and M Hartmann to Hines family, May 1864.

Timeline of diary

1863	14 August: Adolf Hartmann accepts call to be a missionary in Australia. Start of ongoing diary
1863	29 December: Wedding day of Adolf Hartmann and Mary (Polly) Hines
1864	23 January: Adolf and Polly Hartmann set sail for Australia on the *Norfolk*
1864	7 May: Adolf and Polly Hartmann arrive at the Ebenezer mission station, on Wotjobaluk country, in the Colony of Victoria, Australia
1872	9 March: Adolf and Polly Hartmann, with children Eleanor (born 14 December 1865) and Henry (born 20 November 1868), leave Australia for England
1873	23 January: Adolf and Polly accept a call to be missionaries to the 'Indian Mission in Canada' to the Lenni Lenape (also known as Delaware) at New Fairfield, Canada
1873	6 April: Hartmann's first Sunday in New Fairfield, Canada
1873	19 July: Last entry in the diary, written in New Fairfield, Canada

Adolf and Mary (known as Polly) Hartmann's Diary, 1863–1873

Diary entries written or partly written by Polly/Mary are indicated by an asterisk (*). Her entries are further indicated by a different font.

* * *

This diary was commenced in Fulneck[1] in the year 1863 on Friday the 24th of July.[2]_

January

1 January 1864
Salem[3]_ In the evening there was a tre teaparty in the schoolroom's , & after it there was a good deal of speechifying, when I had to get up & say a few words about Australia.[4]_

---

1   Fulneck, Moravian settlement, now part of greater Leeds. The Moravian settlement was established there in 1744. In the 1750s, boys' and girls' schools, including room for boarders, were established. Adolf Hartmann was a teacher at the Moravian boys' school in Fulneck when he received his call to Australia, Ref: 14 August 1863.
2   Actual start of the diary Ref: 14 August 1863.
3   Salem, UK, where Adolf and Mary (Polly) Hartmann spent a few days on honeymoon after being married on Ref: 29 December 1863.
4   Adolf received his call to Australia on 13 August 1863, the day before he commenced the diary.

EBENEZER MISSION STATION, 1863–1873

1 January 1865

[Sun] New year in Ebenezer[5] in Australia Wimmera District.[6]

1 January 1866

[Mon] All of us to Antwerp[7] to see the Christmas (or rather new years tree. Spieseke[8] & family in the Spring-cart; Polly,[9] Nelly,[10] & myself in the buggy. There were present also M̄ & M̄ˢ H[enry]. Ellerman[11] from the lake.[12]_

---

5   Ebenezer mission station run by Moravian missionaries, in operation from 1859 to 1904. Established on the traditional country of the Wotjobaluk. The site was *Banji bunag* (also written *Bungo budnutt/ Punyo Bunnutt* or *Binio ponyip*), near a massacre site where the mother of Jim Crow (also known as Willie Wimmera) was killed. See: *The Periodical Accounts relating to the Missions of the Church of the United Brethren Established among the Heathen* (hereafter *Periodical Accounts*) 23 (1858), 167.
6   The Wimmera Shire was established in March 1864 through the local government *Electoral Act 1863* (Vic). It was on traditional Wotjobaluk country. The Wergaia language group has four major dialects, being Wudjubalug/Wotjobaluk; Djadjala/Djadjali; Buibadjali; Biwadjali. The first was the dialect of the site where the Ebenezer mission was established.
7   Antwerp was a station claimed by Horatio Cockburn Ellerman. He was one of the first squatters of the area and a supporter of the Ebenezer mission station. He became an ordained minister of the Presbyterian Church in 1866 (Ref: 16 May 1866). He was married to Anne Westgarth, whose brother was William, active in Melbourne government and literary circles. See: Anne Longmire, *Nine Creeks to Albacutya: A History of the Shire of Dimboola* (North Melbourne: Hargreen Publishing Company, 1985), 21.
8   First mention in diary (First Ref:) Ref: 20 May 1864. Friedrich Wilhelm Spieseke (1821–1877), married to Christina née Fricke. In 1849, he was called to be a missionary in Australia. In October 1848, he travelled to Australia with Br. Andreas Täger to establish the Lake Boga mission station, near Swan Hill. At the end of 1856, Spieseke, Täger and another missionary, Br. Hansen, left Australia without permission from the Moravian Church Board, which was unusual and controversial. In 1857, Spieseke was called again to be a missionary in Australia, this time with Friedrich August Hagenauer. They arrived in Australia in May 1858. In August 1859, the two missionaries established the Ebenezer mission station near Antwerp in the Wimmera district. In May 1861, he married Christina Fricke. In September 1876, Spieseke resigned from active missionary duties. He died on 24 June 1877 at Ebenezer. Christina Spieseke returned to Europe after his death. See: Felicity Jensz, *German Moravian Missionaries in the British Colony of Victoria, Australia, 1848–1908: Influential Strangers* (Leiden: Brill, 2010), doi.org/10.1163/ej.9789004179219.i-274.
9   First Ref: 17 September 1863. Polly being Adolf's nickname for Mary Hartmann, née Hines. Born 1838, Nottinghamshire, England to John and Ann Hines. Died 1916, in Bethlehem, Pennsylvania, USA.
10   First Ref: 15 December 1865. Eleanor Hartmann, known as Nelly, was born at Ebenezer on Ref: 14 December 1865. She moved with her parents to Canada in 1873, and spent her later years in the USA.
11   First Ref: 26 December 1864. Henry Clarence Ellerman, brother of Horatio Cockburn Ellerman of the Antwerp station. The first name of Mrs Ellerman is not recorded in the diary.
12   Lake Hindmarsh (also written Hindmarsch), is the largest fresh water lake in Victoria. It is about 25 km north of the mission. Known as *Gurru* (also recorded as *Guru*) in the Wergaia language, the story relates that Barra, the red kangaroo, made the lake when he stopped to eat grass. In 1865, Lake Hindmarsh was under squatting license from the Trust and Agency Co. See: Story translated by Kylie Klimpton Kennedy, 'Wergaia Guli', *Culture Victoria*: cv.vic.gov.au/stories/aboriginal-culture/nyernila/wergaia-barra/ (site discontinued; accessed 15 June 2021); Phil Taylor, *Karkarooc: Mallee Shire History, 1896–1995* (Yarriambiack Shire Council: Warracknbeal, 1996), 12; Anonymous, *The Squatters' Directory, Road Guide, and Key to the Squatting Map of Victoria* (Blundell & Ford: Melbourne, 1865), trove.nla.gov.au/version/264832355, 19.

1 January 1867

[Tue] A very hot day so there was not much done out of doors, I finished the letters for spelling[13]

2 January 1864

[Mon] Went back again to Fairfield[14] to the little cot;[15] to spend but a few more days in the same, as we heard from London[16] that our vessel the "Norfolk"[17] was to sail on Jan 20.[18]_

2 January 1867

[Wed] There was a hot wind & towards evening there was a tremendous blast sweeping along about a mile from us on Stuarts run;[19] the dust it sent up looked like fire, Although we did not ^get^ the worst of it, we had so much of it that our mill[20] came down, yes down it came, & the wings broken all to bits_ Judy[21] who came here was spoken to, that if she wished to stay with us leaving her husband Little[22] we would protect her._ Jerry[23] gone to the camp with his blanket & we think he will bolt with one of Littles wives._

---

13   These letters were to be used in the mission school, which was first established in 1859.
14   Fairfield, near Manchester, UK, was a planned Moravian settlement established in 1785. For more on Moravian settlements in England, particularly earlier ones, see: Colin Podmore, *The Moravian Church in England 1728–1760* (Oxford: Clarendon Press, 1998), doi.org/10.1093/acprof:oso/9780198207252.001.0001.
15   Sleeping quarters.
16   London, England, UK.
17   *Norfolk*, a sailing vessel of 1,000 tonnes. Captain Jonkin. Left Plymouth on 28 January 1863, arrived Hobson's Bay, near Melbourne, Australia on 15 April 1864. Passenger list, in which Hartmann is written Hartman, can be found in 'Unassisted passenger lists of the Public Record Office Victoria, Record Series Number (BPRS)': 947. See: prov.vic.gov.au/explore-collection/explore-topic/passenger-records-and-immigration/unassisted-passenger-lists (accessed April 2020).
18   Actually sailed later (Ref: 28 January 1864).
19   Stuarts run, also known as Marsh and Stuarts (Stewart) run, was next to the mission. However, it is not listed in *The Squatters' Directory* of 1865.
20   Windmill used for irrigation. Adolf spent much of 1866 building the windmill.
21   First reference. Judy was recorded as being one of Little's wives, the other wife being Charlotte. Judy was recorded as being the mother of George, also known as Bupbup and many other iterations (see footnote at Ref: 19 February 1865). Unclear if this Judy refers to the mother of Kitty, whose father Old Jack died Ref: 18 February 1865. See: *Periodical Accounts* 25 (1863), 288.
22   First reference. Little was recorded as having two wives, Judy and Charlotte; scant other information is available on him in this diary.
23   First Ref: 30 January 1865. Jerry was an Aboriginal man from the Tatiara district (also written Tatta Yarra) in current-day South Australia. He was the husband of Martha (Ref: 17 January 1867).

2 January 1868

[Thu] Bobby[24] + Tarpot[25] ~~left~~ left us to-day going back to M[r] M[c] Leod.[26] Tarpot speaks of coming back again._ Matthew[27] began putting up the walls of his new house using the boards I made some time ago._ There is the [W]hooping cough[28] at our place at present Christina[29] Minnie[30] & Emma[31] have it there is a great deal of coughing amongst the boys. we fear it may spread._ Sp[ieseke]: is busy making shelves & hoocks for the boys room,[32] previous to plaistering[33] the same._

---

24   First Ref: 26 March 1867. Bobby, a young person, brother of Maggie (also written Maggy) and Lizzy, 'collected' from the Mac Millan run on Ref: 26 March 1867.
25   This is the only mention of Tarpot in this diary. Anne Longmire reports of a Tarpot, who travelled with on the Aboriginal Cricket Tour to England in 1866. Longmire, *Nine Creeks to Albacutya*, 14.
26   Adolf first mentions Mr Hugh McLeod at Lochiel on Ref: 25 June 1867. In 1869, the Hartmanns went on a journey west and brought back with them the 'half-caste' boy Henry and his aunt Nancy from McLeod's place (Ref: 18 December 1869).
27   First Ref: 8 May 1864. Matthew Elliott (formerly Liberty) was baptised on Ref: 8 May 1864, on the same day as Philip (formerly Charley Charley) and Rebecca (formerly Jessie, married to Philip). He was already connected to the mission in 1862. In 1866, he was recorded as being 23 years old. He had a sister called Nancy. Matthew was married to Margaret on Ref: 18 August 1864. She was suggested as a wife for Matthew by Rev. Chase. According to Adolf, the 'Murray Blacks … found fault with Matthew marrying Margaret saying that she was his sister' (Ref: 22 August 1866). Together they had three sons, Joseph (Ref: 8 February 1866; 24 February 1866), Robert (Ref: 5 November 1867), and Charles Arthur (Ref: 25 July 1870). Matthew died in November 1870. See: *Periodical Accounts* 27 (1868), 514; Melbourne Association in Aid of the Moravian Mission, *Further Facts relating to the Moravian Mission Read with the Report of the Committee at the First Annual Meeting of the Melbourne Association in Aid of the Moravian Mission* (hereafter *Further Facts*), *Fifth Paper* (Melbourne: WM Goodhugh & Co, 1866), 5; *Missions-Blatt aus der Brüdergemeine* (herafter *Missionsblatt*), No. 10 (1864), 189.
28   Pertussis (whooping cough), a highly contagious respiratory disease caused by bacteria.
29   First Ref: 26 November 1867. Christina, a 'half-caste' girl, was brought to the Ebenezer mission Station by her father, Peter Mac Guinnes, who worked on Adam Smith's station Mosquito Plaines. This could refer to the Aboriginal man Peter MacGuinnes (ca. 1846–1911), who was also known as Jowley, and was said to be the last survivor of the Yarrikuluk clan of the Wotjobaluk. Taylor, *Karkarooc*, 22–24.
30   First Ref: 26 March 1867. Minnie is referred to most often in 1867, but there is not defining information about her in the diary.
31   First Ref: 14 June 1864. Emma, a young girl, was reported to be the only unmarried woman of the 'tribe' in 1865. She was reported to be nine years old in 1866. In December 1864, Polly and Adolf visited Emma, reported to be about seven or eight years old, and her parents, who were living near Scott's station of Warracknabeal. Her parents 'allowed her to return' to the mission on Ref: 23 January 1865. Her father was Paddy (Ref: 14 June 1864). See: Moravian Archives Bethlehem, Pennsylvania, USA [MAB], Personal Papers [PP], John Adolphus Hieronymus Hartmann [HJAH], 3, Letters, written by Adolph and Mary Hartmann to their parents and siblings (1864–1871), Polly Hartman to Hines family, 15 December 1864; *Periodical Accounts* 25 (1863), 509. See also: *Further Facts*, *Fifth Paper*, 5.
32   The two male missionaries, Spieseke and Hartmann, and the Aboriginal men Mark and Philip were working on building a sleeping room for the boys in the school. Ref: 8 July 1867.
33   Plastering.

3 January 1865

[Tue] Drove to the 9 creeks[34] with Polly to purchase sundry things, a lock for Phillip,[35] a new grindstone £ 1.1 among the things. There were a good many Blacks about the inn;[36] talked to them: all of them very friendly & glad to see us._ Stopped at Edol's[37] for dinner._ B[r][other] Meissel[38] was riding with us on Browns[39] horse. A close day._

3 January 1868

[Fri] Spieseke drove to the Nine Creeks to spend ~~XX~~ £ 20 (remainder of the wool money[40] on behalf of the people buying useful articles for them. Not all the Blacks at the Station got something but only those who have

---

34   Nine Creeks was the former name of Dimboola: the latter was first surveyed in 1862, however, the settlement was referred to as Nine Creeks throughout this diary. Anne Longmire, a historian of the shire, suggests that the location was called 'Watchegatcheca', meaning wattle tree and white cockatoos, by the Wotjobaluk. See: Longmire, *Nine Creeks to Albacutya*, 33.

35   First Ref: 8 May 1864, the day of his baptism. Philip (sometimes spelt Phillip), formerly known as Charley Charley. He was Nathaniel's brother. In 1866, he was recorded as being about 28 years old. His wife, Rebecca, was formerly known as Jessie (sometimes Jessy). She was described as 'one of the remaining three young women of this "tribe"'. Philip died on 16 August 1873. See: *Periodical Accounts* 25 (1863), 188; *Periodical Accounts* 29 (1873), 79–80. See also: *Further Facts, Fifth Paper*, 5; Robert Kenny, *The Lamb Enters the Dreaming: Nathanael Pepper and the Ruptured World* (Melbourne: Scribe, 2007); Phillip Pepper and Tess De Araugo, *You Are What You Make Yourself To Be: The Story of a Victorian Aboriginal Family 1842–1980* (Melbourne: Hyland House, 1980). See also Hagenauer's account: *Periodical Accounts* 30 (1879), 381–87.

36   In 1861, Horatio Ellerman, a supporter of the mission, protested against the establishment of the public house in Nine Creeks, due to concern that 'every endeavour to better the condition of the aborigines will be set at naught, and the recognized usefulness of the mission destroyed'. See: *First Report of the Central Board Appointed to Watch Over the Interests of the Aborigines in the Colony of Victoria* no. 39 (Melbourne: John Ferres, Government Printer, 1861), 23. Reports in this series hereafter referred to as, e.g. *First BPA Report*.

37   First Ref: 12 August 1864. Thomas Edols held the Upper Regions squatting run from 1858 to 1872, some 14 miles from Ebenezer. Edols also held the Bonegar squatting run. Ref: Longmire, *Nine Creeks to Albacutya*, 21; *The Squatters' Directory*, 31.

38   First Ref: 9 December 1864. Gottlieb Meissel was one of four missionaries sent out in 1864 by the United Elders Conference (UEC) of the Moravian Church, located in Herrnhut, Germany. They were to establish a mission, possibly at Cooper's Creek, with the exact location to be decided once the men were in Australia. The decision to send out missionaries had been made by the UEC in October 1863, with the men, Br Heinrich Walder, Carl Wilhelm Kramer, Wilhelm Julius Kühne and Gottlieb Meissel, arriving in December 1864. Walder and Meissel went to Ebenezer, while Kramer and Kühne were sent to Ramahyuck to support the mission before their own missionary field was decided. See: Jensz, *German Moravian Missionaries*.

39   First Ref: 25 December 1864. Brown was reported as being an Indigenous man being instructed by the missionaries. He was recorded to be 26 years old in 1866. In July 1866 he reportedly requested to be baptised. He was baptised, taking the name Samuel, on Ref: 13 August 1866. See also: *Further Facts, Fifth Paper*, 5; *Periodical Accounts* 26 (1866), 247.

40   The wool clip for 1867 was 2,000 pounds. See: *Sixth BPA Report*, 14.

fairly settled down & worked the station during the last year._ S[pieseke]: brought Miss White[41] with him to stay with us for a little while (She is the governess at the manse[42])

4 January 1865

[Wed] A very close day, horizon clouded_ After school, when at work, Nathanael[43] came back from looking after the Sheep, & said that he had heard a man, inside the Antwerp gate crying out, but thinking it might be a bushrangers, he did not venture to go near. Well. S[pieseke]. myself & Walder[44] with a number of Blacks went out to see what it was, & we found a man of the name "Bruce" from M[r] H. J. Ellerman's[45] Station, having been thrown by his horse, lying on the ground, & his leg broken between the ankle & knee_ When at the gate, & attempting to open it, a box of wax-matches fell out of his pocket, ignited and burned the horse so that it got wild & jumped & not only threw, but also kicked him, so breaking his leg. I went back immediately with Walder & one of the Blacks to fetch something to carry him to our place._ We quickly made a litter of an old ladder, put ~~my~~ ᵒᵘʳ sofa mattras upon it, and down we went again to take up this poor man to our place. This carrying was rather hard work, but there being many Blacks with us, we managed the ¾ of a mile pretty well._

---

41   Ref: 17 August 1867.
42   The manse was the dwelling associated with the Presbyterian church in Dimboola. The church, a log cabin, was built was 1861. See: Longmire, *Nine Creeks to Albacutya*, 33.
43   First Ref: 19 May 1864. Nathanael (also Nathaniel) Pepper, was baptised on 12 August 1860 being the first baptised Indigenous person at Ebenezer. On 21 May 1863, he was married to Rachel Warndekan, an Aboriginal woman from Western Australia, who was raised at Anne Camfield's 'Institution for Native and Half-Caste Children'. Rachel died on Ref: 23 March 1869. After her death, Nathaniel Pepper moved to the Ramahyuck mission in Gippsland Ref: 3 May 1869. There FA Hagenauer, also a Moravian missionary, worked. Nathaniel was married again in February 1870 to the 16-year-old Louise Arbuckle, a Christian woman of the Bratowoloong people. He died on 7 March 1877 at Ramahyuck. His brother Phillip (Charley Charley) and half-brother Lanky also lived on the Ebenezer mission. His brother, Light, the first husband of Kitty (Amelia) died in 1862. He also had a sister, name unrecorded here. Nathaniel's father was Toney (baptised name of Joshua) and his mother Lina (also spelt Linna). For more on Nathaniel see: Kenny, *The Lamb Enters the Dreaming*; Pepper and De Araugo, *You Are What You Make Yourself to Be*. Tess De Araugo, 'Pepper, Nathaniel (1841–1877)', *Australian Dictionary of Biography*, accessed 22 April 2020, adb.anu.edu.au/biography/pepper-nathaniel-13148/text23799. See also Hagenauer's account: *Periodical Accounts* 30 (1879), 381–87.
44   First Ref: 9 December 1864. Heinrich Walder was one of the four missionaries sent out by the UEC to Australia in 1864 to establish a mission. See: Jensz, *German Moravian Missionaries*.
45   The proximity would suggest that this refers to Horatio Ellerman's station at Antwerp.

We put M[r] Bruce into Mary's[46] room on her bed, & then I cut with a razor his boots off, & then bathed the injured leg in cold water. He felt much better towards evening, & said that he felt the inflamation going down. Phillip was despatched to Horsham[47] to fetch D[r] Johnson[48]_ Meissel Walder volunteered to watch with M[r] Bruce during the night._

Edward[49] went of with our cart & mare to Walmar[50] to fetch part of the things of M[r] M[eissel]. & W[alder]._ A number of new blacks, 5 alltogether came_

5 January 1865

[Thu] D[r] Johnson came at 1 p.m. he looked at M[r] Bruce's leg & did not find it as bad as he expected. He said that M[r] B[ruce]: must be taken down to Horsham before he could do much in the matter, consequently we prepared a swinging bed in our spring-cart, not without some trouble, though, as we had to alter the ~~plan we~~ arrangement we had to put up first. When he was was got into the cart at last, there was some difficulty whom to send

---

46 First Ref: 28 May 1864. Mary was the daughter of the deceased man Isaac. In 1865, she was reported to be about 13 years old and worked as a house girl for the missionaries. Mary took on the name Elizabeth when she was baptised on Ref: 27 July 1865. She married the baptised man David on Ref: 7 May 1867. See: *Periodical Accounts* 25 (1863), 126, 509.
47 Horsham, the largest European settlement in the Wimmera, had settler colonists living there from the 1840s.
48 First Ref: 4 June 1864. Doctor Johnson from Horsham, some 50 kilometres away, attended on occasion to the mission inhabitants.
49 First Ref: 17 September 1864. Edward was baptised on Ref: 26 July 1865 and took the name James. He was reported as being a man of around the age of 30 in 1866. He was said to have the same father as Kitty, being 'Old Man Jack'. He married Ruth in early 1866, and together they lived in one of the huts build on the mission. He died on Ref: 4 November 1868. See: *Further Facts, Fifth Paper*, 5; *Periodical Accounts* 27 (1868), 193; MAB, PP HJAH, 3, Letters, written by Adolph and Mary Hartmann to their parents and siblings (18641871), Polly Hartman to Hines family, 15 December 1864.
50 Walmer (often written Walmar in this diary), near Horsham, was the property of Charles Wilson, Esq. Wilson was a supporter of the Ebenezer mission. By 1869, it was also a location for which the two Wilson men, Charles and Alexander, were honorary correspondents for the Central Board, with the latter being at Vectis.

with him. The Blacks did not seem very willing, and as we got Daniel[51] & Corney[52] at last, we were not sure whether we could trust them & so S[pieseke]: went with them as far as the 9 creeks to see how things would get on. All this caused a great stir & not much else was done during the day. D[r] Johnson was went up away before our cart started.

<u>Uncle Mark Hines;[53] father's brother departed suddenly at in Manchester aged 52.</u>

5 January 1868

[Sun] Tobsy[54] the wife of Timothy[55] was deliverd of a boy this afternoon; it came about 2 months too soon & it seemed as if the little thing would not live, but the endeavours of M[r] Spieseke & Polly were blessed to keep it alive._

---

51   First mention in diary Ref: 22 May 1864. Daniel, previously known as Young Boney (sometimes Bony), was baptised on 6 December 1863. A man named Boney was reported to have spent some time in late 1863 and early 1864, before the Hartmanns arrived at Ebenezer, on the Lorquon station that Hugh Campbell managed. This station had a number of Chinese shepherds working on it, with Boney often associating with Chinese people of the station and other stations of the area. Young Boney/Daniel's brother Talliho (also written Tallyho, Taliho and Dallio), was baptised on the same day as Daniel and took the name Timothy. Boney (Daniel), Talliho (Timothy), and Corney were reportedly the first three scholars of the school which Spieseke and Hagenauer had established while still residing with Ellerman in January 1859. Daniel's father was Old Boney, his mother was old Mary, who died mid-July 1867. In April 1864, Daniel expressed a wish to Br Spieseke to travel into the interior with the four Moravian missionaries to Coopers Creek, Br H Walder, CW Kramer, WJ Kuehne and G Meissel. Daniel went with the three Moravian missionaries to establish a mission in the interior of Australia (Lake Kopperamana); however, he died in the evening of 11 October 1865 in Adelaide before he could reach the interior. Already in Geelong he had complained of a pain in his leg and was operated on. Cause of death was said to be consumption. See: *Periodical Accounts* 23 (1858), 168; *Periodical Accounts* 25 (1863), 187, 468–469; *Periodical Accounts* 26 (1866), 35, 38, 340. See: Melbourne Association in Aid of the Moravian Mission, *Facts relating to the Moravian Mission, First Paper* (hereafter *Facts, First Paper*) (Melbourne: WM Goodhugh & Co, 1860), 4. See: Unitätsarchiv (UA), UEC Minutes, 7 July 1864, #4. See also: The Dimboola and District Historical Society Archive (DDHS), The Lorquon Diary of Hugh Campbell, 19 October 1863 to 27 February 1864, copy of the diary supplied by Mr MDN Campbell, a descendant of Hugh Campbell.
52   First Ref: 13 June 1864. Corney/Corny/Korney was one of the first men to make a connection with the mission in 1860. He left Ebenezer in 1865 to work at a station near Horsham. See: *Periodical Accounts* 25 (1863), 508; *Facts, First Paper*, 11.
53   First Ref: 15 December 1863. Mark Hines was Polly's uncle. Polly and Adolf visited him before leaving England Ref: 16 January 1864.
54   First Ref: 5 December 1865. Topsy (also written Tobsy) was married to Timothy on Ref: 5 April 1867. Topsy was referred to as a 'half caste' girl aged 15, from Balmoral. Ref: 5 December 1865; Ref: 13 January 1866. She was said to be an orphan, who at the age of three was 'taken in' by a squatter, the Philip family. See: *Further Facts, Fifth Paper*, 6.
55   First Ref: 28 May 1864. Timothy, formerly known as Talliho (sometimes Tallyho), was the brother of Daniel (Young Bony), both baptised on 6 December 1863. Timothy's first wife, Susanne (also known as Susan) died on Ref: 12 February 1866. He married Topsy on Ref: 5 April 1867. In 1866, he was reported as being 23 years old. Timothy died in November 1870. See: *Periodical Accounts* 27 (1868), 514; *Further Facts, Fifth Paper*, 5.

6 January 1868

[Mon] Mr Lloyd[56] sent the things Sp[ieseke] bought last Friday[57] & they were distributed among the people. Sp[ieseke] begins to lath & plaister the boys schoolroowm. I am proceeding but slowly with the iron oven._

6 January 1870

[Thu] Philip sent off a letter (written by himself) to the Central Board[58] asking for land on their own account.[59]_

7 January 1865

[Sat] Finished the door in Phillips house & Walder finished the front window (very nicely done, alltogether Br W[alder]: is a very practical, clever, & neat worker). The Back window was also done by Wa him._ S[pieseke]: ma finished the Bed stead, & is going to make a wash stand next._

Edward returned from Walmar with W[alder]. & Meissel's things; our spring cart also came back, infor & the people informing us that Mr Bruce had got to Horsham safely. In the evening we got all those in that get meat & had a good speaking with them that they sh[ou]ld work in the afternoon, or else not come the next morning to fetch meat, they all acquiesced._

---

56 First Ref: 25 July 1864. William Henry Lloyd was a shopkeeper in Nine Creeks (Dimboola). Originally from Somersetshire, UK, he was a hawker before working in the Dimboola store from April 1863. See: Longmire, *Nine Creeks to Albacutya*, 34.
57 Ref: 3 January 1868.
58 The Central Board for the Protection of Aborigines (the Central Board or BPA) was established in 1869 through the *Aboriginal Protection Act 1869* (Vic). It replaced the Central Board Appointed to Watch Over the Interests of the Aborigines and was the governmental body for the administration of Aboriginal affairs in the Colony of Victoria.
59 The issue of access to land was dominant during the 1860s. On 10 March 1871, 1,710 acres were added to the Ebenezer mission reserve for 'Aboriginal Purposes'. See: *Seventh BPA Report*, 27.

7 January 1866

[Sun] We had our lovefeast[60] in according to the pra^(c)tice of our Mission congregation. We gave a collecting-card from the Melbourne association[61] to our people to try what they could do in the collecting way._ They seemed to like it._

7 January 1868

[Tue] I took the candidates for baptism from B^r Sp[ieseke] & began to-day taking Torr's lectures. _ Old Peter is very sick so we went down to see him & speak to him, but he seems to be closed up._

8 January 1865

[Sun] We had a lovefeast in the afternoon, w^[hlich] we ought to have had at Epiphany[62]_ Our turkey[63] hatched 5 eggs out of 9:[64] well pretty little things they are._

8 January 1867

[Tue] Since the 3^(rd) of Jan after the coming down of our mill I was at it putting up the new pump, to-day every thing about it was finished satisfactorily._ Among the additional things made is a tin box at the juncture where the pipe leads into the tank, at the bottom of this box I made an outlet to draw the water in case the tank gets full._ I had a good of trouble with the new pump as we ommitted to put a perforated box at the end of the suction pipe; an a great deal of sand & sticks was sucked up & discharged into the pipe leading to the garden so that I had to take it to pieces & clean some of them out._ Another strange behaviour of Timothy's. His old father[65] going to Antwerp had a blood vessel burst, but T[imothy]. came home & said nothing about it, till Sp[ieseke]: got to know about it from other Blacks.

---

60   Lovefeast is a Moravian custom in which primarily the service consists of hymns, with no address. The eating of sugar-cake, another Moravian speciality, and coffee concludes the service. Called 'Singstunde' in German.
61   Referring to the Melbourne Association in Aid of the Moravian Mission to the Aborigines of Australia, established 1861. From 1863, known as the Victorian Association in Aid of the Moravian Mission to the Aborigines of Australia. A collecting card was used to collect funds for the mission.
62   Christian religious festival, usually celebrated on 6 January.
63   A present to the mission from Mr Rutherford of the Wonwondah Station in the West Wimmera, Ref: 23 November 1864.
64   Ref: 13 December 1864.
65   Timothy's father was known as Old Boney (later Old Frank).

T[imothy] when spoken to said that S[pieseke]. would not lend him the cart (of course thinking so) afterwards he was saucy to boot._ Well I could not help speaking about his behaviour in chapel, It really requires much patience & strength from above to bear with the peculiar tempers of the people._

8 January 1868

[Wed] It began to rain in the morning & rained the greater part of the day: the rain came from the east._ Philip returned from his trip to the east &, Teddy[66] who went with him is about 12 miles from here bringing 6 more children 3 boys & 2 girls. How to bring them under will be the question.[67]

9 January 1865

[Mon] Made a commencement for a stand for the new grind stone._ There are some more candidates for baptism. Edward[68] & Kitty[69] & Brown.[70]

---

66   First Ref: 2 June 1864. Teddy was recorded as being a 32-year-old man attending the missionary school in 1866. He was married to Mary Ann. She died on Ref: 25 June 1865. He does not seem to have been baptised; however, he spent some time at the mission and went on tours collecting children to raise on the mission. He stated before the coroner's inquest into Amos Mackenzie's death in 1869 that he was Amos's brother. See: *Further Facts, Fifth Paper*, 5; DDHS, 'Proceedings of Inquest Held upon the Body of Amos Mackenzie at Dimboola District of Wimmera Received at the Crown Law Office 4th November 1869'.
67   According to Spieseke, Philip returned from this missionary tour with 19 people, including the six children. This brought the number of children to be provided for on the mission to 14. Included in the people brought back by Philip were old Hamilton and Isabella from Lake Boga, as well as (Jackson) Stewart and Dan with wives, and Stewart's child. Stewart's wife was Susan (not to be confused with Timothy's first wife, Susan). Lake Boga was the first Moravian mission site at which Spieseke was station and which closed in 1856. See *Periodical Accounts* 26 (1866), 420. For reference to Hamilton at Lake Boga see: *Periodical Accounts* 21 (1853), 46; *Periodical Accounts* 22 (1856), 202–3. See also: UA, UEC Minutes, 16 April 1868.
68   Baptism Ref: 26 July 1865, took the name James.
69   First Ref: 24 November 1864. Kitty was already known to the mission when the Hartmanns arrived in May 1864, with Spieseke going on a mission tour to visit her in the months after the Hartmanns arrived. According to missionary reports, she had the same father as Edward, being 'Old Man Jack'. She was married to Light, Nathaniel Pepper's brother, who died at the beginning of 1862. Thereafter she left the mission with her father and mother, returned to their 'native country' and married again. In late 1867, Kitty returned with Spieseke on one of his missionary tours west with Diana, asking to be baptised. The date of her baptism is not recorded, but Kitty took on the name Amelia at her baptism. She subsequently married Dick-a-Dick (later Paul). She died around the start of April 1871, leaving behind a young daughter. See: MAB, PP HJAH, 3, Letters, written by Adolph and Mary Hartmann to their parents and siblings (1864–1871), Polly Hartman to Hines family, 15 December 1864; *Periodical Accounts* 26 (1866), 420; UEC Minutes, 12 November 1864, #11, 161; *Periodical Accounts* 28 (1871), 126; *Further Facts, Third Paper*, 6; *Further Facts, Fourth Paper*, 3–4.
70   Baptism Ref: 13 August 1866, took the name Samuel.

9 January 1868

[Thu] Joe[71] (Mary's[72] husband) died to-day._ Towards evening ^little^ Teddy arrived with a number of Blacks & half-castes from Morton Plains[73] the name of the children are as follows (boys Robroy, Bob

girls

besides these then came also a ~~number~~ ^few^ of the Blacks from Mr Scotts[74] Sintax,[75] Harry, Bandel[76] etc._

10 January 1865

[Tue] According to an invitation of Mr Simpson[77] from Horsham that one of us sh[ld] come down & be present at the soirée,[78] ~~I took~~ it was settled that I sh[ld] go down this time. _And as Mr Ellerman[79] wanted to give a holiday or 2 to his governess, Miss Fraser,[80] he requested me to drive down Miss F[raser]. in his buggy & with his horse. So I walked to Antwerp with Polly who thought it would be well to stop with M[rs] Ellerman whilst I was off especially as M[r] Ellerman was going to be absent for the whole ~~wo~~ week._ As Miss Fraser was rather timid about the horse, they gave us a very old horse "Claude." The horse went very well as far as the 9 creeks._

---

71 Joe and Mary had lived on the mission from May 1864. Ref: 24 May 1864.
72 Polly had engaged in a reciprocal gift-giving with Mary in 1864. Ref: 30 May 1864; 13 June 1864.
73 Mortons Plain is about 100 kilometres north-east of the Ebenezer mission, and some 10 kilometres south of Birchip. On Ref: 29 March 1866 about 40 people from Morton Plain came to the Ebenezer mission. In 1865, the squatting run was held by GC Macredie. See: *The Squatters' Directory*, 17.
74 Scott's station at Warracknabeal (also spelt Warracknebel) some 28 miles from Ebenezer, where the Moravian missionaries occasionally preached to the local white population. See: *Further Facts, Second Paper*, 5. See also: *The Squatters' Directory*, 23.
75 Possibly referring to Syntax. Ref: 2 June 1864.
76 Peter Bandel, Ref: 6 June 1865.
77 First Ref: 28 June 1864. Rev. Patrick Simpson was the Presbyterian minister in Horsham. On Ref: 8 May 1864 he baptised Philip (formerly Charley Charley), Rebecca (formerly Jessie) and Matthew (formerly Liberty). He had to leave Horsham in 1868 as he was often intoxicated (Ref: 21 March 1868).
78 An annual missionary tea meeting in Horsham, according to Spieseke, where the converted married couple Rebecca and Phillip spoke. See: UA, UEC Minutes, 2 May 1865, #17, 126.
79 First Ref: 23 May 1864. Horatio Cockburn Ellerman was one of the first squatters of the area, taking on a 128,000-acre licence for an area he called Antwerp in April 1847. In 1851, he married Anne Westgarth, who was from a prominent family in Melbourne. In 1852, Henry Clarence Ellerman, Horatio's brother, joined them in their squatting run, extending their leases to include Pine Hills/Lake Hindmarsh, until 1857. Ellerman was an honorary correspondent of the Central Board, resigning his appointment after being ordained a Presbyterian minister in 1866. In May 1864, they were described as having five children, the eldest a boy. See: MAB, PP HJAH, 3, Letters, Adolf and Polly Hartmann to Hines family, May 1864; *Periodical Accounts* 25 (1863), 188; *Sixth BPA Report*, 41. See also: Jensz, *German Moravian Missionaries*, 115–16.
80 First Ref: 8 October 1864. Miss Fraser was already employed as a governess and was preparing to leave Ref: 30 September 1865.

Our cart also went down with Phillip & Rebecca,[81] & the 2 brethren riding alternatively on horse back, the horse for the cart & for riding was also given by Mr Ellerman.

10 January 1866

[Wed] Polly sent off a collecting card to Mrs Stedman,[82] also a small note to Mrs Simpson.[83]_ I despatched a letter to uncle Charles asking him & aunt to be godfather & godmother to our little pet.[84]_

10 January 1868

[Fri] This morning Topsy's poor little Baby died.[85] Evidently it was too young & weak to live being a 7 month's child._ Topsy having a bad cold the little thing most likely caught it, & so it was taken home to the Saviour. Poor Topsy is crying much & wants comforting._

10 January 1869*

Caroline[86] our sister was married to Oswald Heyde,[87] of Peilan: a nursery gardener. She had to leave the congregation, as he was not a member.

---

81   First Ref: 8 May 1864. Rebecca (also Rebekah) previously called Jessie was baptised on Ref: 8 May 1864. She married Philip (formerly Charley Charley) on the same day. In 1866, she was reported to be 22. See: *Further Facts, Fifth Paper*, 5.
82   Mrs Stedman had sent Polly a letter and present on Ref: 3 August 1865.
83   Wife of the Presbyterian minister in Horsham.
84   First Ref: 14 December 1865. Reference to Mary Elanor (Nelly) Hartmann.
85   Born premature. Ref: 5 January 1868.
86   First Ref: 19 November 1863. Adolf's sister, Caroline Heyde née Hines, (1839–1903).
87   Only Ref. Oswald Heide, a gardener, had been in the army and due to his itinerant lifestyle was no longer in the Moravian Church, which meant that Caroline was also no longer a member of the church. This caused much anxiety in the family. He was the brother of Wilhem Heide (also spelt Heyde) a missionary in Tibet. Caroline and Adolf's sister was Maria Heyde, who was a missionary in Tibet for almost 50 years. Polly described Oswald as the 'brother to her [Caroline's] sister's [Maria] husband [Wilhelm]', MAB, PP HJAH, 3 Letters, Mary Hartmann to Hines family, Ebenezer, 10 August 1869. For more Maria Heyde, see: Felicity Jensz, 'Miscarriage and Coping in the Mid-Nineteenth Century: Private Notes from Distant Places', *Gender & History* 32, no. 3 (2020): 270–85, doi.org/10.1111/1468-0424.12478.

11 January 1865

[Wed] Left Edols[88] at about 10 am. & got to Walmar about 2 ½; as usual received very kindly._ Oh our our poor horse Claude_ Tired as it was, it was put into harness again to pull us to Horsham in the evening._ During the tea I made myself useful in handing about the tea etc. Afterwards when the speaking commenced, there was a very full chapel about 300 were in._ M[r] Scott was chosen chairman; there were some more ministers who spoke besides M[r] Simpson._ Whey my turn came to speak I of course made it all to be about the Blacks what they did to the white, & what the whites did to them._ I then made a request for some bullocks & a dray. Phillip then stood up after me & said something he was rather nervous & so did not get out very much, but there was great clapping & cheering when he made his appearance.[89]_ Walder & Meissel also spoke a little. Got back to Walmar rather late: had M[r] Flemming[90] with me, poor old Claude could hardly get on anymore._

12 January 1864

Tues: Left Fairfield for London 7 ½ a.m._ Took train from Manchester to Rugby & there got out & saw uncle John Horn[91] at Lawford Lodge._ (very foggy weather.)

12 January 1865

[Thu] From Walmar to Horsham again & stayed for dinner at the manse M[r] Simpson thrown from his horse._ Back to Walmar._

12 January 1866

[Fri] A disagreeable affair between S[pliesekel] & Mark,[92] originating, as Mark would have it that S[pliesekel] did not give him notice that he had to fetch his own rations w[h] Kitty had fetched hitherto & cooked for him._

---

88   Edols, sometimes written Edolls, referred to the squatting run of Thomas Edols, who had the Upper Regions squatting run from 1858 to 1872. Ref: Longmire, *Nine Creeks to Albacutya*, 21.

89   Philip is reported to have spoken at another tea meeting in late 1864, however, that event might be a conflation with the event in early 1865. See: Longmire, *Nine Creeks to Albacutya*, 13.

90   First Reference of Flemming, who was subsequent leaseholder of Antwerp, once Ellerman left. Ref: 4 May 1866.

91   Father of Jane Horn, bridesmaid at Adolf and Polly's wedding. Ref: 29 December 1863.

92   First Ref: 22 May 1864. Mark (also known as Thomas Marks) was recorded being at the mission already at the Hartmanns' arrival Ref: 22 May 1864. He was married to Lizzie (later Esther).

13 January 1864
Got to London at about 6 p.m._ We lodged in Hatton Garden[93]

13 January 1865
[Fri] Left Horsham at 1 pm._ Meissel i[n]vited by Mrs Wilson[94] stayed behind for a week or so._ Very hot day & poor old Claude[95] got very tired. Mr Edolls[96] overtaking us about half way took Miss Fraser into his buggy.

13 January 1866
[Sat] Sp[ieseke] got a letter from Re^{vd} Henderson[97] (Balmoral[98]) that Mr Phillip would bring (Topsy) to our place on the 23rd of this month. _ Been trying several days to manage the dry process according to Russel,[99] but could not get the plates to produce a picture._ Mark is not gone away but seem in a depressed state of mind._ Preparatory meeting for the communion, Matthew & Margaret,[100] & Timothy admitted._

---

93 Hatton Garden is a street and area in the district of Holborn in the London Borough of Camden, London, UK.
94 Wife of Charles Wilson Esquire, of Walmer, near Horsham.
95 Claude, the horse.
96 Also Edols, Ref: 11 January 1865.
97 First Ref: 5 December 1865. The Reverend James Henderson was a Presbyterian minister who spent over 40 years in the Balmoral district, retiring in 1906. See: 'Departure of Rev. J. Henderson', *Hamilton Spectator*, Sat 2 February 1907, 4. Via: trove.nla.gov.au (accessed 13 July 2020).
98 Approximately 80 kilometres south-west of Horsham, in the current shire of South Grampians.
99 According to a contemporaneous photography instruction manual, Major Russel's dry process, also known as *tannin process*, was one of two popular in England, France and Germany. The other being the *collodio albumen process* of M Taupenot, which Adolf switched to in April 1865, Ref: 3 April 1865. See: Désiré van Monckhoven, *A Popular Treatise on Photography*, translated by William Henry Thornthwaite (London: Virtue Brother, 1863), 72. Available via: archive.org/details/populartreatiseo00moncrich/mode/2up (accessed 13 July 2020).
100 First Ref: 25 June 1864. Margaret, wife of Matthew Elliott, was brought to Ebenezer in August 1864. The missionaries had applied through Rev. Chase for her to marry Matthew Ref: 25 June 1864, She married Matthew (formerly Liberty) on Ref: 18 August 1864. She was described as being a young mother around 17 years old in 1866. She was at Yelta, where she was taught about Christianity by the missionary Thomas Hill Goodwin. In March 1863, she was baptised at St Paul's Church, Melbourne. Mr Chase recommended her to be a wife to Matthew. Together they had three sons, Joseph (Ref: 8 February 1866; 24 February 1866), Robert (Ref: 5 November 1867) and Charles Arthur (Ref: 25 July 1870). See also: *Further Facts*, Fifth Paper, 5–6.

14 January 1864
Went to the young men's association[101] with Dan:[102] & attended a prayermeeting._

14 January 1865*
[Sat] Old Claude could not go any more: he was lying down all the time so Mr Edolls was kind enough to give us a horse, a very lazy fellow though & I had to use the whip most desperately to make him go. Walder stopped to preach to-morrow._ Got to Antwerp about 1 p.m. & found my Polly still waiting for me._ We had a very pleasant walk home._ We found that S[pieseke]. had sent out some Blacks with the cart to shoot a wild bullock & that they succeeded in getting a nice young fellow, so we have splendid beef at present. We shall have to get some more to ~~safe~~ save our flock wh has so much been killed down that we must touch young sheep if we want any m~~i~~utton._ We should have had the communion this evening but it was postponed, chiefly on account of Br Walder & Meissel's absence.

15 January 1863
Stood Godfather to <u>Alfred Oxley</u> born Nov: 28, 1862.

The other ... was Theophilus Kramer, & Godmother Mrs Dickson the minister was Rev Libbey. _

15 January 1864
Friday._ In the morning I went to the East India Dock[103] with Polly & had a look at our vessel "Norfolk" we were much pleased with her, she ~~being a~~ looking to be a fine vessel._ In the afternoon I went with Br Fisher & bought an Harmonium for £ 14.10._ £11 Polly & I had collected the remainder was sent from the Continent._ In the evening, Daniel, Polly & I went to Exeter Hall[104] & heard the Creation,[105] most splendid affair, on our way home we had an oyster supper._ Bought also a washing machine. ~~that~~ to-day.

---

101 Possibly referring to the Young Men's Christian Association, first established in London in 1844. The Moravians did not have a Young Men's Association.
102 First Ref: 24 December 1863. Daniel, known as Dan, Hines, Polly's brother.
103 East India Docks in London Borough of Tower Hamlets, UK, established in 1803.
104 Exeter Hall, on the north side of the Strand, London, England, built around 1830. It was known for evangelical meetings and anti-slavery meetings. It could hold up to 4,000 people in its large auditorium.
105 Joseph Haydn's (1732–1809) *Creation*, sung by the Sacred Harmonic Society, conducted by Mr Costa. See: 'Advertisement', *The Musical World* (London), 42, no. 2, Saturday 9 January 1864, 1.

15 January 1865

[Sun] S[pieseke]. went to Antwerp to keep the meeting in the evening. Walder came back in the evening._

15 January 1866

[Mon] a very hot day (130 Fahrenheit in the sun[106]) S[pieseke] drove to Loyd's[107]

16 January 1864

Sat._ Went out with Br Charles Linder & bought; 1, a gun an necessaries; 2 a good supply of tools; 3 a lamp._ In the evening we set out for Clapham Park terrace to see uncle Mark Hines.[108] & a very pleasant Sunday we spent there; uncle Mark a very nice man._ I partook of the communion in the Church of England for the first time._

16 January 1865*

[Mon] We had this evening a preparatory meeting for the Communion. Br Spieseke kept it. Subject. Isa. 4 V. 1.2.[109]

17 January 1865*

[Tue] We had the communion this evening. Nat[haneal]. was gone to Nine Creeks & did not return in time. Br Meissel was at Walmer. Br Spieseke held it. Of our people, Philip, Rebecca, Daniel, & Rachel[110] attended.

---

106 130 degrees Fahrenheit is 54.4 degrees Celsius.
107 Lloyd's being the store in Dimboola (Nine Creeks).
108 Died Ref: 5 January 1865. Father of cousin Eliza Hines.
109 King James Version of the Bible (hereafter KJV). Isaiah 4:5 'And the LORD will create upon every dwelling place of mount Zion, and upon her assemblies, a cloud and smoke by day, and the shining of a flaming fire by night: for upon all the glory shall be a defence'.
110 First Ref: 19 May 1864. Rachel Warndekan, wife of Nathanael (Nathaniel) Pepper. She was a teacher at the Sunday School. She was a central female Aboriginal figure on the mission. Together with Nathanael had a son, who died shortly after birth in February 1864. In 1866, she was reported to be 21 years old. Rachel was confirmed on Ref: 19 May 1864. She died on Ref: 23 March 1869. For more on Rachel see: John Harris, *One Blood. 200 Years of Aboriginal Encounter with Christianity: A Story of Hope* (Sutherland: Albatross, 1990), 194, 202, 266. See also: *Further Facts, Fifth Paper*, 5.

17 January 1866
[Wed] Baptism of our Nelly[111]

17 January 1867
[Thu] Not been putting down anything for a long time, for we had fearfully hot weather, since Xmas, & nothing particular occurred._ The new pump is at last securely fastened does not leak anymore & works well._ Commenced a box for the letters, for spelling._ Sp[ieseke]: went to the camp again & shot another dog[112] whereupon old Boney[113] rushed at him & pulled the gun (my gun)[114] out of his hand injuring it somewhat._ S of course did not yield any resistance but went away rather badly bitten by one of the dogs belonging to the boy Albert.[115]_ Old Boney was very sorry for his behaviour lying on the ground & crying out. Afterwards he offered S his hand to make all straight being sorry for his bad behaviour, but S ~~was~~ said it should be all right again if he would poison that dog that bit him to w^h the old man reluctantly consented. Another row between Jerry & Martha[116] the former setting fire to the new house he is building, of course a stop was put to it, & he was threatened with the law if he would repeat it.

18 January 1864
Monday/ Followed an invitation of Mr Leech to spend the evening with him._

---

111 Mary Elanor (Nelly) Hartmann. Born Ref: 14 December 1865. On 17 January 1866, two Aboriginal men and two Aboriginal women were also baptised. Neither this event nor their names were recorded in the Hartmann diary. However, Adolf did communicate these baptisms, but not the names, to the Moravian Church. See: *Periodical Accounts* 26 (1866), 31.
112 On Ref: 28 December 1866 four or five camp dogs were destroyed because they killed some six sheep and injured eleven more. Ian Clark suggests that the deliberate killing of domesticated dogs was a particularly distressful action for Aboriginal people. See: Ian D Clark, *'That's My Country Belonging to Me'. Aboriginal Land Tenure and Dispossession in Nineteenth Century Western Victoria* (Melbourne: Heritage Matters, 1998), 165.
113 First Ref: 17 September 1864. Old Boney was the father of Young Boney (baptised as Daniel, 6 December 1863) and Tallihо/Tallyho (Timothy). He was the partner of Mary (Old Mary), and the diary suggests that he also had the name 'Frank'. Ref: 31 August 1866. See also: *Facts, First Paper*, 11.
114 Purchased Ref: 16 January 1864.
115 First Ref: 9 July 1864. One of the 'boys' of the mission. Often noted in company of (George) Boopboop. In 1866, Albert, known in other sources as Albert Coombes, was reported to be about 13 years old, and a 'half caste'. He was born at Antwerp in 1852. See also: *Further Facts, Fifth Paper*, 5.
116 First Ref: 24 January 1865 under the name Sarah, baptised Ref: 27 July 1865. She was the widow of Lanky (also written Lanke), half-brother of Nathanael. Lanky died Ref: 15 August 1865. Martha left the mission with Jerry (Ref: 30 January 1865), who was not a Christian, Ref: 24 November 1865. In October 1866, she was at Mount Elgin, near Nhill, working for Mr and Mrs Telford (Ref: 6 October 1866). See also: *Periodical Accounts* 26 (1866), 29.

19 January 1864

Was on board the Norfolk again to see that things were properly managed, stopt there till dark._ In the evening to Exeter Hall & heard a lecture about "Missions & Missionaries."

19 January 1865*

[Thu] M[r] & M[rs] Spieseke[117] went to Antwerp, for a short visit, & left Anna[118] with me. They returned at dusk. We sent off English letters_ to the home party, to M[rs] Clough,[119] a note for M[r] F Latrobe,[120] & Adolf's journal, & notes to B[p] Libbey & Kramer. Adolf got at last an answer from Johnson & O'Shanessy. They gave him information, but do not sell goods. He wrote off at once, for more particulars, enclosing £1 for the information, & also a list of goods to be obtained of Chas Johnson & Co.[121]

20 January 1864

Once more to the vessel to look after our things in the Cabin. John[122] was there, too._ In the evening we were at M[r] Shipton's to tea & supper; a very pleasant evening._

20 January 1865*

[Fri] M[r] Walder went to Upper Regions,[123] on his way to Horsham, to fetch Mr Meissel, who has been staying a week at Walmer.

21 January 1864

In the morning we wrote our last letters home from London: a very busy morning._ We spent the evening being the last with Dan: & John at the formers lodging._

---

117 First Ref: 24 May 1864. Christina née Fricke. Born 28 December 1828 near Hannover, died 19 June 1888 in Königsfeld, Germany. Arrived in Australia on 14 May 1861, married to FW Spieseke on 29 May 1861 in Melbourne.
118 Anna Spieseke.
119 The Hartmanns received a letter from Mrs Clough on Ref: 8 November 1864. No further reference to her in the diary.
120 Frederick La Trobe, Adolf's best man at his wedding. Ref: 29 December 1863.
121 Photographical chemicals arrived Ref: 20 March 1865.
122 First Ref: 24 December 1863. John Hines, Polly's brother.
123 A station 14 miles from Ebenezer, licence held by Thomas Edols. See: *Facts, First Paper*, 10; *The Squatters' Directory*, 31.

EBENEZER MISSION STATION, 1863-1873

21 January 1865*

[Sat] Nathaniel brought us a wild goose; a rare occurrence for one to be shot in this neighbourhood. In the afternoon English letters came, a large packet, containing good news_ as also two photographs _ 1 _ M^r & Mrs H. Shawe,[124] & Mrs Harvey. Spent the evening over the letters;_ which were from Father, Mother, Dan, John, Mr H. Shawe, & B^r Reichel.[125]

22 January 1864

Left London for Gravesend[126] accompanied by Daniel, and got on board our vessel[127] there safe & sound; then we parted from Dan._ _ As the vessel did not sail that day we had a nice time to arrange our Cabin and it took us the whole afternoon to get it into somewhat a comfortable condition (For particulars of our voyage see PB 88)[128]

22 January 1865*

[Sun] Some of our people had had colds: Philip, Kitty, Jacky's[129] Lilly[130] tc. had the roast goose, & our first cucumber.

---

124 First Ref: 21 January 1865. Henry Shawe had been a teacher at Fulneck, see footnotes in Ref: 24 October 1863.
125 First Ref: 9 September 1863. Levin Theodore Reichel of the Mission Department in Herrnhut.
126 Gravesend, in the Shire of Kent, UK, was a site from which boats departed for non-European ports.
127 The *Norfolk*, Ref: 2 January 1864.
128 MAB, PP HJAH, 10, Diary, written by Adolph Hartmann, Insert written by Mary 'Polly' Hartmann, Voyage to Australia. The first entry reads: 'January 22nd [1864]. Left Hatton Garden at 10.15, & drove to Fenchurch St, where we were joined by Dan and John. The latter saw us off in the train, and Dan accompanied us to the vessel. On arriving at Tibury, we found a boat immediately to take us to the Norfolk. I was at once first quite at a loss to know how I was to mount the steep narrow perpendicular steps by which the vessel was reached. My perplexity was soon removed, for a chair, in appearance like a large barrel with one side open and a seat in, was let down for me. In this I was drawn up, and reached the deck in safety. As soon as our cabin door could be opened (for the key could not be found,) we began the work of arranging and beautifying our cabin. Between whiles we had dinner, Dan with us, consisting of soup, meat of several kinds, and bread and cheese. After dinner Dan left us. Ah! This parting! But such is life! We had tea about 7. We walked afterwards on the deck in the moonlight, but it was not clear. We worked and wrote till after ten and then had prayers and went to bed.'
129 First Ref: 23 May 1864 from Jacky. He and Lilly (First Ref: 5 December 1864) were recorded as already being married in 1863. They were baptised on Ref: 13 August 1866 and took the names Stephen and Lydia. See: *Periodical Accounts* 25 (1863), 186.
130 First Ref: 5 December 1864. Lilly, married to Jacky (later Stephen), was baptised on Ref: 13 August 1866 and took the name Lydia.

23 January 1864

Sat._ A 10 ½ we moved off from Gravesend, but wind being had the Captain did not know whether we should get out to-day; did not get out that day._[131]

23 January 1865*

[Mon] At last Emma's parents have allowed her to return to us. She returned with Old Jenny;[132] & seemed pleased to be here again. Napoleon[133] also came. Adolf finished his grindstone._

The fine Lowan,[134] caught some days ago by Old Charlie[135] for the Acclimatisation Society,[136] was last night killed by native cats.[137]

24 January 1865

[Tue] A comet visible in the southern hemisphere.[138]_ Phillip & Rebecca moved into their new house._ I made a small kiln & burnt some lime for washing the background in my gallery._ The cook who at present is Sarah[139] was to have the house in w^h Phillip was, she & Lanke[140] took possession of it.

---

131 Polly also describes this day in the diary of the ship voyage. MAB, PP HJAH, 10, Diary, Voyage to Australia: 'Jan^{uary} 23rd [1864] Saturday Had a comfortable night. Rose at 8, & had prayers. Adolf decided to read the Harmony of the Gospels in the morning, & the morning portion; & in the evening the Psalms & evening portion. Breakfast at nine, then a walk on deck, where I noticed the peculiar manner in which the sailors sing while pulling up the ropes to spread out the sails. We noticed 24 pulling at one said at once, half the rope on one side & half on the other. They sing altogether while pulling the rope. After dinner we walked again on deck. In the evening we anchored again opposite Southend. After tea, Adolf gave me the first lesson in chess. I went early to bed, not feeling well.'
132 First Ref: 24 May 1864.
133 First Reference in the diary. Napoleon was reported to be a youth of about 14 years in 1866. In December 1864, he was residing about a mile away from Scott's Warracknabeal station. See: MAB, PP HJAH, 3, Letters, Polly Hartman to Hines family, 15 December 1864. See also: *Further Facts, Fifth Paper*, 5.
134 Alternative name for a malleefowl. Also known as lauan.
135 First reference in the diary. Old Charley collected other natural objects for the mission, such as emu eggs Ref: 4 July 1865. He died Ref: 24 September 1866.
136 The Acclimatisation Society of Victoria was established in 1861 to introduce exotic game animals and birds both into Australia as well as from Australia to Britain and other colonial spaces. See: Deborah Tout-Smith, 2003, 'Acclimatisation Society of Victoria', *Museums Victoria Collections*, accessed 14 July 2020, collections.museumsvictoria.com.au/articles/1803.
137 Native cat, or native pole-cat, was a settler-colonist term for a quoll (belonging to the Dasyuridae family), once common in Victoria.
138 This comet was commented on in the local newspapers of the time. See, for example: 'The Comet', *Mount Alexander Mail*, Saturday 28 January 1865, 2. Available via: trove.nla.gov.au (accessed 20 April 2020).
139 First Reference in the diary. Sarah (later Martha, Ref: 26 July 1865) was Lanky's wife. Lanky was the half-brother of Nathanael/Nathaniel. Sarah was already working in the mission house in late 1863 with Spieseke stating that 'she is more helpful to us than I ever would have expected from a Black' (my translation). See: *Misisonsblatt* 3 (1864), 64. See also: *Periodical Accounts* 25 (1863), 126.
140 First Ref: 22 October 1864. Lanke, also written as Lanky. Died Ref: 15 August 1865.

25 January

26 January 1864

~~Friday~~ ^{Tuesday}. Arrived in Plymouth sound at 9 p.m.

26 January 1866

[Fri] Early in the morning we heard distant thunder, but we did not think that there would be much rain. We were mistaken, though, for it came up thicker & thicker, thundering & lightening very much & then there came such a rain down as we had not had since we came to this country. All the forenoon thunder & lightening & heavy rain & so it was that by dinner time, the dry soil was soaked about a spade deep. The thunder & rain came from a westerly direction, & there was all the time an easterly current of wind blowing. Splendid splendid!

26 January 1867

[Sat] Commenced, H (properly) the building of the new mill, repairing the rings first ~~reotting~~ drawing the rivets more tight & putting rollers between the 2 rings to make them go more easy._ Spieseke finished laying down the floor in Davids[141] house._ Finished eating the apricots. We counted the stones 250.

27 January 1864

Wednesday. Went ashore_ bought sundry things in Plymouth & spent a few hours with B^{r[other]} & S^{is[ter]} J.D. Libbey at Devenport._ We were sorry not to be able to stop any longer with them, as our vessel was to set sail that night._ got back to our Norfolk between 6 & 7 p.m.

27 January 1867

~~[Sat] Commenced yesterday to~~

[Sun] There was some rain & thunder._ We had the first melons 2 fine fellows._

---

141 First Ref: 25 April 1866. David was a man about 26 years old in 1866. David married Elizabeth (formerly Mary, Ref: 27 July 1865) on Ref: 7 May 1867. See also: *Further Facts, Fifth Paper*, 5.

28 January 1864

Thursday Set sail from Plymouth at 4.30 p.m.

28 January 1865

[Sat] Made a still for getting water pure for my photographics. at the thing all day.

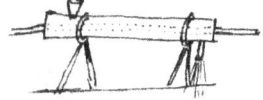

[Here Adolf included a small sketch of the still] the still._

Our sofa at last was finished to day as regards the covering it with chints,[142] looks very spiff though._ Very hot day 108[143] in the shade 115[144] in the sun._ We had the first peaches & watermelon to-day.

28 January 1867

[Mon] S[pieseke]. went off to Dimboola & to Locheal[145] to get several things & some cow hides for ~~mender~~ rebarking our roof.

29 January 1865

[Sun] A good many Blacks are here at present. This morning when I went to the camp I heard a queer story._ Jacky Lake told me that Edward yesterday threatened to shoot him with a pistol he produced from his pocket after he, Jacky, had thrown Edward in wrestling with him._ Well this sounded rather serious; so I went & told S[pieseke] about it & we both had a talk with Edward. A queer story we were told again; he E[d] said that Jacky wanted to take his wife from him & give her to another Black because, as the Blacks in the camp said; he had driven Timothy out of the hut they were living in together for some time, & that he had been the cause that Susan[146] had gone to the Camp & left Timothy._ The whole thing was a regular Blacks concern, somehow we managed to settle everything amicably & spoke strongly to the people about the way they sh[ou][ld] live together

---

142 Possibly 'chintz', a printed cotton fabric.
143 108 degrees Fahrenheit is 42.2 degrees Celsius.
144 115 degrees Fahrenheit is 46.1 degrees Celsius.
145 Locheal, also spelt Lochiel (correct spelling), was a pastoral run held by John Holt. See: *The Squatters' Directory*, Correction and Errata page.
146 First Ref: 28 May 1864. Susan, also known as Susanna, was the first wife of Timothy (formerly Tallyho, also Talliho). They were married some time in 1863, before the Hartmanns arrived in Australia. See: *Periodical Accounts* 25 (1863), 126. She died Ref: 12 February 1866.

30 January 1865

[Mon] Jerry a Black from Tatta Yarra[147] showed some extra ordinary feats on a wild horse w[h][ich] King Cole[148] had fetched from the Lake to take down to M[r] Ale[x] Wilson.[149] Well such a bucking! but he kept his seat admirably & made the horse do as he liked. We all looked on; it was quite a sight._ S[pieseke]. rode to the 9 creeks in the evening to look for some sheep w[h][ich] M[r] Edols had promised

30 January 1866

[Tue] S[pieseke]. came back from Horsham & brought Tobsy with him a young half cast girl, from Balmoral near the Glenelg river). _ She is 17 years old, & was brought up in a family there[150]

31 January 1865*

[Tue] After school this morning Adolf was the means of stopping a fight between two or three blacks, wh[ich]. might have led ended in bloodshed. Teddy had been offended in school by Hearty's[151] laughing at his mistakes in reading figures. A saw T[eddy]s eyes flash fire, & expected, what proved to be, the result. He heard a noise in the camp afterwards, & on going down, saw Teddy, Corny,[152] & Doctor Charley, & Hearty with sticks & spears confronting each other. No blow had as yet been struck, but words ran high between them. Adolf was enabled with our Saviour's help, to make all straight & quiet. In the afternoon I was enabled to bring about a reconciliation between some of the women, who had quarrelled. In the evening I went down to the camp with A[dolf]. to see Susan, who has not attended school or church for some time. She does no work, & gets no rations. We hope our visit may be productive of good results.

---

147 Tatiara, in current-day South Australia. Ref: 13 February 1865. Often people from this area came to the mission.
148 First Ref: 26 August 1864. A man named King Cole took part in the 1868 Aboriginal Cricket team tour of England in 1868; he died of tuberculosis and was buried in London, England, in June 1868. There is reference in the diary of King Cole killing Lady, his wife, Ref: 9 October 1864.
149 In 1865, Alexander Wilson held the Vectis pastoral lese, as well as Wyn-wyn, Muckindar, Arapiles and Darragon in the West Wimmera. See: *The Squatters' Directory*, 45.
150 Topsy was said to have been brought up by the Philip family. Ref: 5 December 1865.
151 First Ref: 10 June 1864. Hearty was also referred to as Harty (Ref: 10 November 1866). In December 1864, Hearty was living near the Scott's run at Warracknabeal. See: MAB, PP HJAH, 3, Letters, Polly Hartman to Hines family, 15 December 1864.
152 More commonly written Corney.

31 January 1868

[Fri] Nahri was buried this afternoon;[153] if ever any expressed faith in our Saviour in her dying hours it was Nahri & we believe she is now resting from her labours. _

February

1 February 1868

[Sat] There are really now 5 houses building. Matthew (stone house) Samuel,[154] Mark, Nathanael, & Stuart (Werimanda)[155] the 4 last mentioned are ~~stone~~ wood houses._ A very sad thing about Pearce[156] that he intends to leave our place & go back to the Murray. The boy a half caste (very light) is in a peculiar temper, he has fallen out with some of the other boys living in the school, is at present very touchy about anything one speaks to him, sulks & lives in the camp.

2 February 1866

[Fri] Managed to get some good ~~vewes~~ ~~wewes~~ wievs[157] from the chapel. Mean to print some to sell them, in order to get some chemicals etc._

3 February 1865

[Fri] Helped Edward to put a few more logs to his house he is building._ Very slow work with the people, not only that they are not handy, but also ~~that~~ lazy for working._

---

153 Only reference to Nahri in this diary. Her death was reported in the *Periodical Accounts*, albeit without reference to her name. Nahri had attended the school for women run by Polly. Her death was attributed to 'her previously vicious life'. See: *Periodical Accounts* 27 (1869), 193.
154 First Ref: 25 December 1864 under the name of Brown, who took the name Samuel on Ref: 13 August 1866.
155 First Reference in the diary. He was also referred to as Wirremande Steward Ref: 9 March 1870.
156 First Ref: 27 October 1866. Pearce was said to be about 10 years old, and came to the mission with about 80 people from the Murray in June 1866. According to the missionaries, he expressed his wish to go to the mission school. See: *Periodical Accounts* 26 (1866), 247.
157 This should be 'views'.

3 February 1866

[Sat] Tobsy[158] & Elizabeth[159] went into the kitchen to be our cooks; rather young cooks but we hope they will do well._ No success in photography like yesterday, cant tell why not!!!_ M^r Ry^{a}n & another from Melbourne was here Wet (Westly).[160]_

4 February 1865

[Sat] Went with S[pieseke]. to look at the new fence some of people were making, to fence off our run from Mr Stuart's._ Matthew & Margaret are not going on well they quarrel so much together and everything in their house seems to go wrong, they break everything we give them *und die ganze Wirtschaft geht hinter sich.*[161] We don't know what to do, to exclude[162] Matthew only would not do; this is a trouble but we are sure the Lord will help us in this matter._ Got a piece of black wood to make some handles to some of our adxes, fine wood to work in._

4 February 1866

5 February

6 February 1865

[Mon] A very strong West wind blew all day; it was rather a warm wind. The sky gradually got covered & in the evening it began to rain. A very pleasant noise to hear the drops of rain falling down, there has not been a shower for a long time. Of a number of vine cuttings w^h I set a while ag ago, & w^h I watered well & protected from the sun, one is starting out very nicely._ The peaches are all eaten up._

---

158 More commonly referred to as Topsy. Ref: 5 January 1868.
159 First Ref: 28 May 1864. Elizabeth, formerly Mary, was baptised Ref: 27 July 1865 the same day as Martha (formerly Sarah). Elizabeth married David on Ref: 7 May 1867. She was recorded as being 14 years old in 1866. See also: *Further Facts, Fifth Paper*, 5.
160 Wesleyan.
161 Literal English translation: 'and the whole economy goes behind them'.
162 Exclusion from the congregation for a period of time was a punishment for un-Christian behaviour.

6 February 1866

[Tue] S[plieseke] & wife off to the lake for a short visit._ The Blacks from Scotts came, & among them that young Peter,[163] so I went down & told him that he could not stop here because of Matthew & Margaret._

7 February

8 February 1865

[Wed] Polly & I & Mr Walder & Meissel started for a visit to Mr Scott._ It was a cold morning & a cool day although the sun was shining brightly. Scott's at home._ Their garden in splendid order._ Plenty flowers & fruit._ A very clean & neat house._ Everything kept in splendid order._

8 February 1866

[Thu] Towards night Margaret was delivered of a fine healthy baby a boy;[164] they[165] seem both to be very happy about it._ The Ellermans came from Horsham & stayed a few days, when they will move to the new manse built for them._

9 February 1865

[Thu] In the morning the b^m & I went to see the brick making that was going on then at a little distance; learnt something by it._ Then we went to see the new building that was being erected for Mr Scott's men. The brickmaker who was building it payed 12^s to each of his men besides finding them rations per day._ In the af^t we saw the few Blacks that were then near the Station; poor fellows! especially the old man Jack.[166] Kittys father; a deplorable figure. _ The Blacks said he would die in a fortnight about. I could not do much for him; the old man was rather dull & stupid although not unwilling to listen to what I said. He is not willing to leave the place although he had a chance quite lately; so I think he will die at Scott's.[167]_

---

163 First Ref: 6 June 1865. Not much more information is given on Peter Bandel in this diary, except for his affair with Margaret (Ref: 6 June 1865).
164 First Reference. Joseph was baptised on Ref: 24 February 1866.
165 The parents of Joseph were Margaret and Matthew.
166 Adolf reported that Jack was blind. See: *Periodical Accounts* 25 (1863), 358.
167 Old Jack died on Ref: 18 February 1865.

10 February 1865

[Fri] Got back to our place at about 5 p.m._ We stopped a few hours at Antwerp._ When we arrived Sp[ieseke]: was in the camp keeping the meeting there._ A good many blacks had arrived whilst we were off, so there are about 60 at present. They had pitched their camp a long way off our place & the evening of the next day after we left for Scotts they had a small "corroborie" Sp: not knowing anything about it He gave it them well for it he said._ There was lime burning in the kiln._ Sp: in great rage about the Blacks' dogs, said he would set poison to kill them._ We filled up the kiln with some more lime in the evening._ Polly tooth-ache._

11 February 1865

[Sat] Trying to make a sort of brick of a mixture of lime & small stones, no go; wants too much time to set._ In the evening we had the preparatory meeting for the communion._ After it hearing a noise in the far off camp, I went down with the b^m & Phillip, but there was nothing._ Great many Blacks in the camp about 50._

12 February 1865

[Sun] A very warm day. Few people came to the morning meeting._ Polly had head ache all day._ No singing in the afternoon._ Felt very low spirited. Was revived though in the evening when we had the Lord's supper._ M^r H^or & H^en Ellerman[168] present._ Polly got so well that she could play the harmonium for us._

12 February 1866

[Mon] At 2 a.m. Susan[169] the wife of Timothy died, & we believe she is with the Lord._ She was sick for some days or rather weeks, & whenever I spoke to her I found her composed at the prospect of death, she put her trust in the Saviour. Her life was one of those useless ones apparently, & we were never g pleased with her conduct, but it seems she found the Saviour in the at the eleventh hour._

---

168 Horatio and Henry Ellerman.
169 Spieseke noted that she died of consumption. See: UA, UEC Minutes, 26 April 1866, #3, 115; *Periodical Accounts* 26 (1866), 30.

13 February 1865

[Mon] Some of the Blacks gone off to Scott's others to meet the Tatiara[170] Blacks who are coming._ Very warm again._ Worked with Phillip & Edward at their house but found it too much of a good thing, it being 106[171] in the sun._

13 February 1867*

[Wed] Dicky[172] & Lily[173] went to Vectis[174] to work out a debt there, & took Rosa[175] with them. She has been with us more than two months, had everything comfortable, ate with us, was treated with: had just begun to read nicely, & to take a pleasure in learning, & yet her parents could not be persuaded to leave her here.

14 February 1865

[Tue] Very ^hot^ warm again._ The Blacks moved their camp to the other side of the river,[176] & it takes a long time for them to come to chapel after the bell has been wrung._ We are afraid that some disturbance may take place between our people & the Tatiara Blacks who are expected soon to arrive here, because old Boney speared one of them last year._

15 February

16 February 1865

[Thu] Got the home letters, amongst them the first from Caroline.[177]

---

170 Also spelt Tatta Yarra (Ref: 30 January 1865) and Tata Yarra (Ref: 4 July 1864).
171 106 degrees Fahrenheit is 41.1 degrees Celsius.
172 First Ref: 18 May 1865. Dicky was reported to be a 'half-caste' youth in 1865. Although he was a candidate for baptism in Ref: 21 August 1865, it seems as though he was not baptised. It was reported in June 1866 that Dicky's people to the west took him and his sister Emma back to them. It is not clear if this is the same Dicky. See: *Periodical Accounts* 26 (1866), 135–36.
173 Referred to as the mother of Rosa. No other substantial information in the diary about her.
174 At Vectis, Alexander Wilson was the honorary correspondent to the Central Board.
175 Spieseke reported to the UEC in December 1866, that he had taken the 'half-white' girl Rosa into his house See: UA, UEC Minutes, 2 March 1867, #8, 219. Alexander Wilson of Vectis reported that Rosy, a 'half-caste' girl, daughter of Lily, was sent to the mission station when Lily 'bolted'. See: *Seventh BPA Report*, 21.
176 Known as Barringgi Gadyin by the Wotjobaluk People, known from the colonial period as the Wimmera River.
177 Adolf's sister, Caroline Heyde Ref: 10 January 1869.

16 February 1866

[Fri] S~~plieseke~~l came back from Calders,[178] to w^h place he went to see some blacks; there were about 15 there._ S: got a letter from Mr Officer[179] from Mount Talbot[180] informing him that the 2 black girls might be fetched any time, but he thought there would be some difficulty in obtaining the voluntary consent of the Blacks that have a claim upon her; he, M^r O, said he would try to persuade the Blacks to give them up._

16 February 1867*

[Sat] M^r & Mrs Fleming[181] & Miss Hastie[182] came over this morning and brought their new hose to be sewn with our machine. Two pieces were soon finished to satisfaction. The home mail arrived.

17 February 1865

[Fri] Spiesecke washed his lime: ~~he made a great mistake first, he just got the lime in a heap & poured water over it.~~

17 February 1867*

[Sun] ~~We heard~~ To day ~~that~~ Mrs Fleming of Antwerp, has a little daughter rather unexpectedly.

18 February 1865

[Sat] In the forenoon we had a visit ^from a Miss Little, Miss Smith, Mr Smith,[183] Mr White[184] they came over from Antwerp. P.m. I rode to Antwerp on Bobby taking with me the home letters._ The Blacks who were at Scott's came all here to-day. The old man Jack died shortly after we had

---

178 Robert Calder leased the Polkemmet Station in the West Wimmera. See: *The Squatters' Directory*, 26.
179 CM and SH Officer held Lingmer and Mount Talbot runs, both in the West Wimmera. See: *The Squatters' Directory*, 39.
180 Mount Talbot is approximately 45 kilometres south of Horsham, Victoria. In 1865 it was leased by CM and SH Officer. See: *The Squatters' Directory*, 18.
181 Of Antwerp. The diary does not provide much information on this couple.
182 Also of Antwerp, but no further information available in the diary.
183 Unclear if this is the Mr Smith of Mosquito Plains, '12 miles beyond the Boundary', Ref: 26 November 1867. In *The Squatters' Directory* of 1865 there is a run called 'Boundary North' held by Smith and Wynne. See: *The Squatters' Directory*, 10.
184 First Ref: 8 August 1864. Mr and Mrs White were at Lake Hindmarsh. Left the area in Ref: 1 November 1865.

left, poor Kitty, his daughter, seems to feel it much, we hear her sobbing in her house._ The rams were taken out of the flock on the other side & all the sheep put over._

18 February 1867*

[Mon] Mrs Spieseke and I commenced our long-talked of knitting school for the women & girls. They seemed to like it, & pick it up pretty fast.

19 February 1865

[Sun] In the afternoon after the usual singing I proposed reading to them, stories, suitable for Sunday in the school; the people enjoyed it very much._ In the evening we went to the camp to have the meeting there, it was my turn._ The Tatiara Blacks had just arrived when we came to the camp, their faces painted & evidently intending to fight. George's[185] mother Judy[186] had also come & there was a scene when she saw her boy._ Well talk about the people having no affection, why they cried like little children._ It was a large meeting although a a great many did come near & join the circle. I spoke about Tim 2, 4-6,[187] & then Phillip & Nathanael spoke & the latter prayed too._ It did not seem to be settled yet whether there would be fighting or no, at least when we got home some of our people said that they were sure to fight in the morning._ There are alltogether 97 Blacks here._

19 February 1867*

M[rs] Spieseke & I drove over to Antwerp to see M[rs] Fleming.[188] Adolf rode on Max.

---

185 First Ref: 22 May 1864 under the name Booppoop. This spelling of this boy's name varied from George Bupbup (Ref: 26 February 1865), Booppoop (Ref: 22 May 1864; 18 October 1864), Boop-poop (Ref: 29 May 1864), Bopoop (Ref: 9 July 1864), Bubbub (Ref: 11 July 1864; 14 July 1864), Boopboop (Ref: 2 September 1864). He was connected intermediately to the mission. His mother was Judy. He died suddenly on Ref: 25 December 1867.
186 First mention in the diary. Judy was the mother of Kitty. See: *Periodical Accounts* 25 (1863), 288.
187 KJV. 1 Timothy 2:4-6. 'Who will have all men to be saved, and to come unto the knowledge of the truth. For there is one God, and one mediator between God and men, the man Christ Jesus; who gave himself a ransom for all, to be testified in due time.'
188 Mrs Fleming had given premature birth to a baby girl, Ref: 17 February 1867.

20 February 1865

[Mon] We had a large attendance this morning._ S[pieseke] & I went down to the camp early to see about the fighting, but it was all quiet, it did not look fighting at all thanks be to our Lord that so many Blacks have been brought to our place to hear the Gospel. After school I commenced flooring Matthews hut B[r] Walder helped, S[pieseke]. pulled down the little walls of the little room in w[hich] the girls slept to make them of stone entirely. Chapel almost quite full not quite 2/3 of them women._ Helped S[pieseke]. giving out rations._ King Barney[189] made peace between the 2 tribes

20 February 1867*

[Wed] Some blacks arrived from the East, & wish to take away Lizzie,[190] Marks lubra, because she had "bolted with Mark", without the permission of her relations.[191] Lizzie did not want to go, & as she put herself under our protion, M[r] Spieseke has taken the matter up, & will not allow them to drag her away. She lives for the present with our girls in the kitchen.

21 February 1865

[Tue] Just managed to finish the floor in Matthew's hut before tea, rather a hard days work,_ very warm._ the perspiration run off my in drop._ None of Blacks came to the meeting to-night; there was a ceremony, the going away of Emma. Well as they did not come in time for rations S[pieseke]. made them wait a good while; it seemed to have a good effect for they came well the next morning._

---

189 Only reference in the diary. Spieseke described King Barney, who lived in the mid-1860s at Mr Scott's station at Warracknabeal, as 'a regular sorcerer', who in 1866 treated Old Neptune, who was very sick in mid-1866. See: *Periodical Accounts* 26 (1866), 135–36.
190 First Ref. Lizzie was married to a man called Mark, also known as Thomas Marks, who was connected to the mission. She would subsequently be called Esther.
191 Adolf reported this incident in a letter to the UEC in Herrnhut in which he added more details. In the letter, he stated that they had given protection to a young woman from the Avoca River, without giving her name, who lived at Ebenezer with a 'Black'. She was given protection, as her uncle, who, Adolf noted, was a 'half-white', wanted to violently take her away. The young woman, he wrote, was not converted, had a somewhat insolent manner, but seemed, however, not to want to follow the 'horrible' customs of the 'Blacks'. Furthermore, Adolf reported that 'they wanted namely to have her in the Camp, to satisfy their carnal lusts. She does, however, not want this.' See: UA, UEC Minutes, 8 June 1867, #13, 235.

21 February 1866

[Wed] Some days ago, some Blacks in the camp exchanged wives w[h] was told us by some of the boys; of course we spoke decidedly against such proceedings. Well Paddy[192] one of them, beat amongst others our Elizabeth.[193] This we could not allow to get unpunished, so a warrant was get from M[r] Calder to take up Paddy.[194] Timothy went for it & came back to-day with a warrant. The Policeman came too, so we proceeded to the Camp & found Paddy quite willing to give himself up to the Policeman._ Some of our people amongst them James[195] showed too much sympathy with P[addy]. the latter giving him his best coat & shirt to put on. We were much displeased with all these tokens of pity that shaking of hands & doing nicely with Paddy, because he had done wrong & so B[r] S[pieseke]. & I spoke against it in Chapel, trying to make it clear to the people that a man who had done wrong should not be sympathized with; he should be pitied & prayed for._[196]

21 February 1867*

[Thu] M[r] Ellerman arrived late in the evening on ~~the~~ his way to Nine Creeks where he expects to meet M[rs] E. on her return from Melbourne.

---

192 Unclear if this is the same Paddy as the Paddy at Vectis, who was reported to be 33 years old in 1871. On Ref: 14 June 1864 a Paddy asked for his daughter, Emma, a child of around 7 years old, back from the missionaries.
193 First Ref: 28 May 1864 under the name Mary. Elizabeth was baptised on Ref: 27 July 1865, had been the house helper for the missionaries.
194 Paddy was confined in Dimboola on counts of assault on 19 February 1866, and then in Horsham on 1 March 1866. He was discharged without a sentence. See: *Sixth BPA Report*, 45.
195 First Ref: 17 September 1864 under the names Edward. Took on the name James at baptism on Ref: 26 July 1865. Married to Ruth in early 1866. Died Ref: 4 November 1868.
196 For more on this incident See: *Periodical Accounts* 26 (1866), 30.

21 February 1869*

[Sun] Adolf preached in Horsham on Matt. XV. 30[197]_ I stayed in Walmer with the two children:[198] where A. preached in the evening on Rev. VII. 13-17.[199]

22 February 1865

[Wed] Very hot again; a bit of a hot wind._ All day in the tool shop making Matthew a new door. Towards evening Matthew spied a mob Blacks coming on the other side of the river. S[pieseke]: & I crossed in the boat; they were Wimmera Blacks John their king.[200]_ They had their faces painted of course._

22 February 1866

[Thu] Started early, with Mona[201] & the cart, taking with me Timothy & Teddy, for the salt-lake[202] near Locheal Station to get some salt. _ There was plenty salt, just a little water here & there._ There is a mud about one foot deep all over the lake, on that mud when the water is sufficiently evaporated a crust of salt is formed, hard enough to hold a boy but not an upgrown person._ The salt is obtained by scraping the loose ^wet salt, lying on that crust, together with little boards, as I did not provide myself with proper boots, I got my feet somewhat cut by the hard crust of salt._ We brought home with us 4 sacks full of beautiful salt._ On our way back Timothy shot a black swan & a native companion.[203]

---

197 KJV. Matthew 15:30, 'And great multitudes came unto him, having with them those that were lame, blind, dumb, maimed, and many others, and cast them down at Jesus' feet; and he healed them.'
198 The two Hartmann children, Mary Eleanor, called Nelly (born Ref: 14 December 1865) and Henry (born Ref: 20 November 1868).
199 KJV. Revelations 7:13-20, 'And one of the elders answered, saying unto me, What are these which are arrayed in white robes? And whence come they? And I said unto him, Sir, thou knowest. And he said to me, These are they which come out of great tribulation, and have washed their robes, and made them white in the blood of the Lamb. Therefore are they before the throne of God, and serve him day and night in his temple: and he that sitteth on the throne shall dwell among them. They shall hunger no more, neither thirst any more; neither shall the sun light on them, nor any heat. For the Lamb which is in the midst of the throne shall feed them, and shall lead them unto living fountains of water: and God shall wipe away all tears from their eyes.'
200 First mention Ref: 25 August 1864. King John was at the station in the first quarter of 1872, just before Hartmann left, being diagnosed as consumptive. See: *Eighth BPA Report*, 17.
201 Mona, the horse.
202 Presently known as Pink Lake, just north of Dimboola.
203 Native companion is a former term for the 'brolga' (*Antigone rubicunda*).

22 February 1869*

Went over to Horsham, saw Mrs Robertson & family[204]_ stayed to dinner. Miss Williams there too. Went to see Mrs Gain[205] & Mrs Kelly.[206] Langlands[207] moving their shop.

23 February 1865

[Thu] Finished nailing together Matthew's door, & then commenced mending his key, half of the same been broken off some time ago._ A fight between some Blacks was reported to have taken place this afternoon._

23 February 1866

[Fri] All day in the toolshop planning the boards for Edwards house._

23 February 1869*

Went again to Horsham. Got baby[208] vaccinated. Called on old Mrs Langlands.[209] Mr Wilson[210] lent us his buggy. We left Nelly with Topsy at Walmer.

24 February 1865

[Fri] Just strengthened the grindstone-stand._ An then put up Matthew's door, having mended his broken key._ Margaret cleaned the house nicely & so everything looks proper._ Oh that peace & happiness might enter

---

204 Mr Robertson being the minister in Horsham from around Ref: 21 August 1868.
205 Mrs Gain from Horsham was the midwife at Henry Hartmann's birth (Ref: 20 November 1868).
206 Possibly the Mrs Kelly who was the midwife at Nelly Hartmann's birth (Ref: 11 December 1865; 15 December 1865).
207 George Langland began trading in Horsham in 1849, building a brick building in 1854. George died in 1861, however, the company continued. See: LJ Blake, 'Langlands, George (1803–1861)', *Australian Dictionary of Biography*, National Centre of Biography, The Australian National University, published first in hardcopy 1974, accessed 30 August 2021, adb.anu.edu.au/biography/langlands-george-3988/text6305.
208 Henry Hartmann, born Ref: 20 November 1868.
209 Betsey Langlands (1806–1898). See: 'Langlands, Betsey (1806–1898)', *Obituaries Australia*, National Centre of Biography, The Australian National University, accessed 16 July 2020, oa.anu.edu.au/obituary/langlands-betsey-17087/text28927.
210 Charles Wilson Esq, residing at Walmer, near Horsham, was a friend of the mission and an honorary correspondent for the Central Board Appointed to Watch Over the Interests of the Aborigines in the Colony of Victoria in 1864. Together with his brother he held multiple pastoral leases. He resided at the homestead Walmer. He left the district and returned to England in 1870. See: *The Squatters' Directory; Misssionsblatt* 10 (1870), 246.

into the house too & take their abode in the hearts of the 2 young people._ The whole Ellerman tribe came unexpectedly in the afternoon & stayed over tea._

24 February 1866

[Sat] In the afternoon was the baptism of Matthews child; he became the name of Joseph[211]_ Rebecca, Philip & Timothy being witnesses

24 February 1869*

We left Walmer after dinner, went round by Vectis, & reached Mr Calder's[212] towards tea-time. Enjoyed a quiet chat with Mrs Calders while the rest were all out playing croquet. Later in the evening had some music: chief performer Miss Hood.

25 February 1865

[Sat] Polly came to me when still in bed telling me that the young Black Timpo[213] died last night very suddenly._ This is a event & of course does put a stop not only to the corrobories of the Blacks in the camp, w^h as we are told are held pretty frequently, but will also be the cause of their leaving our place soon._ The Blacks moved their camp to our side again: I think they did so partly because Mr Steward's boundary rider had put a good deal of poison about, as the dogs of the Blacks had bitten some of his sheep._ We had the evening meeting in the camp; Phillip spoke to a congregation of about 60 or 70 Blacks._

25 February 1866

[Sun] S[pieseke]: & family set off this forenoon for Horsham, partly for the sake of Paddy, to present at his trial for beating Elizabeth,[214] partly for having a spell._ Anna was left with us._ I nailed the door of for James'

---

211 First Ref: 8 February 1866, Joseph was the son of Matthew and Margaret.
212 Polkemmet Station.
213 First Ref: 27 February 1865 under the name Timpi. He, Timpian (another version of his name) is said to have stood up to fetch some water and suddenly died. MAB, PP HJAH, 2, Letterbook, containing copies of letters written by Adolf Hartmann to family members (18641871), A. Hartmann to Br. Reichel, Ebenezer 25 March 1865.
214 Ref: 21 February 1866.

house together._ I gave to Sp. a number of my views[215] to give them to Mr Simpson to sell them for me._ (From the 21st to the 25 the accounts kept should be a day on so this should stand on [Mon]26th of Feb.)

25 February 1867*

[Mon] Some blacks went away to Scotts; among the rest Old Frank,[216] & Corny.

26 February 1865

[Sun] The hottest wind blew to-day w^h we had this year & there came a nice rain in the evening but soon gave over._ I cleaned out the tool-shop. As the Tatiara Blacks are about to go back we have tried our best to keep George Bupbup[217] here for another year or 2, but it seems to be no go._ Judy his mother is determined to take him away, well we are sorry for it, very sorry; he ~~was~~ ^is such a promising young boy, well our prayer ~~it~~ is that the Lord would continue the good work that has been commenced in this boys heart._

26 February 1867*

[Tue] Adolf has been occupied for some 5 or 6 weeks in making the new windmill, 4 times the size of the former one, this time the shutters of tin. He began to put it up to-day.

27 February 1865

[Mon] There was no school as the people went down to make the grave for Timpi.[218] Well as was to be expected the boy was not buried in the forenoon._ S[pieseke]. myself & Meissel went down to the camp to see about the people in general._ The Tatiara Blacks were getting their things ready to leave the place._ I took a new testament with me & gave it to George, who was indeed to leave our place._ By & bye there was a small row about Matthew's sister Nancy.[219] Our camp Blacks at least some of them said

---

215 Photographs.
216 First Reference in the diary. There is scant information about Old Frank in the diary. There is a suggestion that Frank was another name for Old Boney, Ref: 17 January 1867. He was living in the camp on the mission on Ref: 19 December 1867.
217 George Bupbup was known under many names. See footnote at Ref: 19 February 1865.).
218 Died on Ref: 25 February 1865. Alternatively called Timpo.
219 Nancy died on Ref: 15 August 1866. Two Nancys are mentioned in the diary, for another Nancy was fetched by Phillip and Rebecca from Lochiel on Ref: 13 October 1866, which may be the same Nancy who was the aunt of the 'half-caste' Henry, from Hugh McLeod station at Vectis.

that she should stop here instead of George & even our Matthew claimed his sister, to keep her & instruct her. This was opposed by Little, but we soon made him quiet._ We then made the thing depend upon Nancy's own decision. But she would go away._ There came news also from Neil[220] that an old Black had died there._ Meissel & I shot the 2 goats, because they were found not only to be useless but also cumbersome animals. We were called by the people to come down to Timpis burial just as we were to have our dinner; we went down. Nathanael made a short speech & S. prayed. The Tatiara Blacks went to-day._

27 February 1866

[Tue] We had visitors to-day M^r & Mrs Edols & Mrs Whalley; they came just about dinner-time, when we did not expect any body. Mr E. came in his new family carriage, w^h holds 9 upgrown people, was made at Geelong & cost him £100._

28 February 1865

[Tue] Our cultivation paddock fence was commenced: Phillip, Hearty & Lake Jack[221] agreed to do it_

29 February 1865

Myself in the toolshop making a box for keeping prepared plates, did not like the wood & did not succeed well either so I left it._ Some of the people cutting boards for the new room, they are paid for it._ (This should be on the 1st of March.)

March

1 March 1865

[Wed] Fetched a small Blackwood from the other side of the river nearly opposite to Mr Ellerman's & cut it into boards to make a plate box of them by & bye._ I shall soak the boards well in the river that they may not split as they are rather thin._ (This should be on March 3rd)

220 Nhill.
221 First Ref: 25 December 1864.

1 March 1866

[Thu] Our brother John Hines finished his apprenticeship in London.

1 March 1867

[Fri] Sp came back from Scotts Station where he went yesterday in the buggy to see the Blacks._ They promised to come soon. Emma is rather sick._

2 March

3 March 1866

[Sat] S[pieseke]. & family came back from Horsham, Helene & ~~Anna~~ Mary[222] having sore eyes, & so Anna who had stopped with us got them too._ Paddy got off without punishment, but was charged to keep the peace.[223]_ Dear Polly who had had a gathering in her face (the left cheek) for some days felt better._

3 March 1870

[Thu] The piano[224] arrived a present from Mr G Mackie[225] & his friends._

4 March 1867

[Mon] Mr & Mrs McDonald from Niel[226] came here to spend a few days with us. Sp: with some of the people commenced the rebarking of our house._ I got Mark & Nathanael to help me at the mill.

---

222 Mary Christine Spieseke born Ref: 17 March 1865 or 18 March 1865.
223 Paddy was charged with assault and discharged on 1 March 1866. See: *Sixth BPA Report*, 45.
224 Adolf requested the Rev. George Mackie to help him purchase a piano for the mission. Mackie procured one with a mahogany frame from Mr Glen, Music Seller of Collins St for £27.10. Mackie also raised funds for the purchase. See: MAB, PP HJAH 3, Letters, Adolf Hartmann to Hines family, Ebenezer, 21 February 1870.
225 The Rev. G Mackie was a Presbyterian pastor, who ended his career in a position in South Yarra. He died in 1872. He was the moderator of the General Assembly in Victoria. He had been a minister in Horsham for two years and was a strong supporter of the Ramahyuck mission. See: *Periodical Accounts* 28 (1871), 229.
226 Referring to the current-day town with the name Nhill, also written Nhil and Nhiel in the diary. The name for the town apparently has its origins in a local Aboriginal word, *nhill*, referring to a swamp, meaning 'white mist wreathing up from the water'. As cited in Jill Giese, 'Yanggendyinanyuk (c. 1834–1886)', *Australian Dictionary of Biography*, National Centre of Biography, The Australian National University, published online 2020, accessed 16 March 2022, adb.anu.edu.au/biography/yanggendyinanyuk-30059/text37299.

5 March 1865

[Sun] Rode on Bobby to the 9 Creeks to preach there; very pleasant ride._

5 March 1867

[Tue] M︎ʳ & M︎ʳˢ Stuart (lately married) & M︎ʳˢ Marsh[227] with children came here & so we had the house pretty full; they left us towards evening._

6 March 1867

[Wed] M︎ʳ & M︎ʳˢ McDonald left for Nhiel to-day._

7 March 1867

[Thu] The new windmill was finished, & there was a good wind blowing so to work it was set, well! well! I thought before that something would break! It worked beautifully as long as there was a moderate wind, but when the puffs came it seemed too much for the pump having a long stroke of 17 inches, it pumped so hard that the water spurted out of the top of the pump. During dinner a puff came w︎ʰ settled broke the bar across the top ring; happily everything being well fastened the wings did not come down. The crank was bent too. Well & so there was and end of pumping. The bottom of the pump had come off from the solder & was leaking. I took then everything down again & set to work renewing & strengthening all the things that required it._

8 March 1865

[Wed] Yesterday & to-day I was at it making a gate for our cultivation paddock._ M︎ʳ Walder made a water-balance to be used when putting up the irrigation._

9 March 1865*

[Thu] Put my gates together & in the afternoon went out with Albert & Napoleon getting 2 posts for putting it up._ Matthew & Nathanael are getting nails, posts etc to fence of a small piece of ground near the river for

---

227 Marsh and Stuart (also written Stewart) held the run next to the mission. The diary does not mention which run it is.

a garden._ Sp[ieseke] finished the wall of the little room._ This day Father & Mother[228] removed to the house which had been repaired & improved for them: viz:_ the one in which B^r & Sr Elliott lived formerly.

9 March 1866

[Fri] A trip to the lake[229] to see M^r & Mrs Ellerman, & also to see the windmill he made._ The pump of his is good, & very powerful filling a tank containing 400 gallons in one quarter of an hour, the mill & all about it rather poor dont think it will keep together very long._ M^r & M^rs E: are rather in straits about their station, there is a baillif at their place for some time already._ The country dreadfully bare not a bit of grass to be seen._ Our Nelly was troubled with sore eyes._ Mrs E. was sick too, & had been so for some time_

9 March 1870

[Wed] A letter arrived, addressed to Wirremande Steward,[230] from the office of lands & works stating contrary to our expectation that sufficient land should be added so as to ~~support~~ carry 3,000 sheep.[231]_

10 March 1865

[Fri] Put up the cultivation paddock gate; had some trouble to get the posts firm, the ground being so dry._

10 March 1866

[Sat] Sister S[pieseke] got sick & had a miscarriage, she could not account for it._

11 March 1865

[Sat] Communion_ Mrs Ellerman present._ A good many more Blacks went away to Locheal._

---

228 Referring to the Hines.
229 Lake Hindmarsh.
230 Also referred to as Stuart (Werimanda), Ref: 1 February 1868.
231 Ref: 22 November 1869. See also: *Periodical Accounts* 27 (1868), 408.

11 March 1867*

Nelly had a bad fall this afternoon & I was for some time afraid she had got seriously hurt, as she could not walk properly, limped, & occasionally fell: but after some time, we were very thankful to see she regained the proper use of her limbs.

12 March 1866

[Tue] Sister Sp[ieseke]: is getting better out of danger:[232]_

12 March 1869*

[Fri] Dick a Dick,[233] who has been with the cricketers to England came here today.[234] He looks a fine black, & speaks very well.

13 March 1865

[Mon] Got at last a good heavy rain in the afternoon; quite refreshing that Was out fetching some wood for windmill, but could not find pieces to my satisfaction._

13 March 1867*

[Wed] Received a letter from Miss Dennis[235] of Colac containing £3 for collecting card,[236] which Mr Spieseke forwarded to Mr Chase.[237]

---

232 Ref: 10 March 1866.
233 Within the diary, there seem to be two men called Dick a Dick. This man here seems to be a man also known as Yanggendyinanyuk (c. 1834 to 1886), who toured England on the Aboriginal Cricket team from May to October 1868. He was born near Nhill and was also known under the names of King Richard, Richard Kennedy, and Richard Barney. A well-known tracker, he was the leader of the group to find the Duff children in mid-August 1864. See: Giese, 'Yanggendyinanyuk (c. 1834–1886)'; Bill Edwards, 'The Fate of an Aboriginal Cricketer: When and Where Did Dick-a-Dick Die?', *Australian Aboriginal Studies* 2 (Fall 1999): 5961. This seems to be a different Dick a Dick to the man who would become Paul after his baptism. Ref: 26 July 1869.
234 For a popular history of the 1868 tour see: Ashley Alexander Mallett, *The Black Lords of Summer: The Story of the 1868 Aboriginal Tour of England and Beyond* (St Lucia: University of Queensland Press, 2002).
235 Miss Dennis visited the mission on Ref: 24 August 1865.
236 Collecting card of the Committee of the Victorian Association in Aid of the Moravian Mission to the Aborigines of Australia.
237 The Reverend Septimus Lloyd Chase was a Church of England minister and supporter of the Ebenezer mission. First incumbent of St. Paul's Anglican Church, now St Paul's cathedral, in Melbourne. Member of the Committee of the Melbourne (later Victorian) Association in Aid of the Moravian Mission to the Aborigines of Australia.

14 March 1867*

[Thu] M^r^ & Mrs Spieseke & children started for Upper Regions on their way to Horsham. M^rs^ & Miss Hastie[238] were here having been fetched over in the morning to spend the day. Later in the afternoon, M^r^ & Mrs Fleming Mr Wallace,[239] & Mr Brookes[240] came over & stayed a short time. They all left about 4 p.m. Philipp & Rebecca started about dinner-time on their trip to the Lake.

14 March 1868

[Sat] B^r^ Hagenauer[241] arrived very unexpectedly. B^r^ Sp: was absent having gone to the manse ~~a few da~~ to assist Mr Ellerman in the communion

15 March 1865

[Wed] Almost everybody[242] went off to the 9 Creeks, either on foot, or in vehicles, or on horseback._ Myself & Polly had Ellerman's buggy with our Bobby in it, Jimmy Reed going with us. Sp[ieseke]: came a little later on horseback._ There was a good gathering of people, about 100._ The tea was laid out in the chapel in fine style._ All our Blacks & ourselves got in gratis._ The main object of the meeting was to present a buggy to M^r^ H[oratio] Ellerman for his faithful services in ministering to the spiritual want, of the people in the N W. Wimmera._ Mr Simpson took the chair for Mr Edols_ M^r^ M^c^Donnald[243] presented the buggy[244] the Mr Ellermann._ Phillip made a somewhat successful speech._ As it was a nice moonlight night, myself & S^p^ returned that night ~~at~~ & got home at 2 am._

---

238 Mr and Mrs Hasting visited the area, first mentioned Ref: 28 October 1866.
239 Mr Wallace was the manager of the Lochiel run (licensed by John Holt). Ref: 15 March 1867.
240 Mr Brooks was in the service of Mr Edols, of the Lochiel run (Ref: 26 March 1865). Possibly also the same Mr Brooks who was a relative of the Edols family (Ref: 20 July 1870).
241 First Ref: 19 May 1864. Friedrich August Hagenauer, Moravian missionary, sent out to Australia with Spieseke in 1858. Established the Ramahyuck mission station in Gippsland in 1862. Later a paid member of the Board of the Protection of the Aborigines. See: Jensz, *German Moravian Missionaries*.
242 Everybody refers here to all the inhabitants of the mission, who were invited to the tea meeting. MAB, PP HJAH, 2, Letterbook, containing copies of letters written by Adolf Hartmann to family members (1864–1871), Adolf Hartmann to Mrs. Hines, 18 March 1865.
243 Unclear if this is the Mr Mc Donnald, a Presbyterian minister from Melbourne (Ref: 19 October 1865) or a local settler (Ref: 4 October 1866).
244 The buggy was worth £70. MAB, PP HJAH, 2, Letterbook, Adolf Hartmann to Mrs. Hines, 18 March 1865.

EBENEZER MISSION STATION, 1863-1873

15 March 1867*

[Fri] Had a visit from a M̲ʳ̲ Mc Niece a friend of M̲ʳˢ̲ Hastie,[245] & whose brother is to succeed M̲ʳ̲ Wallace as manager at Lochiel. He stayed an hour & looked about the station. This morning several blacks started off to M̲ʳ̲ Scotts. Mark & Lizzie, Matthew, ~~Brown~~ ˢᵃᵐᵘᵉˡ, Stephen[246] & Lydia.[247] There is some dispute about Mark having married Lizzie, & they go to settle it.[248] The only men left on the station are Nathaniel, Timothy, James & David.

16 March 1865

[Thu] Fetched a pretty heavy log of ~~to out a~~ ʷʰⁱᵗᵉ ᵍᵘᵐ to season for the windmill._

16 March 1866

[Fri] Nathanael came back & Rachel too._ Poor March[249] was so knocked up that he could not get on any more & so Nathanael had left M̲ʳ̲ E.[250] 7 miles from her, & came to fetch a horse from us._ M̲ʳ̲ E:, on his way to Horsham, stopped over night with us._

16 March 1867*

[Sat] ~~The~~ The Archdeacon of Geelong[251] paid us a visit this afternoon. He was driven over from Upper Regions by M̲ʳ̲ Brookes, & was accompanied by M̲ʳ̲ Bolton of Horsham. He did not stay more then ¾ hour. Cant say his visit afforded us much pleasure. Adolf has at last got the pump watertight, & put up the wings etc again & hopes to have the mill working again in a day or two.

---

245 The Hasties are mentioned throughout the diary, but not clear from the context where they live.
246 First Ref: 23 May 1864. Previously called Jacky, married to Lydia (previously Lilly). Baptised on Ref: 13 August 1866, with Lydia (formerly Lilly) and Samuel (formerly Brown).
247 Previously called Lilly, married to Stephen (previously Jacky). Baptised on Ref: 13 August 1866, with Stephen (formerly Jacky) and Samuel (formerly Brown).
248 Ref: 20 February 1867.
249 March, the horse.
250 Not clear if Mr Ellerman, or Mr Edols.
251 Theodore Carlos Benoni Stretch was the Archdeacon. He officiated at a wedding in Horsham on the 19 March, 1865. See: *The Argus* (Melbourne), 26 March 1867, 4; James Grant, 'Stretch, Theodore Carlos Benoni (1817–1899)', *Australian Dictionary of Biography*, National Centre of Biography, The Australian National University, accessed 16 July 2020, adb.anu.edu.au/biography/stretch-theodore-carlos-benoni-4655/text7691.

17 March 1865

[Fri] Sis: Spieseke was delivered of a healthy girl, w^h is to be called Mary after my dear Polly._

18 March 1865

[Sat] Yesterday & to-day cutting with Matthew, Nathanael & Phillip the white gum log we fetched on Thursday, hard work cutting that wood._

Got the Home letters too & had a very enjoyable evening in reading them. There was the sad news that uncle Mark had been called away suddenly.[252] In the morning Sis: S[pieseke]: was delivered of a little girl.[253]_ S^p finished also the little room w^h he commenced on Feb: 20th; the wall of the same.

18 March 1867

[Mon] The new mill was at last put up again & this time it went well; nothing broke. It is only to be regretted that the pump wont stand heavy pumping, it being made of galvanized iron sheets. I commenced watering, Pearce helping me._

19 March 1865

[Sun] The afternoon singing meeting not being attended well; S[pieseke]: said in the evening meeting, it would be well if it was dropped for some time._

19 March 1866

[Mon] M^r S[pieseke]: spoke to the people about the rations, that he could not any more distribute to all of them, that only those who always live with us could have rations till government would send some more. (The ~~reu~~ result of this was that many of the Blacks left our place to look out for some job

---

252 Ref: 5 January 1865.
253 Ref: 17 March 1865.

EBENEZER MISSION STATION, 1863–1873

19 March 1867

[Tue] Mark & some others came back from Scotts, the former of course without Lizzy,[254] with whom he had bolted from the Avoca.[255] The Blacks took her away from Mark & gave her to Paddy. Mark should have followed our advice & not have gone to Scott's for if he had stayed with us we could have prevented the Blacks taking her away. Mark came to me & asked me how he could get Lizzy back again Of course I could not say anything definite about it, but told him that I would speak to Spieseke when he was back._

20 March 1865

[Mon] My chemicals from Johnson & Co at last arrived all in good order, Mark carried over the box from Antwerp._ Mended my Gallery w^h had sadly suffered from the wind._ My back ached very much & I could hardly do anything.

20 March 1868

[Fri] Drove Hagenauer[256] in our buggy to Horsham, went only as far as Mr Edol's to-day_ Donald[257] on riding on Bobby_

Donald agreed to m go with B^r Hagenauer to get married to Miss Bessy Flower,[258] being school mistress at Ramahyuck, if he liked the place & her also, if not H[agenauer]. was to pay his journey back to our place_ Further if Donald should stay at R[amahyuck]: his brother Pelham[259] was to go to R[amahyuck] too if he wished to do so._

---

254 Also Lizzie.
255 Ref: 20 February 1867.
256 Hagenauer arrived unexpectedly on Ref: 14 March 1868.
257 First Ref: 14 September 1867. Donald Cameron, a man of mixed heritage, who went to Ramahyuck to marry Bessy Flowers. See: Bain Attwood, 'Cameron, Elizabeth (Bessy) (c. 1851–1895)', *Australian Dictionary of Biography*, National Centre of Biography, The Australian National University, accessed 16 July 2020, adb.anu.edu.au/biography/cameron-elizabeth-bessy-12834/text23167. See also: Jensz, *German Moravian Missionaries*, 174-77.
258 Much has been written about Bessy Flower, with some of her letters in Elizabeth Nelson, Sandra Smith and Patricia Grimshaw (eds), *Letters from Aboriginal Women of Victoria, 1867–1926* (Melbourne: The University of Melbourne, History Department, 2002). See also: Bain Attwood, '"In the Name of All My Coloured Brethren and Sisters": A Biography of Bessy Cameron', *Hecate: A Women's Interdisciplinary Journal* 12, no. 1–2 (1986): 9–53.
259 Only mention in the diary. Pelham Cameron, born 1854 at Morton Plains, stayed at Ebenezer and married Blanche. They left the mission with their children in 1880. See: *Periodical Accounts* 29 (1873), 353; *Periodical Accounts* 31 (1878), 348.

21 March 1865

[Tue] Had a bad night. Felt ill in the morning, quite stiff & knocked up, xx pain in the head, back & throat; stopped in bed all day, & took some medicine, homeopathic.[260]_ (aconitum[261] & nux vomica[262]) Got a little better towards evening, & managed to get up & write a letter to Johnson & C⁰ ordering some Jodide of Potassium._ Mʳ Walder going to Horsham for Mʳ S[pieseke]: as we, besides 22 more settlers had been summond for not sending in the marking of sheep, took the letter for me to Horsham._ S: flooring the little room._

21 March 1868

[Sat] Down to Walmar_ most cordially received._ Just in time for dinner; there was there a clergyman "Murdock" to preach for some time in Horsham, since Mr Simpson left._

(Mr Simpson had to leave Horsham because he got intoxicated) Miss Hughes told me that it was a constitutional weakness of Mr S:; having the heart decease, & being prescribed by the doctor to take a little brandy, he went too far, because he was in such an excited state when feeling the decease. _

22 March 1865

[Wed] Felt sufficiently strong to get up after the meeting, went to the school & kept it as usual; improved much during the day, so that I was able to work at getting things ready in the photographic line._ Dear Polly rather much to do at present.[263] Spoke to the people about their playing for money, & tried to make plain to them the foolishness & wrong of doing so_ S: got a bad attack of tooth-ache._

---

260 Many Moravians used homeopathic medicine. Spieseke, for example, also used homeopathic medicine, asking the UEC to send him a book by Dr Lutze on homeopathic medicine. His reasoning was that the Australian doctors were very expensive. See: UA, UEC Minutes, 1 May 1869, #6, 111. For use of homeopathic medicine by other German missionaries in Australia see: Regina Ganter, *The Contest for Aboriginal Souls: European Missionary Agendas in Australia* (Canberra: ANU Press, 2018), doi.org/10.22459/CAS.05.2018, 177.
261 *Aconitum napellus* is a homeopathic remedy commonly used at the beginning of an acute illness. Commonly known as monkshood or wolfsbane, it is a flowering plant from South America.
262 *Strychnos nux-vomica* is a homeopathic remedy commonly used for colds and everyday complaints. The seeds of this native Indian plant are used in alternative medicine.
263 Particularly as Sis. Spieseke had just given birth Ref:18 March 1865.

22 March 1868

[Sun] Hagenauer preached in Horsham. We all drove to Horsham in <u>the family coach.</u>_

At Ebenezer another incedent occurred. At evening prayer Dina & Kitty[264] were not be found having attempted to run away At 11 p m they roused us by their unexpected return & seemed very much ashamed._

22 March 1869*

Borrowed today from Mr Charles Wilson 100 lbs tea. 168 lbs Sugar. 20 lbs. tobacco.

23 March 1866

[Fri] Finished the alteration we commenced a few days ago, with our pump._ We ~~pump~~ put it down 3 feet, & made a wooden box above it to have a good body of water above the sucker, the thing seems to answer well._ Had some trouble to get that box watertight._ There was a nice shower this morning

23 March 1868

[Mon] Had a drive with H[agaenauer] to see a post & wire fence; it was a round about way towards the gate leading to the Dimboola road._ We missed somehow the fence, because there was too much talking going on between us. Well we drove to Horsham inquired at Borders for the ~~mail~~ coach fare, then we saw Mrs Musslan. Back again to Horsham stopped at Dr Purvis'[265] waited for the mail & then drove back to Horsham the same way we came On the way Hagenauer, to whom I had told my wish to see my uncle[266] gave me £10 towards accomplishing this my journey.

---

264 Diana and Kitty, who Spieseke brought to the mission from one of his trips westward in November–December 1867. Prev. Ref: 4 December 1867.

265 Possibly referring to Doctor WL Purves, coroner in Horsham from November 1867. Ref: 30 October 1869.

266 Adolf's uncle, Carl Hartig, who lived at Chinamans Creek, near Castlemaine. Adolf and Polly went on a trip of almost four weeks to visit his Uncle and Aunt Hartig in May 1868, Ref: 6 May 1868. Adolf received a letter from him in 1864 (Ref: 19 May 1864).

23 March 1869

[Tue] Poor Rachel died this morning at 10-30 a.m. at the Pleasant Creek Hospital[267], whither she went about three weeks ago. No particulars were told us except that her disease was enlargement of the liver & spleen.

24 March 1866

[Sat] There was a fog this morning, the first this year, & in the afternoon a thunderstorm came up from the west; it seemed to be very partial, for south & north there was blue sky; well we got it, & that very nicely. During the shower 2 more visitors arrived. Mrs Archibald[268] & one of her sons. A very comfortable old elderly lady. She it was who adopted little Archie[269] the black boy & gave him the name too: Alltogether Mrs Archibald is one of those few people who are kindly disposed towards the Blacks, _& I think the Blacks like her, too._ A black snake was killed near the river 4 feet long this is the 3rd snake I have seen since we are here._

24 March 1868

[Tue] At 9 a.m. Hagenauer left Walmar for Horsham & I for home. Bobby I tied behind the buggy & it went very well. Made the way to Edol's in a little more then 3 hours At Edols there were the Calder's and presently Mr A. Wilson wife & baby came too, on their way to Antwerp. I invited them to come & see us._ Back to Ebenezer at sunset._

25 March 1796

Birthday of my Father Johann Gottlieb Hartmann.[270] Gebhardsdorf n^r Marklissa. Died on the 5th of May 1844 in Charlottenburg.[271]

25 March 1865

[Sat] Distilling water very convenient way to do it with my new still. Cleaned out my dark room & got things ready inside._

---

267 Opened in 1861 as a medical facility for the population of Stawell and district.
268 From beyond the lake (Ref: 27 September 1866).
269 First Ref: 21 October 1864. Archie (Archibald) was a boy of around seven or eight years old in 1866. He attended the school. According to Hartmann, Archie was a full orphan. See: *Periodical Accounts* 25 (1863), 357. See also: *Further Facts, Fifth Paper*, 5.
270 Johann Gottlieb Hartmann was a missionary in Suriname, the country where Adolf was born.
271 Suriname.

25 March 1866

[Sun] There was a hot wind this day, & so the mill pumped very well, after the improvement made to it._ In the afternoon Mrs Archibald & son left for the 9 creeks.

25 March 1867

[Mon] Left for M$^{r.}$Scotts with Mona & the spring cart, to fetch some of the Black children that were there; the Blacks had sent word that I we might come for them. When I arrived I heard that they had gone away some to Bell & Macguiness[272] & others to Mac Millans.[273] So I made up my mind to go after them to the latter place._

26 March 1865

[Tue] Should be on March 28._

Made a tea box to contain 9 prepared plates for the dry process._ Phillip & Matthew & some others after wild cattle, did not get anything Sp[ieseke] in the garden all day made use at last of my arrangement to pull up the tub on the sledge I made._ B^{rn} Walder & Meissel off to see Mr Hny[274] Ellerman & Scott's._

26 March 1865

[Sun] Mr Crosswell[275] & Brooks[276] on a visit the latter about to leave Mr Edoll's service._

26 March 1866

[Mon] Off to Horsham with Polly & the baby, taking Rachel with us_ Stopped at Edol's for the night._ We took Miss Donovan[277] back to Mr Edols._

---

272 In 1865, McGuiness and Bell leased the Corong, Minapree and Lake Wilhelmina runs. All three were in the Swan Hill area. See: *The Squatters' Directory*, 12.
273 Possibly a run leased by Archibald McMillan. In 1865, he was the leaseholder of the Irrewarra (West Wimmera), and Sheep Hill (East Wimmera) and Glenwyllan (East Wimmera) runs. See: *The Squatters' Directory*, 37–38.
274 Henry Ellerman.
275 Single reference to Crosswell in the diary.
276 Possibly Mr Brookes.
277 No conclusive information is given about Miss Donovan in the diary.

26 March 1867*

[Tue] Off to Mac Millans. Found the Blacks we were in search for & I succeeded to get 5 young people._ Lizzy & her sister Maggy[278] & her brother Bobby & then Minnie[279] & Emma. Back again to M[r] Scotts._ M[r] Dykes[280] arrived from the Mission Station._ Also M[r] Mac Millan came. M[r] Dykes preached a beautiful sermon on, Luke 13-13-14.[281]_ He had previously visited us here at Ebenezer, & though he did not stay long ²ʰᵒᵘʳˢ he left us with a favourable impression of his piety, humility & Christian. He spoke very nicely to the blacks in a little impromptu meeting which we had during his visit.

26 March 1869*

Good Friday. Sandy[282] started with his two children for Vectis.

27 March 1865

[Mon] Getting my camera light tight, the wood very much shrunk in it I- Made also a ~~roof~~ rough box to contain the rags for cleaning glasses._

27 March 1866

[Tue] Drove to Walmar, & as usual were well received & entertained

27 March 1867

[Wed] Back to our place. Took me about 7 hours to get there._

---

278 Also known as Maggie.
279 First mention. Minnie decided to stay at the mission (Ref: 5 September 1867). She had departed by 1880. See: *Periodical Accounts* 31 (1878), 347.
280 No further reference to him in the diary.
281 KJV. Luke 14:13-14, 'And he laid his hands on her: and immediately she was made straight, and glorified God. And the ruler of the synagogue answered with indignation, because that Jesus had healed on the sabbath day, and said unto the people, There are six days in which men ought to work: in them therefore come and be healed, and not on the sabbath day.'
282 First Ref: 28 August 1866. In 1869, it was reported that Sandy was a 32-year-old man. According to Alexander Wilson, in November 1869, Sandy was looking after his two little daughters, three-year-old Minnie and 18-month-old Laura, himself after their mother, Fanny, died in 1868, and his sister also passed away in November 1869: 'He declined to send them to the Mission Station, or to go with them.' See: *Seventh BPA Report*, 21–22. By 1876, Sandy, now baptised and known as Nathan, was living on the Ebenezer mission station with his daughters. Laura died on 8 June 1876, aged 10. Cause of death was not given. See: *Periodical Accounts* 30 (1876), 125–26.

28 March 1866

[Wed] Drove to Horsham_ Stopped at the manse_ Spoke to Dr Johnson to get baby[283] vaccinated, he had no matter just then & said he would send us some, when I could vaccinate it myself._ Went a stopping with Langlands with the Simpsons._ Saw the Bowdens.[284]_ In the evening there was a prayer-meeting preparatory to the communion next Sunday

28 March 1869*

Easter Sunday. We had a lovefeast in the afternoon. Very warm.

28 March 1870

[Mon] A visit from Mr & Mrs Townsend, stayed one night, promised some sheep._ Sarah Topsy Franklin went with them to stay with them a little while

29 March 1866

[Thu] As there were a good many Blacks at Longernong,[285] & as we wished to see Mr & Mrs Samuel Wilson, we put our Mona into Mr Simpson's buggy, w^h he kindly offered to us._ What a splendid house & place in this wilderness. We were well received._ Every thing quite fashionable. Mr S took me about in his garden & showed me many very interesting plants etc._ In the Towards evening we went down into the wood to see the Blacks, there were about 40 of them mostly from Morton plain. We spoke to them first separately & then before we went away I preached to them Jesus; may the Lord bless what I said!_ We believe that many of the people living there are addicted to drink, & the temptation is very great as a public house has been built there._

283 Baby being Eleanor Mary Hartmann, born Ref: 14 December 1865.
284 Acquaintances of the Hartmanns in Horsham.
285 Longerenong, Wimmera. In a report to the Central Board in 1866, Samuel Wilson states that the youngest member of the group was 30, with no young women, and four deaths in the past 12 months see: *Sixth BPA Report*, 30.

29 March 1869*

We had a one or two thunder storms in the evening, & a good fall of rain in the night, which was very acceptable.

30 March 1866

[Fri] Good Friday_ Got back to Walmar at about 2 p.m._ I brought some plants from Longernong; strawberries, jessamine, passis-flower, & some seeds of desert pea, fruit ba^earing passion flower & s some rock melon seed._ We gave Mona a rest, & Mr Simpson drove us in his buggy with his own horse to Walmar._

30 March 1870

[Wed] M^r & Mrs March from Glenlee came on a short visit

31 March 1865

[Fri] The b^m Walder, Meissel having come back yesterday I commenced operations this morning[286] but did not succeed well. Miserable affair that_

31 March 1866

[Sat] In the afternoon to Horsham to attend church_ Mr Simpson preaching _ Back to Walmar._

31 March 1870

[Thu] Mr Ellerman came & brought Eliza his daughter with him to stay with us a week or so._

---

286 Meaning working on his photography.

April

1 April 1865

[Sat] Mr Walder, Meissel & Daniel[287] left us to-day after dinner.[288] We prayed before we parted in our dining-room. Daniel & his father[289] & mother[290] being present. Sp[ieseke]: drove the b^rn to the 9 Creeks._ Tried hard in morning to get a good likness[291] of Daniel but it was no go._

1 April 1866

[Sun] To Horsham for the communion. The first time that I partook of it in that Church.[292] It lasted 3 hours._ Back to Walmar, Mr Boxborough Mr Simpson curate[293] going with us to preach at Walmar._

2 April 1865

[Sun] Went to the Camp to see the people._ Heard in the afternoon that they quietly had gone away to the 9 Creeks, almost all of them except the women; this I consider to be wrong

2 April 1866

[Mon] Off again to Horsham for the missionary meeting, w^h Mr Paten[294] conducted on behalf of the Mission in the New Hebrides.[295]_ Had no chance given me to speak._ There was a sale on behalf of this mission._ Back to Walmar again._ Mr Calder & whole family there_ Got an invitation to visit them

---

287 In April 1864, Daniel expressed a wish to Br Spieseke to travel into the interior with the four Moravian missionaries to Coopers Creek, Br H Walder, CW Kramer, WJ Kuehne and G Meissel. See: UA, UEC Minutes, 7 July 1864, #4.
288 Walder, Meissel and Daniel travelled towards Melbourne, however, Daniel began to complain of pain in his legs and was operated on in Geelong on 10 April 1865. He subsequently died on 11 October 1865: See: *Periodical Accounts* 25 (1863), 468–69; *Periodical Accounts* 26 (1866), 38.
289 Old Boney.
290 Old Mary.
291 Meaning trying to get a photograph.
292 Presbyterian Church in Horsham.
293 Curate being the assistant clergy.
294 The Rev. John Gibson Paton was a Protestant missionary to the 'New Hebrides' (now Vanuatu). He was born in the south of Scotland in 1824 and travelled as a missionary to Vanuatu in 1858. In 1865–66, he was in Australia on a recruiting tour. In in April 1865, he had already been in contact with the Moravian missionaries Walder and Miessel at a tea meeting in Melbourne organised by the Melbourne Young Men's Presbyterian Association. See: *Leader* (Melbourne), Saturday 22 April 1865, 2. Via: trove.nla.gov.au (accessed 20 April 2022).
295 Current-day Vanuatu.

2 April 1870

[Sat] Off with Polly & Nelly to Nhil[l], as I had accepted an arrangement to preach for M̲ͬ Ellerman at Bleakhouse[296] & Nhil[l].

3 April 1865

[Mon] Experimentalizing in my dark room I found that I got something like a good picture from the old bath & Pontings collodion,[297] but I found out too that strong light coming against my camera made my picture thick & foggy._ Cleaned some plates in the evening to have one more try tomorrow._ Sp: came back from the 9 Creeks in the evening._ Sent away Peter with a letter to M̲ͬ Clarke containing a number of my prints, as he requested me to send some that he might tell how to remedy faults.[298]_

3 April 1866

[Tue] Left H̶o̶r̶s̶h̶ Walmar for M̲ͬ t̶h̶e̶ Edol's._ Found M̲ͬ Whally had arrived._ As he was rather an accomplished musician & singer we had a very enjoyable evening

3 April 1869*

[Sat] We heard to-day that M̲ͬˢ Hagenauer is on her way here at last. M̲ͬ Spieseke also heard some particulars respecting Rachel: - that she was taken suddenly worse (was walking about the n̶i̶g̶h̶t̶ day before;) she was visited by lay reader: & was observed praying to the last. (We also heard that B̲ͬ Walder[299] has a call to Jamaica:[300] & B̲ͬ Meissel[301] to Surinam.[302])

---

296 Location near Nhill.
297 Collodion is a chemical solution needed for the wet-plate photography process.
298 Adolf had already been in contact with Clarke in January 1865, requesting him how to get 'warm brown tone' in his photographs. See: MAB, PP HJAH, 2, Letterbook, containing copies of letters written by Adolf Hartmann to family members (1864–1871), A. Hartmann to Clarke [no date, January 1865].
299 Heinrich Walder received the call to the West Indies while still in Australia. He left Adelaide on 19 July 1869 to London. In England, he married Anna Charlotte Less and they both arrived in Jamaica on 3 April 1870. Information from his *Dienstlauf* (Service history), copies held in Moravian archives including MAB, UA, and Moravian Church Archive and Library, in London.
300 The Moravians established a Christian mission in Jamaica in 1754 to African slaves on the plantations.
301 Gottlieb Meissel received the call to Suriname while in Australia. He left Melbourne on 26 May 1869, arrived in Paramaribo, via San Francisco, on 25 October 1869. He worked in Suriname until late 1883, when he was transferred to the mission field in Jamaica. Information from his *Dienstlauf* (Service history).
302 The Moravians first sent Christian colonists to work in Suriname in 1735.

4 April 1865

[Tue] Once more I tried to get some good pictures, but cannot manage. I felt very much disappointed, very, for I have been trying my utmost & then it seems that Sp: does not want to help me in it I cannot get any material when I want to do something for my gallery w^h by the by is very defective, well well I must wait till I get an answer from Mr Clarke_ There is great trouble again about Matthew & Margaret, so much so that Margaret slept last night in our dining-room. Although Matthew has a very bad temper & may be the ^{chief} cause of these disturbances, Margaret, Polly & I think has a good share in it, too, & we hope to be able to find it out in time to come._

Mr Bailey a former settler in this district & friend of Mr Ellerman visited here._ Sp: with a number of the people mended the fence along the river._

4 April 1866

[Wed] Back to our place at 3 p.m._ Found them all well & a good number of Blacks present._ We both felt refreshed & strengthened to take up our work again._ Planted out some jessamine[303] & passion-flower near some of the verandah posts._ Very happy to be again in our own little rooms._

5 April 1865

[Wed] All of us except S^{is} Sp[ieseke]: went off to Antwerp to eat a goose._ did not enjoy it much as my stomach was not in proper order Tried Mr Ellerman's new plough (Spoke my mind to Sp: finding some trouble to get on with him)

5 April 1866

[Thu] We had a visit from M^r & Mrs Edols, M^r & Mrs Whally & Miss Donovan Of course there was not much work done that day on my part & on nobody's part. Mr Whally was kind enough to give as £2 for the Mission._ They left us in the afternoon._

---

303 Alternative form of 'jasmine'.

5 April 1867

[Fri] Topsy was married to Timothy. They were not married in the chapel because Timothy was still excluded because of the sins he committed a little whill while ago.[304] B^r S. married them as I am not licensed to do so The whole was done without any ceremony, some blunders being made, too._ When the papers were signed S[pieseke] rang the bell & we had a singing meeting. We sang some verses in behalf of Topsy & Timothy & commended them to our dear Saviour in prayer._

6 April 1865

[Thu] Was much troubled last night with diarrhea, & felt very weak all day. Took some homeopathic medecin (Arsenic)._ In the evening Sp[ieseke] came back from the 9 creeks having bought 4 bullocks etc_ Phillip & Edward also came back having shot a large beast about 8 miles from our place._

6 April 1867

[Sat] It began to rain during the night & rained uninterruptedly almost all the forenoon. It was a regular soaker. 1 inch & ¾ of rain fell._

7 April 1865

[Fri] Early in the morning a number of the people went off to see about the big bullock Phillip had shot yesterday._ Myself & Edward & 2 of the boys left with the cart after breakfast_ A very hot day._ After a long drive through very wild country, through Mallée & shrubs & bush we came to one of the cuttings the surveyors had made through the mallée; here we whistled & cooed & got an answer by the others who were a long way in the Mallee.[305] We had now to cut our way through about 2 miles of Mallee to get to the place where the bullock lay._ Near one of the swamps, on our way back we

---

304 Timothy had been reprimanded for his behaviour by Adolf in chapel in January. Ref: 8 January 1867. According to the UAC Minutes, in January 1867 four people were excluded from the religious community for a period of time as they had engaged in improper fornication, being Timothy, Stephen, Magdalene, and Nathanael. See: UA, UEC Minutes, 4 July 1867, #4, 25.
305 The area called the *Mallee* is named after a distinctive *Eucalyptus dumosa* tree, known as *Mally* in a local Aboriginal language. The term 'Malle' appeared on settler maps from 1846 and is also spelt Marlie, Marlee, malley and Mawley. Taylor, *Karkarooc*, 318.

stopped; the people made some fire, by shooting some cotton out of my gun, & then we had some of the beef, & a little tea w[h] Edward had provided for._ Got back about 5 p.m., when the meat was cut into pieces & salted._

8 April 1865

[Sat] Commenced making a ladder to be used when putting up the irrigation In the morning I had first to grind 2 of the adces[306] out of w[h] big pieces had been broken, took me some time doing. Nathanael helped me adcing[307] the posts for the ladder._ A strong wind all day_ It is getting much cooler_ Polly got suddenly sick when at tea, an old thing she had had some years ago troubling her, hysterics.

9 April 1865

[Sun] Baptism of Sp[ieseke]'s child[308]_ Polly stood godmother; the little one was baptized Mary Christine._ I stood proxy for a certain Schulz in Niesky.[309]_ Polly getting a little better._ It being a coldish day I made a little fire & enjoyed it much._ The singing in the afternoon fell out last sunday & this because the people came so badly._

10 April 1865

[Mon] After school went out with Matthew to cut down a nice tree for making the wings of my windmill, fetched also some more wood for the ladder._ Shot a hawk behind Tony's[310] house, sitting on the tree._ Sp began the wall of the little store

11 April 1865

[Tue] Grubbing in the garden before breakfast, at the shrubs._ After school cut that tree into half I fetched yesterday; Matthew helped._ In the afternoon adcing the halves into proper shape for the wings._ Timothy went to the

---

306 Adze or adz, an axe-like tool used to dress timbers roughly.
307 Adzing, verb meaning to dress or shape wood with an adze.
308 Ref: 17 or 18 March 1865.
309 Niesky was founded by the Moravians in 1741. The town is some 38 kilometres north-north-east of the main Moravian settlement in Germany, Herrnhut.
310 First Ref: 19 May 1864. Tony/Toney (later, Joshua Ref: 29 December 1867) was mentioned frequently before his baptism, but not after. He was an older man who had frequented the school already in 1864, and was the father of Phillip and Nathaniel, and the husband of Lina (also spelt Linna, and Lena, Ref: 6 July 1864). See: *Periodical Accounts* 26 (1866), 420.

9 Creeks to fetch our bullocks & team, so Albert came & asked whether he might not go with him to fetch his parents, but I forbade him, as I feared that he would not return._

12 April 1865

[Wed] Cut & prepared the beams for the windmill & put them into the water to season; after that went at the ladder again._ There was a mist this morning but it was soon driven away by a south wind & we had a clear day._ In the evening we had a meeting preparatory to the Lord's supper._

12 April 1866

[Thu] Napoleon & Albert went away to-day with a mob of Blacks to mount Elgin[311] or somewhere about there. We spoke hard against it but it was of no use._ Poor boys!!

13 April 1865

        Maundy Thursday

[Thu] Had the Lord's supper in the evening; kept it._

14 April 1865

[Fri] Good Friday._ After dinner M[r] Brooks & Harry Ellerman came from Antwerp in M[r] E[llerman]'s buggy, carrying a note from M[rs] E[llerman]: to Polly requesting her to keep her company till Monday, as she would be alone; we thought it better to refuse going there._ There was no work done to-day; kept it as much as we could, as they keep it at home-

15 April 1864

[Fri] Arrived in Australia.[312]_ The anchor was cast at 8 ½ pm. in Hobson's Bay.[313]

---

311 South-west of Nhill.
312 Left England Ref: 28 January 1864.
313 Hobson's Bay is the most northern point of Port Phillip Bay, Melbourne.

15 April 1865

[Sat] A Lovefeast in the afternoon at 3; kept it._ Worked at the ladder_ A very nice & gentle rain came down, & we hope that it will go on raining, it being so very dry._

15 April 1867

[Mon] Had a little more rain to-day. The country begins to look green._ I have taken for some time the feeding of the horses in the morning._ There was a difference between Tobsy & Timothy to-night but S[pieseke] managed to make it somewhat straight again. Making new harrows for the harrowing in the new crop of hay. The paddock is just being ploughed.

16 April

17 April 1865

[Mon] Worked all day hard at my ladder & finished it[314]_ Felt rather tired at night but nevertheless I helped Polly translating a birthday verse for father._ Polly & M^{rs} Sp[ieseke] had a drive to Antwerp by themselves.

17 April 1869*

[Sat] Mr Mackie[315] Convener of Presbyt. Mission Committee[316] arrived from Melbourne, accompanied by Mrs Hagenauer, Sissy,[317] & a black girl named Betsy.[318] Mr Spieseke fetched them from Horsham. They came early, & caught us in the midst of our Saturday morning's work. Mr Mackie had a good look at the place, people, tc.

---

314 Began the ladder on Ref: 8 April 1865 with the help of Nathanael.
315 George Mackie, born in Scotland, had been the Presbyterian minister at Horsham.
316 Presbyterian Church's Chinese and Aborigines Mission Committee in Victoria from later 1860 to May 1862. See: Alan Dougan, 'Mackie, George (1823–1871)', *Australian Dictionary of Biography*, National Centre of Biography, The Australian National University, published first in hardcopy 1974, accessed 27 October 2020, adb.anu.edu.au/biography/mackie-george-4110/text6571.
317 Sissy was born in Gippsland on 14 September 1863, and baptised under the name 'Mary', but called 'Sissy' by the family. She was the second of the Hagenauer's nine children. See: *Periodical Accounts* 25 (1863), 189.
318 First Mention. Married Cogle at Ebenezer on Ref: 1 May 1869. It is possible that this is the Betsy mentioned by Adolf Hartmann in Robert Brough Smyth, *The Aborigines of Victoria: With Notes relating to the Habits of the Natives of Other Parts of Australia and Tasmania. Compiled from Various Sources for the Government of Victoria, vol. II* (Melbourne: John Ferres, Government Printer, 1878), 2 (available via: archive.org). The book refers to her as a 21-year-old woman around 1870.

18 April 1865

[Tue] Matthew & Timothy went off early to shoot a bullock, but Matthew returned in the afternoon leaving Timothy in pursuit of a beast, w^h he shot too, but could not bleed as he had no knife; so we are not going to fetch the beast._ Made a new water-balance, the one Mr Walder had made of wood, being no good, made mine of tin & it answers very well. So I once more made out the level from our garden to the river & marked a tree at the proper height to be cut off._ A rather warm day, but beautiful

18 April 1869*

Mr Mackie preached this morning & there, on Joseph's words "See that ye fall not out by the way." After service he started for Nine Creeks having to preach there at 12, & again in Horsham at night: We were very sorry he could not stay longer.

19 April 1865

[Wed] Phillip & Edward went off early to shoot a bullock as they failed to do so yesterday; they were successful._ Towards evening the beast was brought in the cart, skinned & hung up for the night to dry, to be salted next day._ So there is a prospect of some nice beef._

20 April 1865

[Thu] Walked about our grounds looking out for trees for posts for the windmill._ Sent off the home letters also notes to Jackson Shawe[319] Caroline,[320] Miss Jackson, Cousin Jane, an extra birthday letter to father & letter to B^r Reichel._ Phillip followed an invitation of Mr White to come to him for a little time & shot some wild cattle._

---

319 Jackson Shawe was at Fulneck with Adolf. This is the only reference to him in the diary, with Adolf only writing one letter to him during his time in Australia. In this letter, Adolf informs Jackson Shawe that the latter can gain information about Adolf and Polly from Br Hines at Fairfield, demonstrating the second order of transfer of information through letters to family members from missionaries. See: MAB, PP HJAH, 2, Letterbook, Adolf Hartmann to Jackson Shawe, 19 April 1865.
320 Adolf's sister.

20 April 1867*

Adolf & Mr Spieseke had a long talk about school affairs, & came to an understanding that A[dolf]. was to have the correspondence connected with the school, as was arranged by the U. E. C.[321]

21 April 1865

[Fri] Cut down 3 small trees in the Durrock paddock, Mark & Toney[322] helping. As the horse could not pull them as they were, we left them to be adced on the place._ Stopt at home after dinner & got our blinds in order, w^{h} were very badly tacked to the rollers etc

21 April 1867*

Easter-Sunday. We had a lovefeast in the afternoon for our members. Polly began to be sick. It turned out to be the commencement of a miscarriage.[323]

22 April 1865

[Sat] Off all day with Nathanael, Matthew & Timothy adcing the 3 posts we cut down yesterday, rather stiff adcing & felt my bones in the evening._ There were no letters, the mail having been changed._

22 April 1867*

[Mon] Had a visit from Mr Hastie to-day. He returned to Antwerp soon after dinner. We had expected Mrs Hastie also, but she could not come.

23 April 1865

[Sun] Head again our usual singing in the afternoon, w^{h} had been dropped because the people did not come well._ King Peter[324] just came to see how our Blacks were, & went away._ Mark & Matthew I found reading the Bible in the hut of the latter._

---

321 Unity Elders' Conference (in German *Unitätsältestenkonferenz*), the General Directory of the Church responsible for making decisions on Church matters between the General Synods.
322 Also written Tony.
323 Polly suffered a further miscarriage on Ref: 24 August 1870.
324 First Ref: 10 July 1864. Reported by Spieseke as being the supreme head of the tribe, King Peter opposed the marriage of Phillip (Charley Charley) and Rebecca (Jessie). Spieseke called the police at Nine Creeks who threatened King Peter with three months jail for potential arson. Due to this disruption, he was commanded to leave Ebenezer for three months in December 1863. See: *Periodical Accounts* 25 (1863), 188; HG Schneider, *Missionsarbeit der Brüdergemeine in Australien* (Gnadau: Verlag der Unitäts-Buchhandlung, 1882), 170. *Missionsblatt* 4 (1864), 76–77.

24 April 1865

[Mon] Went & cut down, with Toney one more tree for a post for the windmill, as it was standing near a water hole & leaning towards the same. I tied with a rope to another tree, that when falling it might come over to the land, well I did not quite succeed but some of the people being near, we managed to fetch it up._ In the afternoon I adced it with Nathanael._

25 April 1865

[Tue] Got the home mail in the evening. Besides the usual letters there were others, from Badham,[325] Reichel & Johua Taylor, the latter asking for my likenesses & asking also about some information about the squatting going on here._

25 April 1866

[Thu] Spieseke finished the ~~valls of th~~ building of the walls of the house for David._

26 April 1865

[Wed] Last night about 1 o'clock there came a good thunderstorm; it awoke both of us, & we could not sleep after it for some time._ There was some rain falling in the night._ There was another thunderstorm in the afternoon accompanied by a terrific shower._ I was in the toolshop all day cutting out the revolving circle for the wind mill to rest upon._ Mr Holt[326] & Mr Wallace payed us a visit._ The cabbages w^h S[pieseke]. planted some time ago are thriving well._

27 April 1865

[Thu] In tool-shop all day working at the ring for windmill. Nathanael for whom S[pieseke]. bought a nice pair of boots, from a hawker, promised to h^{e}olp me at the windmill._ P.m. we had some more rain._ When a hawker comes the people seem to be mad about spending money; they would spend

---

325 Thomas Leopold Badham, assistant secretary of the Moravian missions, until the death of Peter La Trobe in 24 September 1863, whence Badham became secretary. He was also long-time editor of the Moravian *Periodical Accounts*, a missionary periodical. See: J Taylor Hamilton, *A History of the Church Known as the Moravian Church, or the Unitas Fratrum, or the Unity of the Brethren, During the Eighteenth and Nineteenth Centuries* (Bethlehem, Pennsylvania: Times Publishing Company, 1900), 444.

326 John Holt held the Lochiel run. See: *The Squatters' Directory*, Correction and Errata page.

every penny they have got, if we did not check them. Well Matthew came & wanted his 10/s for milking in advance (he had 4 more days to milk) but as he wanted to buy a hat for Margaret S[pieseke]. did not feel inclined to give it him. Well M[atthew]. next morning did not milk (very silly) so S. engaged Peter to milk._ Such is Matthew at times._

27 April 1867*

Heard to day of the compulsory flight of the Brethren[327] from Kopperamana[328] their station; they took refuge with the Lutheran Missionaries at Kilalpanina.[329] They had a narrow escape of their lives, as they heard afterwards that the blacks intended to shoot them on the very day they escaped. About a thousand were collected in the neighbourhood. Their watchword was "Down with the whites".[330]

28 April 1866

[Sat] Last Wednesday week Polly's eyes began to be sore last Wednesday a week ago & & last Wednesday Tuesday they got so bad that she could do any more work as her eyes could not bear the light any more, so she kept in bed, the room being darkened, & I took the cooking, as M^{rs} Sp[ieseke]: was still laid up from her miscarriage.[331] Polly's eyes are much better to day; last night she had good rest._ Made a new kind of yeast to day as the other does not seem to answer._ What a dry season no rain yet._ The school had been omitted for a fortnight because the people were engaged in carting manure from an old sheep yard to improve our cultivation paddock.

29 April 1865

[Sat] Sp[ieseke] finished the wall of the little store, & covered also the floor with lime._

---

327 Br Heinrich Walder, Carl Wilhelm Kramer, and Gottlieb Meissel. Wilhelm Julius Kühne stayed at Kadina and later married an English woman.
328 More commonly written: Kopperamanna. See Jensz, *German Moravian Missionaries*, Chapter 5; Ganter, *The Contest for Aboriginal Souls*, particularly Chapter 2.
329 More commonly written: Killalpaninna. It was the Lutheran mission at Cooper's Creek. For more see: Harris, *One Blood*, 376–83. See also: Ganter, *The Contest for Aboriginal Souls*, particularly Chapter 2.
330 A description of the situation is given in the *Periodical Accounts* 26 (1866), 294–97.
331 Ref: 10 March 1866.

30 April 1865

[Sun] A quiet day; no singing in the afternoon the women going to Antwerp

30 April 1868*

[Thu] Started for Castlemaine[332] went as far as Horsham.

May

1 May 1865

[Mon] Mark & Timothy went off to Walmar to fetch some sheep for killing, presented by Mr C^h Wilson._ Phillip came back from the Lake having earned about £2._ The flock was also fetched to this side._ The grass is just beginning to grow, & a few lambs have made their appearance._ Some more of our people went to Antwerp to help mustering sheep._ <u>Prepared some plates to try the dry process according to Russel[333] but did not quite succeed</u> at least there was only one picture that came out a little._

1 May 1869*

[Sat] Cogle[334] & Betsy were married. As we had heard some talk of Cogle wanting to return to Lake Boga[335] at some future time, a written agreement was required of him that he would not take her away from the Mission Station against her will.

2 May 1865

[Tue] Put in another yellow glass in my dark room to get a little more light into it. It seems to be quite another affair now._ Wrote a letter to Walder, also, sending him a pattern of the size of my watch-glass to get me

---

332 Journey to Uncle Hartig at Chinaman's Creek, near Castlemaine. Ref: 23 March 1868. Castlemaine was the major town in the Mount Alexander diggings of the goldfields. It became a town in 1853. It is on the land of the Dja Dja Wurrung.
333 Ref: 13 January 1866.
334 First Ref: 6 November 1868. There is sparse mention of Cogle in the diary. There is a mention of Cogle in the *Periodical Accounts* 30 (1876), 212–13. A Coyle is also mentioned in Smyth, *The Aborigines of Victoria*, 2, from information provided by Adolf Hartmann.
335 Lake Boga was the first mission station that the Moravians established in Victoria. See: Felicity Jensz, 'Writing the Lake Boga Failure', *Traffic: An Interdisciplinary Postgraduate Journal*, no. 3 (2003): 147–61.

some in Melbourne._ Asked him also to get me "Russel's tannin process.³³⁶_ Requested him, too, to speak to Mʳ Clarke why the same did not ~~write~~ answer my letters.³³⁷_

2 May 1866

[Wed] In the forenoon I finished the inside of the house of James, except the paving of the fire-place. A very neat & comfortable house it will be._ In the afternoon went off to Locheal with Mona & the cart to borrow 2 bags of flour for our people; Dicky went with me. Got there just by sunset & stopped the night; Mʳ Wallace & Perkins³³⁸ being at home.

2 May 1867*

Mʳ Spieseke whitewashed the dining-room. We have had very dry weather since the nice rain Apl: 6ᵗʰ.

2 May 1868*

[Fri] Travelled from Horsham to Pleasant Creek:³³⁹ - arrived at Mʳ Matthews³⁴⁰ late in the evening.

3 May 1865

[Wed] Sp[ieseke] In his religious instructions he gave to the Candidates for baptism, found it good to separate the women from the men, keeping the instructions for the women in the afternoon._

3 May 1866

[Thu] Off to the nine Creeks to by sundry articles & to fetch our buggy from the Blacksmith. On my way through the creeks I stopped for a little time with the Blacks camping near the road. They were as usual very glad to see me. I spoke to them about Jesus & invited them to give their hearts

---

336 Referring to: Charles Russell, *The Tannin Process* (London: John W. Davies, 1861). Available via archive.org.
337 Ref: 3 April 1865.
338 Mr Perkins often mentioned in conjunction with Mr Wallace (Ref: 14 March 1867). In the district since at least June 1864. He reportedly brought alcohol to Aboriginal camps in exchange for sex with women. Ref: 25 May 1866.
339 Near Stawell.
340 Rev. W Matthews, Presbyterian clergyman (not connected to a colonial church) from Pleasant Creek.

to that dear Saviour. Neptune[341] was very sick; spoke to him & found him to be have a knowledge of our Saviour; endeavoured to strengthen him._ Then I spoke very seriously to Albert who had left our place some time ago trying to get him back with to our place, but it was no use; he seems to be hardened & determined to keep away poor boy!! Left for home at 1 pm. with a good load of for our Mona to pull; it took me 4 hours and ¼ walking all the time of course._

3 May 1868*

[Sun] Adolf preached for Mr Matthews in the evening: church full.

3 May 1869*

[Mon] Mrs Hagenauer & Sissy left us having been here a fortnight,[342] a much shorter visit than we had hoped. Adolf took her as far as Horsham. Nathaniel is gone with her to Gippsland, where it is probable he may settle down & try to be useful to his countrymen.

4 May 1865

[Thu] Fetched with Nathanael 4 pine trees 25 feet long for putting up a scaffold round the tree. Preparatory meeting for the Lord's supper in the evening "Phillip expressed himself to S[pieseke]: that he did not feel towards the Saviour as he should & that he thought he had better not come to the Lords supper, he did not think he was worthy of it. He came nevertheless spoken to by Sp._ Had some trouble as regards getting the fire lighted in the schoolroom in the morning so I put up a slate on the mantle piece with a name of one of the scholars on it, to point out who had to make the fire; this arrangement seemed to answer._

4 May 1866

[Fri] S[pieseke]. & myself drove to Antwerp after dinner (with the new buggy for the first time) to welcome M^r & Mrs Flemming. The M^r & Mrs Scott were at Antwerp waiting for their arrival. At 4 ½ they arrived in a

---

341 First Ref. Neptune, an older man, was reported to have engaged a 'heathen sorcerer'. In December 1865, he was living with other people, including Biddy, near Scott's Station at Warracknabeal. In May 1866, he was brought from Nine Creeks to the mission, but left soon after to be treated by 'medicine men or sorcerers of his own people'. See: *Periodical Accounts* 26 (1866), 246; MAB, PP HJAH, 3, Letters, Polly Hartman to Hines family, 15 December 1864; UA, UEC Minutes, 10 November 1866, #7, 158.
342 Ref: 17 April 1869.

new carriage & new horses. We were asked to stay dinner but it being late, already, we did not accept the offer._ The appearance of Antwerp much improved since M̲ͬ Flemming got into possession of it; the rooms in the house especially have been got up very nicely, it is alltogether another affair._

4 May 1867*

Amos[343] & Magdalene[344] returned from Stewart's, with the news that Margaret & Matthew are gone to the Lake.

4 May 1868*

Started for Ararat:[345] a nice drive up hill & down dale.

5 May 1865

[Wed] Began to put up a scaffold round the tree on wh the windmill is to come in order to be able to have easier working; Nathanael helped me putting it up._ Rev̲ͩ Matthew's from Pleasant Creek came to our place on his way to mount Elgin; he promised to come back here on his way home & stay over night._ Mark & Timothy came back from M̲ͬ C̲ʰ Wilson's with a flock of 140 sheep, as a present from M̲ͬ C̲ʰ Wilson; there are 20 beautiful fat weathers among them for killing._ Got at last a letter & photograph from M̲ͬ Clarke._

5 May 1866

[Sat] Finished the fireplace in James' hut & asphalted with limed stones the front of it._ Got a letter from Johnston & C̲º about my photographs

---

343 First Ref: 5 August 1866. The baptised man, Amos, was married 'according to the law and rites of the church' to Magdalene already in 1866. He was recorded as being 28 years old in 1866. He died on 27 October 1869, with his body being exhumed on 30 October 1869 and a post-mortem examination undertaken by the coroner, WL Purves. The coroner's inquest recorded his name as Amos Mackenzie. Teddy stated that he was the brother of Amos. Amos was at Lorquon Station when he took ill, then was brought to the mission where he stayed in a Miamia, attended by other Aboriginal people and with a possum rug to keep him warm. He was recorded as a peaceful man, who was not feuding with anyone, with his death described as natural. Ref: 30 October 1869. See also: *Further Facts, Fifth Paper*, 4; DDHS, 'Proceedings of Inquest Held upon the Body of Amos Mackenzie'.
344 First Ref: 14 July 1866. Magdalene was reported as being 23 in 1866. She died on Ref: 22 July 1869. See also: *Further Facts, Fifth Paper*, 5.
345 On Djab Wurrung land. Settled by Europeans in the 1840s; gold found there in 1857 with a large Chinese miner population.

5 May 1868

[Tue] Started from Ararat by coach to Ballarat;[346] very crowded.

6 May 1865

[Sat] Finished putting up the scaffold round the tree, very nice now to get at it

6 May 1868

[Wed] Left Balarat[347] for Castlemaine. Had a pleasant journey. Met Uncle[348] at the Archdeacon's:[349] & rode after tea by moonlight to Chinaman's Creek_.

6 May 1869*

[Thu] Adolf returned from taking M[rs] Hagenauer to Horsham.

7 May 1864

[Sat] At 2 o clock in the afternoon we arrived at Ebenezer (The account of our journey from Melbourne to this place & also what we did the first few days in small book p. 128.[350]_

7 May 1865

[Sun] Left E[benezer]: with Polly at daybreak for the 9 Creeks, as I had to preach there._ As it had not been made known that somebody was coming, there was but a poor attendance (text Luke 18, 31 etc[351]) Had a walk in the afternoon with M[r] Edolls to see the Blacks that were camping some where near Locheal, but taking a wrong turn we got to the other side of the river just opposite the camp, so I just had a chat as well as I could. Got a little tired from the walk (text in the evening Heb:III last verse[352]) (M[r] Perkins riding M[r] E's mare that she dropped her foal)

---

346 On Wathaurung land. Settled by Europeans from the late 1830s, gold found there in 1850s, with many miners flocking to the area in the gold rush period.
347 Ballarat.
348 Uncle Hartig at Chinaman's Creek.
349 The Church of England Archdeacon in 1868 was Archibald Crawford. See: *Mount Alexander Mail* (Castlemaine), 26 May 1868, 3.
350 The pages 127 to 144 are missing from the small book. MAB, PP HJAH, 10.
351 KJV. Luke 18:31, 'Then he took unto him the twelve, and said unto them, Behold, we go up to Jerusalem, and all things that are written by the prophets concerning the Son of man shall be accomplished.'
352 KJV. Hebrews 3:19, 'So we see that they could not enter in because of unbelief.'

7 May 1866

[Mon] Set James to whitewash ~~his~~ the walls of xx his rooms, myself went at his chimney._ S[pieseke] & some of the people commenced work on the paddock spreading the manure that had been carted into it._ Philip & Timothy returned from Mount Elgin. (Martha in a sad state, quarrelling with Jerry & wishing to come back in fact she asked Philip to get Sp to send the cart to fetch her, but we think if she really wants to come she will come in spite of anything that might get into her way._

7 May 1867*

David & Elizabeth[353] married to-da[y]:. M^r & Mrs Fleming & Miss Hastie were present. We gave the couple a tea in the evening with our girls. Philip returned from Mr Scotts, reporting that a number of blacks are there, some of whom Napier,[354] Dicky &c wish to come here.

7 May 1868

[Thu]

8 May 1864

[Sun] In the afternoon Charley Charley,[355] his lubra Jessie[356] & ~~Matt~~ Liberty were baptized, there were a great many friends present (Charley ~~Ba~~ received the name Phillip, his wife Rebecca & Liberty, Matthew.[357]

---

353 Elizabeth, previously known as Mary before her baptism on Ref: 27 July 1865, had been the house helper for the missionaries.
354 Only reference in diary. Napier was described as being a young boy in 1861 living at Scott's station. See also: *Further Facts, Second Paper*, 5.
355 Nathanael's brother Charley Charley, subsequently Phillip Pepper. A Charley Charley was mentioned as visiting the Lorquon Station, Hugh Campbell, in December 1863. See: DDHS, The Lorquon Diary of Hugh Campbell.
356 Jessie (Rebecca) Ref: 10 January 1865.
357 According to Spieseke, there were some 50 white people and 20 to 30 Aboriginal people present at the baptism. After being baptised, Phillip and Rebecca were married on the afternoon of their baptism by the Rev. Simpson from Horsham. See: *Periodical Accounts* 25 (1863), 233.

8 May 1865

[Mon] 9 Creeks Had a good boating in the morning, after w^h we started for home, Polly walking with Mrs Edolls & Miss Donnovan to the Chapel whilst I drove Bobby._ Had some shopping & then a very nice drive home; there came also some showers of rain._ Mr Matthew's arrived soon after ~~ourselves~~ us to spend a night at our place._ he kept the meeting in the evening._ Matthew had left for the lake to look out for some job._

8 May 1866

[Tue] Put up James' chimney railing on shingles m instead of bark Mona our horse got fits this morning & we did not know for some time time till she threw a dead foal. We were not aware of that she was with foal. Sp most likely will not be able to use her for ploughing the field as he intended. No rain yet._

8 May 1867*

M^r & Mrs Spieseke & children started for Upper Regions.

9 May 1865

[Tue] Mr Matthew's again addressed the Blacks._ He left after dinner for the 9 Creeks. (We had a little argument about the use of the lot in our Church.[358]} M^r M: did not agree that the lot sh^ld be used._ A little rain in the afternoon._ I straightened some wire I had got from Mr Edols to make bolts of for the ring of the windmill._ Sp[ieseke]: got a letter from Walder, from Melbourne, stating that 3 of the b^rn & one Black would go to Cooper's Creek.[359]_

---

358 Moravians throughout the eighteenth and into the late nineteenth century used the lot to ask God's divine will in matters of importance. From 1741, the lot was systematically introduced into Moravian committees to decide on matters such as appointments to committees, missionary appointments, marriages, and the establishment of new mission fields. Usually a question was formulated with a 'yes/'no' answer, or a question with three alternative names or answers. After a prayer, a marker was drawn from a box. If the question was formulated with a yes/no answer, three markers were included in the box: one with a 'yes', one with a 'no' and a blank marker. If this latter marker was drawn, it could indicate that the question should be asked again at a later date, that that the question should be reformulated, or that the Church Elders should themselves decide. The use of the lot in official committees stopped in 1889. For use of the lot in the Moravian missions in Australia see: Jensz, *German Moravian Missionaries*, 25–27, as well as Chapters 4 and 5.
359 Walder, Meissel and Kramer with Daniel, who died in Adelaide before he could reach Lake Kopperamanna.

10 May 1866

[Thu] Bʳ & Sis Sp[ieseke] with their children drove over to Antwerp to pay a visit to Mʳ & Mʳˢ Flemming._

10 May 1868*

[Sun] Uncle drove us to Castlemaine to church. Heard the Curate. Deut VI.6.7.[360]

11 May 1864

[Wed] Commenced my school with the Blacks, something rather novel.[361]_

11 May 1865*

[Thu] A strong howling wind awoke us this morning, and cheered our hearts as the precursor of rain. Nathaniel shewed us a peculiar insect, about 4 inches long, which he picked up in the yard. He said it always came with that wind, & was a sign of much rain. A[dolf]. preserved the insect in spirits. In the evening Lanky[362] arrived with the bullocks. He had left the dray about a mile distant on the road, the bullocks being too knocked up to bring it further. After dinner the rain came. Addie[363] got wet through, & was very poorly in the evening. He went early to bed, underwent a process of perspirations, & was better in the morning.

11 May 1866

[Fri] A strong North wind, like last year, blew the greater part of the day, clouds gathered thickly, & although we did ~~not~~ got but a very few drops of rain, in other places they must have more for there seemed to be some heavy showers moving at a distance._ Sp[ieseke]. made a pig-sty, to keep the pigs in, because they went to the hay-stack & destroyed a good deal of hay._ I finished the chimney & all about James' house except the furniture inside.

---

360 KJV. Deuteronomy 6:6, 'And these words, which I command thee this day, shall be in thine heart: 7: And thou shalt teach them diligently unto thy children, and shalt talk of them when thou sittest in thine house, and when thou walkest by the way, and when thou liest down, and when thou risest up.'
361 Ref: 19 May 1864.
362 First Ref: 22 October 1864. Lanky (also written Lanke), was described as the half-brother of Nathanael/Nathaniel. He was married to Sarah some time in 1863. Lanky returned to the station in mid-1863 after some four years absence. He worked as the gardener at the mission. Died Ref: 15 August 1865. Buried on Ref: 17 August 1865. See: *Periodical Accounts* 25 (1863), 126.
363 Adolf.

12 May 1865*

[Fri] Showers all day. Addie kept much in the house, not being quite well. He tried to temper steel, but failed. Mark & Lanky fetched the dray this morning. B^r Spieseke intended to have started for Horsham but the weather prevented.

12 May 1869

[Sat] Painted the new wheels of our buggy, dark brown, & took the box of the buggy down to mend it._ Several small showers of rain._

13 May 1865*

[Sat] The blacks went in a body to the cultivation paddock, provided with hoes, spade, & picks to turn up the ground, ready for the oat seed. Adolf dug hard ~~the~~ in our own garden. Still windy & showery.

13 May 1866

[Sun] There were some slight showers of rain during the night, & in the morning it looked very much like rain, & indeed it turn^{ed} out a regular wet day, raining almost all the day ~~N~~ (wind NW.). It cleared up towards evening._ What a blessing such a rain is after such a season of drought we have had._

14 May 1865*

[Sun] Wet & stormy. Tremendous gusts of wind wh. shook the house. Torrents of rain. In the evening finished Vol I of Cröger's *"Geschichte der erneuerten Brüderkirche"*[364]. ~~(Evening) Tried the~~

14 May 1866

[Mon] Sp. commenced ploughing the field. He put Mona & Bobby abreast but that would not answer, Bobby being too quick; I then suggested to take Mona by herself & it went well, after a little while we put Bobby before

---

[364] Ernst Wilhelm Cröger, *Geschichte der erneuerten Brüderkirche* (Gnadau: Buchhandlung der evangelischen Brüder-Unität, 1853). This volume is dedicated to the period from 1722 to 1760, which is the beginning of the renewed Moravian Church in Herrnhut to the death of the spiritual leader of the Church, Count von Zinzendorf in 1760.

Mona, w^h answered very well; The Horses both of them were led. I was occupied with mending the box of our buggy. The people mended the river fence in the Durrockpaddock & put the sheep in ~~for a little~~._

14 May 1868*

~~Went to church at Walmer, where we heard a Mr Abson preach.~~

15 May 1865*

[Mon] The men had no school, & in order to get the paddock ready sooner for the oats, no plough being obtainable at present. Adolf made a kind of harrow (Evening) The harrow answers very well so far, but I com^mended a heavier one to be pulled by the horse._ As we shall get Mr Ellerman's heavy plow there is a prospect of having finished our cultivation paddock much sooner than we expected the people will only go on digging where the stumps have not been taken out_____

16 May 1866

[Wed] Mr Ellerman's ordination at the 9 creeks._ Sp[ieseke]. I [Adolf] & Polly went off to the 9 creeks in our buggy._ There were a good many gentlemen & ladies, among others also M^r & Mrs Charles Wilson. We S & I were requested to associate in the ceremony by the imposition of our hands. Revd Megaw from Ararat preached a very good sermon about, "the excellency of the knowledge of Christ". We had to leave the meeting in order to get home in time. A drive in the dark, got against a stump, but did not break anything.__ Great joy in finding that the home mail had arrived, besides the usual letters there was one from Caroline[365] containing a photograph of herself & of Emma my brother Henry's[366] eldest._

17 May 1865

[Wed] Worked a little in cultivation paddock._ Mr Stone Clergyman of the Church of England from Pleasant Creek arrived, & stayed ~~a little while~~ with us overnight. Mr Henry Ellerman also made suddenly his appearance coming back from the nine Creeks where he went to meet a flock a sheep

---

365 Adolf's sister.
366 Joh Heinrich (Henry) Hartmann was a Moravian missionary in the East Cape in Southern Africa from 1849 to 1881. Married to Bertha Emilie (née Bonatz). Worked amongst the Xhosa.

he had bought._ The government stores arrived,³⁶⁷ & as all the Blacks were off hunting, there was some trouble in getting the things unloaded, but the German carrier with his man helped & so we got it into the store all right._ Another little try at photography & there seems to be a success at least I managed without much trying & difficulties to get a pretty fair picture._

17 May 1866

[Thu] In the evening Mr & Mrs Cʰ Wilson according to a promise they made yesterday, arrived, to stay for a night & so we had a very pleasant evening.

17 May 1868

[Sat] At my uncles³⁶⁸ Chinamans Creek 4 miles from Castlemaine, received a letter from Br Spieseke informing me that the Central Board for the protection of the Aborigines has made me the Correspondent, & commissioned me to buy the stores

18 May 1865

[Thu] Sent off the home letters, & one to Mr F. Latrobe; Polly a note to Miss E. Shaw. Polly sent of E.: bell _ According to Mr Herny Ellerman's advice I began to take a cold bath in the morning; a desperate undertaking, but somehow it seemed to agree with me._ Sp[ieseke]: brought our home letters from Antp very late at 10._ Old Jenny; the boy Dicky & Maggie³⁶⁹ came back from Locheal where they had been staying a while._

18 May 1866

[Fri] Mr & Mrs Cʰ Wilson went off this morning. In the afternoon Polly & I drove to Antwerp to pay our respects to Mr & Mrs Flemming. A windy & cold day._ Neptune³⁷⁰ was fetched in our buggy about half way from here

---

367 The government, through the Central Board or the subsequent BPA, distributed stores to Aboriginal people. In the year from 1 August 1864 to 31 July 1864, Ebenezer received: flour, tea, sugar, tobacco, rice, oatmeal, soap, blankets, serge shirts, twill shirts, trousers, boy's jumpers, dresses, chemises, tomahawks, and pint and quart pots. They did not receive petticoats, although 24 of the total 39 stations did. Ebenezer also received measurements of flannel, print, and linsey-woolsey, as well as camp kettles, axes and axe handles. For the exact quantities see the BPA annual reports. For 1864–65 see: *Fifth BPA Report*, 19.
368 Uncle Hartig.
369 First Ref. Maggie was reported as being a pupil in the girls' school and some 30 years old in 1866. See also: *Further Facts, Fifth Paper*, 5.
370 Ref: 3 May 1866.

18 May 1868*

[Sun] Went to Walmer church: heard Mr Abson preach.

19 May 1864

[Thu] My way of teaching at present is, I Spelling & reading in w$^\text{h}$ I set the more advanced to teach those less so._ II Writing III A little arithmetic at present only mentally quite easy addition sums IV Conclude with reading a chapter out of Rep. of day._ My regular duties at present When it is my wife's week of cooking I get up in the morning a little earlier, look after the boys in school that they get washed, & give out meat_ After breakfast about 8 meeting_ After that school till 11 or 11 ½_ Then try to occupy boys; difficult thing sometimes to find employment for them.__ Before dinner helped to pull down old loghouse w$^\text{h}$ was to be divided into 2 & put up near Tony's._ Ab$^\text{t}$ dinner finished railing in the grave of Nathaniel's child,[371] helped in this by Phillip his brother._ Then prepared block for sharpening saws. Whilst at it letters arrived from home. Heard also that our things had got to Horsham._ At night Rachel was confirmed._ Sent off letters to Rev$^\text{d}$ Goethe,[372] Chase, a letter in season of my uncle Hartig; also short notes to M$^\text{r}$ Morris[373] & Hagenauer._ We have splendid moonlight nights; rather cool in the evening & morning._

19 May 1865

[Fri] Some trials at photography somewhat better than before but not the thing yet._ In the evening we had a reading of home letters._

---

371 Nathaniel and Rachel's child was born in around the beginning of February 1864 and was to be baptised with Charley (also known as Charley Charley, brother of Nathanael, who took on the name Phillip) and Liberty (who took on the name Matthew) as soon as the Hartmanns arrived. The baptism of Charley, Jessie (his wife, subsequently called Rebecca), and Liberty was held on Ref: 8 May 1864. See: UA, UEC Minutes, 31 May 1864, #11.

372 Matthias Goethe was a Lutheran pastor in Melbourne, originally from Germany. Influential among the Lutheran community in Melbourne. See: SM Tarnay, 'Goethe, Matthias (1827–1876)', *Australian Dictionary of Biography*, National Centre of Biography, The Australian National University, published first in hardcopy 1972, accessed 23 April 2021, adb.anu.edu.au/biography/goethe-matthias-3625/text5633.

373 No further reference to Morris in the diary.

19 May 1866

[Sat] The bullocks went off this morning to assist the men getting up the stores to our place. Well soon ~~Richard~~ David came back telling us that the man had broken his leg, by a tree, w^h he burned down falling unto his leg. We sent Mona with the Spring cart to get the poor Man down to the 9 Creeks, & Philip very bravely resisted the attempts of some men who wanted him to get the man down to Horsham. The stores arrived then

20 May 1864

[Fri] Made a list to see better who comes to school._ S[pieseke]. & family left for a visit to Horsham for a week._ With the horse & cart we got up some more of the old log house; some of the Blacks very hard to get to help._ After I had rung the Bell for the evening meeting a bullock team with the rest of the stores, so I set the people to work to unload; after that it not being dark yet. I got them all to chapel & hearing that a number of them were going to leave the place, I spoke to them on that point (telling them about the danger to go without Jesus: in fact I tried to persuade them to stop) Did not give provisions to some who had absented themselves all day & done no work according to S's advice._ About 7 p.m S. came back on horseback from 9 creeks having met the coming stores giving me some directions how to manage them (a beautiful warm & sunny day.)

20 May 1865

[Sat] Digged a little in the field & in the afternoon I ~~filtered~~ distilled some water for use in the photographic department; Nathanael helped me. In the afternoon Mr H^or Ellerman called on his way to Locheal; he was kind enough to promise to help us next week in ploughing our paddock._

20 May 1868*

Left Chinaman's Creek for Castlemaine, on our return home. Spent a very happy time with the Archdeacon. Afterwards called at Mrs Blackwell's,[374] & Mrs Newcombe's, & ~~saw~~ spent the evening at Mr Niebuhr's: then to our Temperance hotel for the night.

---

374 Mr and Mrs Blackwell were at the savings bank in Castlemaine. Ref: 28 May 1868.

21 May [Missing, page ripped out, no indication why]

22 May 1864
[Sun] I w rang the bell at 11. The Blacks go dressed very nicely on Sunday._ I spoke to them about the institution & observances of Sunday._ (Matthew Daniel[375] & Mark go on satisfactorily) In the afternoon we got together as many as we could round Nathaniel w[ho] was lying out in the open air & had some singing with them, they seem to like it._ Booppoop's foot much better, some more poultice._ I can manage now to ring the Chapel bell properly; even this wants learning.__

22 May 1865
[Mon] The Blacks' dogs trouble our sheep very much & so S[p[ieseke]] set poison round the camp & managed to kill one of them, but we were told this morning that one of the dogs had been after the sheep & killed one, so S: went down with poison but the dog would not take it, & so he fetched Phillips gun & managed to shoot that dog; well this caused a great row; old Bony & his Mary making a big noise about it (the dog shot belonged to Teddy who happened to be absent) It seems they were much touched about shooting & would not make so much ado about poisoning.[376]_ I took to-day & view & succeeded very well, so I shall give up taken trying to take likenesses till I can succeed better._

22 May 1868*
[Fri] Stayed in Ballarat at the Earl of Zetland Hotel: doing business.

23 May 1864
[Mon] Had no school to-day as they were all building at the log houses & I helped them all myself all day & got very tired about it._ In the morning a number of Blacks went off. On my way to the camp I met Daniel who also intended to go away; I tried to persuade him to stop_ Jacky[377] &

---

375 Formerly called Talliho.
376 The poisoning of dogs occurred on a number of occasions (Ref: 17 January 1867; Ref: 25 February 1865).
377 Jacky later Stephen (Ref: 13 August 1866). Not clear in diary if this Jacky is also Jacky Lake (Ref: 29 January 1865).

Makenzie[378] before going came to me to shake hands & said that they liked to be at our place but they had to go to M͏ʳ Ellerman to drive in some cattle, but they would soon be here again._ Nathaniel feels worse to-day having caught a fresh cold as he says._

23 May 1865

[Tue] Felt somewhat vexed this morning before school, as nobody showed any willingness to make fire; & I had some words to Matthew, who when the fire was made was about to take his place near to the same; well he moved away from it & said "I dont want the fire"_ After a few more words from my side, that he should show a little more acknowledgement for the troubles I took, & less selfishness & more gratitude, he left the school_ This is one of a little trouble._

Attempting with Nathanael to fetch 2 box logs from the other side, by boating them accross, the boat upset & I ~~took~~ partook of an unwelcome bath, but was none the worse for it._ In the afternoon & evening I prepared my new dark box for going about to take views._

23 May 1867

[Thu] Our long contemplated trip to Walmar came off. We took the buggy & Mona. Before we started I had some trouble to fit on the new ~~herrnes~~ harness on her, it is alltogether rather small & the traces too short, so I took the old traces. Of course being in a hurry to be off we forgot some things amongst others some cuttings of thyme for M͏ʳˢ C Wilson._ The roads were rather wet from the late rain._ Stayed over night at M͏ʳ Edol's_ A governess there Miss Glassford_ The house well got up & newly furnished. A row in the boat a mile up the river_

23 May 1868*

[Sat] Coach to Ararat: fearfully crowded.

---

378 First Ref. Makenzie was reported to be a candidate for baptism in April 1864. Was married to Lilly (sometimes called Lilly M). Not to be confused with Jacky's wife Lilly (sometimes called Lilly J). See: MAB, PP HJAH, 2, Letterbook, A. Hartman to Simpson, Ebenezer, 12 April 1865.

24 May 1864*

[Tue] I made my first attempt at butter-making, having watched Sⁱˢ Spieseke the week before. It turned out very well. It is sometimes so cold in the mornings when I go to skim the milk, that I can hardly use my hands. I spoke to Jenny & Joe's Mary about not coming to prayer, trying to shew them how good & necessary it is for them to learn about Jesus. I was glad to see these two present in the evening. Sometimes I feel very sad about these poor ᵒˡᵈ lubras. They are so entirely ignorant, seem to understand very little English, & even when spoken to in their own language, can take in so very little. But our Saviour can give us wisdom to speak to them, & he can speak to them himself by own means. So we sow the seed in hope. "Blessed are they that sow beside all waters.³⁷⁹"

24 May 1865

[Wed] Digged again in our little front garden as I did already some mornings ago._ Harry Ellerman came & stayed over dinner; he told us that he was going to leave home to-morrow to go to a school about 35 miles from Ballarat; He is going down with his father & are going to take a number of their horses down to Ballarat to sell them. I worked all the afternoon at my dark box & very nearly finished it. Lanke ~~who getting~~ having been sick a good while, but getting better now begins to go on building his house which has been left standing for a long while._ Polly transplanted several things in the flowergarden & sowed also sundry seeds._

24 May 1866

[Thu] Sp[ieseke]: walked with Matthew to the 9 creeks to see the Blacks. I was engaged all the week, (almost) in painting the buggy._ A North wind rose during the night

24 May 1867

[Fri] Got to Walmar in good time, were well received. Shortly after our arrival Francis Annie Wilson broke the blade bone of her shoulder, happily it was not seriously fractured & D͟r Pervis set it. I studied a little work about tricks & manufacture of the same._

---

379 KJV. Isaiah 32:20.

24 May 1868*

[Sun] Stayed in Ararat, went to Presbyterian church in the morning. Spent the afternoon with M^r & Mrs Leopold. Very kind people.

25 May 1864

[Wed] I ~~found~~ roasted some coffee & Polly put the clothes & dresses in order in the storehouse._ At 2 p.m. S[pieseke]. came back from Horsham. Had school in the afternoon. After the meeting I went to the loghouses to see how they got on, when I heard the distant sound of wheels; I walked off to meet the wagons for I knew that they brought my ^our things. What a blessing they have come at last. We went at once at unpacking them. Got first the Harmonium out & played a bit on it to the great amusement of the Blacks standing by._ We worked till late at night._

25 May 1865

[Thu] Fastened some iron hooks on the side of the dark box to put 2 sticks through to carry it about._ Prepared a plate in the box & took a view tolerably well._ In the afternoon I pulled down my poor old gallery felt somewhat vexed that I had to pull it down without having succeeded to get a decent likeness._ At tea letters came one from our uncle Hartig,[380] & the other containing a bill from Dr Johnson from Horsham £3, rather much for 2 bottles of medicin & one consultation._ Sp put some people to topping the fences, from our gate to the horsepaddock._ (Ascension day) was not celebrated by stopping works._

25 May 1866

[Fri] Sp: came back about dinner time, & with him came Albert & Napoleon (Mr Perkins, as the Blacks told Sp: seems to have brought grog to the Blacks camp at the 9 creeks, to make use of the women). A very strong N. Wind all day._

25 May 1867

[Sun] Rode with Mr C Wilson to Horsham for the morning service. Mr Simpson preached. In the evening I preached in Walmar._

---

380 Carl Hartig lived near Chinaman's Creek. The Hartmanns visited him in May 1868 and were away from the mission for four weeks.

25 May 1868*

[Mon] Stayed at Mr Leopolds: went to the Botanical Gardens in afternoon

26 May 1864

[Thur] First of all got the Harmonium to chapel. When it was played before the meeting commenced some of the people laughed right out, it was too much for them._ All day we were at unpacking & arranging things. In the evening Mr Ellerman & family came & we had a very pleasant tea together. (Daniel seems to keep to the place.

26 May 1865

[Fri] Cleared the ground where my gallery stood making the place tidy._ Made a new handle into my hammer w^h by a mistake I broke._ Digged in the garden in the afternoon._

26 May 1866

[Sat] Heavy clouds coming up from N W. & very soon a good rain came down. It rained till about 4 p.m with but little interruption. Mr Ellerman with us to-day. I was all day in the toolshop commencing a perambulator for Nelly._ The moon shining brightly, but still there is a nice shower of rain._

26 May 1867

[Mon] Went with Polly to Horsham to see the Simpson's, Mrs Simpson very weak, indeed she looked as if she would not live long._ Had a conversation with M^r S[impson]. about our work & about our land_ squatters all tough to give any as it seems from M^r S's statement._ Something also about the school grant; would be a blessed thing if it passes Parliament. Saw several Blacks Dicky Lilly & Rosa.[381] Got promised that I might take Rosa with me._ Dicky drunk._

26 May 1868*

[Tue] Started for Pleasant Creek_ put up at Munro's. Spent the evening with Mrs Cobham[382] & family.

---

381 First Ref: 28 November 1864. Rosa, the 'half-caste' girl, was taken by Dicky and Lilly to Vectis, east of Horsham early in 1867. Ref: 13 February 1867.
382 Wife of Mr Francis McCrae Cobham, who was from 1866 the inspector of the police of the Wimmera district. Ref: 1 July 1866.

27 May 1864

[Fri] The first thing in the morning I put a new spring (of brass) into our sitting room door lock; then I made a shelf about above our cupboard in sleeping room._ Polly very busy in arranging things & getting the linen & bed in order._ Well we got almost everything straight that day & our rooms looks now very comfortable yet there are still many things to be done to make it complete._ S[pieseke]. went off to Antwerp towards 4 p.m. on some business._ Matthew not quite well complains of a cold in the chest; gave him some of my stockings & advised him to take care of himself especially at night time._ A cloudy day & now & then a sprinkling or rain._

Aunt Elisabeth Hines mother's sister departed at Fairfield, aged 67.

27 May 1865

[Sat] Digged all day in the front garden & just managed to get it done before the rain came down, w^h had threatened all day, & it did rain nicely all the afternoon._ I scraped some little channels to make the water run well into the beds._ The rain prevented us having a meeting._

27 May 1867

[Tue] Drove to Vectis alone & saw Sandy & Fanny[383] & another old woman._ got back to Walmar at dark._

27 May 1868*

[Wed] Started early for Horsham. Stopped at Ledcourt Bridge Hotel, where we met Mr Wilson, Mr Scott, Rev^{ds} Matthews, Megaw, Ellerman, & Robertson. Mr Wilson paid our bills, about 15/. Arrived late in Horsham.

28 May 1864*

[Sat] Again we were at our things for the whole day & got everything straight._ M^r S[pieseke]. & family went off the lake for a visit to return on Monday next._

---

383 First Ref: 28 August 1866. Fanny, Sandy's (later Nathan) wife, is only mentioned four times in the diary. Fanny died in 1868, leaving behind two small daughters, Minnie and Laura, who died on 8 June 1876, aged ten. See: *Seventh BPA Report*, 21; *Periodical Accounts* 30 (1876), 125–26.

We gave Susan Timothy's lubra, a new dress tc, & talked to her about keeping herself clean & tidy. She is much improved since we came but we have much trouble ~~with her~~ as regards ~~keeping~~ her clothes in order. In the afternoon Mary became poorly. I gave her a little medicine "Gregory's Powder", took her early to bed. In the evening I made gruel for Matthew & Mary.

28 May 1865

[Sun] There was some rain during the last night, but this morning it began to pour in right good earnest, & rained with little breaks nown & then till night when it cleared up._ There was no meeting in the morning, & in the afternoon Sp held a meeting in the school, it being too cold to do so in the chapel. Well the earth is now well drenched & things will go nicely now._

28 May 1866

[Mon] A good rain in the afternoon. Timothy & James are cutting boards for their houses._

28 May 1867

[Wed] Again to Horsham for the purpose of fetching Rosa[384] but could not get her as the Mother[385] would not let her go: very vexacious affair._

28 May 1868*

[Thu] Came back again from a trip to Castlemaine to our uncle & aunt just been away 4 weeks._ Uncle & Aunt making us heirs of their land 80 acres_ They wanted us to stop but that could never be_ Brought home a hive of bees[386]_ In Castlemaine made the acquaintance of M^r & Mrs Blackwell at the savingsbank, also of the Archdeacon Crawford_ At uncles we got to know Mr Cheliers & Anton Stosser. (long account of our journey & experiences in ~~some~~ book $^{letter\text{-}copying}$)

Glad to get home, & people seem glad to see us.

---

384 Adolf believed that he had permission to take Rosa from her parents. Ref: 26 May 1867.
385 Lily, wife of Dicky, mother of Rosa.
386 These bees came to an untimely end, when yellow ants attacked the hive around October 1869. See: MAB, PP HJAH, 3, Letters, Adolf Hartmann to Hines family, 6 October 1869.

29 May 1864

[Sun] A cold night_ a thick hoar frost covered the ground._ The day was beautiful & warm._ In the morning I read our litaney & then spoke about Daniel V chapter.[387] In the afternoon we had the people together in chapel & taught them to sing "Promote we pray thy servants' good etc" They all liked it & we intend to form a Sunday school. In the evening I went to Nathaniel & read to him a little tract "The man under the tree". Found Boop-poop reading his Bible. In the afternoon I had a walk through the grounds looking after the sheep: there were plenty of little lambs._ Mary ^{the} _{black girl} is much better to-day, but has a rash.

29 May 1865

[Mon] The rain having moistened the ground thoroughly I made the proposal to Sp[ieseke] to have another day's good digging in our field with all the people we can muster, so we went at it & dug a very large piece of ground._ In the evening although feeling rather tired I nevertheless set to work mending the old clock on the dining-room mantleshelf.

29 May 1866

[Tue] Went to Antwerp with Bobby & the cart & fetched our new pump & also the iron bedstead for Nelly_ Some of the people were ploughing with the bullocks to break up the new ground: it went very well._

29 May 1867

[Thu] Off for the 9 Creeks_ Mrs Wilson presented ~~us~~ Polly with some nice linen, she had just received from Europe._ At Edol's we had a good singing evening.

29 May 1868

[Fri] Was engaged putting in the raspberries & blackberries & strawberries I bought from uncles,_ the people ploughing I set the plough for them & ploughed a few furrows, about 7 inches deep._ Began digging my flower garden.

---

387 Biblical story of Belshazzar's feast and the writing on the wall.

EBENEZER MISSION STATION, 1863-1873

29 May 1873

[New Fairfield, Canada] (For the new Fairfield diary see the loose leaves at the beginning of the book._) With Jeremiah Stonefish I had long conversation. There is a talk about him afloat that he is carrying on unlawful intercourse with Martha Dolsen. He denies it. It seems only to be a talk, as no decisive proof has yet been brought forward that it is so. He seemed to take the advice & warnings I gave him quietly. Oh! There is such a talking amongst the Indians against one another. Whiteeyes too has a quarrel of long standing with John Peter ~~zen~~ ^{sen}.

30 May 1864*

[Mon] Having got all my things straight in our rooms I began again my school._ After it I changed the little washing table we had on board the vessel into a working one for Polly._ Then I commenced arranging the toolshop._ Got a key for the lock to have it shut_ I managed also to get that spring in the big vice all right w^h had puzzled me for some time._ At 5 p.m. S. & fa^{ly} came back from the lake._ I took my easy chair to Nathanael to sit in it._ I tried to make bread with baking-powder, but having taken bad flour, it did not turn out well. Mary $^{Joe's\ lubra}$ brought me a basket wh. she had made of long coarse grass.

30 May 1865

[Tue] Phillip, Matthew & Timothy went off to the lake to shoot bullocks for the people there. Edward also went off to Campbell's[388] for emu-eggs as she says._ I had some more work finishing the old clock._ Then I planted out the strawberries (50 shoots I had raised from one plant). Polly & I also planted ~~xx~~ a ~~time~~ thyme border in our front garden._ There was a hawker here to-day from Maryborough & he had a Malagasy travelling with him, ~~This~~ who had fled from his country losing his father, mother & etc in the rebellion[389]_

---

388 Possibly referring to Hugh Campbell, who managed the Lorquon Station.
389 Could refer to the *coup d'état* in Madagascar in 1863 in which King Radama II lost his life.

30 May 1867
[Fri] Stayed at Edol's_ M.r Cobham[390] & M.r & M.rs Ellerman from the Manse also arrived & there was a full house._ Singing again in the evening

31 May 1864*
[Tue] Began to paper our sitting room, all day hard at it._ Polly got an attack of face-ache very badly towards night & spent a rather restless night. Joe & Mary, who had before talked of going away, are now persuaded to remain.

31 May 1867
[Sat] Back again in safety to our place.

~~31 May 1868~~
~~Polly's complaint returned, & badly too.~~

31 May 1873
[New Fairfield, Canada] Went with Mary & the Children to London yesterday & returned to-day We bought a good many things & amongst others a new carriage. Paint & oil etc for painting the inside of the house._ M.r Cornelious Brown who had taken a field for new peas contrary to the contract wanted to S stop ploughing because the ground got rather dry, but I insisted upon his keeping the agreement. Mary was not well during our trip to London & feel the work alltogether rather heavy

---

390 Francis McCrae Cobham (1823–1902), inspector of police in the Wimmera district. He joined the police force in January 1853. He was stationed at Swan Hill District then at the Benella district (Ref: 1 July 1866). In 1870, there was a parliamentary inquiry into his conduct, with charges of gross misconduct, mostly in relation to financial and administrative misconduct. See: *The Argus* (Melbourne), Saturday 17 December 1870, 4; State Parliament of Victoria, second session, *The Report and Proceedings of the Board Lately Appointed to Inquire into the Charges Brought against Mr. Cobham, Superintendent of Police of the Wimmera District,* 16 December 1870, www.parliament.vic.gov.au/papers/govpub/VPARL1870_2ndSessionNoC3.pdf. (accessed 30 April 2020).

June

1 June 1864

[Wed] All day at papering_ at it very late at night._ A good many of the people feel sick, & Nathanael seems, more & more, to approach his end.[391] The sheep were driven ^(accross the river) to this side & S[pieseke]. had a deal to do to look after them.

1 June 1865

[Thu] A letter arrived from the board of education in Melbourne refusing the grant of schoolmaterials I ordered some time ago, & so I shall apply for them in London at the english & foreign school society[392] & see whether something is to be got there._

1 June 1866

[Fri] The ploughing of the cultivation paddock was finished, & ~~some of~~ ^(the oats in) the first ploughed bits are springing up nicely._

1 June 1873

[New Fairfield, Canada] Whit Sunday.[393] 21 children at the Sunday School. The services were attended mi^(d)dling well only._ The Singing practise in the afternoon was well attended. We are in hopes to get Rebecca Jabobs (daughter of Joshua) in place of Lucy Jacobs who left us a little while ago._ So we shall help again._

---

391 According to the local doctor, Nathaniel was so sick that he was expected only to live for a month. This prognosis turned out to be false. See: *Missionsblatt* 10 (1864), 191.

392 By this Adolf means the British and Foreign School Society, established in the early nineteenth century to provide affordable education and school material to the working classes. Connected to the evangelical movement.

393 Meaning Whit Sunday, the seventh Sunday after Easter Sunday.

2 June 1864*

[Thu] Finished our room in the forenoon._ Commenced school again in the afternoon w^h I had omitted the 2 previous days._ Some more Blacks arrived to-night_ Sintax[394] Richard Teddy. I went with S[pieseke]. to the camp after tea & found some of them to be very agreeable men._

After chapel I stayed and played a few tunes. Rachel stayed too to hear the music, and I had a little quiet talk with her about the hymns we sang. Altogether I have great hopes respecting both her & Rebecca, as regards their state of mind.

2 June 1866

[Sat] The sheep were taken out of the Durrockpaddock, (being all breeding ewes) & the rams taken out. The country begins to look green._ Finished the 3 iron wheels of my perambulator.[395]_

2 June 1867

[Tue] Began digging my flowergarden._ School again._ Renewed our hearth in our sittingroom & fastened the new firesafe before our fire place_ M^r & Mrs Ellerman came on their way home. In the evening at about 8 o clock we heard a shriek from Lizzy,[396] & rushing out we found the place in commotion for a strange looking & painted Black had struck Lizzy on her head on going out of her house. Happily she was not struck seriously._ The Black according to her saying looked a short & stout fellow, & after hitting her rushed away past the smithy. There was much talking among the people about how to proceed in this matter. May our Saviour graciously watch over us & our place._

---

394 Also written 'Syntax'. In 1869, a 'Syntax' was reported to be at Carr's Plains. See: *Seventh BPA Report*, 20. In November 1887, the *Periodical Accounts* reported that: 'a beloved member of the congregation, Alexander Harrison (formerly called Syntax), peacefully departed this life in November'. See: *Periodical Accounts* 34 (1887), 179.
395 Ref: 26 May 1866. The pram being constructed for Nelly, Adolf and Polly's daughter.
396 Also spelt Lizzie. First Ref: 20 February 1867.

EBENEZER MISSION STATION, 1863-1873

2 June 1873

[New Fairfield, Canada] The new carriage (a rockaway) was fetched by Albert from Bothwell. Levi Jacobs came to buy the old farm wagon $25 2 wanted for it & he is willing to pay it. The ground being very hard & dry Cornelius Brown objects to plough & plant all the pieces he agreed to do. I objected & insisted on his keeping to the agreement._

3 June 1864*

[Fri] Polly got the room into nice order & I busied myself getting the toolhouse straight_ put the working bench into good order._ Nathanael more lively today_ The other Blacks getting better, too._ heavy hoar frost in the morning & alltogether a rather cold day._

I, Polly, visited Nathaniel after school, found him a little better, read to him from the "Cottager[397]" a story about "poor Jospeh." I am sorry to say he is unable to use our chair, because he cannot lie on his back. It is very painful to him to be obliged to lie, & nearly always in the same position.

3 June 1865

[Sat] Had the Lord's supper at 8 p.m._ The dark box I made for taking likenesses proves not to answer, the pictures getting foggy; So I tried to prepare some plates in the dark room carrying them to the the spot my camera stood; the pictures were a little better, but the prints are not good yet, so I must try again.

3 June 1867

[Tue] Began digging the flowergarden._ S & wife went on a visit to Scott's leaving Helene with us_ Almost all the men went out to see whether they could not find any tracks of the fellow that hit Lizzie, but nothing at all was found, so it was generally believed that it was imagination on Lizzie's part, knocking her head against the door in opening it to call out for Mark._ put the new turkey stones stone into a wood M.r Edol's gave me into a wood

---

[397] Referring to the Reverend Leigh Richmond's *The Young Cottager*, an edifying Christian story with great popularity published in different versions from the 1830s.

3 June 1873

[New Fairfield, Canada] Washed our 7 sheep & 2 lambs with Albert's help in the river. A hot day again. The Indians ~~came with their~~ brass band came & played before the Mission house._

4 June 1864

[Sat] In the morning I fastened the big vice I brought._ At 2 p.m. we both dove to 9 creeks, as I was to officiate to-morrow in that place._ There happened to come a good many visitors_ Mr Mack_ Thomas_ Dr Johnson of Horsham_ Made the particular acquaintance of Mr Mitchill, Mr Edoll's cook, a very peculiar sort of man_ I walked to the postoffice, despatching 2 parcels I had by mistake taken to Ebenezer._ We had some music & singing_ As the house was rather full I had to sleep on the floor ~~of~~ in the dining room & Polly slept with Miss Donovan._ Just when we were about to leave E: Mr Selinger & Forense (Hawkers) arrived at our place & took dinner with us._

4 June 1865

[Sun] A cold day_ No singing in the afternoon._ Richard expressed himself to B^r S[pieseke]: rather pleasingly about the state of his heart yesterday[398]_ May it be true that the Saviour takes possession of the heart of that man._

4 June 1867

[Thu] A part of this year's rations came from Langlands in Horsham._ Timothy commenced tempering the clay I intend to use for the bricks._ Our people believe that Lizzie has not seen any wild Black fellow at all & the women think that she shrieked out as she did, to induce Mark, who would often go to the camp to stay with her._ Some of them especially Philip seems to be angry with her._ Samuel begins to plaister the inside of his new house._

---

398 It was common Moravian practice to ask people about the state of their hearts and an indication of the spiritual process of people under Christian instruction.

EBENEZER MISSION STATION, 1863–1873

4 June 1873

[New Fairfield, Canada] A hot close day. Thunder & rain in the afternoon. Albert & myself shore the 7 sheep & 2 Lambs, getting 43 ½ ^{lbs} of wool from them. Rebecca Jacobs came to day, to be our servant. Might she stay a little longer than Lucy._

5 June 1864*

[Sun] Kept the service in the little chapel at nine Creeks._ My text "What think ye of Christ"_ Mr Wallace & Mr Perkins at Mr Edoll's._ Afternoon & evening we spent in the house._ sang, read, & talked.

5 June 1865

[Mon] Very cold weather all this while_ Have such a trouble to get my pupils to make fire in the morning in the schoolhouse, they wont do it on their own accord, & so I must put up again a slate with the name of that one on it, who has to make fire_ Helped digging in the cultivation paddock till dinnertime. Afternoon cleaned B^r Spieseckes clock, & towards evening got one of our large boxes prepared to contain my tools, so as to have them handy._

5 June 1873

[New Fairfield, Canada] Th: Visiting the first time in the new carriage. Saw Nancy Anthony her baby being ill._ The more I hear & see of that woman the more hopes I have. She seems, although a comparatively ignorant & heathenish woman, nevertheless a virtuous woman from what I hear about her._ She herself looks tidy & her house is also clean & neat._ Met also the wife of Jeremiah Stonefish; her husband seems indeed to be guilty of adultery being (as I am told) very often with Martha Doslen. Albert & myself were sprinkling the potatoes with Paris green to kill the bugs. M^r & Mrs Bryson paid us a visit._

6 June 1864*

[Mon] Left Edoll's at 10 a.m. & drove home part of the way on the middle road & found it to be much worse than the upper._ Got to E[benezer]. at 1 p.m._ I put some handles on the harmonium to facilitate its being carried about._ In the evening at 8 we celebrated the Lord's supper._ We had it in our dining room & I kept it._ We fetched the harmonium for it, & Polly played it. Nathanael & Rachel were present, the former lying on a sofa._ It was a blessed evening, such as we have not had many._ We all felt very happy & got strengthened._ Nathanael, weak as he was, expressed the wish, when asked how he felt & whether he enjoyed it, that he hoped to join us once more_ if it were the Lord's will. He liked the music; it was the first time he had heard it.

6 June 1865

[Tue] Sad news this morning about Margaret._ Nathanael came & told us that Peter (Bandel) had been with Margaret all night._ (Her husband Matthew was at the Lake) Well what we feared then has at last come to pass, we did not trust Margaret for some time past as regarded her moral conduct. It is a sad affair indeed!! Sp[ieseke]: spoke to Margaret, ~~during~~ whilst we were at the meeting_ Peter who came into my school, as if nothing had happened I sent out, & Sp: spoke to him about his sin & told him also to leave the place w^h he did._ We are somewhat troubled about Matthew's return._ p.m. I walked to Antwerp with the letters, was received more friendly than I thought I would._ Mrs Westgarth,[399] M^{rs} E's mother being at a visit we had a good chat about sundry things. Kept prayers at Antwerp & had a nice walk back it being a moonlight night._

6 June 1866

[Wed] Finished my perambulator, & it only remains to be painted._ I shall give it a dark green colour._ There are a great many Blacks here at present about 80; & there is some trouble about the rations, of course they all want some, but we cannot give to all as we would be short of them before the year is gone._ There is even a Black here from the place Tobsy comes from (Sem-down[400]) is his name, most likely looking out for Tobsy.

---

399 Mrs Christina Westgarth, Christian, née Thomson, wife of John, mother also of William and Sophia. See: Geoffrey Serle, 'Westgarth, William (1815–1889)', *Australian Dictionary of Biography*, National Centre of Biography, The Australian National University, published first in hardcopy 1976, accessed 10 April 2020, adb.anu.edu.au/biography/westgarth-william-4830/text8057.
400 Only reference to Sem-down in the diary. Topsy was from Balmoral, Glenelg Ref: 5 December 1865.

6 June 1867

[Thur]M^r Sp: returned from Mr Scott's in the afternoon. I was making some more trials about finding the proper proportions of clay sand & lime for making bricks._ Very dry weather we have had for a good while._ There seems to be such a number of lambs this year._

7 June 1864*

[Tue] I was in the tool house again all day._ The rain w^h we looked for all this while, seems to be coming now; a pretty strong wind was blowing & we had some good showers._ Rain is much needed, it being very dry._ Some Blacks in the camp shot an emu, consequently not many came to chapel._ B^r Spiesecke bought two eggs of them, & blew them. The yolks make excellent puddings. They ^{each} containe as much as five or 6 hen eggs.

7 June 1865

[Wed] Mr Ellerman came in the forenoon & ~~we~~ stayed over dinner; after dinner we had a talk together about the preaching at the 9 Creeks. It was settled, that every first Sunday in the month one of us sh^{ld} go, yet Mr Ellerman was to let us know every time, or we should inform him beforehand whether we could come or not._ The thing was arranged in that way to prevent all appearance from our side, of a regular engagement in ministerial duties apart from our own work_ M^r E: also informed us that he intends to leave off sheep-farming, & ~~that the~~ enter the ministry._ Margaret keeps herself shut up in her house._ Tried to make a hole punching machine by means of a lever, but could not manage as the things give way._

7 June 1866

[Thu] Looked very much like rain in the morning, & it did rain, too, almost all the day, but ~~only~~ not much, in the evening some heavy puffs of wind, came & a good shower, but soon cleared again._ Commenced painting my perambulator, & finished ~~our bugg~~ the painting of our buggy._ Nathanael Philip, Jacky & Richard are engaged by Sp: to cut bark for our house._ Sp: was looking out for lambs to-day & there were ~~xx~~ about 7 come_

7 June 1867*

[Fri] Towards evening there was thunder & lightening accompanied with some nice showers of rain._

7 June 1868*

Mr Spieseke went to preach at Nine Creeks. Polly's complaint returned, badly.[401]

8 June 1864

[Wed] In my school I commenced gathering native words; there is some good laughing about it now & then._ In toolshop all day._ In the evening just before the meeting Mr Ellerman & family & with them Miss Hamilton came on a short visit; we had a very pleasant tea._ Some more Blacks have come & others are about to go._ The Ellermans went home about 7 o'clock.

8 June 1865

[Thu] Tried once more at the punching machine, but no go_ So I managed to get the holes punched by means of a chisel 6 heavy hammer._ Matthew having come back last night Sp[ieseke]: spoke to him about his wife & her wickedness[402]_ He seemed at first to misunderstand the matter thinking that Peter was at fault alone. Matthew went to Antwerp to get a warrant for Peter, but Mr Ellerman did not give him one._ Sp: managed to get Matthew to understand the thing properly, namely that his wife was as much at fault as Peter O Lord convert that poor fallen woman!_

8 June 1867

[Sat] Finished the mould for making brick_ Had a good rain during the night ¼ inch fell. Rode on Mona to Antwerp to fetch some letters & see the Flemmings._

8 June 1873

[New Fairfield, Canada] Sun: Sunday school well attended: the children sang a little better._ It is amazing to see some of the Indians lie on the ground, before the Church during service time. Gave out that Mr Mackenzie was coming on Wednesday to pay the annuity & requested the Indians to have the business transacted in their own School on the reserve_ Singing in the afternoon not well attended. Few at the evening service also. Spoke on the

---

401 Polly suffered from 'nervous weakness'. MAB, PP HJAH, 3, Letters, M. Hartmann to Dan Hines, 9 August 1870.
402 Ref: 6 June 1865.

text "Christ tasting death for every man._ Some Indian must have lighted a heap of rubbish that got carted a while ago to the riverbank This improper thing on a Sunday I have to comment on next Sunday._

9 June 1864*

[Thu] Finished the toolshop._ There was plenty of rain to-day; it does not rain here as it does at home, but it comes in shocks & that pretty hard, too._ The country begins to look green^{er} already. A german Personenen Urban (a *Holsteiner*[403]) came to-day & brought us some fruit trees._ Rachel feels rather sick & so we intend to send her to Horsham to the Doctor. [gap] I succeeded in making bread with baking-powder.

9 June 1865

[Fri] At punching holes into bar-iron all day, interrupted ♭ in it by the coming of Mrs Ellerman & her mother,[404] & Mr Ellerman. They just had a peep & then drove again._ Polly commenced cutting out baby clothes!!![405]

9 June 1866

[Sat] Sp[ieseke] put the rams into the flock on the other side, there being about 30 ewes in it, to try how the lambs will do at a later season than usual._

10 June 1864*

[Fri] I commenced taking Matthew by himself to teach him more thourroughly than the others, he seems to me to be a most promising young man, with good abilities, & by the grace of God may yet prove to be useful among his countrymen._ Nathanael is improving. Some more Blacks have come among them. Hearty a clever one in all handywork._ I made cakes, & while baking them in the kitchen had a long talk with Mary alone. I am not without hopes of her, although like the rest, she appears very indifferent.

---

403 A Holsteiner is a person from the Holstein region of northern Germany.
404 Christina Westgarth.
405 Reference to Polly's pregnancy with her first child, Eleanor Hartmann, known as Nelly, born at Ebenezer on Ref: 14 December 1865.

10 June 1865

[Sat] Commenced putting together the ring for the windmill, riveting the circular slabs of wood together. S^[plieseke] went off to Horsham for a trip, took Helene with him.

10 June 1866

[Sun] There was a heavy frost last-night. In a basin I had standing out with water there was ice ¼ inch thick._ In the afternoon, I whilst Polly had her Sunday school, I gave our Nelly the first drive in the perambulator._

10 June 1867

[Mon] Last [Sat] when in Antwerp our horse Mona got her tail cut off very short when standing in the stable (& as I got to know to-day when riding over again to investigate the matter by some travellers)) I was very very glad to find that to be the case, as I thought Arnold Mr Flemmings man had done it. I the morning the remainder of the stores arrived, we just took a hurried breakfast as the bullockdrivers wanted to be off quickly & then unloaded the 8 tons of flowur._ A good many of our people went to Locheal for a few days to gather beer[406] & also to have a holiday. Before they went we had them together in the school & talked to them about their garden how to divide them that every one who wanted a garden might have a nice piece of his own. As it now stands there is one picking here & one picking there in the piece of ground that Timothy & Toney have fenced in._

11 June 1864

[Sat] Commenced operations for my dark room to take likenesses_ made the frame for the door & a small sliding window with a wooden-slide._

11 June 1866

[Mon] There being a want of food of food, because of the bad season tt to keep 2 pigs, we <u>killed</u> one of them to-day._ Most of the people, because they cannot expect regular rations intend to leave our place, but breaking up too late most of them came back again to camp once more; so we think there will be regular start to-morrow.

---

406 Honeysuckle from the desert banksia.

11 June 1868*

[Thur] A fearful thunderstorm in the evening tremendous rain, very welcome.

11 June 1873

[New Fairfield, Canada] ᵂ· Mʳ Mackencie came to pay the annuity to the Indians. The affair lasted until Friday morning at 3 oclock._ (See notes)

12 June 1864

[Sun] S[pieseke]. going off the Antwerp to keep the meeting there I preached in the morning._ I feel sometimes heavy & find myself in difficulties about what I shall say to the Blacks, but our good Lord has helped me through hitherto & I trust will do so in time to come._ I have sometimes gone to chapel not knowing what to say, but somehow words were given to me when I commenced speaking._ In the afternoon we had some of them in Chapel teaching them to sing "Come ye sinners poor & wretched". S. came to back shortly after the a.m. meeting. In going he had seen some sheep tracks leading out of our Paddock, & he thought somebody had been to steal sheep; but it proved to be Mʳ Ellerman's rams that had been driven out by Phillip._

12 June 1865

[Mon] No work to day with the people as they all went off hunting_ I worked at the ring_ Cold frosty morning, & a clear warm day._ My cold baths I commenced some time ago do me much good._

12 June 1867

[Wed] First thing in the morning I fetched some rafters & small pine saplings to build a small shed for drying bricks under._ Mʳ & Mʳˢ Thomas Scott came to see us stayed but a little while._ Some of our people returned from the Locheal._ Mʳ Charles Wilson answered Mʳ Sp: letter asking for some killing sheep. Mʳ C. W. did not only promise the sheep but inclosed also a £ 10 note to be spent for the Mission._ There was frost last night & the night before._ Timothy & David are tempering the clay for the bricks. A drive to Antwerp with Polly & Nelly.

12 June 1869*

[Sat] Rec^d news from home of the engagement of my friend Miss E. Shaw with Mr Frederick Pansel of Ockbrook.⁴⁰⁷ To be married in July.

13 June 1864*

[Mon] Got Timothy & Corney to fetch sand & lime to build my dark room._ Somehow I felt ill & weak to-day, so I took a Seidlitz powder⁴⁰⁸ before I went to bed, & it did me good._ I gave Mary to-day a bag which I had made for her according to promise. She will collect together etc to fill it for a pillow. I gave her also an old shirt for Joe, & an old cracked looked hand-looking glass of a pretty form. When she had rec^d these, she ran into the kitchen, & threw her arms around Jessie Rebecca, our cook, shewing her the things. They were given as a kind of encouragement, because she has been more industrious lately, & also for the basket.⁴⁰⁹

13 June 1865

[Tue] There was a little disagreeableness about the meat this morning, some come & fetch when they have no business to do so._ All went off working at the fence._ I began the top ting_ Cold frosty morning again, but beautiful & warm day._ Got Russel's tannin⁴¹⁰ from town & read in it all night._

13 June 1866

[Wed] During the instruction meeting, for the baptized people, w^h Sp[ieseke] kept;__ Dicky, Emma & Napoleon packed quickly their things together & ran away to the other Blacks that were camping near Antwerp._ This was rather an unexpected blow for we did not think that the children would do such a thing for both of them applied themselves well to their studies, both were candidates for baptism & we all thought that they had received an impression of the truth. We don't know what to think about. M^r Sp: will go to-morrow early to see whether he cannot get them back._ I finished the bedstead for James. James is helping Sp: digging a trench round the tank to plant roses in.

---

407 Village in Derbyshire, England.
408 A common nineteenth-century powder used to aid digestion.
409 Ref: 30 May 1864.
410 Referring to the book. Ref: 2 May 1865.

13 June 1867

[Fri] Another frosty night._ Sp: left with Philip for the west to see how many Blacks there were to be found._ One of the Squatters McClellan[411] having asked for rations for the Blacks, & the Board in Melbourne asking us to look into the affair whether is was advisable or not._ The people came back from Locheal all very glad to come back._ Built a small shed for drying the bricks under. Got our old mare Bessy fetched in._

13 June 1873

[New Fairfield, Canada] ^{F.} A married young white woman (whose husband is in jail I suppose) came & offered herself to enter our service. We dont like the looks of the woman. My wife did not want her. We learnt afterwards that R. Jacobs was intinded to leave impressed by the woman to do so._ We would not take that woman on any act._

14 June 1864*

[Tue] Commenced building the wall for my darkroom._ S[pieseke]. working hard in the garden these days; I sh^{ld} like to help him but have so much to do that I cannot for the present._ I got the ^{my} gar flower-garden a little in order, divided large roots of mignionetter pinks &c set young sweet-williams, also seeds of Hollyhocks, convolvulus, Canterbury bell; sweet Williams &c &c_ We were much disturbed today by Paddy asking for his little daughter Emma, a nice gentle little girl of about 7 or 8 years old, who has lived in the Mission-house for some time. We spoke to him about the good she was getting here in every way, shewed him her work, books, doll, the picture books we have to shew her, but I do not think all these w^d have availed, had the child herself been willing to go. But when he saw her tears of sorrow at going away, he relented, & promised she sh^d stay. Before night however, he had changed his mind, the mother he said cried so much at leaving her, so we must let her go afterall, hoping soon to get her back again. When we think of the vice wh wh. is practised in the camp, & the wild, uncivilized habits of the people among whom she goes, it makes us feel very sad. But we trust that the Good Shepherd will watch over this little lamb. & teach her himself.

---

411 On advice of the missionaries, the BPA was informed not to provide rations to Mr McClellan. Ref: 22 June 1867.

14 June 1865

[Wed] The same work & weather as yesterday only that the day was perhaps more beautiful than yesterday._

14 June 1866

[Thu] Sp: came back but without Dicky & Emma; they seemed, at least Dicky did to wish to have a change. Paddy said to Sp that the children should come back after 2 month. Napoleon came back._ We had a little rain in the morning, & a sort of drizzling rain all the day through; the country looks very fresh._

14 June 1869*

We started on a visit to Mr Scotts, taking Rebecca with us. I ^{Polly} was very sick on the way. We found them_ not at home.

15 June 1864*

[Wed] To-day our pig was killed_ I killed it_ We had a great hunt for it to catch it_ Made a sieve to sieve the lime w^h is full of stones & very inconvenient for building._

[from letter extract] <u>Wednesday June 15th</u>. Adolf killed our pig. It was but small, but very wild. The blacks had great trouble to catch it. A. Also made a sieve for the lime, as it was so full of stones, he could not work it into mortar for his photographic room.[412]

15 June 1866

[Fri] Finished a table for James._ Tried to push on Timothy as I had done many times before already, to be a little sharp about getting his boards cut, but he seems not to care much about it as he said at least, & so I shall not trouble him any more, let him just do as he likes._ Some boxes of caps were missing xx from our little store & we found that Albert had stolen them._ What a sad thing about that boy! If he only does not leave our place._ A dull day_ Wind North._

---

412 MAB, PP HJAH 3, Letters, Extract from our Diary, commencing June 15th [1864], enclosed in letter from Polly [Mary] Hartmann to Dan and John Hines [June 1864].

15 June 1867

[Sat] Finished in the forenoon the shed for protecting the bricks to be made Fetched the home mail in the afternoon. There was a letter for Rachel too from W Australia; in it she was told that 5 young girls were one the way to Melbourne,[413] some of them to go to Hagenauer, & some to us, this is rather astonishing news, as it seems that we have not written for any girls.[414]

15 June 1869*

Returned from Mr Scotts. Had a more pleasant drive than yesterday. Called at Antwerp & gave the horse a feed.

16 June 1864

[Thu] Cut up the pig & salted it._

16 June 1866

[Sat] Nice gentle rain almost all the day._ Fine warm growing weather.__ I made two stools for James; a put up also a board over this fireplace & made a little shelf for his plates etc & for his books. He took possession of his new house & the & his wife Ruth[415] are very happy to have a snug & comfortable dwelling

16 June 1867

[Sun] Began a sort of sunday school with the men & boys in the chapel reading & explaining to them some interesting stories, & sing with them at the harmonium teaching some of them to sing bass._ In the evening a gentle rain commenced coming down

---

413 These five women from Anne Camfield's 'Institute for Native and Half-Caste Children' in Albany, Western Australia were: Nora White, Rhoda Toby, Emily Peters, Ada Flower and Bessy Flower. Much has been written about Bessy Flower, with some of her letters in Nelson, Smith and Grimshaw, *Letters from Aboriginal Women*. See also: Attwood, '"In the Name of All My Coloured Brethren and Sisters"'. On the marriage of the other women see: Felicity Jensz, 'Controlling Marriages: Friedrich Hagenauer and the Betrothal of Indigenous Western Australian Women in Colonial Victoria', *Aboriginal History*, no. 34 (2010): 35–54, doi.org/10.22459/AH.34.2011.02.

414 Hagenauer had been in communication with 'friends in Western Australia' in March 1867 regarding the sending over of more girls. See: *Periodical Accounts* 26 (1866), 236.

415 First Ref: 5 August 1866. Ruth was said to be 28 years old in 1866. She and James (previously Edward) were baptised and were married in the first half of 1866. Ruth attended the mission school. She died on Ref: 15 November 1867 See: *Further Facts, Fifth Paper*, 4–5.

17 June 1864*

[Fri] Feeling rather stiff in my back I commenced cold baths; for the present only sponging in the morning & evening._

[from letter extract] <u>Friday</u>. Adolf cut up & salted the pig. He also commenced cold baths.[416]

17 June 1865

[Sat] S[pieseke]. came back from Horsham where he had been on a visit. In the forenoon I finished putting the ring of the windmill together, I had been at almost all the week.

17 June 1867*

[Mon] James & Stephen went to Walmar on horseback to fetch the sheep M̠ͬ C Wilson promised some ^{little} time ago._ Made a little bit of commencement in making a bricks, made just a few towards evening to try whether I can make use of the pallet moulding or whether I must adhere to the slop moulding process._ A good rain during the night

17 June 1869*

Adolf received We were delighted by a visit from M̠ͬ & M̠ͬˢ Ellerman They were on their way to M̠ͬ Scotts for Sunday. Stayed the night.

17 June 1873

[New Fairfield, Canada] ᵀ Albert finished sprinkling the potatoes (this is the second time) It took about 1 ¼ ˡᵗ of green for all the potatoes about 1 ½ acre. The strength is 2 small table spoons full dissolved in a pail of water._ It is very dry weather, quite discouraging to do anything in the garden. The corn & peas M̠ͬ Macarthen & Cornelius Brown sowed are not coming up.

18 June 1864*

[Sat] Whilst building at my dark room in the afternoon I got a letter from my uncle Hartig_ he lives at Ca near Castlemaine,[417] it was a very nice letter.

---

416 MAB, PP HJAH 3, Letters, Extract from our Diary.
417 Uncle Hartig Lived near Chinaman's Creek.

[from letter extract] Saturday 18th Adolf worked at his dark room. We received a letter from A's uncle, whom he has found out. He lives near Castlemaine on a place of his own. They are very anxious to see us. They are old people & have no children.[418]

18 June 1867

[Tue] Good heavy rain last night._ Strong rain almost all the day it gave over at about 3 p.m. Not much done of course._ Had a pretty long school._

18 June 1869*

The Ellerman family went on to M[r] Scotts, leaving Dolly & Gussy here till Monday.

19 June 1864

[Sun] The first Sunday since the baptism that we & S[pieseke]. were together_ Feeling rather unwell in the afternoon we had no singing in Chapel._

19 June 1865

[Mon] Making a box to contain the draining stand for the dry process. In the afternoon writing at the home letters._

19 June 1867

[Wed] Some very heavy rain last night for about 2 hours & a half. Tremendous puddles all over._ Hagenauer wrote to Sp 2 letters about the girls coming from the west. In the first they were not arrived yet & he asked Sp: to come to M[elbourne]: & arrange matters with him_ In the 2nd they had arrived & he wrote that as they could ^(or would) not be separated he had taken them all to his place.[419]_ Letters from Kennedy & from M[r] Cobham the former telling us that the pla pipes etc were on the way, the latter that he had ordered the carling plate & that it would be sent as soon as possible. Hagenauer also announced that he would be pay us a visit about November or October from him also we learnt that our B[rn] at Coopers Creek have been obliged to leave the place, being attacked of the Blacks.[420]_ This is sad news!_

---

418 MAB, PP HJAH 3,Letters, Extract from our Diary.
419 Ref: 15 June 1867. None of the women came to Ebenezer.
420 This mission was subsequently closed.

19 June 1869*

[Sat] Adolf received a letter from the Church Mission Committee asking if he could temporarily supply the post at Lake Condah,[421] or recommend any one. He subsequently wrote to say he could not, & gave them a hint as regards the small salaries they give their Missionaries

19 June 1873

[New Fairfield, Canada] Th The singing practice was well attended. Learnt in four parts "Children of Jerusalem;" Here we suffer grief & pain"_ The bass & tenor require but little practice they nearly sing it from the notes. There was a ploughing bee in Fred Jacobs field to give him a start in the ploughing for fall wheat._

20 June 1864*

[Mon] Had an attack of tooth-ache. S[pieseke]. went in the evening on a short visit to Antwerp & intends to come back to-morrow._ The last 4 or 5 days we had plenty of rain._

[from letter extract] Monday 20th A. had toothache very badly. Br & Sr. Spieseke & children went to Antwerp to spend the evening. We have had ^{much} rain these last few days.[422]

20 June 1865

[Tue] Polly & I had a walk to Antwerp, taking there the home letters & expecting to bring back English letters, but there was no mail at all that day. It was dark when we came back._

20 June 1873

[New Fairfield, Canada] ^F Hot day. First swarm of bees came out. Boxed them myself._ Began painting the windows, after I had given them a good washing w^h took me 2 days._

---

421 The Lake Condah mission was supported by the Church Mission Society. It was established in 1867 and closed in 1913. In the first decade had a high turnover of staff, including some former Moravian missionaries.
422 MAB, PP HJAH 3, Letters, Extract from our Diary.

EBENEZER MISSION STATION, 1863-1873

21 June 1864*

[Tue] S[pieseke]. came back from Antwerp at 12 oclock_ he brought Eliza[423] with him who presented us with a little dog from her Parents_ we called the little fellow Prince._

[from letter extract] Tuesday 21st Mr & Mrs Spieseke returned, & brought back one of <u>Mrs Ellermanns</u> little girls to stay with he us for a few days. The latter brought us a present of a little dog, which we call Prince. It is a little black terrier.[424]

21 June 1865

[Wed] Killed one of our pigs, a nice fellow. I was the butcher. We managed everything much better than last year._ Both S. & I ha are driving hard the people to stick to their houses to get them done._ Not an easy matter to get them to stick at their own work._ The sheep were all driven to the other side; plenty of food there._ Our cows, too, having been driven accross for a day gave more milk_

22 June 1864

Mr Spiesecke made out of my harmonium boy a meat safe_ Our little dog[425] gets at home with us._ I am still building at my darkroom it takes more time then I thought as I prepare everything myself. Mr Ellerman kindly offered to get me chemicals if I should want such.

22 June 1865

Cut up the pig with Polly's ^{help} & salted it._ Mr Wallace from Locheal came & stayed over dinner. He promised 2 other pigs like last year to be fetched at any time convenient. We also got permission to shoot wild cattle on the Mr Holts run.[426]_ In the afternoon we all set to work making sausages & succeeded pretty well._ Mary Ann[427] Teddy's wife rather sick with the old decease & not expected to live. Got from town "Graham on infants"[428] also some seeds"

---

423 Eliza Ellerman.
424 MAB, PP HJAH 3, Letters, Extract from our Diary.
425 Prince, the dog, was a present from the Ellermans. Ref: 21 June 1864.
426 Holts's run was Lochiel, which Wallace managed until March 1867 (Ref: 15 March 1867).
427 There is little information on Mary Ann in the diary. She died Ref: 25 June 1865.
428 This reference to a medial book on infants reflects Polly's early stage of pregnancy as announced in the diary on Ref: 9 June 1865. Eleanor Mary Hartmann was born on Ref: 14 December 1865.

22 June 1867

Today & yesterday I made about 200 bricks._ Sp: came back from his tour to the west he had been as far as at M͜cClellan's._ He is going to write to the Board[429] that no rations should be given there.[430]_ Sp had an idea of making a station in that district rather than giving rations into the hands of squatters._

22 June 1873

[New Fairfield, Canada] There was a good rainfall during the night. A thing we have been looking for for a long time. Everything looks so fresh after it. <u>The Lord is good.</u>_

23 June 1865

[Fri] Made to-day the models of the axle-tree for the windmill etc, all of wood to be taken to to the 9 Creeks to get Mͬ Cook the blacksmith to make the things of iron._ Helped a little bit at the houses of Edward & Timothy._ Mary Ann is rather sick & not expected to live, it is the old decease with her she does not seem to be without some good impressions, but when spoken to just now she does not answer._

23 June 1866

[Sat] Came back from Edol's where we had gone 2 days ago to pay a visit as we had not been there a long time

24 June 1865

[Sat] Fetched a log & cut it into thick laths for a roof on the windmill

24 June 1867

[Mon] James & Nathanael were sent off to M͜cClellans to induce the Blacks there to come to the Mission station._ Put the bricks I made last week into the shed I made._ ~~Some~~ David & Elizabeth[431] went to Locheal for beer gathering

---

429 Central Board Appointed to Watch Over the Interests of the Aborigines in the Colony of Victoria.
430 The Central Board had asked Spieseke if they should supply rations for Aboriginal people at the squatter McClellan's place. Ref: 13 June 1867.
431 David and Elizabeth (formerly Mary, Ref: 27 July 1865), married Ref: 7 May 1867.

EBENEZER MISSION STATION, 1863-1873

25 June 1864*

[Sat] Finished the wall to my dark room._ S[pieseke]. & myself sent off letters to Mr Chase in quest of a wife for Matthew, we applied for Margaret[432] at Mr Burchills; for particulars see copy of letter._

[from letter extract] Saturday 25th Adolf finished building his dark room. Mr. Ellermann has promised to get him chemicals or anything he wants.[433]

25 June 1865

[Sun] Mary Ann, Teddy's wife, died during the morning service. After the meeting I went to the camp, when I heard the wailing at some distance._ A cold day._ A good shower of rain accompanied by hail at noon._

25 June 1867

[Tue] Took 2 bags of flowers & 1 bag of sugar to Mr Edol's, in our spring cart. It was a heavy pull for Bobby.[434]_ See & To Locheal in the evening made the acquaintance of M^r McLeod.[435]_

25 June 1873

[New Fairfield, Canada] W. An attack of "bilious Colic", rather painful kept me all day in the room but thanks to the Lord's help ^after the medicines, injections, & the throwing up oof a deal of bile I felt better towards evening._ Albert went to Monseytown for the week having his place filled up by it Kennedy Snake.

26 June 1864*

[Sun] B^r Spieseke started this morning for Nine Creeks, where he was to officiate. He took Matthew with him. Adolf preached from Matt. XXII. 1-14.[436] especially "All things are ready."[437] In the afternoon etc & I sang a little together out of "Messiah",[438] & afterwards we had our singing with the blacks. We taught them tune 39. ^b & I.22.[439]

432 Rev. Chase recommended Margaret. UA, UEC Minutes, 12 November 1864, #10.
433 MAB, PP HJAH 3, Letters, Extract from our Diary.
434 Bobby, the horse.
435 Ref: 2 January 1868.
436 Parable of the wedding feast.
437 KJV: Matthew 22:4.
438 'Messiah' composed in 1741 by George Frideric Handel.
439 In 1849, an English-language hymn book of the Moravian Church was collated by the Moravian poet James Montgomery, containing 1,260 hymns. See: www.hymnologyarchive.com/james-montgomery.

[from letter extract] Sunday 26th Mr. Spieseke went off this morning to preach at Upper Regions & Nine Creeks. He took Matthew with him. Adolf preached from All things are ready. In the afternoon A & I sang a little from the Messiah with the ~~afternoon~~ harmonium, & afterwards taught the black a new hymn & tune.[440]

26 June 1866

[Tue] Very bad tooth ache (or rather tic doloreux)[441] stopped in the room all day & could do nothing at all._

26 June 1867

[Fri] Saw the Blacks in the morning prayed with them & then took sick Nancy & Joe with me into the cart & brought them to our place._ I got my stomach deranged too & did not feel ~~ve~~ well at all._ M^r Sp caught a bad cold too & was in bed all day

27 June 1864*

[Mon] S[pieseke]. who had been off to 9 creeks to preach there, coming back brought sundry things with him; he brought also a letter copying book for us & 5 lt: of tobacco for me._ I was to-day in the toolshop making a horse[442] for Polly to dry linen._ In the morning before prayer Phillip informed me that some ducks had settled down near our place, so after prayer I gave him my gun, & he managed to get one of them, it flew down into the water & we had to fetch the boat to get it_ It was very interesting to me to watch Phillip in search of the ducks; he spied them after some time sitting on a gum tree._

[from letter extract] Monday 27th B. Spieseke returned. Adolf made a large horse for drying & airing our clothes.[443]

---

440 MAB, PP HJAH 3, Letters, Extract from our Diary.
441 Tic douloureux, also trigeminal neuralgia, is a long-term nerve pain disorder affecting the trigeminal nerve in the face.
442 Clothes horse.
443 MAB, PP HJAH 3, Letters, Extract from our Diary.

27 June 1865

[Tue] Mary Ann[444] was buried before dinner. S & I were present & spoke to the people. I spoke to them about the rich man & Lazarus

27 June 1867

[Thu] ~~Mar~~ Nice rain last night & a little bit in the morning._ Made a roller to day & almost finished it. ☦ It is to be used for rolling the flat I am making the brick on, and also to be used for a garden roller._ The sheep were taken from the other side into the Durrock paddock._

27 June 1873

[New Fairfield, Canada] ᴱ Susan Tobias came this morning to take the place of Rebecca Jacobs_ She seemed anxious to come, as my wife asked here a few days ago. Kennedy Snake is certainly a better worker than Albert he does fully half as much again. I must speak to Albert about this._ He does not work enough for the pay he gets._ Helped Bʳ Peter sen: mending his pump._ Let a field of hay to Stonefish & Peter sen: their shares being half the hay._ No singing because nobody came._

28 June 1864*

[Tue] Finished the horse I commenced yesterday._ In the evening just before the meeting Mʳ Ellerman & Simpson made their appearance; the latter had been through the land a long way, saw also our old station on Boga Lake & as he wished to speak to S[pieseke]. about it & they going back that evening. S. went with them, in our conveyance._ Mʳ Ellerman on coming to us in his vehicle had an accident, he ran against a stump & broke the axeltree

[from letter extract] Tuesday 28ᵗʰ Mr Ellermann came over in the afternoon with Rev. Simpson of Horsham, who had been on a ministerial visit as far as Lake Boga, the scene of our former mission. He says the blacks are fine fellows & want much to see Br. Spieseke again. It is most probably that the latter will soon pay them a visit. Mr. S. & Mr. E. returned late in the evening to Antwerp.[445]

---

444 Died Ref: 25 June 1865.
445 MAB, PP HJAH 3, Letters, Extract from our Diary.

28 June 1865

[Wed] After much thinking I at last settled how to do the roof of the windmill made it to be screwed off & on at leisure._ Cold weather!_ S: helps Edward & Timothy putting up the roof, first time S: helps at that new house._

29 June 1864*

[Wed] In the forenoon all that could be got went off to mend our fence along the river to prevent the sheep getting across; rather hard work this topping of fences._ We got back at 12 & presently Revd Simpson, with his wife & little daughter Martha came. After dinner we had a meeting in the chapel & Revd Simpson spoke to our people on_ "The blood of Jesus Christ his son cleaneth from all sin"_ After the meeting we looked about our place & saw all the Blacks._ Mrs Simpson is a most amiable, pleasant & also pious woman, when we went about seeing the people she had a word for each of them; she stopped some time with Nathanael & prayed with him._ We then got all those that come to school to the schoolhouse, & made them read to Mr Simpson out of the Bible. At 3 p.m. M^r & Mrs Simpson left for 9 Creeks where they intend to stop over night & then proceed to Horsham_ I made a hut for our little dog Prince & he forthwith, when I put it there took possession of it, the little fellow is very pleasant._

[from letter extract] Wednesday 29th. Mr Spieseke, Adolf & all the available blacks went off to finish a piece of fencing, to secure the sheep. They returned at 12. About the same time came Mr. Simpson in his conveyance from Antwerp on his way home to Horsham, bringing with him his wife & little girl who on account of illness, had been a way for change of air. They were here only a few hours, but long enough to shew he us how much business an earnest Christian can do for his heavenly Master in a very short time, & how we may let our light shine, without any unnecessary glare. They went round with us to see the blacks & the new huts which some are building. Mrs. Simpson had a quick word for each, managing somehow to get them aside, & to speak to them of Jesus. She visited Nathaniel, & as I heard afterwards, prayed with him. Altogether she is a most amiable, pleasant, pious woman, & I wish I was like her. They left us about 3 p.m. but before they went, we had a meeting in the chapel, & Mr. Simpson spoke to the blacks on John I 7. Afterwards too, all our scholars went to the schoolroom, & read to them of out of the Bible.[446]

446 MAB, PP HJAH 3, Letters, Extract from our Diary.

29 June 1866
[Fri] Finished digging my flower garden, or rather Polly's, cutting the thyme ~~boar~~ border. Looks very neat now._

29 June 1867
[Sat] Matthew began building the wall of his new house. I directed him in getting the foundation correct._ Sp: was planning the boards for ~~the boy~~ flooring the ^boys^ bedroom in the school._ Since Mr C^h Wilson's sheep came 4 have been killed a week.

30 June 1864*
[Thu] The flood came during the night & we found the water risen about 2 feet. & it kept on rising steadily all day. After school I set to work making a pair of oars for our boat, all the other Blacks we sent out fetching wood, we spoke to them about fetching wood & told them it would be best to ~~fetch~~ set every weaek a day apart & fetch plenty for the whole week; they all agreed to do it._ We got letters from Hagenauer in the afternoon._ Polly commenced to stuff our sofa._ After tea fearing, the water m might fill our lime kiln we took out all th. lime by candle-light, Matthew helping._

[from letter extract] <u>Thursday 30th</u> . The rive rose about 2 feet during the night. Adolf made a pair of ours for the boat. We got letters in the afternoon from Br. & Sp. Hagenauer in Gippsland. In the evening Mr. Spieseke & Adolf got out the lime from the lime kiln, lest the flood should come & spoil it.[447]

30 June 1866
[Sat] A ride to Antwerp on Bobby fetched the letters, & also a good number of strawberry plants, as I intend to grow them upon the spot towards the chapel gate._ Sp. put up the roof on Davids house._ All the week fine warm weather & much of a drizzling rain very fruitful weather.

---

[447] MAB, PP HJAH 3, Letters, Extract from our Diary.

July

1 July 1864

[Fri] Made a small improvement on the oars, outing some iron round the wooden pegs that they might not wear out so fast._ In the afternoon we shipped the goats to the other side, they making too much nuisance about our house, then I helped Polly with the sofa_ In the evening I washed some wool for stuffing our sofa, as we had not enough material.

1 July 1865

[Sat] Off with Polly to the 9 Creeks to preach._ pleasant drive_ saw on the way a wild turkey (buzzaard)[448] very big bird_ Got almost a bite from one of Mr Edol's dogs._

1 July 1866

[Sun] During the morning-service M‍r Edols & M‍r Cobham suddenly made their appearance in our chapel. M‍r Cobham at present inspector of the police of the Wimmera district, & having his residence at Pleasant Creek, was formerly stationed in that district[449] [gap] & it was under him that Morgan[450] the bushranger was caught._ They both left in the afternoon._

1 July 1867

[Mon] We commenced reading to the people in the school. William's missionary enterprise in the south sea islands,[451] taking it in turn on Monday & Wednesday night

---

448 Perhaps referring to a malleefowl.
449 In 1857, Francis McCrae Cobham was the inspector of police in the Swan Hill district, and subsequently in the Benalla district, at the time that Daniel Morgan, bushranger, was shot. See: *The Argus* (Melbourne), Thursday 5 March 1857, 6; also State Parliament of Victoria, *Report and Proceedings of the Board*.
450 Daniel Morgan (1830–1865), bushranger. See: John McQuilton, 'Morgan, Daniel (Dan) (1830–1865)', *Australian Dictionary of Biography*, National Centre of Biography, The Australian National University, published first in hardcopy 2005, accessed 5 May 2021, adb.anu.edu.au/biography/morgan-daniel-dan-13109/text23717.
451 First published in 1837, *A Narrative of Missionary Enterprises in the South Sea Islands: With Remarks upon the Natural History of the Islands, Origin, Languages, Traditions, and Usages of the Inhabitants* (London: John Snow, 1837), by the London Missionary Society's John Williams, became a classic of the evangelical missionary movement.

2 July 1864*

[Sat] Worked at my stand for the camera & almost finished it, it seems to be a substantial tripod._ In the evening we celebrated the Lord's supper & Nathanael according to his wish, when partaking it 4 weeks ago, to be present at the next was present. He is getting better

[from letter extract] Saturday July 2nd We thought of Father all day & wished him many happy returns. We had communion together in the evening. Nathaniel and his wife were present.[452]

2 July 1865

[Sun] Preached at the 9 Creek's chapel about "and that knowing the time Rom 13 II 453" Mr Edols seems to be a little disturbed about the new land bill[454] that has come into force; could notice it in his manner & behaviour._ In the evening I spoke about "whose I am & whom I serve". Acts 27.[455]_

2 July 1866

[Mon] Planted out the strawberry plants I got from Mr Flemming about 230 plants

3 July 1864*

[Sun] In the morning at 10 Polly & I went off to Antwerp, I to preach there & were as usual well received._ We took our little dog[456] with us & the little chap felt very comfortable & at home with his brothers & sisters._ I spoke in the morning about "I go to prepare a place for you"[457] & in the evening about John XV 1,2.[458]_ In the afternoon Mrs Ellerman & children, Miss Donovan & ourselves took a walk into the Mallé; it was a fine afternoon.

---

452 MAB, PP HJAH 3, Letters, Extract from our Diary.
453 KJV. Romans 13:2, 'Whosoever therefore resisteth the power, resisteth the ordinance of God: and they that resist shall receive to themselves damnation.'
454 Under the 1862 Land Act (known as the Duffy Act), 10 million acres (4 million hectares) in the colony was 'made available' for selectors. In 1865, the Act was amended, providing the ability to subdivide lots so as to encourage smaller-scale agriculture.
455 KJV. Acts 27:23, 'For these stood by me this night the angel of God, whose I am, and whom I serve.'
456 Prince, the dog, was a present to the Hartmanns from the Ellerman family Ref: 21 June 1864.
457 KJV. John 14:2, 'In my Father's house are many mansions: if it were not so, I would have told you. I go to prepare a place for you.'
458 KJV. John 15:1, 'I am the true vine, and my Father is the husbandman. 2. Every branch in me that beareth not fruit he taketh away: and every branch that beareth fruit, he purgeth it, that it may bring forth more fruit.'

[from letter extract] Sunday 3ʳᵈ We walked over to Antwerp to spend the day, as Adolf was to preach there for Mr. Ellermann, who was absent. In the afternoon Miss Donavon, Mrs. Ellermann, the children & ourselves took a long walk into the mallee. It was a beautiful day.⁴⁵⁹

3 July 1865

[Mon] Back from the 9 Creeks at 2 p.m._ rather a cold wind blowing. The Lord's supper in the evening._

3 July 1866

[Tue] S[pieseke]. with wife & Anna & Mary left for Nill⁴⁶⁰ to see the Blacks about that district & also to pay a visit to Mʳ Ellerman's at the new manse._ Cut the vines & the 2 peach-trees. top of the garden._ Mʳ March & Stuart came to see about some boards, but Timothy who was just cutting for his house, did not feel inclined to sell them & very right he did not for his house has been standing a long time._ We thought to night about our tea how nice it would be if we could have tea & breakfast by ourselves._

4 July 1864*

[Mon] We came back by 11 a.m. & S[pieseke]. with Phillip started on horseback for Tata Yarra.⁴⁶¹_ They managed to cross the river & rode as far as Neil._ I finished my tripod & found it to answer very well._ I tried my hand at fishing & got a few._ Matthew asked me to go & help Mʳ Atkinson to find our horse wʰ he had lost_ In the evening a traveller came on his way to Mʳ Holt's station, & as he came rather late & it began to rain heavily I allowed him to stop over night._

[from letter extract] Monday 5ᵗʰ We had a beautiful walk home. Mr. S. started with Philip about 11am his journey to see the blacks at Tata Yarra. Adolf caught a few fish in the river.⁴⁶²

---

459 MAB, PP HJAH 3, Letters, Extract from our Diary.
460 Nhill.
461 Tatiara, in South Australia.
462 MAB, PP HJAH 3, Letters, Extract from our Diary.

4 July 1865

[Tue] Put up the revolving roof for the windmill, upon 4 posts, behind the toolshop._ Gave the roof a sort of blueish colour. Towards evening Mark coming back from the fence brough a "death adder"[463] he had killed there; he skinned it for me, & then I filled it with ~~sand~~ saw dust to keep the shape._ Charley (old) brought us some emu eggs 2 for us & 2 for Sp. of course we paid 2^s 6^d a piece.__

5 July 1864*

[Tue] Gave some shot etc to old Joe; he shot 4 ducks (black & gave us one of them._ In the afternoon I burnt some charcoal, making a big fire & then covering it with sods. I wanted it for drying my dark room, wood making too much smoke._ I roasted coffee_

[from letter extract] Tuesday 5th. One of the blacks shot four ducks with some powder & shot which Adolf gave him, & he brought us one. They are delicious eating. Adolf roasted coffee, & made an attempt at making charcoal.[464]

6 July 1864*

[Wed] When I came to the school house this morning to keep school I found Nathanael standing on his legs, making an attempt to walk, so I took him under the arms & helped him a little. Lena his mother seing N. walk was so touched that she began to sob whether for joy or pity I know not._ At any rate it shows that the people have a fine feeling & affectionate hearts_ We had for dinner another duck which old Joe shot._ I gathered some more charcoal to dry my dark room with_ My attempt to make charcoal proved a failure._ There was a good heavy shower in the afternoon._ After tea we finished the stuffing of our sofa._ Matthew returned tonight._

[from letter extract] Wednesday 6th. Nathaniel walked a little for the first time since his illness. His mother cried for joy. This evening we finished stuffing our sofa.[465]

---

463 The common death adder does not habituate the Wimmera.
464 MAB, PP HJAH 3, Letters, Extract from our Diary.
465 MAB, PP HJAH 3, Letters, Extract from our Diary.

6 July 1865

[Thu] Made a yoke to carry water more easily. M^r Sp[ieseke] got letters from Walder Meissel & Daniel, & I got those watch glasses w^h I asked Mr Walder some time ago to get for me when still in Melbourne but as they were just about to start from Melbourne I did not get them then.

6 July 1866

[Fri] Very bad tooth-ache all day

6 July 1867

[Sat] Finished the making of the bricks I commenced a week or so ago. The weather for brick making was most unfavourable or I would have finished long ago, made 989 bricks._ At tea time a great quarrel broke out between Stephen & Lydia, Tobsy & Timothy, Mark & Lizzie, also fell out so there were great troubles about the place._

7 July 1864*

[Thu] After school I helped Nathanael, in walking to our room where he sat for some time: he seemed to enjoy it very much._ I then took an early dinner & then went off with Matthew to fetch some nice pine trees, to be sawn into boards for making our doors (Matthew's hut & my dark room) I took my gun with me hoping that something would turn up but I got nothing. I just got home in time to escape a heavy rain that was coming up. Polly was working at our sofa cutting the chintz to cover it; it is now a nice & comfortable sofa._

[from letter extract] Thursday 7th. Nathaniel paid us a visit, & sat for a long time looking at pictures &c. Adolf took an early dinner, & then went off with Matthew to get some large pine trees about 3 miles off, suitable for sawing up to make doors. They did not return till evening.[466]

7 July 1865

[Fri] Put our sheep into the Durrock paddock; letting them through the gate we counted the sheep & lambs: 700 of the former about & only 85 of the latter._ This is a poor lambing, as we expected 300._ What a dry season! & such frosty nights. Beautiful clear days all the time._ Mr Ellerman was with us & brought us some vine cuttings; pleasant evening._

---

[466] MAB, PP HJAH 3, Letters, Extract from our Diary.

7 July 1866

[Sat] Killed the other pig, very successfully. Philip helped me._ Sp[ieseke] & family returned from their trip to Niel & the manse all well._ This was again a wet week, no heavy rains to be sure, but a good deal of drizzling rain, & some showers at night time

7 July 1867

[Sun] In the morning we had all the married men together & spoke to them about how they should live together with their wives, we had also the women together in the afternoon. We were enabled to bring together again Stephen & Lydia_ Mark & Lizzie but Tobsy is at present in our house, away from Timothy

7 July 1869*

[Wed] Esther[467] had a little boy[468] in the night. We had sent for the doctor, as she was very weak last night, & had been bad 40 hours. D[r] & M[rs] Parvis came about dinner-time. Stayed two or three hours, & then returned to Upper Regions.

8 July 1864*

[Fri] Whilst I, after school was mending the bark roof over my dark room, Polly came in great excitement telling me that Timothy was beating his wife [Susan]; I just came in time to see Rebecca standing between Tim: & Susan keeping him off. Timothy entirely forgot himself & was in a fearful rage, he ran to his hut & fetched a stick to beat his wife but she having gone away he threatened old Jenny, but I stopped him there, begging him to be quiet, but I hardly could restrain him._ Now all this schocking noise & excitement arose, by somebody having taken away old Jenny's bag, containing 2 shillings, some

---

467 First Ref. Esther McGuinness (née Robinson, as referred to in Nelson, Smith and Grimshaw, *Letters from Aboriginal Women of Victoria*) was the wife of Thomas Marks, referred to in the diary as Mark. Adolf Hartmann provided Robert Brough Smyth with measurements and details of Thomas for Smyth's monograph, *The Aborigines of Victoria*, published in 1878 (see p. 2). Thomas Marks was born at Lake Hindmarsh in 1844. Esther was the daughter of a woman called Kitty, who had another daughter with Robertson, also referred to in Smyth, called Maggie. Esther and Thomas married in 1867. This child was one of some 12 children they had. When Thomas Marks died in 1889, Ester married Peter McGuiness, and possibly had more children with hm. She died at Goyura on 7 January 1918. See: MAB, PP HJAH, 3, Letters, Mary Hartmann to Hines family, Ebenezer, 10 August 1869; Nelson, Smith, and Grimshaw, *Letters from Aboriginal Women*; Smyth, *The Aborigines of Victoria*, 93.
468 The boy would be baptised with the name Andrew. Ref: 25 July 1869.

pieces of tobacco & other little things, & Susan was suspected to have taken it & buried it somewhere. It was dreadful to see old Jenny going about & shrieking for her things: & then Timothy in that excitement. Well I left Timothy by himself that day & did not speak to him, as I would let him let him first cool down thoroughly but I spoke to Susan trying to get something out of her, but she gave me no answer at all, then I said, (she was sitting behind Toney's hut) now Susan get up & bring me those things & I will make it all straight, well after a while when I had left her, she got up, but I saw no more of her that day._ In the later part of the afternoon Mr H. Ellerman & family arrived, Mrs Ellerman intending to stay here for a few days._ I was much pleased with Matthew, m by the manner in w^h he spoke to me about Timothy & Susan entirely disapproving of their conduct.

[from letter extract] Friday 8th We had a disturbance this morning. One of our lubras had stolen a bag from old Jenny, containing some tobacco two shillings, & other little things. When it was found out old Jenny shouted & screamed, & chattered at a fearful rate, & when the husband of this lubra heard of it, he was so vexed (& more especially ^{because} some of the blacks thought he had told her to do it) that he began to beat her close to the back of our house. I ran to find Adolf, & meanwhile Jessie or Rebecca our cook stood between him & his lubra to protect her. We managed to prevent anything further, except the screaming & chattering which was kept up for a long time. Of course Adolf had a good talk with all the parties afterwards. In the afternoon Mr. Ellerman came over to spend the evening & later Mr. Henry Ellerman & family.[469]

8 July 1865

[Sat] Two rams of Mr Ellerman's having got amongst our flock Sp[ieseke] & I with Richard went through the paddock & fetched them out._ Hung up the bacon._ Change of weather_ Planted the vines w^h Mr Ellerman brought yesterday._

8 July 1867

[Mon] M^r Sp: is about making some stretchers for the boys sleeping room Mark & ~~Timoth~~ Philip cutting the wood for him

---

469 MAB, PP HJAH 3, Letters, Extract from our Diary.

9 July 1864*

[Sat] M^r H Ellerman went back to his place this morning_ I took all the Blacks present, got the sheep to the drafting yard & cut the ^lambs ~~weathers and ewes~~._ (90 weathers & 83 ewes) then I counted all the young & found there to be 195._ In the evening after tea when it was dark all the Blacks suddenly started off to see what had happened to old Joe; he had gone off after morning prayer with his gun & did not come back all day, when about the said time a shot was heard about a mile off, & after it a shrieking; the boys Bopoop & Albert told me some queer story about a wild Black fellow, gellem gulum,[470] who goes about killing other Black fellows_ All the Blacks off, we cannot get the sheep killed w^h I intended to do with Matthew._ It turned out after all that it was but a false alarm about old Joe, for he had only been caring for old Sam.[471]_

[from letter extract] Saturday 9th. Mr. H. Ellerman went home, leaving Mrs. H. E. & family for a few days.[472]

9 July 1865

[Sun] Nice rain in the forenoon._ We had been looking out for it for a long time._ ⊦ At night it set in raining & did so all the night through

10 July 1864*

[Sun] After the morning service I spoke to Timothy about his behaviour ~~the day be~~ a few days ago, he was sorry for it, but said that he could not help himself because he was suspected through Susan. He said he would not live with her any more but take her to his father who was camping some 8 miles off A good number then went away to that place (Matthew, Daniel, old Joe & his Mary, old Jenny, Susan & Timothy, to return soon again as they said_ They told me that old King Peter was there also very sick._

[from letter extract] Sunday 10th Some of the blacks went away to see old King Peter, ^who is dying. They promised to return tomorrow.[473]

---

470 The term 'gulum gulum' is reported to refer to foreigners, that is, people from other clans or languages without ties to the Wegaia language. Taylor, *Karkarooc*, 19.
471 Only other mention of Old Sam in the diary Ref: 12 July 1864.
472 MAB, PP HJAH 3, Letters, Extract from our Diary.
473 MAB, PP HJAH 3, Letters, Extract from our Diary.

10 July 1865

[Mon] Sp[ieseke] again after the 2 rams of Mr Ellerman's, w^h had got again into our paddock._ I made a screw holder for cleaning plates._ The wind shifted in the morning towards south & so the rain gave over._

10 July 1867

[Wed] Mr Edols came to-day and made arrangement about the land he promised some time ago. The fence will be continued from ours & carried on through the mallee till it meets his fence._ Philip is trenching a piece of ground along the tank in our garden to put a few more vines. I began a few days ago pruning the old vines & digging the ground about them._ M^r Sp went to see the Blacks at Locheal

11 July 1864*

[Mon] There was some trouble this morning as regards the milking; as all the Blacks had gone off we had nobody to do it. Well Rachel said that she could do it, so I went down to the ~~yard~~ paddock with the 2 boys Albert & Bubbub got the cows into the yard & we commenced operation, but soon found out that Rachel was a bad milker & we got, although we tried in turns myself & Rebecca & Rachel only a little milk out of the 2 cows, ¼ of a bucket._ This took us such a time, that as M^{rs} H Ellerman wanted to go to Antwerp in our conveyance, I had no time to keep the meeting but had to get the gig ready & drive her to Antwerp._ I stay^{ed}~~ed~~ there over dinner & took Miss Donnovan, who had been there for a visit for some time, to our place where she intended to stay a little while._ On coming back I found a hawker to have arrived._ I was glad to find Polly a little better, who was sick when I left in the morning.

[from letter extract] <u>Monday 11th</u> Nobody was founded who could milk, so Adolf had to try. The cows here are very wild & do not readily give their milk. About 11 a.m. Adolf drove Mrs. H. Ellerman, her two children & nurse over to Antwerp & brought back Miss Donovan on a visit to us.[474]

---

474 MAB, PP HJAH 3, Letters, Extract from our Diary.

EBENEZER MISSION STATION, 1863–1873

11 July 1865

[Tue] S^{p[ieseke]} having received from Edward a good confession of faith, & also from Sarah⁴⁷⁵ asked me, if I would not baptize them this time (the time of baptism not yet fixed) We had a good deal of talking about the people._ The Lord is blessing our work._

11 July 1867

[Thu] Got all the people together after the school & set to work with all of them to enlarge their garden.⁴⁷⁶ We took all the ᵒᵘʳ fences out & build a new one, so setting apart a piece of ground 245 feet by between 186 and 156_ We all went to work in a right good spirit & if we had had enough mallee sticks we would have finished the whole._ There was a nice rain during the night; alltogether it it is a very wet season._

11 July 1868*

[Sat] A. & I started for the Manse. Had a beautiful drive, & picnic at the dam. Could not call at M̶r̶ Nhil on account of the measles. Arrived about 3-30 & found to my disappointment, that Mrs Ellerman was not at home, having joined Mr Ellerman at Carngham.⁴⁷⁷

11 July 1873

[New Fairfield, Canada] Sat Albert my servant left me dissatisfied with his wages $ 3. I did not induce him to stay as he was rather late in coming in the morning & did also very little work for the money he got._

12 July 1864*

[Tue] Milked myself to-day & got a little more milk than yesterday_ Toney & old Sam went away._ In the afternoon I took the young mare & rode round our fence to look after the sheep, found them all right, lambs getting nicely._ No black man left on the station but Nathaniel & he is getting better._

[from letter extract] Tuesday 12th. Adolf's milking improves, but it is hard work for him, & rather dangerous as the cows are so wild. Today the other black men went away. We have now for a few days only Nathaniel his wife,

---

475 Sarah was baptised on Ref: 27 July 1865, taking the name Martha.
476 Prev. Ref: 10 June 1867.
477 Former goldmining town 25 kilometres west of Ballarat.

& mother, Rebecca, a girl, & two boys. We are told that in a few days a great number of blacks are coming. Adolf rode after the sheep. He has to do all the hard men's work himself. Nathaniel still improves.[478]

12 July 1865

[Wed] Finished 3 leveling stands I commenced yesterday._ Had a hunt after a duck but did not get it.

12 July 1866

[Thu] Vaccinated Nelly with ~~some~~ vacine matter sent to us from Horsham by Dr Johnson. That dear little pet is prospering wonderfully._ Off this afternoon to cut down some fine long pine trees for this new wings for the windmill 21 feet long._ M^r & Mrs Flemming called again._ The tooth ache I suffered from is almost healed by some homeophathic Threosod I took 2 days ago__

12 July 1867

[Fri] Divided the garden we enclosed yesterday: took me nearly all day._ The Blacks fetched some more Mallee. Mark & Nathanael are beginning to cut the boards for the nursery I am going to build. Sp[ieseke]: came back from Locheal bringing news that Frank's[479] Mary was very sick, & likely not to live very long._ Towards evening some of the Blacks came from Locheal bringing the news of Mary's death. We believe she died in the Lord, for she put all her trust in the Saviour._

12 July 1868*

[Sun] A. preached at the manse; more people came than we expected, among the rest_ the Macphersons (three.)[480]

13 July 1864*

[Wed] Milking better still than yesterday; white cow showed me her horns rather awkward that, but I managed her._ After milking I had to fetch water, & cut wood, then we hung up the bacon to dry. Letter writing in the

---

478 MAB, PP HJAH 3, Letters, Extract from our Diary.
479 The diary suggested that Frank was an alternative name for Old Boney. Ref: 31 August 1866.
480 No other reference to them in the diary.

afternoon & evening as they must be off to-morrow. Yesterday & to-day we had frosty nights but most lovely days. The river has risen a good deal since yesterday._

[from letter extract] <u>Wednesday 13th</u>. We hung up our bacon & hams. The river rose last night about a foot and a half. We have most lovely days, but very cold frosty nights. The blacks are not yet returned.[481]

13 July 1868*

[Mon] A. went over to Mr Elgin, to fetch some pigs Mr Jelford[482] had promised us, I was not at all well, & was glad to remain quietly at the Manse.

14 July 1864*

[Thu] Walked to Antwerp with the 2 boys Albert & Bubbub despatching our letters. River rising still._ So much to do all day that I could do nothing at my dark room._

[from letter extract] <u>Thursday July 14th</u>. Today we must send off our letters. Adolf will ride over to Antwerp with them this afternoon. Miss. D. is still with us. We have had some very pleasant walks together.[483]

14 July 1865

[Fri] Took up the wings of the mill to finish them. Sp[ieseke] speaking the people still, & finds out that some do not feel the need of the Saviour as they sh^{ld} do, They do not know themselves yet, they do not see that they are poor sinners, but on the contrary think that they are good having left off their former bad ways & tried to live a moral life._

14 July 1866

[Sat] Magdalene had a miscarriage, she got very ill after it especially as she had caught a severe cold._ Polly & I had a drive to Antwerp._ The country looks ver nice & green but the grass is very short, consequently the sheep are rather poor there is not a fat sheep among the whole lot.

---

481 MAB, PP HJAH 3, Letters, Extract from our Diary.
482 No other reference to him in the diary.
483 MAB, PP HJAH 3, Letters, Extract from our Diary.

14 July 1868*
[Tue] We started for home, called at M̲r̲ Macdonald's & had lunch. When arrived we found that many of our people had gone for a holiday to Lochiel.

15 July 1864
[Fri] The river has risen so much that the water begins to run into the creeks, so I took the mare & rode along the river to see whether the sheep were all right, found them to all this side of the creek._ In the afternoon I took the 2 boys to help me driving the sheep together to get a weather for killing, which I killed myself being directed by Nathanael how to do it, I could hardly re from restrain him him from helping me; he is improving marvellously._ Miss Donnovan left for Antwerp in the afternoon, & so we are quite alone again._ In the afternoon I had a little time left to watch the water running into the creek, filling hole after hole._

16 July 1864
[Sat] In the afternoon I get off for a little duckshooting, I shot 3 ducks & another bird On my way home, having crossed the river & coming back to recross I spied S[pieseke]. & Phillip coming back from their visit to the Blacks.[484]_ I was very glad to see them again because I had too much to do when alone._

17 July 1864
[Sun] After morning service w̲h̲ S[pieseke]. kept he went to Antwerp for a short visit taking with him the boys & Rebecca, Mary._ In the afternoon Matthew, Timothy & Tony came back._ I spoke to them about the promise they had made to return sooner, & they seemed to feel it much._

17 July 1865
[Mon] Matthew wanting to go to the lake & take his wife Margaret with him, we objected to his taking her along with him, knowing that she would exposed there to a great many temptations. M[atthew]. agreed to leave her here & went himself with old Charley to shoot a bullock for M̲r̲ Hny Ellerman

---

[484] Ref: 4 July 1864.

17 July 1866

[Tues] M̲r̲ & M̲rs̲ Scott & his mother, also M̲r̲ & M̲rs̲ Flemming came & stayed just a little bit to see the place & people._ I was adzing the poles for the new wings for the windmill._ The vaccination on Nelly's arm does not seem to take quite well._

17 July 1867

[Fri] Matthew beginning to put up his wall I set the boards for him & the thing answers well. P.[485] received a letter from Ballarat containing medicine

18 July 1864

[Mon] In the morning I mended some of our chairs which were in a rather dilapidated state, then I made some iron hooks to hold the ~~the~~ beam in the sawpit; I made these hooks out of the rails for my tram way._ Sharpened a crotchet saw. We ~~drov~~ drove also the 2 horses Spider & Bobby into the river & made them swim to our side, when S[pieseke]. & P̲h[illip]̲ came on S̲at̲ last they left on the other side of the river_ It has been very windy & cold yesterday & to day._ The river is going down a little._ In the evening Daniel came back._ <u>The meeting was kept by Phillip</u> He spoke indeed very nicely about the first few verses of the first chapter of S̲t̲ John's gospel. It was a most edifying matter to see this black man proclaim the gospel to his brethren. The Lord indeed do~~e~~th wonders.

18 July 1865

[Tue] Getting on nicely with my wings for the mill._ S̲p̲ is going to make a new gate, is going to make a well finished one. Mark & Phillip cutting for him in the pit some white gum for the ~~ga~~ gate posts etc._ There were some nice showers during the day & at night there was one of the most splendid rainbows we ever saw. It looks like fine wet weather after that great dryness we have had for so many days._

---

485 Likely to be referring to Phillip.

18 July 1866

[Wed] Went to the Durrock Paddock with Nathanael & Teddy & cut down a red gum tree to be cut into posts for raising ~~up~~ the mill._ Harty came back from the Murray._ Magdalene is not getting better yet but rather worse._

18 July 1869*

[Sun] Started early for Nine Creeks, for the Communion. Adolf assisted Mr Ellerman, & preached in the evening. I went in for the sermon, leaving baby asleep at the manse. Had a bad sick ~~head ache~~.

18 July 1873

[New Fairfield, Canada] ~~Sat~~ F Sent off a letter to Roederer Neuwied requesting him to find me a suitable sister to be our servant._ (See copy book) Also a letter to Koch for Lense & chemicals._

19 July 1864

[Tue] Kept school again; had not had any all the last week. Nathanael also comes again to school_ After school I went to the sawpit having previously prepared a log of pine, for cutting boards; we found it rather hard to get into the way, but by & by we managed pretty fairly. We got rather tired about it._ B^r & S^{is} S[pieseke]. in the afternoon drove to Antwerp on a small visit; they found our boundary gate smashed, w^h had been done by a bullox dray coming from the lake_ Some of our Blacks Phillip, Daniel & Toney have gone to Antwerp helping to drive the sheep in._

19 July 1865

[Wed] Several showers during the day._ There arrived a Mr Swan editor of a Ballarat newspaper.[486]_ He wants to report about the Blacks & so he came up to see about our place._ He seemed to be satisfied with what he saw.[487]_

---

486 Referring to *The Ararat & Pleasant Creek Advertiser and Chronicle for the District of the Wimmera.*
487 Ref: 25 August 1865.

19 July 1867

[Fri] Wrote a letter of thanks to the Attorney-general[488] thanking for the interest that had been taken on behalf of the Blacks by including them into the Education bill[489] that was brought into Parliament by the royal Commission[490] inquiring into the Sp: signed the letter._ The Lambs were cut to-day & showed a per centage of 90 – very good.

19 July 1869*

Left the Manse & went on to Upper Regions. Took a walk with Mrs Edols while baby slept. Called to see a sick woman.

19 July 1873

[New Fairfield, Canada] Sat Been without a servant for 3 days, doing all the work myself. Milking the cows too; very hard work for the hands in the beginning._

20 July 1864

[Wed] Our people did not go to Antwerp to-day._ I went on with Matthew sawing boards & finished one log getting 7 very nice boards out of it._ B^r S[pieseke]. made a new gate for the one that had been broken & I helped him a little after I had done sawing._ Nathanael is getting on beautifully, he expressed a great desire to help me in sawing e.t.c._

20 July 1865

[Thu] Fetched the mail myself on Bobby._ Received letters from home: H^n Shawes & his sister E; Sist Harvey & daughter, & cousin Marie Hemm._ Sent of letters home; a small note to B^r Badham, aunt Kate & cousin Annie._ Heard of our B^r Dan's[491] engagement to a Miss Clarke._

---

[488] George Higinbotham (1826–1892), attorney-general from 27 June 1863 to 5 May 1868. Gwyneth Dow, 'Higinbotham, George (1826–1892)', *Australian Dictionary of Biography*, National Centre of Biography, The Australian National University, published first in hardcopy 1972, accessed 15 March 2022, adb.anu.edu.au/biography/higinbotham-george-3766/text5939.

[489] George Higinbotham established a Royal Commission in 1866 into the operation of the *Common Schools Act 1862* (Vic) which ultimately helped usher in free and secular education under the *Education Act 1872* (Vic). See: www.nma.gov.au/defining-moments/resources/free-education-introduced.

[490] *Report of the Royal Commission to Enquire into and Report upon the Operation of the System of Public Education* (Melbourne: State Parliament of Victoria, 1867).

[491] Daniel Hines, Polly's brother.

20 July 1869*

Returned from Upper Regions. Max gave us a fright when we started, reared tc. We called at the Manse with peacemaking intent, as a misunderstanding had arisen between them & M̲ͬ Edols.

20 July 1870*[492]

A party came from Mr. Edol's to fetch Miss Mayes[493] home, including Master Edols, two Misses Edols, Mr. Brooks their cousin, Miss Brooks, his sister, & Miss McPherson. They stayed dinner and then returned in the afternoon, taking Miss Mayes with them. Miss Brooks is a splendid player, & our little piano got well used that day, as all the party played in turn. Adolf too, of course.

21 July 1864

[Thu] I was plaistering inside of my dark room._ In the afternoon M̲ͬ Ellerman & Simpson paid us a small visit._

21 July 1865

[Fri] Finished the wings for the mill I had been at all the week._

21 July 1866

[Sat] Very hard frost during the last four nights, I think the hardest frost for many years as they say. It looks like a change to-day._ Went with the people to hunt ducks to the swamp 5 miles off._

21 July 1867

[Sun] <u>The flood came during the night</u> & a very nice & full river it was._

21 July 1869*

[Wed] M̲ͬ & M̲ͬˢ Spieseke went on a visit to Nine Creeks Manse & Upper Regions

---

492 This is not entered in the entry, rather in a letter to the Hines family from Polly. MAB, PP HJAH, 3 Letters, Polly Hartmann to Hines family, Ebenezer, 9 August 1870.
493 Miss Mayes was the governess at Edols, who had come for a short visit to the mission and ended up staying three weeks. MAB, PP HJAH, 3, Letters, Adolf Hartmann to Hines family, Ebenezer, 9 August 1870.

21 July 1870*494

We had a visit from the new doctor, who had been sent for Dick-a-dick, he being very ill. The other doctor had to leave, as he lived extravagantly, & could not make both ends meet. Dr. Lawton is a single man, not very young, but not such a one as I could confide in in a serious case. I therefore did not consult him, though for a month or more I had been troubled with my nervous weakness. It was proposed that I should to Melbourne and consult an experienced doctor, stopping there for a regular course of treatment, but happily for me on July 22nd my nervousness most unaccountable left me (I say happily, for from the state of the roads, I promised myself a fearful coach ride the first half of the journey).

22 July 1864

[Fri] Again at plaistering the dark room. Our bull calf was cut by the Blacks, & Toney took our young horse (a stallion) to Antwerp & Mr Ellerman cut it._ The Blacks played a great deal at marbles lately & especially to-day so we hinted to them that they might occupy their time a little better than that. S[pieseke]. worked in the garden almost all day._ We had a very misty morning, a fine day & rain in the evening._ The river hay fallen very much._

22 July 1866

[Sun] Some showers of rain nice pleasant weather

22 July 1867

[Mon] Went on a visit to Mr Scott with Polly & Nelly. As P[olly] had not been there for 2 ½ years we were very glad to go those lest they should think we did not care for their friendship._ The people began the putting up of the fence & there was a great deal of talking & arranging. 12 of the people accepted the job._ £6 was promised if finished in 4 weeks. £5 if more time was spent over it._

22 July 1869*

[Thu] Early this morning Magdalene departed after a lengthened & painful illness, We have to reason to hope she is now with her Saviour. When visited yesterday, she expressed her trust in Him, and said she was not afraid to die.

---

494 This is not entered in the entry, rather in a letter to the Hines family from Polly. MAB, PP HJAH, 3, Letters, Polly Hartmann to Hines family, Ebenezer, 9 August 1870.

23 July 1864*

[Sat] S[pieseke]'s birthday._ Polly & I last night agreed to sing a few verses for S in the morning before he got up. "Auf gib an deinem"[495] & Sei du ihm nur immer"[496] Well we got up in good time, but when we were going to commence singing a laughing fit came upon both of us, but we managed to sing the 2 verses._ Sis S. had baked a birthday cake for her husband._ I was engaged in my dark room all day stretching some strong canvas over the ceiling of it & pasting paper over it & wherever I thought dust might enter._ In the evening prepared my sermon for 9 creeks. The Whites from the Lake were here to dinner, on their way to Upper Regions. They invited us to visit them.

23 July 1867

[Tue] Asked M[r] Scott in the evening to present us with a few sheep. He consented, but said that it could not be immediately, but he would write to M[r] Sp: & inform him about it

23 July 1869*

This afternoon Magdalene was buried.

24 July 1864*

[Sun] At 8 a.m I started, accompanied by Matthew, for Upper Regions to preach there. I had a good attendance, & the Lord gave me words to speak to them. A very sad accident had happened to M[r] Edoll's oldest boy. He had been thrown from a horse, & so much injured that they thought he would not recover; he was insinsible for a good while, & D[r] Johnson was present for some days._ The D[r] declared him out of danger, & left the Monday morning I left._ In the evening I spoke about the words "Remember how thou hast received & heard & hold fast";[497] I was led to dwell strongly on the grace of God procuring Salvation for us, & that we are saved by simply believing it._ After service there was a little conversation about what I said_ At home we had a pleasant day. In the afternoon we had some nice singing of the simple pieces wh. the people know, such as "Here we suffer", "There is a happy land". &c. &c. Evening. Philip kept the meeting & made again a very nice prayer.

---

495   English translation: 'Give up on yours'.
496   English translation: 'Be you forever his'.
497   KJV. Revelations 3:3.

24 July 1865*

[Mon] Adolf started for Nine Creeks, but found his order at the blacksmith not yet executed. Mͬ Edolls was much troubled about the Land Act.[498]

24 July 1866

[Tue] Finished cutting the posts for heightening making the mill higher Nathanael helped me._ (There arose at dinner a controversy about the candidates for baptism; I had received some people for the instruction who came on their own accord & sat down. I spoke to them that came what this meeting meant & whether they would wished to come to Jesus & on their answering in the affirmative, I allowed them to stop with the others, considering them to be candidates for the time being, for I could not send them away, conscientiously, but considered myself bound to instruct them, praying the Lord that he would give them grace._ S[pieseke]. said these could not be candidates & yet he would not give me his plain opinion about what the qualifications of a candidate should be. Then the matter ended & we thought it best to write to the board[499] about it._

24 July 1867

[Wed] Returned from Scotts_ had a nice drive home although the roads were rather heavy

25 July 1864

[Mon] Bought 5 dozen of fishing hooks at Mͬ Lloyd's, then we drove to Mͬ Holts station to fetch some pigs that had been promised to us, but nobody was at home & so we could not get any. It was a very cold morning & showers of rain falling now & then._ Phillip went off on a Missionary tour to Lake Hindmarsch to speak to the Blacks & induce them to come back._ In the afternoon I commenced making the door to my darkroom. In the evening we had a thunderstorm & heavy rain.

---

498 The *Amending Land Act 1865* (Vic), was an amendment of the *Land Act 1862*, itself known as Duffy's Act, which had allowed for free selection before survey for the price of £1 per acre. What Mr Edol's concerns were are not noted. He had voiced his concern before Ref: 2 July 1865. See: ([186-?]). *The Land Act, 1862 and the Amending Land Act, 1865: together with the regulations and forms under the Act* (Melbourne: George Robertson), nla.gov.au/nla.obj-71931024.
499 The board he was referring to was the Mission Board of the Moravian Church in Herrnhut, Germany.

25 July 1865*

[Tue] A. returned from Nine Creeks.

[extract from Adolf's letter to the Hines][500] evening. I had Edward in, one of the candidates for baptism, & spoke to him. Whilst I questioned & taught him Ed was much affected. He could not answer for some time, but pointed to his hear said "he felt his heart sometimes so much, that he did not know what to do. We thought he meant bodily sickness, but found out that his heart was melted with the love of Jesus, the thought of which moved him to tears.

25 July 1866

[Wed] Several nice showers during the day. The people men & women are much engaged in gathering & making things for the Melbourne exhibition.[501] Polly & I are at it gathering a vocabulary of the native language to be sent in.[502]_

---

500 This letter, dated 19 August 1865, was transcribed by Bill Edwards in 1998 before the new ordering of the MAB, PP HJAH files.
501 The Ebenezer mission was asked to send something to the Melbourne Exhibition. Spieseke noted in July that he was not sure that they would be able to. The exhibition mentioned was the Intercolonial Exhibition of 1866–1867, which was established to prepare items for the Paris Exposition Universelle of 1867. The official catalogue records that in Class IV–Manufactures and Useful Arts under Section 14–Articles of Clothing, Lace, Embroidery, Specimens of Native Workmanship, the Central Board submitted objects. The following items numbered 93–125 were made by 'Aborigines at the Mission Station, Lake Hindmarsh, and were forwarded by the Rev. F.W. Spieseke'. They were: '93, 2 Double barbed Spears; 94, 2 Single barbed Spears; 95, 5 Smooth Spears; 96, 2 Waddy Shields; 97, 4 Instrument for Throwing the Spear (Karrick); 98, 2 Boomerangs; 99, 6 Waddies; 100 1 Opossum Rug, made by Nathaniel, Philip, and others; 101, 3 Kanneys; 102, 1 Necklace; 103, 1 Basket; 104, 2 Bags; 105, 1 Pinafore—made by Ruth; 106, 1 Child's Frock; 107, 1 Necklace; 108, 2 Bags; 109, 2 Nets for the Hair—Rebecca; 110, 1 Petticoat; 111, 1 Bonnet; 112, 1 Pincushion—Margaret Elliott; 113, 1 Frock; 114, 1 Collar and Cuffs; 115, 1 Pincushion—Rachael Pepper; 110, 1 Pinafore; 117, 1 Bag—Magdalene; 118, 1 Chemise—Topsy; 119, 1 Pinafore—Lilly; 120, 1 Pinafore—Elizabeth; 121, 1 Basket; 122, 1 Aboriginal Necklace; 123, 1 Aboriginal Apron—Old Jessie; 124, 1 Basket—Old Linna; 125, 1 Doubled-barbed Spear (Mongile)'. See: *Intercolonial Exhibition 1866: Official Catalogue: Victoria, New South Wales, Queensland, South Australia, Tasmania, New Zealand, Western Australia, Mauritius, New Caledonia, Batavia* (Melbourne: Printed for the Commissioners by Blundell and Ford, [1866?]), 28. See also: 'Melbourne. Intercolonial Exhibition of Australia 1866–67', *State Library of Victoria*, guides.slv.vic. gov.au/interexhib/1866to67 (accessed 5 July 2020); *Periodical Accounts* 26 (1866), 136–37; Penelope Edmonds, '"We Think That This Subject of the Native Races Should Be Thoroughly Gone Into at the Forthcoming Exhibition": The 1866–67 Intercolonial Exhibition', in *Seize the Day: Exhibitions, Australia and the World*, ed. Kate Darian-Smith, Richard Gillespie, Caroline Jordan and Elizabeth Willis (Melbourne: Monash University ePress, 2008), 4.1–4.16 (accessed 5 July 2020).
502 Redmond Barry, President of the Exhibition Commission, sent out a circular letter requesting, among other items, that people collect Aboriginal language for the exhibition. See: State Library of New South Wales, CY979, Miscellaneous papers relating to the Aborigines 1839–1871, Redmond Barry, letter regarding the Intercolonial Exhibition, Melbourne, 5 March 1866, as cited in Edmonds, '"We Think That This Subject"', 4.5.

25 July 1869*

[Sun] Esther's baby[503] was baptized by the name of Andrew. Adolf baptized it.

25 July 1870*[504]

Monday. We went to Nine Creeks for a little change. & spent the first evening at Mrs. Edols. & the next at Mrs. Ellermans's I was invited to come & stay a week or two with each which I intend to do if circumstances permit. I forgot to mention that on 23rd Margaret had a little son, her third.

26 July 1864

[Tue] Made my door to the dark room._ Rather a cool day & now & then a shower._ William Leach Esq departed at 10 p.m London

26 July 1865*

[Wed] Baptism of Edward.[505] See small book. Page. 141.

[extract from Adolf's letter to the Hines][506] Wednesday. Mr Ellerman from Antwerp & Rev Simpson from Horsham came to dinner. At about three the bell rang & the Blacks in holiday attire, obeyed the summons. I baptized Edward. The service was very impressive. The subject of my discourse was from Acts VIII 37 (If thou believest with all thy heart thou mayest be baptized). I myself as well as those present were much affected. Mr Simpson stayed with us. We had a prayer meeting in the evening with the Blacks, Br Sp, Mr Simpson, Nathaneal, Philip, and myself joined in prayer. "It was good for us to be there." We had a pleasant evening. Scripture questions over a cup of nice coffee.

---

503 Born Ref: 7 July 1869.
504 This is not entered in the entry, rather in a letter to the Hines family from Polly. MAB, PP HJAH, 3, Letters, Polly Hartmann to Hines family, Ebenezer, 9 August 1870.
505 Edward took the name James. Adolf baptised him. In a letter to the Hines family, Adolf speaks of Edward's emotive state that evening, writing 'he felt his heart sometimes so much, that he did not know what to do. We thought he meant bodily sickness, but found out that his heart was melted with the love of Jesus, the thought of which moved him with tears'. Of the baptism on the following day Adolf wrote that Mr Ellerman and the Rev. Simpson from Horsham were there, with 'the Blacks in holy attire'. MAB, PP HJAH, 3, Letters, Adolf Hartmann to Hines family, Ebenezer, 19 August 1865. See: *Periodical Accounts* 25 (1863), 509.
506 This letter dated 19 August 1865, was transcribed by Bill Edwards in 1998 before the new ordering of the MAB, PP HJAH files.

26 July 1866

[Thu] Some good showers through the day; ~~in the~~ towards evening there was a very fine rainbow & after that we had a very heavy shower

26 July 1868*

[Sun] M[r] Spieseke went to preach at 9 creeks. We commenced teaching the people to chant the Te deum.,[507] Mornington's chant.

26 July 1869*

Philip & Rebecca, & Dick[508] a dick & Amelia[509] went to the Lake, to hunt kangaroos & get opossum skins.

27 July 1865*

[Thu] Baptism of Sarah[510] & Mary,[511] and visit of M[r] Ellerman & family. See small book, Page 141-2. Timothy's dog, Spring, bit John Ellerman. M[r] Spieseke afterwards poisoned the dog.

[extract from Adolf's letter to the Hines][512] Philip kept the morning meeting in his own language – Text John III 36. Afterwards Mr Simpson heard my scholar read. About 11.30 am Mr & Mrs Ellerman, Mrs Westgarth (mother of Mrs E) their nephew, governess and 4 children, & another lady arrived. They brought with them some provisions – a roast goose, cake, mould of Maizena, jam, bread & milk. A little later we went to church. The two candidates Sarah and Mary appeared neatly dressed, Sarah in a

---

507 A religious chant composed in the fourth century. Translated by Martin Luther and used by various denominations and confessions.

508 Dick a Dick and Amelia (previously Kitty) were together. The missionaries speak of Dick a Dick, who would later become Paul at his baptism on Ref: 30 July 1870, and who died Ref: 3 September 1870. Not to be confused with the cricketer Dick a Dick/ Yanggendyinanyuk (c. 1834–1886) who toured England in March–October 1868. See: *Missionsblatt* 2 (1871), 34; *Periodical Accounts* 28 (1871), 44–45; Schneider, *Missionsarbeit der Brüdergemeine in Australien*, 162–64.

509 First Ref: 27 July 1868. Amelia was known as Kitty before her baptism. Was brought along with Diana to the mission by Spieseke in December 1867. She was the wife of Paul (formerly Dick-a-Dick). She died around the beginning of April 1871, leaving behind a daughter. Ref: 4 December 1867; *Periodical Accounts* 28 (1871), 126.

510 First Ref: 24 January 1865. Sarah, a house helper to the missionaries, took the name Martha. See: *Periodical Accounts* 25 (1863), 509. MAB, PP HJAH, 3, Letters, Adolf Hartmann to Hines family, Ebenezer, 19 August 1865.

511 Mary, a house helper aged 13, took the name Elizabeth. See also: *Periodical Accounts* 25 (1863), 509. MAB, PP HJAH, 3 Letters, Adolf Hartmann to Hines family, Ebenezer, 19 August 1865.

512 This letter dated 19 August 1865, was transcribed by Bill Edwards in 1998 before the new ordering of the MAB, PP HJAH files.

dark dress, a present of Mrs Ellerman, Mary in a light print, presented by Miss Donovan. Both had white cloaks, & white nets tied with ribbons – They appeared very attractive and thoughtful. Mr Simspon performed the ceremony. He gave a most simple practical address on Acts XI "The first named Christians." He spoke of the name Christian, why it was given, what a read Christian is, & does, & what a precious thing it is to be a Christian.

27 July 1867*

[Sat] Little & his two wives came: promise to stay a while. Judy & Charlotte came to school; seem anxious to learn. Guary has been teaching them a little in the bush. A. finished planting the young trees below the tank.

27 July 1868*

[Mon] We heard today that (Kitty) Amelia[513] had gone off from Lochiel with her cousin Judy & Little.[514] She had asked permission a few days previously to go for a holiday to get beer (honeysuckle) & now took this chance to escape from the restriction she was necessarily under here.

27 July 1869*

~~Returned this morning from Upper Regions.~~

Adolf & I made sausages from the pig killed yesterday.

28 July 1864*

I pasted some odd pictures into an old book, which when filled will make a tolerably respectable scrap-book, for the amusement of the blacks &c.

28 July 1865

[Fri] Matthew beat his wife Margaret (the first time) & it seems without any provocation on her part. S[pieseke] & I went to his hut in the evening & talked to him about it._ At first he did not seem to take it in, but after a while he took it in, saying that since he had gone to the Lake, he had got into a bad way of thinking about Margaret. Well he got reconciled to her then._

---

513 Kitty was brought back by Spieseke from a journey west in November–December 1867. Prev. Ref: 4 December 1867.
514 Judy was one of Little's two wives, the other being Charlotte.

28 July 1869*

[Wed] M̃r & M̃rs Spieseke & two children went on a visit to Nine Creeks Manse & Upper Regions.

29 July 1864*

[Fri] We finished preparing our pictures for hanging up, having pasted a strip of black paper round the edge to represent a frame. We fastened up 8 in our room, & find it a great improvement, effected without any expense of money, & very little of labour or time. M̃r Ellermann came to dinner. My flower seeds not having come up, I set more, but not so deep as before.

29 July 1865

[Sat] S[pieseke]. & family went to Antwerp on a small visit; came back in the evening & with them M̃r Ellerman in his new buggy bringing M̃rs Westgarth & Miss Fraser to stay over Sunday._ Lake Lanke whilst working in the toolshop came to me; saying he felt _so_ happy to-day, he had had a dream & was walking in a great light._

29 July 1869*

[Thu] Early this morning Magdalene departed, as we trust to be with her Saviour. When visited yesterday when she expressed her trust in Him, & said she was not afraid to die.

30 July 1864*

[Sat] Was engaged in finishing the interior arrangements of my dark room, making shelves, a watertank etc. I hope soon to be able to commence operations._ M̃r S[pieseke]. & family went off to day to see M̃r Scott, Rebecca going with them. In the evening a Black (long Charley) from the Murray came here on a visit He had been the companion of a gentleman travelling to Horsham, & so he came up to see us._ Yesterday Phillip shot 2 wood ducks & gave them to me. As Rebecca, our cook was away, I had to do all the cooking & washing of. Whilst cooking, I saw a tarantula[515] creeping out of a piece of hollow wood on the fire. I killed it at once with a spade that stood near.

---

515 Australian tarantula species are not found in the Wimmera.

30 July 1866

[Mon] Sent off the sheet containing the language of the Blacks of this district which Polly & I had been at, al the past week to collect.[516] We had Nathanael Philip & Rebecca to give us the words. The bellows I commenced making last Friday I finished to day, by pasting paper on the sides to make it sufficiently stiff so that the wind cannot press them out._ The people are very busy getting the things ready for the Exhibition._

30 July 1867*

[Tue] Mr Spieseke took the girls for a trip to Lochiel in the spring-cart. I took my first lesson in basket making from Rebecca.[517]

30 July 1870*[518]

Dick-a-Dick worse than ever, but rejoicing in hope of the glory of God. It was decided to baptize him, as we had reason to believe his repentance & faith to be genuine. This was performed on his sick bed, in presence of many of the people. He was named Paul.

31 July 1865

[Mon] As it was desirable that the fence towards our gate should be made cattle proof, by topping it, & as all the people were wanted to do it quickly, the school will be dropped for this week_ Drove Miss Fraser to Antwerp & brought Eliza Ellerman back to stay with her grand mother

31 July 1866

[Tue] Agreed to make a little shed behind the toolshop, for smithing purposes, so in the later part of the afternoon I went out & cut 4 posts

---

516 These word lists were collected for the Intercolonial Exhibition in Melbourne of 1866–67, Ref: 25 July 1866.
517 Rebecca, formerly Jessie, was Phillips's wife. Ref: 8 May 1864.
518 This is not a diary entry, rather part of a letter from Polly in diary style to her parents. MAB, PP HJAH, 3, Letters, Polly Hartmann to Hines family, 9 August 1870.

31 July 1867*

[Wed] M[r]Spieseke & the girls returned late in the evening. We heard through the "Australischen Christenbote"[519] that the Brethen[520] in S. Aust.[521] have obtained a grant of land from the Gov[t] of 100 sq. miles, & also the protection of a police-station at Kopperamana.

31 July 1870*[522]

A baptism in the church of two of the candidates, whom we have hope that they will, by God's grace, walk as consistent Christians. These were Charley & Maggie, a middle aged couple, who are now called Walter & Janet.

August

1 August 1864

[Mon] Made some more little things for my dark room, such as plate-holders for cleaning them, & some boxes to keep the clean glasses._ It was raining almost all day._ Phillip helped Mr Ellerman getting his horses._ In the evening after the meeting, w[h] Nathaniel kept Mr Forenzo made his appearance saying that he was asked by M[r] S[pieseke]. to come to us. We found it somewhat awkward, but had to make (eine gute Miene zum bösen Spiel[523])._

1 August 1865

[Tue] Getting things ready for the Tannin process to try again whether it will do or not.

1 August 1866

[Wed] Fetched in the logs I cut yesterday, barked them myself & augured them took me all day._

---

519 The *Australischen Chistenbote* [Australian Christian messenger] was a German-language Lutheran newspaper founded by Rev. Matthias Goethe in Melbourne. See: Tarnay, 'Goethe, Matthias (1827–1876)'.
520 H Walder, CW Kramer, and G Meissel at Lake Kopperamana.
521 South Australia.
522 This is not a diary entry, rather part of a letter from Polly in diary style to her parents. MAB, PP HJAH, 3, Letters, Polly Hartmann to Hines family, 9 August 1870.
523 English translation: 'To put on a brave face'.

1 August 1867*

[Thu] A[dolf]. macadamized[524] our garden walk. Twenty-five more sheep arrived to day, the gift of M[r] Charles Wilson. M[r] Spieseke has summoned M[r] Cassell[525] for giving drink to the Blacks. Little & his two wives[526] are gone to Lochiel, but promise to return soon.

2 August 1864

[Tue] A nice clear day._ Made a footstool for Polly._ At 8 p.m. S returned from M[r] Scott._ My gun is made use of frequently by our people for shooting ducks, to night Nathanael had a try of it but got nothing._ The river begins to rise again in consequence of the rain we had._

2 August 1865

[Wed] A wet day just managed to drive M[rs] Westgarth & Eliza to Antwerp before it began to rain heavily. Some more nice showers during the day._

2 August 1866

[Thu] Finished the logs to-day dug 4 holes & put 2 of the posts in_

2 August 1867*

[Fri] Adolf started to-day for Horsham, going only as far as Upper Regions to-day.

3 August 1865

[Thu] There was a great argument with the people this morning: it was chiefly about poisoning dogs & it arose from S[plieseke] poisoning Timothy's dog[527] for biting John Ellerman._ A good pretext for poisoning, but I dont think it was right as the dog rushed out of Timothy's miami._ Well there was a great deal of talking this & that way & it was finally agreed to some extent that the dogs should be tied & should not be poisoned in the means, but that nobody should complain if his dog running about loose was poisoned._

---

524 A road made by compacting small broken stones into a solid mass.
525 Ref: 7 August 1867.
526 Little's wives, Judy and Charlotte.
527 The dog was called Spring Ref: 27 July 1865.

There came a letter for Polly from M̲r̲s̲ Stedman containing a nice little present. for _

3 August 1867

[Sat] Managed to get to Langland's store in good time to buy all the things I wanted & then to fasten the heavy pipings for our new pup underneath the box of our spring cart on the axel tree, & got to Horsham about 7 o clock Well received of course._

3 August 1868*

[Sun] A disturbance in consequence of drink given by a white traveller[528] to Prince Albert[529] & Peter. M̲r̲ Sp. & A[dolf]. went down & got proof. The case will be brought before the court in Nine Creeks.[530]

4 August 1865

[Fri] Was engaged to prepare my first plates for the Tannin process. got 8 carte de visite size done to have a try._

4 August 1867

[Sun] Rode to Horsham with M̲r̲ C[harles] Wilson attended the morning service, & then asked by M̲r̲ Simpson to preach in the evening, I did so._ M̲r̲s̲ S[impson]: very sick called me in, when I read & prayed with her & had some conversation about different matters._

5 August 1864

[Fri] Swept our chimney, getting up to the top of the roof & brushing the soot down with the end of young green pine tree._

5 August 1865

[Sat] Had a try with the tannin plates I prepared, but it was no go I could not get a picture; the plates seemed to be perfectly insensible. I exposed more than ½ hour & used very strong developers but got no pictures out, dont know either what it may be._

---

528 William Fisher Ref: 2 September 1868.
529 Usually referred to as Albert.
530 Ref: 2 September 1868.

5 August 1866

[Sun] Agreed that I should speak the baptized people that were nonecomunicants, & admit them if nothing was in the way._ Spoke to James & ~~Kate~~ Ruth_ Amos & Magdalene._ The conversation I had with them led me to invite them to join us in partaking of the Lord supper.

5 August 1867

[Mon] Left Walmar at ¼ to 10 & got to Edol's at 6 p.m._

5 August 1870*[531]

The River which was already full, rose last night 2 or 3 feet.

6 August 1864

[Sat] To-day at last I got my photographic affairs so far in order that I could commence operation, but lo & behold I met with a complete failure._ All day I worked away but produced nothing, I tried & tried again but could not discover where the mistake was, till at last I found out in the evening that it was the candle light. So I laboured a whole day for nothing. Satisfactory after all to find out this mistake._ I must then have yellow glass._ Ellerman's family came in the morning & will stay over Sunday._ We got letters to-day from Mr Chase & from our uncle Hartig. The former communicated to us that Margaret[532] is willing to marry Matthew. And that he Mr Chase was on the way to our place with Margaret, & that he would be with her in Horsham the day before this. Now all this came rather suddenly. And it required some thinking on our part how to arrange matters before Matthew had finished his hut. Well M^r Sp[ieseke]: made Matt^h acquainted with it, he seemed to like it very much as well he might. ~~M^r~~ S. will go on Monday to Horsham to meet Mr Chase & Margaret & get them up here, at the same time trying to get something for the couple to be married. May our Saviour who made this thing to come to pass bless this union in time to come._

---

531 This is not a diary entry, rather part of a letter from Polly in diary style to her parents. MAB, PP HJAH, 3, Letters, Polly Hartmann to Hines family, 9 August 1870.
532 Prev. Ref: 25 June 1864.

6 August 1865

[Sun] Felt much encouraged the meeting to speak to the blacks about the text The Lord Jesus Christ shall confirm you unto the end, that ye may be blameless in the day of our Lord Jesus Christ._ There was good attention paid & Richard seemed to get an impression of the Saviours love

6 August 1866

[Mon] A disturbance with Albert._ Some of the Slates were broken so I asked who had done it & as nobody came forward, I questioned Archie afterwards who told me that A[lbert]. had done it; he had seen him breaking one._ Questioned Albert about it he denied it & rushed at Archie beating him, so I pulled him away & gave him a box on the ear. Of course he went away in great anger to the camp. S. & I afterwards went there & got out that Albert had broken one of the slates. & that Dicky had broken 2 more

6 August 1867

[Tues] Got back to our place at 3 p.m. Bobby pulling the heavy load very nicely from Horsham._

7 August 1864*

[Sun] Adolf went to Antwerp at 10 a.m. to keep the service for the men. Mrs Ellermann & family being here, we had a larger congregation than usual. A[dolf]. returned to dinner, & in the afternoon B^r S[pieseke]. proposed that he should go to Horsham, to wh[ich]. A. agreed. M^{rs} E[llerman]. & I went a walk with the children.

7 August 1865

[Mon] Looked after the people how they were getting on (slow work with them) In the afternoon I went again there, took some of the boys with me to get a sheep. Whilst at it S^p came back from the 9 creeks & so we put the sheep into the cart. S^p brought part of the iron work for the windmill A rather warm day so much so that the scents begin to come out of the ground again._

7 August 1867

[Wed] Sp with Philip & Timothy went to the nine Creeks to have the case brought before the court about M‍ʳ Cassel selling grog to the Blacks[533] As was to be expected the f case was lost to us the evidence not being strong enough. D‍ʳ Pervis came here to look at Ruth who is very sick;[534] charged £8.15ˢ. Went to see the people at fence._

7 August 1870*[535]

Margaret's baby was baptized, & called Charles Arthur.[536] Four baptized within 8 days

8 August 1864*

[Mon] We rose before five. A[dolf]. started at 6-30. for Horsham. At 11-30 a.m. M‍ʳ Ellermann returned from M‍ʳ Elgin, & then the whole family took their departure. M‍ʳ White came to a late dinner. I had almost lost my voice from a violent cold. M‍ʳˢ S[pieseke]. sat with me in the evening. Matthew was at work very early this morning, & continued to saw hard the whole day. The old mare went pretty well as far as 9 creeks, to which place I got at 9 ½ a.m._ M‍ʳ Edol's boy I found to have quite recovered from his fall (see 24ᵗʰ of July 1864) I got much frightened by Miss Donnovan about the camels I had to pass on my way to Horsham. (My adventure in this respect._ The old mare would not run a bit, so I got to Horsham just about sun set_ put up my horse & gig at the inn, but lodged at M‍ʳ Simpsons, (he being not at home) M‍ʳ Chase & his comᵖ were not come, but there were letters there, telling he would come on W‍ᵉᵈ next._ (Amusing parrot at M‍ʳ Langlands)._

8 August 1865

[Tue] Went after school to help some of our people putting up a little bit of fence at the upper & lower gate, so as to keep the sheep from going out if the gates should be left open._ Managed to finish both gates._ It is very dry again & so Sᵖ & myself are carrying water for our garden._

---

533 Prev. Ref: 1 August 1867, previously written Cassell.
534 She died Ref: 15 November 1867.
535 This is not a diary entry, rather part of a letter from Polly in diary style to her parents. MAB, PP HJAH, 3, Letters, Polly Hartmann to Hines family, 9 August 1870.
536 Born on 23 July 1870. Ref: 25 July 1870.

8 August 1870*537

We had an unexpected visit from Mr. Robertson, minister at Horsham. He stayed till this morning [9 August]. He would just manage to cross a branch of the river which shuts us in on an island. The river is on two sides of us. & the creek. as it is called, on the other two. The river has risen on an average 1 foot a day since the 5th, & is still rising, so that any communication with world will have to be carried on by boat. Still we have plenty of room to move about, our island being some 3 or 4 square miles in extent. Our horse paddock is under water, & the small paddock in which our house stands partly so. Still it is not so high by 2 feet as the flood of 1867, nor by 4 feet as the flood of 1863.538

Before it reaches our doorstep it must rise fully 10 feet, a height never known to have been reached. But still it rains. Scarcely a day without rain. I shall not be able to pay my visit next week, as intended.

9 August 1864*

[Tues] Busy day. Washing, scrubbing, &c. Blacks returned. Old Jenny, Joe & Mary, & Susan, & another black came whom we have not before seen, named Wimmera Charley. Joe's Mary brought us swan eggs & a grass basket. Br S[pieseke]. very poorly. Philip kept the meeting. I witnessed an interesting scene, the affectionate meeting of Old Jenny & her pickaniney539 Mary. For particulars see small book_ on the characteristics of the blacks. Drove Mrs Simpson & children to Walmar & spent a few pleasant hours there. What a beautiful driving in that carriage over the crab holes compared to ours! On coming back to Horsham Manse Mr Ellerman had arrived to fetch his new governess, but going to the post-office with him, he found a letter there telling him that she was not coming. I also got a letter from Mr Chase informing me & Mr Chase S. about his delay. I took the letter I had written to S. & Polly on Monday evening back again & gave it to Mr Ellerman to take up to our place._ We have had a pleasant evening at the manse_ Mr Ellerman slept with me_ In the afternoon I was at Mr Bowden's & looked about his garden etc, he offered me some rabits.

---

537 This is not a diary entry, rather part of a letter from Polly in diary style to her parents. MAB, PP HJAH, 3, Letters, Polly Hartmann to Hines family, 9 August 1870.
538 The Hartmanns were not in Australia in 1863.
539 Geographically broadly used nineteenth-century term for a 'black child', derogatory in contemporaneous usage.

10 August 1864

[Wed] M͟r Ellerman after much thinking made up his mind to stop & see M͟r Chase arrive._ There was a little rain falling._ Well M͟r Chase & his Com͟p came pretty punctually too._ It was a most interesting evening at the manse. M͟r Chase kept the evening prayer._ Several schemes were laid down as to how to get to Walmar, & at last it was settled that I should go with M͟r Chase & Margaret to Walmar to-morrow, leave W[almer]. on Friday early & try to get to our place before night, so as to celebrate acco͟rd to M͟r Chase's proposal the anniversary of Nathanael's baptism on the next day Aug the 13th [540] & also the Lord's supper. Polly & I wanted to call to mind also that I received my call to Australia.

10 August 1865

[Thu] Finished the night-stool I commenced yesterday, rather a useful article.

10 August 1866

[Fri] Drove to the 9 creeks to fetch my box of chemicals, to by some iron from the blacksmith, and sundry other things from the store._ Among others I got me a pair of trousers & a coat._ The new screwmaker had also arrived, rather an expensive article £2.12.

11 August 1864

[Thu] At 11 a.m. I packed our gig having received very nice presents for Margaret & Matthew & drove Margaret to M͟r Wilson's at Walmar, & as the road was so bad that you could not go on it at all, we drove straight over the crab-holes; dreadful motion that!_ Stopped at Walmar over night & was as usually received very cordially._

11 August 1865

[Fri] Some part of the iron work not being made according to my order I sent Matthew ~~with the~~ to take the things again to the Blacksmith._ Managed during the day to fasten the 2 wings together & put the iron rod through. Matthew came back late at night & brought the iron with him; now made to my satisfaction._

---

540 Nathaniel Pepper was baptised on 12 August 1860.

11 August 1866

[Sat] Was all the week at it building a little log building behind the cartshed to be used for smithing purposes._

11 August 1868

[Tues] Mʳ Ellerman came from Antwerp to Breakfast. He likes Carngham⁵⁴¹ very much, but has not yet got a call.

12 August 1864

[Fri] Left ~~Edol's~~ ₍Walmar₎ early in the morning intending to make my way home with Mʳ Chase & Margaret, but somehow leaving Mʳ Edol's I took a wrong way & got to Mʳ Edol's woolshed instead of getting towards the mission station. Well it was rather late to go back ~~again~~ to Edol's & go on to our place the same day because our poor mare was very tired already, & who knows, what might have happened on the way: Well I took it as a providential hint not to go on but to stop at Mʳ Edol's, although we had had great difficulty just before to get off. I was somewhat vexed about my mistake._

12 August 1865

[Sat] Put the wings of the wind-mill up, & as there was a little wind blowing we let it go, & it went well._ Somehow felt pleased about it as it was not a failure._

12 August 1867

[Mon] As Ruth has to have vapour bath I made ~~for~~ a steaming apparatus, wʰ⁽ⁱᶜʰ⁾ seems to answer very well._

12 August 1868

---

541 Ref: 11 July 1868.

13 August[542] 1864

[Sat] At 11 a.m. I returned from Horsham with Mr Chasse & Margaret, richly laden with presents for Margaret & Matthew. They had been hard at work during my absence to get Matthew's house into an inhabitable state; now it looks very nice already & may our Saviour grant to the couple his blessing & his grace that they be happy together & prosper._ In the evening we celebrated the Lords supper, Mr Chase & Mr Ellerman partaking of the same with us_ It was a blest opportunity._

13 August 1865

[Sun] There was a love-feast in the afternoon to w^h we invited all the Candidates for baptism so that we had a very nice assembly about 30 in all. _ I kept the love feast_ In the evening we had the Lords supper w^h I kept; Mr H^{or} Ellerman joined us._ There were some showers of rain during the day._

13 August 1866

[Mon] The Lords supper which I kept._ Jacky Lilly & Brown were baptized The names they chose for themselves Stephen Lydia Samuel._ I kept the baptism at 3 p.m._ Sp[ieseke] kept the love feast at 5 p.m. and I the Lords

13 August 1868*

[Thu] Had the lovefeast as usual, although many people away. Adolf kept the lovefeast, & B^r S. the Communion in the evening.

14 August[543] 1863

Sent off the letter containing the acceptance of the call I received yesterday (SB. 74)[544] (copy of the letter to be found in the small book.) My call was given out in the evening in the liturgy; the hymn 887.1, was sung._

---

542 Important date in Moravian Calendar. The 13 August 1727 is referred to as the spiritual 'birthday' of the Church as a spiritual awakening occurred in the congregation in Berthelsdorf, near Herrnhut, Germany, on this day.
543 Actual beginning of the diary.
544 Small Book, p 74, not extant.

14 August 1864

[Sun] M̲ʳ̲ Chase rode ~~M~~ with M̲ʳ̲ Ellerman to 9 Creeks to preach there, & S[pieseke]. went to Antwerp to do the same. S. came back rather late & informed us next morning that M̲ʳ̲ Chase would go with M̲ʳ̲ E. to the lake

14 August 1865

[Mon] Sp drafted out some of the old sheep & put them into this paddock <u>About 9 a m the flood came</u>. There was a fog in the morning & we had a few little showers during the day._ I got the net ready wʰ Polly had made to catch some fish._ Lanke is very sick & we do not think that he will live long; his lungs are much affected & he can hardly breathe. One thing, though, affords us joy, he is resigned to his Saviours will; he knows in whom he believes._

14 August 1866

[Tues] Shifted the gate of the middle road to the Durrock paddock a little higher up towards the upper gate to have a drier thorough fare._ The people commenced this business & I went to them after dinner & helped them finishing it._ Kept for the first time, the school in the evening, people seemed to like it.[545]_

15 August 1864

[Mon] Sawed boards with Matthew & managed them much better than last time. S[pieseke]. was at it making a bedstead for the new couple._ We think to get the hut into a decent state by Thursday next, wʰ has been fixed to be the wedding-day of M. & M._ We are much pleased with Margaret, she is a cheerful girl, & commences very nicely._

15 August 1865

[Tue] Lanke[546] died this morning about 7_ As nobody called either Sᵖ or myself we could not witness his last moments, but we felt much assured not only by previous conversations we had with him, ~~I~~ ᵇᵘᵗ also by the accounts we received from others of his state of mind during the night ᵗʰᵃᵗ ʰᵉ ʰᵃᵈ ᶠᵒᵘⁿᵈ

---

545 This was an experiment to hold the school at night for the boys and men three day a week, so that they were free to hunt, fish and work during the daylight hours. See: *Periodical Accounts* 26 (1866), 137.
546 Also written Lanky.

the Saviour._ There was great lamentation for him_ ~~He~~ Lanke is to buried behind the chapel & so the people made the grave for him._ The f river rose considerably._ Worked a little at the mill making ready for putting up._

15 August 1866

[Thu] <u>Nancy died this afternoon</u> Not quite without hope as we think._ I have been busy these 2 last days in putting up the new iron piping for our pump._

15 August 1868*

Two Murray blacks came, & brought grog, wh. Mr Spieseke took away & then ordered them to leave the place. Mary quarrelled with Lizzie for telling.

15 August 1870*

Mr Robertson paid us a visit; stayed all night.

16 August 1864*

[Tue] S[pieseke]. made a table for Matthew out of the boards I cut with M[atthew]. yesterday I was engaged in M.'s hut covering the inside with sacking w^h Polly, Margaret & Rachel had sown together; these sackings are to be white-washed. Phillip came back who had been to Mr Holts station to see some Blacks there, they will come in some time he says._ Mr Chase also came back but went to Antwerp again in the evening to baptize the child of the overseer there, S. went with him & I kept the meeting for him._ I succeeded also to make some yellow paper, w^h stretched over a pane of glass answers for yellow glass in my dark room & found it to answer very nicely. S. & Mr Chase came back on the evening rather late.

~~P~~ I made a wedding-cake for Margaret. M & M went to Antwerp together.

16 August 1865*

[Wed] We intended going to Antwerp for dinner: dressed, & had the horse put in, but it commenced raining so fast that we were obliged to give up the idea of going for that day.

16 August 1867

[Fri] Left with Polly & Nelly for the West Wimmera, partly to assist Mr Ellerman in the approaching communion at the manse on Sunday next, partly to go myself as far as Mr Mc Clellan's to see the Blacks & persuade them to come here, & partly to see some of the friends round about._ To-day we went as far as Nhill, & stayed at Mr McDonnald's.

17 August 1864*

[Wed]. A[dolf]. was busy with the hut, nailing on sacking & whitewashing it. Margaret made a mattress. I made curtains.

17 August 1865

[Tuesday] Lanky was buried this afternoon at 3 o'clock. Mr. Ellerman came just at the time, & stayed to the funeral. All the blacks, as well as ourselves assembled at the grave. A[dolf]. spoke on John XI 25. 26[547] & then read the Burial Liturgy. All were attentive & still. To our surprise the blacks did not make their usual loud lamentations at the grave. They were attentive & still.

17 August 1866

[Sat] Finished the smithing shop & put up the bellows._

17 August 1867*

Drove to the manse, were very cordially received, & also made very comfortable. Miss White[548] a pretty fair piano player._

17 August 1868

Had a children's lovefest for the first time at Ebenezer. Adolf kept it. Present Mrs. Spieseke's 4, our Nelly, Margaret's two, & Ida[549] & Augusta.[550]

---

547 KJV. John 11:25, 'Jesus said unto her, I am the resurrection, and the life: he that believeth in me, though he were dead, yet shall he live; 26. And whosoever liveth and believeth in me shall never die. Believest thou this?'
548 Miss White, governess at the manse in Dimboola (Nine Creeks) Ref: 3 January 1868.
549 First Ref. Ida was referred to as being 16 years old around 1870. See: Smyth, *The Aborigines of Victoria*, 2.
550 First Ref.

17 August 1870*

Present at Children's lovefeast 27 children, 5 mothers, ~~to~~ 2 nurses: including ourselves 38 persons. The children repeated verses & texts in the afternoon lovefeast.[551]

18 August 1864*

[Thu] The morning was passed in finishing the hut, & making preparations for the wedding.[552] This should have been at 3 o'clock, but as the Ellerman family came late, we could not have it till nearly 5. It was a happy occasion. See account in smaller book. Page_ We posted our English letters, & received others from home.

18 August 1867

[Sun] Communion day at the Manse. About 50 people attended & it was an opportunity of much joy & blessing we believe._ A nephew of Mr Mc Clellan riding back to his home to-day about 30 miles I took the opportunity to go with him especially as he made a short cut accross the country._ We arrived at M^r M^c C's about 9 p.m. in the dark. Felt somewhat tired after the long ride.

18 August 1868*

[Tue] ~~We have had~~ A kind of influenza is now going through the place. Mrs Spieseke, Polly, some of the children, & several blacks are poorly with it. Nelly's turned to croup this evening_ a bad attack.

---

[551] MAB, PP HJAH, 10, Diary written by Adolph Hartmann, 148, provides more information on this lovefeast: '1870 Our first children's festival at Ebenezer. Formerly the children had always had their festival with ours on 13th Aug^st there being only so few. But, there being a larger number this year we kept their festival. Children's meeting at 9 a.m. Then a little preparing of verses: and at 3.30 p.m. Lovefeast for children mothers & nurses. The children numbered 27 of whom 2 were ours: 5 Mr. Spieseke's; 11 black girls ^& 2 boys under our care, 7 infants belonging to some of our people; all boys. Besides there came 5 mothers & 2 nurses, which, with ourselves made a congregation of ~~42~~ 38.

First we ~~had~~ sang a few verses, then a short address from A. on the duties of children to parents & teachers. Afterwards a story told by Mr. Spieseke about the children of Nauenbry. Then several more verses. After which, each child old enough repeated a text or hymn, a new experience for them. The whole was then closed with another hymn.'

[552] Wedding of Margaret and Matthew (previously known as Liberty).

19 August 1864*

[Fri] Mʳ Ellerman came over early. We had prayer together just before the departure (at 11 a.m.) of Bʳ Spieseke & Mʳ Chase for Horsham. We were truly sorry to part with Mr Chase, whose visit was a real treat to us all. Adolf had taken a likeness of him. Mʳ Chase took with him the ~~likeness~~ photograph of the wedding party to Melbourne. He will get prints taken from it.

19 August 1867

[Mon] All the day at Mʳ Mᶜ Clellan's. Had a regular good talk with him about the Blacks, & of course could not agree with his having rations as the Blacks would not be much bettered by it; for Mʳ Mᶜ C could not spend any of his time ~~up~~ to give the Blacks some moral training & teaching.

19 August 1869*

[Thu] Government stores arrived late. Adolf had to see them unloaded the same night. Provided by Langlands Blankets &c also from Melbourne.

19 August 1870*

Mʳ Ellerman came & spent the evening.

20 August 1864

[Sat] Quiet day. River higher than ever.

20 August 1867

[Tue] Rode back to Nhiel 37 miles, Bobby doing it all very nicely._ Stopping at Ryans for dinner._ Found Polly & Nelly all right at Mʳ Mᶜ Donalds

21 August 1864

[Sun] Just at the commencement of the morning service 9 travellers came to our place & they all attended our meeting & after the meeting I spoke to them about the salvation of their souls reminding them there was no time to be lost. We gave them 3 testaments & an old textbook & then ferried them accross the river._ At about 12 Mʳ Lloyd from the 9 creeks came with his carriage bringing a Lady (Miss Gollan) who was on her way to Mʳ White's to be the governess there. She stopped with us waiting for Mʳ White to fetch her_

21 August 1865

[Mon] A high wind arose blowing from the north, so that we expected rain. & there came some, too, in the afternoon but not much._ We killed the other pig, Philip helping me._ I keep my class with the candidates for baptism on [Mon] & [Thu]; the Candidates at present are; Mark; Richard; Brown, Dicky, Albert, Napoleon,_ Kitty, Lily, & Susan._ The people prepared some places for melons, on the other side of the river in the old sheep yard, & on this side in the cultivation paddock, & S^{p[ieseke]} set some seeds._ There was again a most splendid rainbow perfect in every way._

21 August 1867

[Wed] Drove from Nhiel to Lorquin[553] Mr Hugh Campbells[554] place, & stayed there over night. Mrs Campbell presented us with a cot, wh we will try to fetch.

21 August 1868

[Fri] The new minister of Horsham Mr Robertson arrived here in the evening & stayed over night.

22 August 1864

[Mon] After a break of a fortnight I commenced school again._ This break was caused by by going to fetch Margaret from Horsham, and also by Mr Chase coming he, & my helping Matthew get his hut ready._ After school I went with the people fetching wood._ In the afternoon Mr White came fetching his governess.[555]_

---

553 Lorquon, 22 kilometres north-east of Nhill, a pastoral run.
554 Hugh Campbell was a manager of the Lorquon run. A copy of his diary is held at the Dimboola and District Historical Society Archive. The diary records information from a period prior to the arrival of the Hartmanns, covering the period from October 1863 to February 1864. In the diary there are references to Aboriginal people such as Boney, Charley Charley, Billy, King John and Kitty. The Aboriginal people on the station mixed with the numerous Chinese shepherds of the station. In December 1863 the station was running some 11,500 sheep. Campbell subsequently moved to New Zealand. See: DDHS, The Lorquon Diary of Hugh Campbell; MDN Campbell, 'Campbell, Hugh McLean 1875–1951', *Dictionary of New Zealand Biography*, updated 22 June 2007, teara.govt.nz/en/biographies/4c3/campbell-hugh-mclean.
555 Miss Gollan Ref: 21 August 1864.

22 August 1865

[Tue] Cut the pig in the morning & salted it, Then I made a kind of squirt to fill the sausages with more ease._ In the afternoon we made the sausages quite a successful affair this time. Felt rather tired at night.

22 August 1866

[Wed] Home letters sent off to Badham & (one to mother for her birthday w^h Polly forgot to put into the envelope so it will have to go next time)_ On Monday I made a heap of dried gum wood to burn charcoal._ Rather a troublesome affair. Made it beyond the second creek, had to run very often to see how it was getting on & could therefore not do much these 3 days, to day I covered up the heap well._ Sp[ieseke] got letters from Hagenauer & from Mr Macredie.[556] The former seems to be in trouble no money forth coming & Mr Green[557] seems to draw away the Blacks from his place_ M^r M tells S. that the Board had nothing to do with the management of the sheep neither did any body object to the way in w^h the thing had been carried on ~~hitt~~ hitherto. M^r M says he wishes we could keep as many sheep again._ The Murray Blacks intend leaving as we cannot supply them with rations: some of them found fault with Matthew marrying Margaret saying that she was his sister;[558] rather a bold assertion!_ Magdalene's desease seems to be a consumption of the bowels, as far as we can make it out; she is very weak & reduced, but has a pretty fair appetite._

22 August 1867

[Thu] Got back to our place about 5 p.m. after a pleasant drive from Mr March & Stuarts. Picked up in the mallee some nice flowers & a creeper w^h I planted out into our garden._ Mr Sp: was somewhat in trouble because the Richardson Blacks had come back & Minnie & Bobby have been in the camp with them for some days, & it is to be feared that they might take them away. Dicky has come back too._

---

556 At Morton Plain.
557 John Green, manager of the Aboriginal Reserve Coranderrk in Gippsland, who also employed by the BPA (from 1860 to 1869 the Central Board Appointed to Watch Over the Interests of Aborigines) to examine Aboriginal missions and reserves in the Colony of Victoria. For more on Green and Coranderrk see: Diane Barwick, *Rebellion at Coranderrk*, Aboriginal History Monograph 5 (Department of History, ANU: Canberra, 1998).
558 In his speech to the Victorian Association in Aid of the Moravian Mission to the Aborigines of Australia in September 1867, Spieseke spoke about the marriage customs of the Aboriginal people (he never used language group names), stating that the 'marriages were not contracted between too near relatives; and even now, if any one can bring forward a pretext that such or such is a brother or a sister to the suitor, this will become a barrier to the marriage'. See: *Further Facts, Sixth Paper*, 9.

22 August 1869*

The fencers did not come home for Sunday, tho' only six miles distant, so Adolf went in the afternoon to those on Stewart's run, with Philip, & kept a meeting for them. He ~~had~~ brought back Elizth & Ida, who had been there for days.

23 August 1864

[Tue] Was hard at work taking likenesses & to my satisfaction succeeded pretty well: M^L White was here again asking for a bag of flow^{u}er_ In the evening after I had sentizised f some paper I got our people together into Nathanael's room & commenced reading to them. "The Pilgrims Progress"[559]_

23 August 1865

[Wed] As a number of our people had undertaken to top a fence, separating Mr Edol's & Ellermans run, & as they went off to-day, I had but few scholars left Dicky, Archie, Albert, Napoleon ((they have to fence 11 miles at £3 10 per mile)) I improved the windmill very much by adding some small slips on the other side of the slant it gained very much in power & now moves in a very slight wind._ We hung up the sausages to smoke

23 August 1866

[Thu] Put up 2 thick logs in the smithy on for the anvil to be placed on the other; the other for the vice to be fixes to; made also a kind of chimney to catch the fumes & sparks of the coal_ In the extra meeting to-night, I commenced by taking the litaney "From coldness to thy merits & death"_ I had a walk over to Antwerp. I brought news that many Blacks die in the Tatiara country & on the Glenelg._ Mr Fleming's lambing rather poor, only 21 pr cent_ Magdalene seems to be getting better, feels much easier to-night

23 August 1867

[Fri] Commenced my school again with the boys, liked it rather as the lads show a mind to learn._ Swam the buggy & horse accross the river_ In the afternoon went again at the fastening up of the new pump._

---

[559] John Bunyan's, *The Pilgrim's Progress from This World, to That Which Is to Come* (1678) was a popular religious edifying tract.

23 August 1869*

[Mon] This morning Augusta went away in spite of all our advice to the contrary. We were very sorry to think of the temptations she might be exposed to & the little probability there is that we shall see her here again for long time.

24 August 1864

[Wed] As my scholars have somewhat improved in reading & writing I gain a little more time & so I commenced with them arithmetic._ Finding that I cannot go on taking likenesses with out a proper background & the light shining to strong on the face of the sitters I made a large stand to stegten calico over & also ~~to ma~~ a topping to moderate the head light._ Somehow I found our people very unwilling to do anything._

24 August 1865*

[Thu] S[pieseke]. & family left this forenoon for a visit to the Lake._ I Commenced painting the wings of the windmill, whilst at it Mr Scott, Ellerman & 2 Ladies, Miss Dennis & Miss Spence came here to see our place. The 2 Ladies stopped with us for the night; were much pleased with what they saw. They both spoke very kindly to our people._ Received a letter from B^r Henry[560] in Africa: the first here.

24 August 1866

[Fri] Sat up the vice & the anvil. Fetched the charcoal I made some days ago; about 1/3 of the wood was not burned; I got 4 sacks out of it

24 August 1867

[Sat] As B^{r}S: is about to go to Melbourne (on agreement) he is busy preparing the points to be brought forward there on behalf of the Blacks._ 1 Application for more land. II Stopping the giving of Government-rations to the neighbouring squatters._ III Endeavour to obtain some power to keep the children here to be taught & to be brought up in a ~~rill~~ ^{proper} way._ I was busy at the pump._ 3 Blacks on horseback came towards nightfall; Paddy & Sandy from Vectis & Jimmy from Glenelg_

---

560 Henry Hartmann. Ref: 16 May 1866.

24 August 1869*

[Tue] Mr Hogg, the new squatter at the lake, fet paid us a visit, came in a fine buggy & pair to fetch goods wh. had been left here.

24 August 1870*

Dear little Henry fell down with his chin on a box, & his tongue hanging: consequently he bit his tongue half through. Polly was in bed, the river was rising, there seemed no chance of crossing the water, so the doctor was sent for. Polly got a shock, & her threatening miscarriage came on.

25 August 1864

[Thu] After much thinking how to make the background for photographing I found it best to stretch old flour-sacks over the stand, paste paper over it & give the desired colours_ Phillip went out after wild cattle but got nothing._ In this evening 2 Blacks from Longernong: Jho^hn (the king) & George._ The first was come up to get his plate[561] back again w^h he had sent to another tribe._ The river is rising a little_

25 August 1865

[Fri] The party that came yesterday went off this morning._ I then finished painting my mill^rs, w^h operation I had been stopped yesterday, & in the afternoon I began nailing up the posts against the tree to put up the mill. It went pretty easy by means of a pulley I had made._ Got up 3 posts._ S[pieseke]. came back in the evening & brought 2 newspapers (Ararat Advertiser) containing a reply of Mr Simpson's to a report, Mr Swan, had written about our mission.[562] The thing seems to create a stir for Mr Swan has somewhat misrepresented to the public, the work we are carrying on in the Lord's name. In the other there was a sharp reply of Mr Swan to

---

561 Referring to a breastplates given out in the pre-Federation period to Aboriginal people considered to be Chiefs, Kings or Queens. See: Chris Healy, 'Chained to their Signs: Remembering Breastplates', in *Body Trade: Captivity, Cannibalism and Colonialism in the Pacific*, ed. B Creed and J Hoorn, 24–35 (Annandale, New South Wales: Pluto Press, 2001), hdl.handle.net/11343/35023.
562 Ref: 19 July 1865.

Mʳ Simpson._ Well as the matter stands we think much of inserting an article into the paper ourselves, to make the public acquainted with our work here in the Wimmera.⁵⁶³_

25 August 1866

[Sat] Cut & fetched myself a small box-tree to be cut into half, lengthways, for the regulator of the new mill, had a long search for the piece of wood._ Got an answer from Johnson & Co to my questions about the ~~Hy~~ Sulpho cyamide, & the dry plates & length of exposure. _ Napoleon went away with Paddy to Vectis⁵⁶⁴_ The weather has been dry for some time._

25 August 1869*

[Wed] The weather continues very dry: day after day there is a promise of rain, but only now & then a slight shower falls. No sign of a flood as yet.

25 August 1870*

The doctor came at dinner-time, put dear Henry under chloroform, & sewed his tongue. In spite of the chloroform he screamed.

26 August 1864

[Fri] Was building the background stretching sacking over it & covering it with paper._ King Cole & Lady came._

26 August 1865

[Sat] Was at it all day putting up the mill upon the tree & managed, too, to get it all up. Mʳ Ellerman, just as if it were to be so, came this morning & helped me putting it up; S[pieseke]. & the Blacks being afraid to get upon the scaffold I had made._ Mʳ Ellerman assisted me very much indeed. All went off, thanks to our Saviour without any accident, except that I got my

---

563 Adolf, in a letter to the Hines family also wrote about Mr Swan, disagreeing with him fervently. According to Adolf, Swan said that 'the Blacks are not fit for civilisation, it is no good to teach them to read & write etc. It is not theirs to live in houses, etc etc. he goes on to say they are children of nature & made to roam about in the woods & says that those attempts to civilize & christianize them drives the sunshine from their faces & makes them sad & melancholy looking beings.' MAB, PP HJAH, 2, Letterbook, A. Hartmann to Hines family, 18 September 1865.

564 In November 1869, Paddy, 33 years old, was still at Vectis. See: *Seventh BPA Report*, 22.

finger a little squeezed. The windmill rests upon 4 posts nailed against an thick gumtree & the hight from the ground to the very top of the little roof in 28 feet._ Sp. is making a new gate & got in the posts to day

26 August 1867

[Mon] The 3 Blacks that came Saturday left this morning.[565] James rode to March & Stuarts with a letter from B^r Sp: informing or asking them (I dont know w^h) that he would ask for 2 miles of their run. The answer James brought back was decided refusal to cede any land whatever, & that they would oppose any attempt made in that direction. About the Minnie & Maggie, it does not seem likely that we shall keep them. Maggie as it seems wants to No marry Bandel (Peter). We have left no stone unturned to keep the girls, force we cannot apply as we do not know whether we could get the case._ Sp: read in the evening the address he has drawn up to be delivered at Melbourne, if possible._

26 August 1869*

[Thu] Philip has gone on a missionary tour to the people who are scattered about fencing &c.

27 August 1863

Tried once more my little steam engine, & found it going very well._ (at Fulneck)

27 August 1866

[Mon] The flood came between 8 & 9 a.m._ Went up to look at it coming_ Seems the flow is stronger than last year._ S[pieseke] & I went down to the crossing at night to see how the water flowed & found that the embarkments dams we had made were still standing & the water flowing just over one of them. (so we think to make up the dams again when the river to nearly gives up flowing._ Matthew & Nathanael went to Scotts to try whether Mr Scott would engage them for shearing. Philip went to Mr Ferris[566] with the same intention_ I adced the piece of box I fetched on Saturday._ Brown or Samuel wanted to go to Vectis but S did not allow him._ Just before prayer we heard something like a thunder, but it could not be as it was

---

565 Paddy and Sandy from Vectis and Jimmy from Glenelg.
566 Only other Ref: 29 August 1866.

a perfectly clear moonlight night, the noise must have proceeded from a meteor, for some of the people at the crossing place saw a very bright body falling from the sky lighting up everything to great brightness & proceeding the thunderlike noise referred to._

27 August 1867

[Tue] B̲ṟ Spieseke left this morning for Melbourne to advocate the cause of our people & if possible to obtain more land.[567]_ Opposition will be met with, as one of our neighbours (Marsh & Stuart) have positively refused, to give up any land whatever. M̲ṟ Holt[568] the other neighbour will not be inclined wither to give up any land as we suppose._

28 August 1869

Excursion to Brimham rocks[569] near Harrogate_ left Fulneck for the rocks by rail at 6 ½ a.m. & came back at 11 p.m._ A very successful excursion_ weather warm & a few showers but we did not get wet._ Our guide among the rocks M̲ṟ Weatherhead, a funny fellow, reciting here & there pieces of poetry to our great amusement._

28 August 1864

[Sat] Gave the background the desired colour with Indian ink. I also finished 2 paper prints but did not suceed well with them. Almost all our people went to Antwerp to day, to wash sheep. I sent a letter to M̲ṟ Ellerman containing a list of chemicals he promised to get for me, & he was kind enough to send me back word, that he would get them for me (although according to my calculation it will cost about £3 12$\underline{s}$._

This ought to be on the preceding page Aug 27.

---

[567] Spieseke spoke before the Annual Meeting of the Victorian Association in aid of the Moravian Mission to the Aborigines of Australia on 30 September 1867. At this meeting, he spoke of some of the traditional practices and beliefs of the Aboriginal people who lived on the land where the mission now stood, as well as some of the events important to the mission. He closed his speech by imploring the meeting to 'let the aboriginal have a decent share' of the rich resources of the colony. See: *Further Facts, Sixth Paper*, 7-17.
[568] John Holt held the Lochiel run. See: *The Squatters' Directory*, Correction and Errata page.
[569] Formerly known as Brimham Crags, eight miles north-west of Harrogate, North Yorkshire, England.

28 August 1865

[Mon] Adzing some small logs for the gallery for the windmill. In the afternoon drove with Polly to Antwerp to see Mrs Ellerman & her baby._ There was a heavy shower of rain there during our stay._

28 August 1866

[Tue] Did different little jobs, first saving the piece I adced yesterday into halves._ fastening the small vice into the place of the former in the toolshop._ taking up the long piece of iron piping lying in the river & soldering in stead of it a piece of lead piping to the other lead pipe._ The sheep were mustered to-day & 120 drawn out for killing; Sp[ieseke] intends to begin to give meat to the people._ There was a talk about Fanny Sandy's wife then at Vectis, & we thought it would be well to try to get her to our place if possible, it was also proposed that Rebecca should write to her & ask her to come to us, with her 2 little children, (girls).[570] _

29 August 1864

[Mon] During my school S[pieseke]. came back from Horsham bringing some more presents for our people. According to the conference kept at Horsham about the Cooper's creek mission an agreement was come to to ~~commence~~ try the above scheme & that 2 of the coming bm with one of our black should go to farthest out Station & see what can be done & that the other 2 bm shld go for the present to Ramahyuck to Br Hagenauer._ I ~~old~~ changed my iron water tank in dark room for a barrel, & made arrangements to distill water._

29 August 1865

[Tue] Cut a log into boards to-day for the windmill, Matthew helping me._ Corney also I taught to cut & he did it very nicely for the first time._ We had a number of little showers during the day._ The remainder of the stores came to-day; clothes, tin-goods axes & tomahawk etc._

---

570 The girls were three-year-old Minnie and 18-month-old Laura. See: *Seventh BPA Report*, 21.

29 August 1866

[Thu] There was a fine rain last night from the East, softened the ground nicely, & made the grass spring wonderfully._ Nathanael & Matthew who had gone to Scott's to shear sheep came back last night without any success, Philip too who had tried at Mr Ferish's Ferris came back._

30 August 1864

[Tue] The boiler ^for of my little engine I took out with me proved to be very useful in distilling water. I distilled about ½ gallon of water; it looks beautifully clear but it remains to be seen whether it will act for photographing purposes._

31 August 1864

[Wed] Printed some likenesses & made experiments in toning & succeeded pretty well, although I cannot get them to my liking yet._

31 August 1866

[Fri] Sent Corney to cut down a long box tree to be used in putting up the new mill by & bye._ On my way back stopped at the camp; there was then much sickness, Jonathan[571] rather poor, & Frank's Mary too (Boney) the latter seems to be rather happy & expressed herself very nicely as regards the salvation of her soul._ Old Charley, too is getting very thin, wasting away, I stopped with him a while, spoke to him & endeavoured to point him to the Saviour. In his superstition he thinks that Stephen gave him Culliwell,[572] & so he goes on saying "me cooking that one along o bark hut cook me". He says, "Jesus Christ give me time"._ I spoke to him in many ways, that he was an old man & that it was his time to die like all other old people. Well he asked me to pray for him & so the old man lay prostate on the ground & I knelt also near his side & prayed, & then Charly prayed himself. I could not understand it all but I felt sure that our Saviour would not disregard the cries of this poor old man, but that he

---

571 Married to Mary. Died Ref: 10 October 1866.
572 AW Howitt refers to a practice called 'Guliwil' employed by the Wotjobaluk in which a bundle of wood is tied up with a piece of an article belonging to 'the intended victim'. Unclear if the 'Culliwell' referred to in this entry is a similar practice. See: AW Howitt, *The Native Tribes of South-East Australia* (London: Macmillan, 1904), 363–64.

would give him light & happiness before his departure._ Sp[ieseke] finished his wall just before breakfast._ Matthew & Napoleon engaged cutting boards for him._

31 August 1867

[Sat] Mr Cobham called here._ I paid him for our cooking plate.[573]

the new pump was finished & went to day in a good stiff puff of wind & nothing broke as I first feared would._

September

1 September 1864

[Thu] Our brother Daniel's[574] birthday._ How different this day is to the one year ago! It has been a blessed & happy time until now._ I resolved, the light being to strong, to make a sort of photographic studio & commenced to-day fetching wood for it._ In the morning meeting after the usual address S[pieseke]. gave to our Blacks a good speaking about their comparative idleness & indifference to assist us in our work._ It seemed to have some effect on them, & they agreed with what S. had said_

1 September 1865

[Fri] A very strong hot wind blew all day, & towards evening there came up from the North a remarkable haze: this haze so much moderated the light of the sun that you could look into it: the sun appeared very white._ I looked into M^r E[llerman]: buggy to make it strong, preparatory, to our journey to Horsham._

2 September 1864

[Fri] No school again, people fetching road in the forenoon & all of them going to Antwerp in the afternoon._ I was hard at work all day building my photographic gallery._ I finished the frame work of the same consisting of [illegible] post rammed into the ground, _ I intend to cover it with

---

573 Ref: 19 June 1867.
574 Daniel Hines.

bark._ Some of our people have applied for baptism Albert, Boopboop, Lilly (Makenzie wife) & Susan. Well it remains to be seen whether they are sincere, or if they seek any outward advantages by it or not._

2 September 1865

[Sat] Left for Horsham Polly & myself at 2 p.m. Stopped at Edol's for the night, but both of us very sick so that we had but little engagment. Polly got so sick & had great trouble in vomiting that we thought we would have to return on Monday instead of going on; & I had tooth-ache._ I was persuaded by M̲ͬ Edol's to take some "pain-killer"_

2 September 1868

[Wed] M̲ͬ Spieseke, I & some of the Blacks, (Albert & Dicky) of course too went to Dimboola to have the case over be present at the case of dr with William Fisher & Albert, the former giving drink to the latter.[575] The case was decided in our favour & W Fisher was fined about £5 of money._

3 September 1864

[Sat] Was about almost all day cutting bark, but did not get much, there being but few trees with good bark, that have not been stripped of it yet._

3 September 1865

[Son] Preached on Gen XLII, 36[576] "All these things are against me; good congregation; In the evening at M̲ͬ E[dol]'s one of the men played the an "organtina" to the singing: a great improvement: Spoke on John IV 30[577] "I that speak unto thee am he". My tooth-ache being bad I was persuaded by M̲ͬ E: to take some "painkiller"._ It began to rain towards evening._

---

575 Ref: 3 August 1868.
576 KJV. Gen 42:36, 'And Jacob their father said unto them, Me have ye bereaved of my children: Joseph is not, and Simeon is not, and ye will take Benjamin away: all these things are against me.'
577 KJV. John 4:26, 'Jesus saith unto her, I that speak unto thee am he.' (KVV: John 4:30, 'Then they went out of the city, and came unto him.') The Luther Bible from 1545 follows the KJV in these two texts indicating that Adolf referred to the wrong verse.

3 September 1866

[Mon] Began putting in the window frames into Timothys house & in the afternoon distilled some water to have some ready for use._ Magdalene seems to be getting better._ Nice warm day._

3 September 1870*

To-day it pleased the Lord to call home the soul of Paul,[578] after he had for weeks past ~~shown~~ given a bright testimony of the power of the grace of God.

4 September 1864

[Sun] Went to Antwerp & preached there,_ As it was just shearing time the service was held in the woolshed._ (M͏ͬ Ellerman lost a good many sheep in the wash they being rather poor).

4 September 1865

[Mon] What a wretched night I had; that "pain killer" completely upset my stomach & I had to keep running all night. Towards morning got a little better, & although rather weak, we could proceed on our way to Horsham._ Polly's health was much improved, too._ It was rather a cool day & were very glad for the rug that M͏ͬ Edols lent us. The road was pretty good considering the season._ Were as usual very friendly received at Walmar, & felt very snug & comfortable excepting my toothache._

4 September 1866

[Tue] Polly sowed a good many flower seeds & ~~mended some~~ I turned tinker mending sundry pots & pans

5 September 1864

[Mon] In the afternoon I commenced covering my photographic ~~gla~~ gallery with whatever I could get hold of, bark sacks & other things._ I find it does not go very fast especially as I have not stuff enough to do it, & have to scrape together all odds & ends._

---

578 Previously known as Dick a Dick. Married to Amelia (previously Kitty). He was baptised on Ref: 30 July 1870.

5 September 1865

[Tue] Stopped all day at Walmar; very comfortable._ In the afternoon we walked with M^rs^ W: to the sheep-wash:_ I applied some Chloroform t against my tooth-ache._

5 September 1866

[Wed] A drive to Antwerp_ M^r^ & Mrs Flemming all well; her sister with her. ~~it~~ for some time as it seems._ Polly began school with the women in the evening in our room at the same time I had mine_

5 September 1867

[Thu] The Richardson Blacks went to-day Harry— & ~~Mary~~ Kitty ^Granny^ Johnny or King John[579] & Mary. The latter took with them Bobby & Maggie[580] but promised very faithfully to bring Bobby back in a short time._ Old Frank has gone with them & will bring him back, so they say. What they are going to do with Maggie we cannot tell. Minnie wonderful to say will remain here; this is more than we expected._ The tin lining in the pump of is of no good at all so I took it out & will try to polish the inside of the iron tube where the sucker works._ I am at present going to the fence with the people to get the work pushed on

6 September 1864

[Tues] All our people went away early with S[pieseke] to Antwerp to wash our sheep. All went off & no sheep died._ The 2 little pigs which we got from Locheal[581] & w^h^ Mr Chantress brought, seem to have taken to their heels._ At my gallery again._

6 September 1865

[Wed] Drove to Horsham with one of Mr Wilson's horses "Paddy" to see Mr Simpson & also to buy some articles at Langland's._ It looked very much like heavy rain coming up. M^r^ S[impson]: well._ M^rs^ S: & baby pretty

---

579 King John was at the station in the first quarter of 1872, just before Hartmann left, being diagnosed as consumptive. He was described by Hugh Campbell in early 1864 as being 'a man of Mrs Little'. See: *Eighth BPA Report*, 17; DDHS, The Lorquon Diary of Hugh Campbell.
580 According to Adolf, Maggie was the daughter of Kitty and a white settler, Robertson. Another daughter by this relationship was called Esther. Bobby was Kitty's son with an Aboriginal man. See: Smyth, *The Aborigines of Victoria*, 93.
581 Ref: 25 July 1864.

well too._ In the afternoon when at Langland's buying some things a good heavy rain came: all day it rained about 7/10 of an inch, consequently we did not return to Walmar that night & spent a very happy evening at Mr Simpson's._

6 September 1868

[Sun] Drove to the Nine Creeks with Polly & Nelly & preached in the fore & afternoon._ texts Luke 7[582] the last verse Rev 7. 14-17.[583]_

7 September 1864

[Wed] We had a lovefeast with our p baptized people; I kept it._ The thing being new to them amused them somewhat, especially the eating & drinking in the chapel. It tickled them so much that they laughed._ It was nevertheless a blessed opportunity, it reminded us of the C^om[584] at home._ The tea was made & served by S^is S[pieseke]. my wife being at the harmonium._ In the forenoon we got our rams shorn._

7 September 1865

[Thu] Got some panes of glass from Spry for Matthew._ Polly & I paid a visit to the Bowden's_ Got some of my shoes mended._ Before we went back to Walmar had a talk with Mr Simpson about ~~the~~ our Mission, as he is going to place a report before the next general assembly of the Presbyterian Church to stir up the interest on behalf of our mission, that the work might be extended, & also that some of our people might be set apart, & paid a salary. for the Home mission.[585]_ Got back to Walmar in good time._

---

582 KJV. Luke 7:10, 'And he said to the woman, Thy faith hath saved thee; go in peace.'
583 KJV. Revelations 7:14, 'And I said unto him, Sir, thou knowest. And he said to me, These are they which came out of great tribulation, and have washed their robes, and made them white in the blood of the Lamb. 15. Therefore are they before the throne of God, and serve him day and night in his temple: and he that sitteth on the throne shall dwell among them. 16. They shall hunger no more, neither thirst any more; neither shall the sun light on them, nor any heat. 17. For the Lamb which is in the midst of the throne shall feed them, and shall lead them unto living fountains of waters: and God shall wipe away all tears from their eyes.'
584 Ambiguous if referring to 'communion' or 'community'.
585 See discussion in the introduction to this diary.

7 September 1868

[Mon] Stayed at M͟r Edols the whole day, I watched his saw mill the greater part of the day. Things begin to grow in his new new large garden._

8 September 1864

[Thu] We the help of a few Blacks I finished my photographic gallery. It looks rather an odd affair, but I think it will answer its purpose._ The Blacks killed a ram, & we found our pigs[586] & drove them back to our place_ Polly made great alterations in our bed room, arranging the furniture differently to what it was before._

8 September 1865

[Fri] M͟r Wilson kind enough to give us "Paddy" again to pull us to the 9 mile recevoir, where we found our Bobby who had been taken there by some of his men early. & so we managed to get quickly to Edol's._ As M͟rs E & family were just about to go to the sheepwash we went with them._ Coming back M͟r Campbell & family had arrived on their way to ~~Bla~~ Ballarat, & so the house was pretty full._ I slept on the floor in the dining room & Polly slept with miss D._

8 September 1866

[Sat] Was for once again in my dark room working all day to get a picture out of those dry plates I got sent from Melbourne, but contrary to all my expectations I did not succeed, could not get a picture at all, well well. This is very sad, very sad. There came a letter in the evening from Mr Lloyd that L A Bang goods had arrived

---

586 Ref: 6 September 1864.

EBENEZER MISSION STATION, 1863-1873

9 September 1863

Wednesday_ Received a letter from B[r] Levine Reichel[587] from Berthelsdorf[588] through Br Latrobe[589] in London,[590] containing an invitation to pay a short visit to Herrnhut[591] before my wedding[592] ((the money for it to d be drawn from B[r] Spence in London))

9 September 1864

[Fri] After breakfast I went to Antwerp with Polly to pay a visit there & see all about the shearing._ It was a nice walk & we enjoyed it very much._ Oh these poor sheep, how they are treated; those shears who went to make quick work of it are not at all particular about cutting the poor sheep & how they are hauled about! A good shearer does about 80 to 100 sheep per day. There happened to be a photographer there, so I learnt a little more about photography & I think I have found out that lens may be used for landscapes also_

9 September 1865

[Sat] Off to our place._ Found them all well._ Polly got a letter & some seeds from Miss Dennis.[593]_ Set the rhubarb plant we got from M[rs] Wilson & then I went to work at once, at to get the gallery done for the pump._ Sp[ieseke]: read a letter from Hagenauer & Kramer[594] from whom we learnt that the b[rn] in Adelaide[595] had not yet started for the interior

---

587 Levin Theodore Reichel was a member of the UEC, and a member of the Department of Missions from 1857. Died 23 May 1878.
588 Berthelsdorf, Upper Lusatia, Germany. From 1722, it was a manor house and property owned by Count von Zinzendorf. Sold in 1732 to his wife. Until 1938 owned by the Moravian Church. Site of some administration of the Church.
589 Bishop Peter La Trobe (1795–1863), secretary of the Moravian Church in England and secretary of missions in London. He died suddenly of heart failure while on a trip to Berthelsdorf, Germany, on 24 September 1863. Peter was brother to Charles Joseph La Trobe (1801–1875), superintendent of the Port Phillip District of New South Wales, and after separation, the first lieutenant-governor of the Colony of Victoria (1851–54). Charles Joseph was also an official advocate for Moravian missionary work. See: JE Hutton, *History of the Moravian Church,* second edition, revised and enlarged (London: Moravian Publication Office, 1909); John Mason and Lucy Torode, *Three Generations of the La Trobe Family in the Moravian Church* (Newtownabbey: Moravian History Magazine, 1997).
590 The Moravian Church had had a continuing presence in London since 1738, from where it spread out to many parts of the country. See: Podmore, *The Moravian Church in England*; JCS Mason, *The Moravian Church and the Missionary Awakening in England, 1760–1800* (Suffolk: The Boydell Press for The Royal Historical Society, 2001).
591 Herrnhut: first settlement of the renewed Moravian Church. Established in 1722 in Upper Lusatia, Germany, on the property of Count Nicolaus Ludwig von Zinzendorf und Pottendorf (1700–1760).
592 Wedding date Ref: 29 December 1863.
593 Ref: 24 August 1865.
594 Karl Wilhelm Kramer (1885–1888). Died at Ebenezer.
595 Walder and Meissel.

9 September 1867

[Mon] Wet weather those last days, was with the people to get the fence done before shearing._ Planted cucumber & melon seeds.

9 September 1868

[Wed] Spieseke & whole family off to Horsham to see M^r & Mrs C^h Wilson

10 September 1864

[Sat] Early in the morning S[pieseke]. with our people drove the sheep to Antwerp to get them shorn, they came back late in the evening._

10 September 1867

[Tue] The people finished the fence they began 8 weeks & 2 days ago._ The river is rising very much again, for the 3rd time this year._

11 September 1864

[Sun] S[pieseke]. to Antwerp to preach_ In the evening Mr Ellerman came here with Mr Simpson's brother, & the same stopped with us over Monday, Mr Simpson is on a tour through the country visiting the different Stations & wool sheds preaching the Gospel to the shearers and other people._

11 September 1865

[Mon] Very few people at our place at present._ The 3 boys Albert, Napoleon, Dicky make themselves very useful; they are all 3 candidates for baptism, & I'm much pleased with Dicky; may the Saviour open his eyes!_ I finished fitting the gallery for the windmill & commenced putting it up at ^on the tree_ Bad tooth-ache_ I'm taking homeopathic medecin (bella Donna)[596] but somehow it wont relieve me._

---

596 Belladonna is commonly used in homeopathic medicine for headaches, sore throats, tonsillitis, coughs, earaches and fever.

11 September 1866

[Tue] S arrived here in the afternoon with our things & the government things well it was a feast, & it took Polly all the evening to get the things in order._ Philip & Steven[597] are engaged by Mr Flemming h during the ~~time of~~ shearing time.

11 September 1867

[Wed] Rode to Antwerp and settled with Mr Fleming that the wages of Philip & Stephen £2. should be added to the money the people get for fencing. Very wet weather_ The river still rising_ received letters from B^r Sp. Mr Chase for the people & read them in the schoolroom to the people._

12 September 1864

[Mon] All ^{the} people again to Antwerp to finish the shearing of our sheep. I was experimentalizing in photographics & had a complete failure, could do nothing & could not find out the mistake either; I felt rather discouraged, but hope to get it when the new chemicals come._

12 September 1865

[Tue] Putting up the gangway of the mill_ tooth-ache._

12 September 1868

[Sat] The remaining stores from Chambers & Maclurcan[598] arrived._

13 September 1864

[Tue] Our sheep were marked to day, and I again tried at photography but no go._

13 September 1866

[Thu] Tried once more at my photographics. The dry process wont do at all

---

597 It is possible that Steven refers to Stephen (formerly Jacky) in the diary.
598 Merchants in Ararat.

14 September 1864*

[Wed] B[r] & S[ister]. Spieseke went to Lake Hindmarsh for a day. Adolf had school again, & after school went fencing with the people. A heavy fall of rain prevented their finishing in the afternoon.

14 September 1867

[Sat] All day away with Donald putting up the 2 other gates. We took the 2 old gates from the Durrock paddock._ It took us nearly all day putting them up._ The 3rd gate we put up the day before yesterday._ The river still rising._

15 September 1864

[Thu] S[pieseke]. coming back from the lake[599] brought home letters for us, the first in answer to ours from Melbourne._ Some failures in photography!._

15 September 1865

[Fri] lifting up a piece of wood amongst our fire-wood, to put it aside for the mill, a snake about 1 ½ foot long crawled away from the place where the wood lay._ There was, of course a great commotion & the snake was killed at once. Now this is the first we met with alive._ Having changed my medecin yesterday,[600] for the tooth-ache, & having taken Camomille[601] I feel much better to-day & the tooth-ache is going._

15 September 1867

[Sun] It rained almost all the day & toward evening there came even a thunderstorm & a very heavy rain._ The river is now nearly overflowing its banks._

16 September 1864

[Fri] More failures in Photography it seems I cannot manage with the present chemicals I have, & must wait for the new one's M[r] Ellerman is going to get for me.[602]

---

599 Ref: 14 September 1864.
600 Ref: 11 September 1865.
601 Chamomile tea is used in homeopathic medicine to treat toothaches, stomach-aches, arthritis and viral infections.
602 Ref: 28 August 1864.

16 September 1865

[Sat] A nice warm day_ Got on a good way with the mill this week, Sp[ieseke] helping me now & then, but I did not finish it there is more to be done than I thought.

17 September 1863

Thursday) After yesterday's conversation I joyfully sent off another letter to Mary[603] ((Copy of it in small book)) p 81.[604]

17 September 1864

[Sat] Another attempt at Photography & another failure so now I shall stop, & S[pieseke]. being willing to get me a few things I have forgotten to ask M[r] Ellerman for, I shall get them. A few more Blacks arrived at night; old Boney & lubra & another Edward. We had a nice warm day after the last 2 or 3 very windy & cold ones._ We had a very busy evening getting our letters ready for home w[h] must be sent off on Monday next._ (Oh for those fleas how they bother one!) It is no use you cannot keep them off your body

18 September 1863

Friday)) A letter to B[r] Seifferth[605] requesting him to forward a call to Mary[606] being advised to do so by B[r] Harvey[607] from Fairfield[608]

18 September 1864

[Sun] A Sunday we were all together. I went to the camp in the morning & was by the outward appearance of our baptized Blacks with that of the few that had come, especially the women, so pretty & nicely dressed._ Matthew

---

603 Mary (Polly) Hines (1838–1916), married Adolf on 29 December 1863.
604 Although a small book exists in the MAB, PP HJAH, 10 file in the Bethlehem archives, pages 71–86 are ripped out, as are pages 127–144, inclusive. These pages corresponded to all references in the large diary.
605 Moravian Bishop Benjamin Seifferth (1795–1876). Consecrated to the episcopate in 1846. For more see: Hamilton, *A History of the Church Known as the Moravian Church*, 480–81.
606 Adolf Hartmann would only refer to Mary Hines as Polly after they met. Prev. Ref. 17 September 1863.
607 Bennet Harvey was a member of the Moravian Church in England. He was a missionary in Antigua in the 1830s. In the 1850s, he taught at the theological seminary at Bedford, before it closed in 1857. He was part of many committees including the committee for the revision of the church Hymnal in the early 1880s. See: Hamilton, *A History of the Church Known as the Moravian Church*, 373, 397.
608 Fairfield, near Manchester, UK.

& Margaret not quite agreeing together_ I spoke to him & Polly to her_ The tempers of these 2 are somewhat different & so it comes that especially Margaret does not find what she perhaps wishes & so she does not seem to care so very much. But we found out when speaking to them that it is not as bad as we thought. Margaret seems to be most in fault_ Little disagreements arising from their difference of disposition seems to be the cause of that little trouble. As our letters have to go to morrow we made them ready to day. Sent also a small order for chemicals to Batchelder & O Neill & wrote to Mr Ellerman not to send Harry this week as we intend to go to the Lake. I added also a letter to B^r Reichels expressing the wish not to be removed to ~~Gippsland~~ Portland,[609] at the same time submitting myself to the lot.[610]_

18 September 1865

[Mon] M^r & M^{rs} Sp[ieseke] with Anna & the Baby went on a trip to Horsham, this afternoon;_ they left Helena with us, so we shall be alone for a week._

18 September 1866

[Tue] Mr Shultz the German carrier from Germantown having passed our place yesterday on his way to the Lake with Goods for Mr Haines the present manager of that Station came back from there on horseback to pay us a visit. S[pieseke]. w^{h}en he came to us yesterday made the mistake, or at least it was found out to have been a mistake not to invite him to dinner for which we were just then sitting down, Mr Shultz being a contributor towards our ~~M~~ work here; & then he knew S from former times._ Well he came to-stay with us ~~for~~ over night

---

609 The Moravians were requested to establish a mission at Portland, but nothing came of this. See: Jensz, *German Moravian Missionaries*, 173.
610 Adolf was referring to the Moravian practice of making decisions through drawing tokens, most commonly three tokens were used with 'yes', 'no' or a blank. For more see: Ref: 9 May 1865.

19 September 1863

Sat: Another letter to Mary[611] informing that a call ^(to her) was on the way.[612] Also a letter to B^r & Sister Hines in Fairfield informing them of it.[613] A small note also to dear Fritz La Trobe[614] in Fairfield. _

19 September 1864

[Mon] Contemplating to make a tin-pan for bathing & for a shower bath, I prepared all the old tin I could get hold of, but as I'm rather in want of solder I dont know ~~whe~~ wether I shall be able to finish.

19 September 1866

[Wed] Mr Shultz[615] left us for the lake accompanied by S[pieseke]. as far as ~~Horsham~~ Antwerp where he wanted to see Philip & Steven engaged by Mr Flemming Another german carrier Schmidt came bringing a few more things for us & left also a few things with us belonging to Mr Scott._

20 September 1864

[Tue] Set off with Polly on a visit to the Lake, to see Mr H. Ellerman & Mr White (account of it in small book page 135.)

21 September 1865

[Thu] Sent of the home letters, & ~~re~~ received them too, & we learnt that mother had been rather sick, but was recovering again._

21 September 1865*

[Fri] I used the new globe for the first time in my school.

---

611 Prev. Ref: 18 September 1863.
612 Her letter of call was sent on 26 September 1864 by Levin T Reichel. MAB, PP HJAH, 8, Letters, written by Moravian officials to the Hartmanns (1863–1873), LT Reichel (Berthelsdorf) to Mary Hines, 26 September 1863.
613 Mary's parents, John and Ann Hines.
614 Frederic La Trobe (1839–1896), fourth son of Bishop James La Trobe. Frederic was ordained as a deacon at Fairfield in 1863 with Adolf (Ref: 10 December 1863). He was ordained as presbyter at Fulneck in 1868. He was also a teacher at Fulneck while Adolf was there. See: Mason and Torode, *Three Generations of the La Trobe Family in the Moravian Church*, 41–43.
615 Ref: 18 September 1866.

22 September 1864
[Thu] Come back from our visit to the Lake at about sunset.[616]_

22 September 1865
[Fri] Finished the joining of the pipes from the irrigation I commenced last Monday, joined them with white lead & rags, & am going to support the joints with a stick tied I-under them._ I had just finished the pipes when M[r] White & his family made their appearance on the other side of the river, so I got them all across & they stayed with us a few hours._ I make the 3 boys, Dicky, Napoleon & Albert look, in turn, at the sheep to see whether all is right, I give them one of the horses to ride._

22 September 1866*
[Sat] M[r] Haines, of Lake Hindmarsh Station paid us a visit

23 September 1864
[Fri] Two new Blacks came to my school, Edward[617] & Mackenzie, the former seems to be a bright man._ After school I went at unpacking our washing machine wh had come yesterday._ A beautiful little thing it is & all is right at it. It took me all day unpacking it & taking the box to pieces & pulling out all the nails._ S[pieseke]. & the people commenced making the fence from the gate up to our river._

23 September 1865
[Sat] There was a strong wind all day & towards evening it came up thick from the west, & we had a drop of rain. I was at the mill putting up some more of the cross-pieces to get up to the top of it for greasing the valve:_ The people also finished the fence between M[r] Edol's & Ellerman's run commenced about 4 ½ weeks ago._

---

616 Ref: 20 September 1864.
617 Arrived at the mission Ref: 17 September 1864.

23 September [1866]*

[Sun] We had the communion together in the dining room on Magdalene's account, she being ill, & attending for the first time. She seemed to enjoy it much.

Old Charley appears to be dying.

24 September 1864

[Sat] Made a black board for my school._ We had our communion in the Chapel this time: Mr Ellerman joined us in partaking of it with us._

24 September 1865

[Sun] There was a nice rain last night, everything looks nice & fresh & the grass which about to dry, will no spring up a bit again.

24 September 1866*

[Mon] Old Charley died this morning. He left no clear evidence of his belief in the Saviour, yet we are not without hope concerning him.

This evening, it being very clear, we saw the total eclipse of the moon. M^r & Mrs Spieseke & two children went this morning to Mr Scotts. Anna remains with me.

25 September 1864

[Sun] Started with Polly for 9 Creeks at ¼ to 8._ Preached from 1 Cor 7.29.[618]_ In the evening at the house I spoke about Luke 21, 33. Heaven & earth shall pass away but my words shall not pass away._

25 September 1865

[Mon] Some of the people charcoaled the posts we got in for the irrigation. I put up everything to the mill to make it work, some how it was so very ackward work. The water would not come up, so I took the lead pipe off & put it on to the other side & then I got some water up. It works very well, but it requires a good wind & the wings of the mill might be a little larger._

---

618 KJV. 1 Cor. 7:28, 'That no flesh should glory in his presence.'

25 September 1866

[Tue] Painted the hose for our garden & made joining of tin instead of the old wood ones w^h ~~were~~ got broken (Photography wants much time & study 2 have not got it & yet I am very ~~loth~~ loath to give it up before I have succeeded so far as to produce a decent picture._

26 September 1864

[Mon] Back to ~~Mr. Flem~~ Ebenezer at 9 p.m._ Very strong wind so that we could not keep on our hats_ A very pleasant drive though._ On returning we found some more Blacks had arrived from Locheal. Commenced making a tin pan for a showerbath, dont know though whether I shall succeed having to make it of old tin. Sister Spiesecke tried the washingmachine for the first time & it proved to do excellent work to the satisfaction of everybody._

26 September 1865

[Tue] There was a nice breeze today & so we let the mill go.

S[pieseke]: & family came back from Horsham just when we had finished dinner They brought a good many things ~~back~~ with them. I took one of the coats ~~of M^r.~~ Mr Simpson had sent & gave one of mine for it._ S: had a good talking with Mr Alex: Wilson as regards the rations he receives from government & w^h induce a good many Blacks to stay at his place. Mr Alex: W. wishes the stores to be continued & Sp: is against it & will write to government._ If the rations are not ~~able to been not~~ stopped at Vectis it is to be feared that more Blacks will be drawn from our place, to live a dissipated & disorderly life_ Made the trap door for the mill._

26 September 1866

[Wed] Old Charley was buried to-day[619]_ S just returned from Mr Scott When we were carrying the dead body to its resting place._ Some nice showers._

27 September 1864

[Tue] ~~If~~ the washing machine, even to the satisfaction of S[pieseke] who did not quite believe in it at first, did some beautiful work to day when used for mangling._

---

619 Died Ref: 24 September 1866.

27 September 1865

[Wed] A very windy day, & rather cold; finished all about the mill excepting the fasting of the lead pipe against the tree._

27 September 1866

[Thu] Mr Archibald from beyond the lake called here & wished to have a Black for a fortnight, so he got James, who was very glad for the opportunity._

28 September 1863

Mon.) Was at Baildon,[620] attending the Mission meetings, a very enjoyable day (SB p 31.)

28 September 1865

[Thu] We went all of us to make a sheep-wash as, for want of water we could not wash at Antwerp._ We managed to get a very decent wash finished to-day We made it near the old crossing place._

29 September 1865

[Fri] Washed our own sheep in the wash we made yesterday, & all went well._ We lost one ewe & one old ram:_ This washing is rather hard work & we all felt very tired when it was done._

29 September 1866

[Sat] Most of the week I was in Timothy's house laying down the floor._ A good deal of sickness among the people in the camp, Jonathan rather ill._ Lydia too seems to have got a bad cold._ Magdalene is getting better it seems. Sp[ieseke] informed us that Mr Mcredie[621] had bought the sawing machine we ordered. I am about ^{making} a letter box for spelling

---

620 Baildon, West Yorkshire, UK.
621 GC Macredie of Morton Plains (Ref: 9 January 1868). Adolf wrote to Macredie already in January 1865 to request his help in procuring materials for the mission, including for the school. See: MAB, PP HJAH, 2, Letterbook (1864–1871), Adolf Hartmann to Maccredie, 25 January 1865.

A day of great joy

30 September 1863

Wed) Another letter from dear Mary,[622] containing her final decisions.[623] I feel so happy ~~at the prospect~~ when I consider what a treasure the Lord has given me in her.

30 September 1864

Left at 3 p.m. for Won Won Dah[624] Mr Rutherford's[625] station to fetch a black infant whose father having been prevailed upon by Mr R: as he told Sp in his letter, to be brought up at our Station & Polly was going to take care of it herself. We stopped the night at Mr Edoll's._

30 September 1865

[Sat] Made an arrangement at the mill so as to be able to unscrew or tighten the lead pipe to the pump without taking the pump._ Mr Ellerman came in the afternoon & it was settled that our blacks should shear our sheep this time to try whether they can do it properly._ Miss Fraser came in the evening with Eliza ^{Ellerman} to pay us a farewell visit, as she is going to leave Antwerp. We had the supper in the evening._

---

622 Prev. Ref: 19 September 1863.
623 In reference to her call from the UEC to be Adolf's husband and be part of the missionary service of the Moravian Church. Ref: 18 September 1863.
624 Wonwondah, also written WonWonda, station, in the West Wimmera held by Quarterman & Rutherford. See: *The Squatters' Directory*, 40.
625 A William Rutherford, Wonwondah/WonWonda, was a supporter of the Moravian mission in the Wimmera, as well as a supporter of other missions, including the 'Native Missionaries on the New Hebrides Islands'. See: *The Age* (Melbourne), Tuesday 14 April 1863, 7. The itinerant Baptist preacher, Joseph J Westwood, noted that John Rutherford held the station Wonwondah in 1864. See: JJ Westwood, *The Journal of J.J. Westwood (Evangelist), or, An Account of Eight Years' Itinerary to the Townships and Squatting Stations of Victoria, New South Wales, South Australia, and Tasmania* (Melbourne: Clarson, Shallard & Co. 1865).

October

1 October 1864

Sat. A somewhat dreary ride to Horsham; the roads very hard & rough having been cut up previously, when soft by heavy drays going over it. Polly not quite well either._ Got to H[orsham]. at about 4 p.m. after a drive of 6 hours. We drove to the manse & were received cordially by Mrs Simpson. Shortly afterward M^r A Simpson arrived with Daniel in Mr Ellermans buggy. In the evening Mr Simpson himself came There was also at the manse Mr Hill, come out from Scottland lately, to take 9 creeks as the place of his ministry._

1 October 1868

[Thu] I rode to Vectis after Stephen who had behaved badly then fighting & drinking. The poor man before he went away, said he had no peace & he wanted to go to a place where he could find peace._ S. had been going about with a ^man Barber driving sheep for Mr White but this Barber most likely got him into a bad way of drinking.

2 October 1864

[Sun] Mr A. Simpson preached in the morning & Mr Hill in the evening. There was a good attendance in the morning. In the afternoon Polly took part ~~of~~ in the sunday school. I had only a look at it.

2 October 1865

[Mon] Drove Miss Fraser to Antwerp, Polly going too. We stayed over dinner._ I was almost all the time at the woolshed, shearing going on, & looked on & tried my hand a bit too. (Matthew who is shearing there, too, did a very foolish thing in ~~spending~~ buying more goods at the hawkers ~~that~~ than he could pay for, so that he was shearing then to pay off the debt he had made, just like him that!)

2 October 1867

[Wed] The river has been highes~~t~~r this morning than I ever saw before. Our gate to Antwerp was half under water & we could just manage to cross the creek on horse back & get the mail from Antwerp M^r Sp[ieseke]: has been in Melbourne now 5 week on Tuesday last.[626]_

---

626 Ref: 27 August 1867.

3 October 1864

[Mon] It began to rain in the early morning & rained hard almost all the forenoon so we thought we would not get off to Wonwonda[627] to-day. We saw Mʳ Bowden & got some stuff given to make a dress for the little girl we are to fetch.[628] Well as it seemed to clear off up we started after all for Rutherford's, but about 2 miles from his station a heavy rain overtook us. We arrived too late to see Mʳ Simpson & his brother & Mʳ C. Wilson, they had gone. We were introduced to some people visiting there Mʳˢ Langlands, Mʳˢ March, & the governess Miss Hallion. (Jenny R's daughter a very peculiar girl of 4 years age)

3 October 1865

[Tue] Mʳ Simpson with Nathanael left this morning for their missionary tour through the country going the Tatiara way._ In the afternoon fetched a whi fine white gum log some of our people to cut boards out for the support of the piper on the scaffold to be erected; had great trouble with Mark in cutting off the slabs.

3 October 1866

[Wed] Started with Polly & Nelly for a tour westward to see the Blacks & also to see some of the Squatters there & get acquainted with them.[629]_ To-day we went as far as Locheal._ Neither Mʳ Wallace nor Perkins were at home so we took possession of the house (Mʳ Semple servant at the manse & who could not agree with the Ellermans.) We went to the camp of the Blacks & found them all there: spoke to them about Jesus & prayed with & for them. <u>Betsy</u> had died last week & there were a good many more sick besides._

---

627 Wonwondah (Ref: 30 September 1864).
628 Ref: 30 September 1864. This plan did not come to fruition as the girl was taken from Wonwondah Station before the missionaries arrived Ref: 4 October 1864.
629 Adolf also described this missionary tour in a letter published in the *Periodical Accounts* in 1866. The published reports mentions a 'young women named Judy', who would come to the mission if it were not for her husband, and reference to Martha and Jerry who is in service at Mount Elgin (under Mr Telford, Ref: 6 October 1866). Jerry, a horse-breaker, subsequently went to Ebenezer. See: *Periodical Accounts* 26 (1866), 196–97.

3 October 1868

[Thu] Returned from Vectis & ^having^ found that Stephen's fighting was caused in a fit of drunkenness,[630] I spoke of it to M̲r̲ A[lexander] Wilson asking him to send Stephen away in case he should not behave well. I spoke also to all the Blacks & exhorted them not to give way to drunkennes & not to accept any challenge of Stephen to fight again. On this my tour I stayed both nights at M̲r̲ Calder's I saw also M̲r̲ Wilsons spout washing & also M̲r̲ Edols._

4 October 1864

[Tue] The very first thing we heard in the morning was ^that^ the Blacks had all gone away, & so we had come for nothing.[631] They got frightened as it seems & cut._ I went to the woolshed with Polly, & M̲r̲ R[utherford]: pulled us some fine wool from off his sheep. A very fine station W.W.[632] is: everything very comfortable. 75,000 sheep are reared on it, & they produce some of the finest wool in Australia. Little music in the evening._

4 October 1865

[Wed] As we could not cut the slabs off the log, the saw having been twisted in some way or other, we split them off as well as it would do & adced it._ The cutting then went very well._ Did not finish to-day though._ M̲r̲ Sp[ieseke]: received letters from the b̲r̲n̲ in Adelaide (there were also 2 likenesses of M̲r̲ Kühn & Daniel) We had asked for some too, but there being none we must ask for them again._ The news in Walder's letter was that they could not proceed yet into the interior for want of rain._ Daniel is sick & has the consumption as the Doctor says, & so they had got him into the hospital & M̲r̲ Walder says that it is not possible for Daniel even if he ~~recovered~~ recovered to go with them as he could never stand the fatigue they would be exposed to, & the best thing would be to send him back by way of the Murray-river._ The old sheep were taken to Antwerp to-night as the Blacks will commence shearing to-morrow._

4 October 1866

[Thu] Off to M̲r̲ Holts woolshed, saw M̲r̲ Wallace & Perkins, stayed but a little time just sufficient to see the shearing etc. We had not proceeded very far towards Niel when we were caught by a heavy thunderstorm. We turned

---

630 Ref: 1 October 1868.
631 Had intended to take a young girl with them. Ref: 3 October 1864.
632 Wonwondah Station (Ref: 30 September 1864).

the buggy round & ~~what~~ wheathered it, but before we got to Niel there came another heavy rain with a very strong wind; we took at first ~~re~~ refuge behind some bushes, but as it did not look like giving over & we were in sight of M̅r̅ Mc'donnalds house we made for it which was not an easy matter in the gale that was blowing. We were very kindly received & very soon got at home with M̅r̅ & M̅r̅s̅ M̅c̅ Donnald._

4 October 1867

[Fri] An arrangement was made to-day that the boys should have their meals in the school superintended by us. Rebecca is willing for a time to take the cooking & the thing seems to answer._

5 October 1863

Mon.) A letter to B̅r̅ T Badham[633] in London about my being naturalized a British subject. _ & also what support my Mary[634] had to expect, in case she sh̅l̅d̅ be left a widow._

5 October 1864

[Wed] Left W.W.D[635] after breakfast taking with us some nice presents_ A waxdoll for Sp[dieseke]'s_ stuff for a dress for S̅i̅s̅ S̅p̅_ an old suit for Nathanael._ Polly got £3 from M̅r̅s̅ Rutherford._ Daniel who had come over from Horsham yesterday rode back with us._ In H[orsham]: I bought ~~a~~ a few things at Langland's._ (We saw also D̅r̅ Jo̅h̅nson!) In the evening we drove to Walmar & stopped there over night._

5 October 1866

[Fri] Off to the Manse; got there safely, & stayed over night. Rather a lonely place. M̅r̅s̅ Ellerman very glad to see us, as she felt very lonely in that place. The house is a good building of stone, but it stands in a very lonely place close to the edge of the mallée. M̅r̅s̅ E gave some stuff for a dress to Polly._ The servant they have at present seems to get on nicely.

---

633 Thomas Leopold Badham, assistant secretary of the Moravian missions until the death of Peter La Trobe in 24 September 1863, whence Badham became secretary. He was also long-time editor of the Moravian *Periodical Accounts*, a missionary periodical. Hamilton, *A History of the Church Known as the Moravian Church*. 444.
634 Prev. Ref: 30 September 1863.
635 Wonwondah Station (Ref: 30 September 1864).

6 October 1864

[Thu] As we had to wait for Dr Johnson we could not leave Walmar before 12 a.m._ On our way to 9 creeks we Polly & I walked over that large plain._ Got to 9 creeks at about sunset._

6 October 1865

[Fri] prepared the boards, I cut with Phillip, by cutting a little out for the pipe to rest in, took me al l day to do._

6 October 1866

[Sat] Off to mount Elgin, 6 miles from the manse,[636] occupied at present by Mr Telford. Saw Martha & spoke to her, Invited her also to come to our place but had to avoid all appearance of taking her wi away as Mrs T. seems to like her very much & did not like to part with her_ Mrs T. a singular woman._ After dinner we started for Nhil & got there in good Time._ As they just had commenced washing sheep I went to the wash to see Mr Mc Donnald_ M^rs M^cD & Mrs H. made also their appearance._

7 October 1864

[Fri] Got back to our dear Ebenezer,[637] & very glad we were._ We found all quite well._ Our young mare had died over getting her foal. Both our cows had calfe calved so we have plenty milk now._ The pigs after much trouble had been caught & been put into the sty._ I set to work on painting the black board over again with oil paint I brought from Horsham._ Then I went on with our bath consisting of a wooden boy lined with linen & painted with oil to make it watertight. In the evening when I was about to keep the meeting, Daniel came & asked me if he might not keep the meeting, as I & S[pieseke]. had nothing to say against it he kept it. He seemed to be very full & could not restrain himself any longer._

7 October 1865

[Sat] Watered a little bit of my garden, by means of the water-tub horse & cart I pumped the water on the mill, and leet let it run down through a pipe into the tub. I had first Boby,[638] but I thought to change him for March

---

636 The Manse at Nhill.
637 Left Ref: 30 September 1864.
638 Bobby, one of the work horses at the mission.

Well March was standing very quiet for a while whilst I was pumping above but suddenly he bolted with the tub full of water, & after a little run along the river, the cart hitting a tree upset & threw the horse down too. When I saw the horse bolt what could I do but ask the Lord to help, & he did in such a way that neither the horse was hurt not the cart broken_ I fetched all in all 11 tubs of water._

7 October 1866

[Sun] At Nhil a quiet & comfortable day. There was but family worship in the morning but in the evening we had a service to w^h the some of the men came.

7 October 1867

[Mon] In consequence of the very very wet weather the river is overflowing its banks We are at present on an island & no more able to ride through the creek outside of our gate & the water is still rising. I am just about putting up a railing outside of our garden fence to keep the cattle away from biting our vines & fruittrees. Not been able to do anything at our mill as the tree is under water & as the water is very low in our tank I put up the small Douglas pump to get it out more easily_

8 October 1864

[Sat] Hard at it, all day making the showerbath_ In the afternoon Mrs Ellerman children & her governess Miss Fraser payed us a visit & took tea with us._ After the meeting I accompanied M^rs E as far as our 2nd gate; it was a beautiful moonlight night. On my way back I stopped at the camp to see the Blacks_ Matthew was there too, & asked me whether he might speak to the people & said they were willing to listen to him. Spieseke happened to be there too, & I had a talk to King Peter I asked him where he thought he would go to when he died, he answered "to heaven" I told him then if he did not come to Jesus before he died he would not go to heaven. He seems to be rather sick._ Considering all things together I would much rather be Missionary amongst our Blacks than being a member of the U E C.[639]_

---

639 Unity Elders Conference (German: *Unitätsältestenkonferenz*) was the administrative direction of the Church between the general synods.

8 October 1865

[Sun] To Antwerp in the morning & preached there; no attendance but the family There was thunder & lightening, but very little rain. There was also a peculiar haze of a brown colour; very close day._

8 October 1866

[Mon] There was rain during the night & it looked a very wet morning so that we thought we would not be able to get home to-day, but it cleared up & so we started. We kept all the way nicely in the track till we came to the big mallee when we took a wrong turn & got into the road to Mr Marsh & Stuart, we soon however found our mistake & turned back into the right road & got home safely._ As the river had risen I crossed in the boat being got over by Sp._ & I went round by the crossing place._

9 October 1864

[Sun] We heard to-day that King Cole has killed his lubra Lady (at Vectis[640]). I made use of this occurrence to speak to the people in the evening meeting._ It was a very warm day & one begins to feel the want of lighter clothes.

9 October 1865

[Mon] All the people off again to Antwerp to go on with the shearing_ I commenced putting up the scaffold to support the pipes that are to lead the water into the garden. After some thinking I found it best to put first, at a convenient distance, posts straight up, to serve for pointers, & although I had nobody to help me I managed to put up the posts although rather heavy._ Some of the candidates show some indifference to spiritual things by keeping away from the meetings._

10 October 1864

[Mon] The first wi touch of a hot wind but not much of it. S[pieseke] & I & some more Blacks were in the sheep yard, marking some old sheep that will be drafted from the flock; we have at present 150 sheep_

---

640 Vectis, squatting run held by Alexander Wilson.

10 October 1866*

[Wed] Jonathan[641] died this morning. Though formerly very depraved & stupid, we have hope in his death. A good many women sick.

11 October 1866*

[Thu] Some blacks came from Lochiel, & brought word that Judy is not expected to live. Others also are sick. We heard to-day that Jonathan before his death, expressed a wish that his lubra, Mary should leave the camp & come up & live at our place, & that she should get the young women to tell her all about Jesus.

11 October 1867

[Fri] To night B[r] Sp[ieseke]: returned from Melbourne.[642]_ Although he has not received a definite promise about the land, he has been assured by the Board that they will look to it that 12,000 acres are secured for the Blacks._ The weather has been pretty fair these last days & the river is falling._ I went to Antwerp in the forenoon to see Stephen & widow Mary[643] both very sick. Stephen seems to put his trust in the Saviour, & expresses himself to be ready to go any time the Lord should call him away._

12 October 1864

[Wed] We killed our old bullock Brown. M[r] Ellerman, who came here with a M[r] Westwood[644] a Baptist minister can & a great admirer of Spurgeon,[645] shot the old fellow in our paddock, & then he & Nathanael skinned him, & jointed him._ M[r] Campbell & wife were here also on the way to their home._

12 October 1866*

[Fri] Jonathan was buried this afternoon.[646] I tried my hand at potting butter.

---

641 Spieseke also reported Jonathan's death as cause of hope that the Christian message was being received by people. See: *Periodical Accounts* 26 (1866), 195, 247.
642 Ref: 27 August 1867.
643 Presumed widow of Johnathan, Ref: 11 October 1866.
644 Only mention of Joseph J Westwood in the diary. By his own accounts, Westwood was the son of Quakers born in Poole, Dorsetshire, England, in May 1828. He travelled to Australia in 1856 and kept a journal from 28 February 1857, which was printed in 1864. He wrote favourably of his day trip to the Ebenezer mission station in his diary, in which he mentions, for example, that Philip was the 'first Christian aborigine I have ever had the privilege of seeing', Westwood, *The Journal of J.J. Westwood*, 466.
645 Referring to Charles Haddon Spurgeon (1834–1892), an influential and widely read Baptist preacher from England.
646 Died Ref: 10 October 1866.

12 October 1867

[Sat] B^r S[pieseke]: went to Antwerp, saw Stephen & brought him over to us. He seems a little better.

13 October 1863

A letter from Mary[647] from Fairfield announcing her safe arrival. I sent off an answer to day telling her that I would be with her to morrow._

13 October 1864

[Thu] At 3 p.m S[pieseke]: set off for Portland[648]_ At parting we had a prayer together commanding him & ourselves to the care of our dear Saviour. I think we may rest assured that he will grant us protection & guidance in what we have to do._

13 October 1865

[Fri] Got in 10 more pine logs for the scaffold for the irrigation Been at it all the week putting it up; Edward & Richard are helping me._

13 October 1866

[Sat] Sp & some of the people made up the sheep wash as we intend to wash next week._ I ~~car~~ charcoaled 30 post to be put up for trellisses for the vines._ Philip & Rebecca drove to Locheal with the spring cart & fetched Nancy[649] who is sick

14 October 1863

~~Wednesday~~ Met my Mary.[650]_ I got to Fairfield at about 5 ¾ p.m. & stopped with her till Saturday (Particulars SB page 32)

---

647 Prev. Ref: 5 October 1863.
648 Spieseke went on a missionary tour to establish if Portland would be a good site for a new mission. Ref: 18 September 1864.
649 This refers to a second Nancy. Ref: 15 August 1866.
650 Prev. Ref: 13 October 1863.

14 October 1864

[Fri] Got a small note from S[pieseke]., written in pencil, on his way to Horsham informing me that a black man Neddy[651] was coming up with 5 bottles of crog.[652]

14 October 1865

[Sat] Had to refuse Mr Ellerman's request to preach for him at the 9 creeks it not being my turn to go, I did so because I feared he would take advantage of it & expect me, if I accepted ~~every~~ proposals ~~to~~ of that kind, to accept them any time w^h of course I could not do._

15 October 1864

[Sat] Neddy having arrived in the evening I went at once to the camp & made inquiries about the grog.[653] It was altogether a story & I was very glad it was such._

15 October 1866

[Mon] A beautiful warm day & so we had our sheep washed. All went well & we did not lose one sheep. The sheep wash had been renewed & improved upon & it answered very much better than last year._

16 October 1865

[Mon] Sp[ieseke]. went of on a trip to Scotts. M^r E from Antwerp lent him his new buggy._ He took Helene, Eliza & John Ellerman with him._ Got the Home letters, & one for my B^r Henry ready to be posted to-morrow._ There was a row with Timothy this morning._ S^p wanted to speak to Matthew about his unwillingness & laziness to do ~~much~~ a thing & then he talked, too, to Timothy about his sulky & surly way he was in for some time, & it came out, at least Matthew, said so, that Timothy last week, in Antwerp, when Sp was urging the people to make up a hole that had burst, had said he would take a board & knock him down, Timothy denied that he had said so, & said to Matthew he would pull him into the fire if he would tell such tales about him._ S^p took up the subject in the morning meeting sharply.

---

651 Only other mention of him on Ref: 15 October 1864.
652 Grog—that is, alcohol.
653 Neddy was presumed to have five bottles of grog with him. Ref: 14 October 1864.

17 October 1863

(Sat.) Got back to Fulneck at 12 ½ & found in my part a letter from S[ir] George Grey[654] from London informing me that I could not be naturalized an Englishman,[655] because I did not intend to stop in the country._

17 October 1864

[Mon] Finished my shower-bath apparatus & hope it to put it up to morrow._

17 October 1866

[Wed] The river is rising again and is now higher than it ever was before this winter. A nice warm day, splendid growing weather._

18 October 1864

[Tue] Plaistered the floor of the end of my gallery where people are to sit. I must try to get some sort of carpet to put over it plaister as the floor would be too white. Our people finished the fence to-day. A beautiful but rather warm day._ I commenced in the evening the instruction with the candidates for baptism. Booppoop, Albert, Susan & Lilly (in S[plieseke] absence)

18 October 1866

[Thu] There was a good heavy shower in last night, but being a fine warm day the sheep got dry & some of them were driven to Antwerp for shearing, to commence to-morrow

19 October 1864

[Wed] Put up our shower-bath, & then it being a rather warm day we had both a try & had felt it to be most refreshing._ I measured to-day the new fence & found it to be 46 chains, & the people that made it shall get for it according to our agreement £13 per mile. £7.9.6._

19 October 1865

[Thu] The old mare bolted this morning when the people (Edward & Dicky) were fetching wood & this time the horse got cut badly about the hind legs & the cart smashed. M[r] M[c] Donnald, perbyterian minister from

---

654 Sir George Grey (1799–1882), British politician. Home secretary three times, including in the period 1861–66.
655 Ref: 5 October 1863.

Melbourne paid us a visit coming from Scotts, he stayed but a few hours & then drove back again to Scotts as he wanted to be present at the tea-meeting to-morrow. I was asked to go too, but as the teameeting was put much earlier than it was made out first, & as I wanted to finish the irrigation this week I declined to go._ Jerry & brown fetched in to-day that hay-filly w^h Mr Wilson had ~~promised~~ ^given^ us some time ago, but w^h we were not able to find until now. Jerry made his first attempt with her to break her in, all went well. So rode to Antwerp to ask Mr Ellerman's advice about the ^broken^ cart & the costs of the repair (seemed to me useless)

19 October 1866

[Fri] Shearing at Antwerp (Somehow S[pieseke]: who had the looking after & arranging it had some trouble with our Black Shearers, they wanting to play the white man not willing to do such little things as radling etc a few sheep. We cannot allow such sentiments to prevail among them as they shear as it were their own sheep._

19 October 1868

[Mon] <u>The Bees swarmed</u>[656] Very unexpectedly too. A strong hot wind blew so of course I did not think they would swarm. Well I think they did so heaving been prevented for some days to swarm, it had always been rather cool weather & so the hive got overcrowded to excess & the heat of the day although very windy made the bees leave the hive; it happened during dinner time

This teaches us to look out for swarms even on hot wind days._

20 October 1865

[Fri] At last the irrigation is so far advanced now, in fact finished so far that water is now running into the garden. We finished to-day the putting up of the pipes, & then let the mill go._ All in order, no leaking, The next thing to be done is the tank in the garden._

20 October 1866

[Sat] Sp[ieseke] had ^yesterday^ some more trouble with the Blacks & had to set them rights about it. I was engaged yesterday & to-day preparing wood for the trellising of the vines

---

656 The Hartmanns brought back the bees from their trip to Castlemaine Ref: 28 May 1868.

21 October 1864

[Fri] Drafted out of our flock some 26 sheep, old ones, for fattening up to be killed._ Went out with Nathanael cutting some posts for the new Washkitchen to be annexed to the back of our kitchen. The little boy <u>Archie</u> from the Lake arrived yesterday, a promising little fellow. _

22 October 1864

[Sat] Was out all the forenoon with Nathanael, Lanke, & Edwaad looking xxx for posts for the washhouse & for the houses they are going to build It was not quite an easy to find some & we only got 4 to-day._ In the afternoon I commenced preparing the posts._

23 October[657] 1863

Friday) Got a very nice letter from my beloved Polly.[658]_ She made me also a present of a small note book._ She sent me also a list of her relatives.[659]_

The following text & verse she drew for me._

>Es sei ferne von uns rühmen, denn
>allein von dem Kreuze unseres Herrn
>Jesu Christi_ Gal. 6. 14_

>Wir rühmen uns des Bluts allein
>Vom Hirten übers Haus;
>denn alles Heil für die Gemein'
>Fließt ewig da heraus.
>O Jesu! gründ uns immermehr
>Auf dein Verdienst u dich.[660]_

---

657 Adolf Hartmann's birthday. Born in Charlottenburg, Suriname, on 23 October 1831.
658 First time that Adolf uses his nickname for Mary. Prev. Ref (to Mary): 14 October 1863.
659 The list is not extant in MAB, PP HJAH.
660 English translation: Far be it from us to boast, for
from the Cross of our Lord alone
Jesus Christ_ Gal. 6. 14

We boast of blood alone
From the shepherd to the house;
for all salvation for the community.
Flowing out of there forever.
O Jesus! Found us evermore
On your merit and you.

23 October 1864*

[Sun] A quiet comfortable day._ We both enjoyed it very much._ In the evening I kept the meeting in the camp._ Matthew interpreted what I said & Nathanael prayed._ I began my women's Sunday class.

23 October 1865

[Mon] Commenced mending our cart; put 2 new spokes ⁿ & part of the ring._ All the people were mustered to pull our hay wʰ is so short that it cannot be mown. Hot day & no wind._

23 October 1866

[Tue] Polly dear made me Putztisch,[661] & some of the women sang before my door "Here we suffer grief & pain, Here we meet to part again._

24 October 1863

Sat) The boys[662] of Fulneck school[663] presented me with a photographic lense & camera._ At 1 oclock after dinner they all gathered in the first room.[664]_ One of the older boys then read to me an address (copy of it in small book p. 32) I then said a few words in return expressing my thanks._ Mʳ Willey[665] then allowed me £2[666] for getting the chemicals[667] at Leeds[668] at Henry Reynold & Fauler's Briggate. I kept the boys for Mʳ Elliott & went out chumping for Nov 5ᵗʰ.[669]_

---

661 Translated as 'a shiny table': PUTZTISCH, abacus, mensa nitidior. See: *Deutsches Wörterbuch von Jacob Grimm und Wilhelm Grimm*, digitalisierte Fassung im Wörterbuchnetz des Trier Center for Digital Humanities, Version 01/21, accessed 25 May 2021, www.woerterbuchnetz.de/DWB.
662 Adolf taught, together with Charles Connor in Room 2, 17 boys, the majority from England, one from Barbados. See: JN Libbey, *In-School Magazine*, Summer 1939, photocopies copied supplied by Robin Hutton, West Yorkshire, UK.
663 Fulneck School, Pudsey, UK, established in 1753 as a boarding school for Moravian as well as non-Moravian boys. A school for girls was established in 1755. Notable pupils of the school included Charles Joseph La Trobe, the first lieutenant general of the Colony of Victoria. See: T Waugh, *A History of Fulneck School* (Leeds: Richard Jackson, 1909); Dianne Reilly, 'Charles Joseph La Trobe: An Appreciation', *The La Trobe Journal* 71 (Autumn 2003), 5–15.
664 Teachers of Room 1 were, at the time, Henry Shawe and Mr Roederer. See: Waugh, *A History of Fulneck School*, 48–50.
665 Joseph Hutton Willey, headmaster of Fulneck School from 1852 to 1879. See: Waugh, *A History of Fulneck School*.
666 In 1860, £2 was equal to 10 days' wages for a skilled tradesman. Conversion undertaken with The National Archives, UK, *Currency converter: 1270–2017*, accessed 2 March 2020, www.nationalarchives.gov.uk/currency-converter/.
667 Chemicals for the photographic process.
668 Leeds, West Yorkshire, UK, some 6 miles from Fulneck.
669 Guy Fawkes Night, 5 November. From 1605 until 1859, the Observance of 5th November Act enforced the celebration of the day to commemorate the failed plot to kill King James I.

24 October 1864

[Mon] Commenced preparing the posts for the new wash house Nathanael & Matthew helped me._ Edward & Timothy ~~fetched~~ ᶜᵘᵗ posts for their own houses._

24 October 1865

[Tue] Got up very early to put the tire on my wheel. I Had to make a big fire & all went well._ People pulling hay._ Very hot again, no wind._ Mr Edol's came here this morning at 8 a.m. had breakfast, looked at the mill & then proceeded to look at the fence our people had topped for him (Edward James[670]) rode with him._ The new horse we called <u>Mona</u> It is a most beautiful mare, so quiet, never bucked yet or played any trick. They had it out to-day pulling a log._

25 October 1864

[Tue] At the washhouse all day but could not do as much as I wished to do my blocks not sticking to me as they sh^{ld} have done. Mr Ellerman came over & presented us with some of his honey._

25 October 1865

[Wed] Very hot again;_ got on with the cart to my satisfaction._

25 October 1866

[Thu] The people finished the shearing to-night._ We had a visit of Mr Gillesbie[671] & ~~M^r~~ his wife, Mrs Hastie, also Mr Andrew Scott, M^r & Mrs Flemming_ They only stayed a short time

26 October 1864

[Wed] The people in the camp being very lazy, I had some trouble to get some to help me cutting logs for the washhouse, but I succeeded to get 3 and with Phillip & Toney I managed to cut 30 logs. We had occasional showers to-day: the river also is rising a little._ Edward & Timothy busy fetching logs for their new houses._

---

670 Edward was baptised and took the name James on 26 July 1865. See: *Periodical Accounts* 27 (1868), 193.
671 No further reference to Gillesbie in the diary.

26 October 1865

[Thu] Finished our cart before dinner._ Afternoon I watered ^(the garden)._ Evening ~~ma~~ washed some lime to white-wash our bed-room._

26 October 1867

[Sat] Having scoured the inside of the pump somewhat smooth, w^(h) I did by means of the windmill & when I had the accident to break a lath of the wings it striking against the post, I put the sucker in & let it pump. It pumped beautifully & we got the tank full again, w^(h) it was not for a month at least._

27 October 1864

[Thu] Nathanael threw his Tomahawk at one of the cows, when driving in the calves. The reason of his doing so I dont know yet. I shall ask him about it by & by when a good opportunity offers itself. Fetched some logs with Matthew from outside the fence. Yesterday & to-day very cold & windy.

27 October 1865

[Tue] White-washed our bed-room_ (About 84 yards of our fence was burned down on the other side at the Locheal gate; it was noticed in good time by Phillip & some other people. It was put out successfully, & S^(p[lieseke]) with Jerry rode after the men that had camped there the previous night, overtook them at Locheal bridge. He got £1 of them & brought also 4 bullocks from Mr Wallace to put up the fence._ should be on the next day)

27 October 1866

[Sat] Finished putting up the trellisses for the ~~vi~~ vines Pearce the boy helping me._

27 October 1867

[Sun] The Lords supper._ Nathanael & Magdalene were received again[672]

---

672 According to the UEC Minutes, in January 1867 four people were excluded from the religious community for a period of time as they had engaged in improper fornication, being Timothy, Stephen, Magdalene and Nathanael. See: UA, UEC Minutes, 4 July 1867, #4, 25.

EBENEZER MISSION STATION, 1863–1873

28 October 1863

(Wed) Went to Leeds to get my large Bible bound; I gave it to Mr Megson._ I bought also the chemicals for my Photographic apparatus;[673] the sum w^{h[ich]} Mr Willey[674] allowed me was £2. but this being not quite sufficient I had to add £3 6^s.[675]

28 October 1864

[Fri] At the washhouse all day with Nathanael._ There was a row between Waape and old Jimmy (account of it in Sketch book). There are 48 Blacks here at present, but we have a bad attendance at our chapel._

28 October 1866

[Sun] Had with us almost all the day Mrs Hastie M^r & Mrs Flemming

28 October 1867

[Mon] Our shearing commenced._ i began cutting our hay, a tremendous crop.

29 October 1863

(Thurs) B^r Stolz[676] from Neuwied[677] arrived here at 3 ½ p.m. I was very glad for it, for now I shall be able to get off soon._

---

673 Adolf had received a camera as a departing present from the pupils at the Fulneck boys' school. Ref: 24 October 1863.
674 Ref: 24 October 1863.
675 In 1860, £3 6s was equal to 16 days' wages for a skilled tradesman. Conversion undertaken with The National Archives, UK, *Currency converter: 12702017*, accessed 2 March 2020, www.nationalarchives.gov.uk/currency-converter/.
676 Br Stolz was Adolf's teaching replacement at the Fulneck Boys school.
677 Neuwied, on the Rheine River near Koblenz, Germany. A Moravian settlement established 1750, originally a French-speaking community.

29 October 1864

[Sat] This morning Mr Green from Coran Darrk[678] about 40 miles from Melbourne, came here with Mr Ellerman. He is travelling about to gather reports about the Blacks of Victoria.[679] According to his statement he seems to have collected about 65 Blacks at his place, who are all doing well, & who seem to settle down doing regular work every day farming e.t.c.

29 October 1866

[Mon] Mr Edols came here about dinner time & stayed with us till evening. His chief object was to enquire from Steven & James about Mr Archibald taking some of ^his (Mr Edol's) ~~both some~~ ^sheep when driving though his paddock.

30 October 1864

[Sun] A very refreshing meeting in the camp Mr Green spoke, as he had done already to the Blacks. The old man Billy[680] very sick expected to die; he is quite blunt, one can get nothing out of him as regards the state of his heart. He never liked the truth & persuaded even other to stay away from us, & now may the Lord be merciful to him, for we can do nothing for him._

30 October 1865

[Mon] Made the additional sails for the windmill

30 October 1866

[Tue] Commenced school again in the morning as it does not answer well to have it in the evening, a good many attended._ A very hot day hot wind._ Schulze[681] the carrier came to our place presenting us with a barrel of colonial wine._ In the afternoon, following an invitation we all went to Antwerp Mrs Hastie still being there, & came back in the evening._

---

678 Coran Darrk referring to Coranderrk. For a detailed history of this Aboriginal Reserve see: Barwick, *Rebellion at Coranderrk*.
679 John Green did so under the auspice of the colonial government. In 1864 he was the inspector of stations for the Central Board.
680 First Ref. Old Man Billy worked for Hugh Campbell in early 1864. Adolf reported Old Man Billy's death in a letter to the Moravian Church in Germany, and suggested that the man was not open to the Christian message. He also gave a report of the burial practices and rites around the burial of Old Man Billy. See: DDHS, The Lorquon Diary of Hugh Campbell; *Periodical Accounts* 25 (1863), 357–58.
681 Ref: 18 September 1866.

30 October 1868
[Fri] Mr Green arrived here & stopped with us for some time._

30 October 1869
[Sat] The policeman Blanc from the Nine Creeks arrived demanding by order of the Coroner Dr Purves[682] that the body of Amos who died on the 27 should be brought to the Nine Creeks to undergo a post mortem examination. Amos had been buried yesterday and so the body had to be exhumed & carted there a very disgusting sort of business. Mr Spieseke & I both wrote to Melbourne to enquire about this affair._ The death of our Blacks had never before been reported at the Creeks but a Dr Purves told M^r S that it ought to be done S did so but unessesarily worded his letter in such a way that the Policeman was in doubt whether an inquest was required or not and therefore proceeded accordingly.

31 October 1864
[Mon] Old Billy died in the morning_ Our people, not the Camp people, made the grave. There was no work done at all to day._ It was very hot too._

31 October 1865
[Tue] 10 ½ a.m. M^r & Mrs Wilson with children arrived & stayed with us till about 3 p.m. There came also just about noon M^r & Mrs Robert Scott[683] from Buninyong near Ballarat, so we had the house full._ There was a nice breeze blowing, so the mill went well. Our visitors were pleased with the thing._ When I mentioned to Mr Wilson about the bullocks we got from Mr Edol's & that the Blacks intended buying 2 new bullocks & we would make up the other 2 he would give them 2 bullocks if they (the Blacks) would buy 1 w^h he would sell them for £5._ The Blacks were told about Mr Wilson proposal & were very glad to accept it

---

682 William Laidlaw Purves, Esq, Coroner of Victoria at Horsham, appointed in November 1867. See: *The Argus* (Melbourne), 9 November 1867, 6.
683 Robert Scott was a supporter of missions and was an annual subscriber to the 'Native Missionaries on the New Hebrides' in 1863, along with other notable supporters of the Moravian mission in Victoria, including Andrew Scott of Warracknabeal and William Rutherford of WonWonda, and Charles Wilson of Walmer. See: *The Age* (Melbourne), Tuesday 14 April 1863, 7.

November

1 November 1864

[Tue] Old man Billy was buried this morning;[684] M[r] Green & I was present I addressed the Blacks present, & begged them to remember their end w[h] must be comming some time or other, & besought them to turn to the Saviour. M[r] White & family paid us a short visit. M[r] White promised me to get in Melbourne where he is going presently to get me 1 lb of Hyposulphite of soda._ 15 grams of Chloride of Gold & 1 oz of Nitrate of silver.[685]_ M[r] Green also left us to go day[686] & went to Antwerp to proceed to M[r] Scott's._

1 November 1865

[Wed] Got our straw mattress stuffed & sown through, & then went out with some of the people to cut logs for the tank in the garden._ M[r] & M[rs] White on their leaving the country called on the other side of the river.

1 November 1866

[Thu] Sp[ieseke]: started this morning for Horsham following an invitation of M[r] Simpson to be present at the Lords supper on Sunday next, he intends also to fetch the doors & windows for his nursery. Engaged a number of people to put up a little yard for the hay stack._ Martha at length arrived here & went for the present to live in the sick house

2 November 1863

Mon) Began to work my photographic apparatus[687] & after 2 days hard working I succeeded in getting a pretty decent negative._ rather a laborious & intricate sort of work._

---

684 Died Ref: 31 October 1864.
685 For photography.
686 Ref: 29 October 1864.
687 The camera was a present from Adolf's students at the Fulneck boy's school. Prev. Ref: 24 October 1863.

2 November 1864

[Wed] M#rs# Edols with her whole family came here very unexpectedly on a visit but stopped only over night & then proceeded to Antwerp. We had some work to accommodate so many in our small house._ tame Blacks gone off but promised to come back again soon._

3 November 1864

[Thu] [Mon] & [Tue] we did no work at all it being rather hot, but to-day we commenced again. I saved a fine log of wood with Phillip for his house, & in the afternoon I worked at the washhouse._ I had an accident. Whilst adzing a log I slipped & touched my leg cutting the skin, but thanks to providence it was not much, & I could work all the afternoon. The weather is getting a little cooler._

3 November 1865

[Wed] Yesterday & to day I was out with the some of the people & cut logs for the tank to be made in the garden cut about 40._ In the evening Jacky killed oneof of our claves a splendid young beast._

3 November 1866

[Sat] Prepared one of the large boxes the Government goods came in for watering purposes, mended the tin & put a sort of tap in to fastened by a screw._

3 November 1868

[Tue] The new water closet was finished to-day_ a comfortable place

4 November 1865

[Sat] Had a somewhat close talk with S[pieseke]: about his treating Matthew._ Matthew said S: was hating him etc. etc. etc. As B#r# S: would not allow that he had treated M. in a wrong way we did not come to much. As one word gave the other, he said that my preaching in the Chapel was not what it should be (NB I went through the old testament) I asked him to put the thing before the U.E.C. but he did not seem to like that & so I begged not to touch upon the matter again if he would not bring it before the U.E.C. to decide.

Mʳ Edols Ellerman & Wallace came to settle about the fence the Blacks had topped.⁶⁸⁸ Well as the Blacks had not done it well, they were not willing to pay the according to the agreement £3,10, per mile. It turned out according to their calculation to be only 4 miles of fence, that our people topped properly, there being 2 ½ mile of mallee fence the people did not do much to & about a mile of log fence. Mʳ E. & E._ said that the Blacks work was not worth more than £14._ So they went away after much talking & said that they would pay £14. Our people after some consideration did not seem to like it & thought they were wronged, saying they topped about 6 miles, & so we will try to get £18 for them._

4 November 1868

[Wed] Mʳ Green left this morning⁶⁸⁹__ Very soon after it James⁶⁹⁰ died as we believe happy.⁶⁹¹_ What a mortality among the poor people 15 died within the last twelve month._

5 November 1865

[Sun] Off with Polly to the 9 creeks to preach._

5 November 1867

[Tue] Margaret had another baby, a boy. (baptized Robert)⁶⁹²

5 November 1868

[Thu] People mending the fence in the durock paddock._ _Planted some more potatoes in the upper garden & a large bed of carrots in the lower._ James was buried to-night behind the Chapel, alongside to his wife.⁶⁹³_ There was also a council kept in the schoolroom about James' house & it was settled that he who wanted ᵗᵒ ᵇᵘʸ it, was to pay £3 wʰ money was to be expended for getting ⁱⁿ clothing for the girls._

---

688 Ref: 19 October 1864.
689 Ref: 30 October 1868.
690 Previously Edward, baptised on Ref: 26 July 1865.
691 Died happy, meaning died a professing Christian.
692 The diary records three sons of Margaret and Matthew being: Joseph (Ref: 8 February 1866; 24 February 1866), Robert (Ref: 5 November 1867), and Charles Arthur (Ref: 25 July 1870).
693 Ruth, died Ref: 15 November 1867.

6 November 1865

[Mon] Had another talk with Mr Edol's about the fence but the result was that Mr Edols got cross about it so I dropped the matter at once._ He paid finally his portion £7. Mr Edol's watering machine for watering the garden a capital thing throwing a great amount of water._

6 November 1866

[Tue] The sowing machine arrived, & also the stuff for the new hose & for the wings of the new wind mill. I put the machine together & then began the study._ The result of all trials was that night a failure that night so I have to try again next morning._ The machine belongs to both Spieseks's & us. Our share was £5 2s 9d it is to be used in turns. The amount was paid by Polly to-day._ The people worked very well to-day at the enclosure of for the hay-stack. I was at the pump for the tank._

6 November 1868

[Fri] Cogle[694] bought the house w^h belonged to James[695]_ I was making new joining for our hoses for water as the old ones are very leaky._

7 November 1863

[Sat] Left Hull[696] for Hamburg[697] at 3 o'clock at night[698]_ A rough passage & felt rather sick, but felt a little better towards the end of the passage._ travelled in company with Miss Edwards. _[699]

Sat) Left Hull for Hamburg at 3 oclock at night, a roughish passage, & felt rather sick, but felt better towards the end of the passage;__ travelled in company with Miss Edwards._

---

694 Cogle married Betsy. Ref: 1 May 1869.
695 James (previously Edward) died Ref: 4 November 1868. In a letter to her parents, Polly stated: 'Just now, the blacks who came here a year ago from Lake Boga, are charged with th having caused the death of James, one of our baptized blacks who died some time ago, or consumption, as we believe. The fear is that the whole of the Lake Boga blacks will be driven aways from our place, which would be a great pity, as they are far before the Wimmera blacks in diligence & good sense & several of them are hopeful candidates for baptism. With them we should also lose six children.' MAB, PP HJAH, 3, Letters, Polly [Mary] Hartmann to Hines, Ebenezer, 21 January [1869].
696 Kingston Upon Hull, UK, ferry port.
697 Hamburg, Germany. In 1863, Hamburg was a city of the Hanseatic League, unifying in 1871 with other Hanseatic cities and kingdoms to form Germany.
698 Prev. Ref: 9 September 1863.
699 This passage is written out twice, once on the left-hand side of open double page, and once on the right. It is unusual and suggests that Adolf had made a mistake in writing the comments for 1863 firstly on the right-hand side of the page.

7 November 1865

[Tue] Commenced digging the tank in our garden with as many people as I could get. We got on very nicely & it may be dug in 3 days. The tank will be 15 feet square._ begun speaking the communicants for the 13 of N^{ov}._

7 November 1866

[Wed] No school_ Set to work again to get the machine straight, & succeeded not only to my ^{own} but also to the others joy_ We took it over then to Sp[ieseke]'s & M^{rs} Sp's did some work that day. When we were at dinner M^{r} S: came back from Horsham. Mr S. spoke out well on behalf of the Blacks & settled with Mr Simpson about some points the latter had been rather quick to arrange wistful to carry out without our consent as to have the school under Government,[700] & to send one of the Blacks to Presbyterian assembly.[701] Both these points were not carried out._

8 November 1864

[Tue] Got at last our home letters w^{h} we had given up as lost, but w^{h} had been kept too long at Grice Summer & Co there was also a letter of F Latrobe[702] & Mrs Clough._

8 November 1867

[Fri] Got our likenesses taken at the 9 creek where we went on a unit to Edol's (poor likenesses) but as I have no time to spend to take them myself we must put up with what we can get._

9 November 1866

[Fri] Put up the wooden pump, I had been at, in the tank, & a big box also containing about 40 buckets of water, to be able to water more expeditiously. The thing seems to answer & S[pieseke] likes it too._ Extraordinary cool & windy weather has set in

---

700 The school could not be under the government's control as Adolf was an ordained minister and thus ineligible to be a government teacher, and further the school was not conducted for four continuous hours a day, as per government regulation. See: UA, UEC Minutes, 9 January 1868, # 5, 28.
701 Phillip (formerly Charley Charley) and Nathanael (formerly Pepper) were selected to go to the Presbyterian General Assembly in Melbourne in 1866, but did not attend. At the previous General Assembly, the suggestion that they should be paid was raised, Ref: 7 September 1865. See also: UA, UEC Minutes, 26 April 1866, #3, 110–16.
702 Possibly Frederick Latrobe, Adolf's groomsman Ref: 29 December 1863.

9 November 1869

[Tue] Dick a Dick & Amelia_ Henry[703] & Diana,[704] ~~lelf~~ left for the west to see their home as they said. Well we hope that they will come back again, but it does not seem quite certain

10 November 1865

[Fri] ~~The~~ The bullocks arrived from Walmar & the Blacks who paid for one of them chose one of them to look upon as their own._

Had <u>Richard</u> in for speaking,[705] he seems to feel the love of the Saviour in his heart and expresses himself pleasingly about the state of his heart._

10 November 1866

[Sat] Martha & Jerry do not agree together, there is quarrelling between the two. Jerry said he was tired of her, & he seemed to have made an agreement with Hᵉarty to take Martha of course we do not countenance the matter & never shall._ Harty[706] is building himself a bark hut like Steven._

10 November 1867

[Son] Margarets boy Joseph[707] was very sick in consequence of a sun stroke his life was almost desparied of, & the doctor sent for but before he came he mended

11 November 1865

[Sat] Had <u>Mark</u> in for speaking[708]_ seems to be seeking yet_ exhorted him to pray to the Saviour to help him._

---

703 Possibly referring to a resident of the mission whom Adolf recorded in his writings to Robert Brough Smyth as being around 24 years old. See: Smyth, *The Aborigines of Victoria*, 2.
704 First Ref: 4 December 1867. Diana was brought with Kitty (baptismal name Amelia) by Spieseke to the mission in December 1867.
705 Meaning discussing his religious state with him.
706 Also referred to as Hearty. See also Ref: 18 July 1866.
707 Born Ref: 8 February 1866.
708 Meaning discussing his religious state with him.

12 November 1863

<u>Thurs</u>) Arrived at Herrnhut[709] ~~in~~ 2 p.m. I went there being called by the U. E. C.[710] to get instructed as regards the Mission in Australia.[711]_

12 November 1864

[Sat] Finished the washhouse except the door & window for w^h I shall have to cut boards first._

12 November 1865

[Sun] Had Dicky in for speaking.[712]_ He seems on the way to Jesus._

12 November 1866

[Tue] Nathanael & Matthew finished cutting the hay to day, it promises to yield fine hay & a good quantity

13 November 1865

[Mon] Had a lovefeast in the afternoon & the Lord's Supper in the evening._ Had a talk, too, with Mr Ellerman who spent the evening with us, about the fence[713] & made everything straight between us._

14 November 1865

[Tue] Drove to Antwerp with Polly, stayed tea; got a few planes given from Mr Ellerman

14 November 1866

[Wed] Got some long letters from Walder & Meissel who were on the way to Coopers creek. Interesting accounts indeed. The dear B^{rn} have some trials to go through; may the Saviour bless their work & labour!_

---

709 Herrnhut, Saxony, Germany is the original settlement of the renewed Moravian Church, established in 1722.
710 Adolf called to Herrnhut by Levin Riechel. Ref: 9 September 1863.
711 All missionaries were given printed as well as individual instructions as to their tasks as missionaries. The individual instructions stated the division of labour between the missionaries already present and the incoming missionary.
712 Meaning discussing his religious state with him.
713 Ref: 4 November 1865.

Mother Hines' birthday.[714]

15 November 1864

[Tue] A large flock of sheep being announced to travel through our paddock I got the old Mare to look after it; I just got in time to drive some small flocks of ours out of the way._

15 November 1867

[Fri] Ruth died to-day having been sick for some time, all our doctoring was of no avail; we believe she died happy.[715] [S]He is the first of those that died having lived in houses for some time.[716]_ Had a visit of M^r & Mrs Hugh Campbell._

16 November 1864

[Wed] Sharpened the pit & crotchet saws & put new handles to the latter having been broken off. Very warm these last days._ I took a bath in the Wimmera for the first time, the water still running it was most delicious._

16 November 1865

[Thu] Mr Ellerman's old buggy he had promised us some time ago was fetched to-day by Davy;[717] Mr E. gave us at the same time a good deal of old iron e t c._ Sp[ieseke] finished papering his room._

16 November 1866

[Fri] The young horse "Max" turns out a most beautiful horse in every way for riding as well as for driving. I did a little in photography this forenoon trying the new collodion I got from Melbourne._

---

714 Mother Hines: Polly's mother, Ann Hines.
715 Meaning that she died believing in the Christian religion.
716 Ruth moved into a house with her husband James (previously Edward). Ref: 16 June 1866.
717 Only mention of Davy in the diary. As noted in the introduction, Adolf took a photography of Davy, indicating that some relationship must have been had between Davy and the mission.

17 November 1863

Tues :| Was at Berthelsdorf before the U. E. C. laid many things before them for which see SB[718] page 40._ Was accepted an acoluth.[719]

17 November 1864

[Thu] Another ~~last~~rge flock of about 5000 sheep travelled through our paddock; no notice was given to me about it; Nathanael informed me about it but thought that our sheep were all right. I commenced making a meat-safe & in the evening before tea I went with Polly to bathe in the river. In the evening we watered the garden again pulling the tub, on a sledge, by a horse w*h* proves to be very convenient sort of work._

17 November 1867

[Sun] Ruth was buried[720]_ ~~to~~ behind the Chapel.

18 November

19 November 1863

Wed) Arrived at Gnadenfrei[721] 9 ¼ p.m. & was met by my sister Caroline had a cup of tea in the *dienerstube*[722] ((slept well that night))._

19 November 1864

[Sat] As our karrosine oil & my photographic chemicals got through M*r* Ellerman had arrived at Antwerp I sent horse & cart to fetch them. As M*r* Ellerman ordered his chemicals through a Chemist, ~~M~~ my order to B*ar* & O'Neil was of no use they most likely not getting my order; at least

---

718 Small Book.
719 An Acoluth is a Brother or Sister who has been accepted to undertake special duties in the religious community. Duties could include special supervision of certain areas of ministry within the local community and serving at communion. Acoluths were often young Brothers who were being training for a religious position.
720 Died Ref: 15 November 1867.
721 Gnadenfrei, Lower Silesian Voivodeship, Poland (current name Piława Górna). Moravian community settled there from 1743 to 1945.
722 English translation: 'service room'.

20 November 1865

[Mon] Wanting some more logs for the tank I made a days job of it by going out side the fence with James, Timothy, Nathanael & Matthew. We took the bullock team with us, cut alltogether 28 logs 15 long & barked them all._ It was very hot work indeed._

20 November 1867

[Wed] Received the large photograph of Father & Mother[723]._

20 November 1868

[Fri] This morning at 4 ½ our boy (Henry John) was born. All went well thanks to our good Lord._ Dear Polly was only 2 ½ hour in labour._ Mrs Gain from Horsham was our nurse._ It rained heavily almost all night, so the hay got thoroughly wet, & will have to be spred again._

21 November

22 November 1869

[Mon] A number of letters were despatched, to the Legislative Assembly of Victoria asking for a grant of land to enable the Blacks to have about 4000 sheep 3 of the letters were written by Stewards, Philip[724] & Matthew & a general petition composed by me & copied by Albert & signed by a number of Blacks._ The squatters are very much against the movement

---

723 Referring to John and Ann Hines.
724 According to Adolf, this letter read:

'Sirs, We are very thankful for what you have done for us and to our race by giving us food and clothing, and now we come to you and thank you for all your kindness, sirs. We have houses and gardens of our own, and we have settle down at this place, but, sirs, we all wish to get [a] little more land, that we might be able to keep four thousand sheep, for we all think that we can work it and earn our own bread by working with our own hands. I have the honour to be &c. Philip Pepper, Aboriginal.' See: *Periodical Accounts* 27 (1868), 409.

but there is no other way to get the people to earn their own living by their own exertion, & at the same time to teach them & give them the advice they are so much in need of._

23 November 1864

[Wed] B^r & S^is Sp[ieseke]: came back from their journey at about 2 p.m.[725]_ We were very glad to welcome them again in our midst. He brought with ~~them~~ him some presents from Mr Rutherford's consisting in a couple of turkeys & a drake to give company to our duck. S. got our spring cart nicely painted at Pleasant Creek.

23 November 1866

[Fri] Mr Green from Corrandrk[726] arrived here on a tour through the Colony looking into the condition of the Blacks._ Made a kind of box ~~on~~ of lattice work to put on the cart for getting the hay in._

23 November 1867

[Sat] Old John died very suddenly this morning (of gall fever as Mr S. thinks) great distress among the people about the many cases of death.

Spieseke started for another trip westward to see the the Blacks scattered in that district

23 November 1869

[Fri] We had 2 tremendous thunder showers one about dinner time and the other towards evening each lasting about 2 hours. The ground got thoroughly soaked & there are large puddles of water standing everywhere._

24 November 1864

[Thu] The building of the 3 houses (all 3 in one) is progressing slowly. I'm putting the posts straight for the people (The houses belong to Timothy Edward & Lanke._ Went to the saw pit on the other side Phillip & Matthew sawing there, I helped them a little._ Our pigs are getting tame, one of them already runs after me._ Edward & Kitty intend to go off to-morrow to see their father who is at Mr Scotts station rather sick._

---

725 A missionary tour to Portland Ref: 13 October 1864.
726 Coranderrk.

24 November 1865

[Fri] Martha[727] who a little while ago had gone to Antwerp, ran away with Jerry.[728] We dont know what to think about her. We can do nothing but pray for her to the Lord, for she has deceived us.

25 November 1864

[Wed] Finished the meatsafe; a circular one enclosed by open canvas. [Here Adolf included a small sketch of the meat safe.]

26 November 1864

[Sat] All day the school taking down the old mantle piece & putting up a new one. The old one was a piece of peculiar patchwork made by Mr Hagenauer.

26 November 1865

[Sun] Being dear Polly's birthday M^{rs} S[pieseke]: got a cake baked & when sitting at breakfast the cake was presented to P: whilst the Black women outside sang "here we suffer grief & pain"._

26 November 1866

[Mon] Got the hay in to-day

26 November 1867

[Tue] Made a present to Polly of a new washstand I made._

Towards evening there came a man named Peter Mac Guinnes[729] from Mr Adam Smith's Station Mosquito Plains, 12 miles beyond the Boundary. He brought with him his daughter Christina a half caste & desired her to be kept & brought up at our place._ She is a very funny & forward girl, but with the Lord's blessing she may be taught in the way she should go._

---

727 Martha (formerly Sarah) was baptised Ref: 27 July 1865.
728 Martha's relationship with Jerry, who was not a Christian, was a source of anxiety for the missionaries.
729 Only mention of Peter Mac Guinnes in the diary. Rather than referring to the settler of the same name, it could refer to the Aboriginal man Peter MacGuinnes (c. 1846–1911), who was also known as Jowley, and was said to be the last survivor the Yarrikuluk clan of the Wotjobaluk. Taylor, *Karkarooc*, 22–24.

27 November 1865

[Mon] Had M[r] & M[rs] Ellerman on a visit, all their children came,_ a pretty warm day after the last 3 or 4 when we had E wind._ Sp[ieseke] went with 2 Blacks Phillip & James to damm up the river so as to keep the water high during the summer._ I was laying the pipes from the tank to the kitchen._

27 November 1866

[Tue] M[r] Green left to-day[730] accompanied by M[r] Spieseke, as far as the 9 Creeks, who is going to see the Blacks there._ Nathanael rode to Vectis to see about Fanny who it was said had expressed a wish to come to our place with her 2 children.[731]_ Many many things were talked over with M[r] Green. It was settled that the rations at Vectis, Longernong & M[r] Officer's[732] were to cease & to be sent to our place.[733]_ It was further thought, that the time had arrived to apply for more land, & M[r] Green was willing to ask that 20 to 30,000 acres of land should be added to our place & that the board should help stocking the land by giving money to purchase sheep & cattle.

27 November 1867

[Wed] Began putting up the new hearth in the kitchen cutting the slabs away & getting the lime ready, Corny who came here yesterday got on[me] some wheelbarrows of stones._

28 November 1864

[Mon] Made the door to my darkroom light tight; it is fearful how the wood shrinks, & then I tried to give my background a proper coulour & succeeded pretty well. Had some difficulty to get a proper coulour; mixed some lampblack with lime._ I think clay will do better mixed with a little glue._ A number of Blacks came to-day among them Commodore,[734] Richard Lilly II with little Rosa a halfcast girl.[735]_

---

730 Ref: 23 November 1866.
731 Fanny, wife of Sandy. Together they had two girls, Minnie and Laura. Prev. Ref: 28 August 1866.
732 Mr Officer at Mount Talbot. See: *The Squatters' Directory*, 18.
733 This was not maintained, as Alexander Wilson was providing government rations to the Aboriginal people around Vectis in 1869. See: *Seventh BPA Report*, 21.
734 In May 1864, Polly described Commodore to her parents as being 'the King of the Horsham tribe', whose 'subjects have almost all died away'. See: MAB, PP HJAH, 3, Letters, Mary Hartmann to Hines parents, May, 1864.
735 The missionaries would try and convince Lily to leave Rosa at the mission station. Rosa would eventually be educated at Ebenezer and then moved to Warracknabeal with Dick. They had at least one girl together. Both Rosa and Dick frequented church. Ref: *Periodical accounts* 31 (1878), 188.

28 November 1866

[Wed] Sp[ieseke]: & Nathanael came back the latter had met the Vectis Blacks on their way to our place._ The new hose w^h was sown last week, I painted with oilpaint, the stuff proving not to be watertight._ Helped Timothy a little, laying the foundation of his fireplace._ Sowed more flowerseeds a few days ago & some of them are coming already._

29 November 1864

[Tue] M^r S[pieseke]. tacked new calico to in to the walls of the schoolroom. Myself fastened the hinges to the washhouse door & made a latch to it. The people who were sent by S. to top the fence on the other side were rather lazy they did hardly anything & played greater part of the time at ball; S. spoke very strongly to them about it in the meeting. The paper on my background cracks from the heat so I must make another alltogether.

29 November 1865

[Wed] Got a calf killed & so we had some splendid veal for a few days._

30 November 1864*

[Wed] Started for Mr Scotts at 8 a.m. very hot drive. Arrived at Werracknebeal[736] at 12.30. Mr Scotts not at home. For account of this visit see small book. Page_

30 November 1867

[Sat] Finished the new hearth; it seems to answer well & is liked

---

[736] 'Werracknabeal' refers to Scott's station Warracknabeal, and is recorded to be an Aboriginal word for gum tree. Taylor, *Karkarooc*, 25. Subsequently a town called Warracknabeal was established in the area.

December

1 December 1864*
[Thur] Visit to the blacks at Mr Scott's out-station. See small book. Page.[737]

1 December 1865
[Fri] Finished the Tank with the people, & then they had the plumpudding we promised them._

2 December 1864*
[Fri] Return home: called at Antwerp. Blacks arrived from the Lake. Rec^d book per post.

3 December 1864*
[Sat] Miss Fraser & the Antwerp children came on a visit. Adolf & B^r Spieseke fencing all morning.

3 December 1866
[Mon] The Blacks Dicky & Lilly gave their daughter Rosa to be with us She is to have her meals with us & sleep in the little room with Elizabeth I fetched with the Blacks & the bullock dray a heavy piece of with to be cut gum to cut the wings of or the is new windmill out of it._

3 December 1867
[Tue] Mr Hugh Campbell sent us 31 old fat sheep 2 of them were lost in the mallée. We had great trouble getting them accross the crossing place._

---

[737] MAB, PP HJAH 3, Letters, Polly [Mary] Hartmann to Hines parents, 15 December 1864. In this letter to her parents, Polly provided more information on this visit: 'About two or three years ago, a black died at that place [Scott's near Warracknabeal], & since then the different tribes have deserted the neighbourhood. We were therefore surprised to hear a short time ago that a large number of blacks were collected there; amongst the rest the aged father of Edward & Kitty (two of our people here), & the little girl Emma, of whose sorrowful removal from us by her parents I told you some time since – Both these were anxious to get to Ebenezer if possible. Now, then, was the time for our long promised visit.' She mentions the names Old Man Jack (Kitty's father) Kitty, Emma, Diggy, Napoleon, Booby and Mary, Neptune and Biddy, Blind Dan, Charles Napier (boy) Hearty, and Jenny.

4 December 1864*

[Sun] Adolf started at 8_30 for Nine Creeks, where he was to preach. In our morning service here we had more black men than I have seen in church before. The men's side was quite full.[738] Had a pleasant time with the women, who were very attentive, & seemed to enjoy our reading. Adolf returned at 7_30. p.m. Evening meeting in the camp.

4 December 1865

[Mon] Our people went all off to the Lake for a weeks holiday. We had promised them that they might do so as soon as the tank was finished._

4 December 1866

[Tue] A full school for some time already. The new system of having the people spell & read together seems to answer better than the old way, giving them singly to the more advanced to be taught by them._

4 December 1867

[Wed] B͟r Spieseke came back from his tour westward & brought with him 2 black women Kitty and Diana. He also got the promise of some more children._ M͟r Calder also promised some sheep although when we applied to him some time ago he excused himself._

5 December 1864*

[Mon] Had additional scholars. Lily_ Richard_ Lily_ Jacky. Rosa. Adolf was contriving a back-ground for his photographic tent. He has much trouble for want of materials.

5 December 1865

[Tue] Off to the 9 creeks store with ~~Moar~~ Mona in the spring cart ~~to~~ & Napoleon to a company me. Mona went splendidly all the way. Coming back we had a heavy load but it did not seem to make very much difference. Once on the way I applied the whip but then Mona kicked frightfully._

---

738 Traditionally, in Moravian Churches men and women sat on different sides of the Church.

S{p[ieseke]} got a letter from Revd Henderson of Balmoral, Glenelg asking him whether he would take a half caste girl <u>Topsy</u> (15 years old) who had been brought up in the family of Mr & Mrs Phillips. Of course we all were glad for this proposal, & Sp forthwith sent off a letter containing our consent._

5 December 1866

[Wed] Philip went off on Mona to Mr Officer's to see about these 2 black children that are there,[739] whether they can be got here ~~or~~ or not.[740] There are a good many Blacks here all the Vectis people except Fanny & her 2 children, & we shall try to get her to our place too, in fact we intend to get as many children from the neighbourhood as we can._

6 December 1865

[Wed] Painted the calico tubes, for ~~our~~ watering the garden._

6 December 1868

[Sun] Henry John Hartman, was baptized by me, this evening. Godfathers & godmother the following (Cousin Henry & his wife & our brother John[741]) B{r} & Sister Spieseke ^{stood} (for the former) & Philip for the latter)

6 December 1869

[Mon] Started in our buggy with the horse Max on our journey westward (Polly, Nelly & myself. Max got the gripes on the way to Walmer about 8 miles from it. We had tremendous work to get on. I took the horse out & tried to lead him to the next water; it was hard work, the horse was nearly falling down every moment, so I got on him & then it went better. Polly with Nelly was pulling the buggy for about 1 ½ miles. Well the horse mended gradually & by the help of the mailman who took our buggy & Polly & Nelly as far as Walmer gate, leaving them there, I managed to get up to them & we got safely to Walmer although rather late._

---

739 These were the children of Fanny and Sandy, being Minnie and Laura. Ref: 27 November 1866.
740 This was at the beginning of the renewed interest in encouraging parents to leave or send their children to the mission. On this particular journey, Philip was not successful. See: *Periodical Accounts* 26 (1866), 195.
741 John Hines, brother of Polly.

7 December 1864

[Wed] S[pieseke]. with wife went to see M̲ʳ H Ellerman & White at the Lake

7 December 1869*

[Tue] Stayed in Walmer, paid a visit to Horsham. M̲ʳ & M̲ʳˢ Robertson not at home. Max ~~selsued~~ went pretty well M̲ʳˢ Wilson in a poor state of health, preparing to go home to England in March.

8 December 1865

[Fri] M̲ʳ Ellerman, paid us a visit & stayed dinner, to-morrow he is going to Melbourne to attend the general assembly of the Presbyterian Church. In the morning I was putting an iron ring between the 2 revolving rings of the wind mill that it might be turned more easily by the rudder._ It seems to work well & will do more so when the iron will be worked smooth._

8 December 1866

[Sat] Finished to-day the cutting of the white gum log I fetched the beginning of this week. It was hard work, as the 2 saws we have would not go well at all. I had a good deal of the saws but they worked better after a little while._ We all went to Antwerp, to see M̲ʳ & M̲ʳˢ Fleming before they went off. I rode Max for the first time Timothy is getting on with his house, he has now done his fireplace & is about giving the inside wall of his house another coat of plaister._

8 December 1869*

[Wed] Started for M̲ʳ Officers.[742] Called at Wonwondah, & dined with M̲ʳ & two Misses Mattheson. Reached M̲ʳ Officers late in the evening after a cold drive with showers. We were very kindly received.

---

742 In 1869, the holding of Mr Officer was at Harrow, near the Glenelg River. He continued to be a supporter of the mission, providing the mission 50 sheep in early 1870. See: *Periodical Accounts* 27 (1868), 513.

~~9 December 1863~~

~~Left Fulneck after a stay of 6 years & 9 months~~[743]

9 December 1864

A letter arrived from Melbourne announcing to us the arrival of the 4 brethren Walder, Meissel, Kühn & Kramer. Walder & Meissel are to come to us for the present & the other 2 to Hagenauer.[744]_

9 December 1869*

[Thur] Started after breakfast for Mr Broughton's, near Harrow. His station, Kout Norin[745] is very prettily situated in a deep valley. The black man Jemmy from Mr Officer's went with us some 12 miles, and put us into a direct road. We arrived in good time, & were kindly received. M^r & Mrs Moffat[746] were on a visit to their parents.

10 December 1863

Left Fulneck after a stay of 6 years & 9 months. _ Took the cab at 11 a m to Stanningley[747]_ Arrived at Fairfield[748] 3 ½ p m_

In the evening at 8 I was ordained a Deacon[749] of the Brethen's Church by B^r James Latrobe.[750]_ B^r Robert Willey[751] & Frederick Latrobe[752] were ordained with me._

---

743 Adolf wrote the entry for 9 December 1863 and then crossed it out. He subsequently wrote Ref: 10 December 1863.
744 Heinrich Walder, Carl Wilhelm Kramer, Wilhelm Julius Kühne and Gottlieb Meissel, all sent out from the German Moravian Church to establish a mission to Aboriginal people in the interior. Walder arrived at Ebenezer on 21 December 1864.
745 Mr RB Broughton, leased Second Kout Narin in the West Wimmera. See: *The Squatters' Directory*, 27.
746 No further identifying information in the diary. The squatters guide of 1865 states that there was a Robert Moffart at Rich Avon, East Wimmera. See: *The Squatters' Directory*, 38.
747 Stanningley, near Leeds, Yorkshire. Some three kilometres from Fulneck.
748 Fairfield, Moravian settlement in the Manchester suburb of Droylsden, UK.
749 Deacon (German: *Diakonus*), the first of the ordained positions of the Church entitled to minister the sacraments and other official acts. Entitled to lead a congregation independently.
750 The La Trobe family were heavily involved in the Moravian Church. There were a number of La Trobe members called James.
751 Possibly son of headmaster Willey.
752 Pref. Ref: 19 September 1863.

EBENEZER MISSION STATION, 1863–1873

10 December 1866

[Mon] Left home for Carr's plains to see the Blacks there & possibly ᵗᵒ induce them ᵗᵒ come to our place.[753]_ Got as far a Polkemit station[754] of Mʳ Calder._

10 December 1869*

[Fri] Left Mʳ Broughton's towards 11 o'clock, (having had some music,) & were kindly accompanied by Mʳˢ Moffatt & boy first to Harrow, & then a good way on the road to Edenhope:[755] till there was no fear of our being lost. Arrived at Edenhope in good time, & kindly received by Mʳ & Mʳˢ Johnson.

11 December 1798

Birthday of my mother Marie Hartmann[756] (b: Lobach[757]) *Turnow in der Hinder Lausitz*.[758] Died on the 30th Dec 1853 in Parimaribo[759]

11 December 1863

Had a visit of Bʳ James Latrobe & his wife whilst putting down things in this books._ He handed over to me my certificate.[760]_

---

753 Adolf Hartmann was encouraged in late 1868 by Mr John Green to go as far as Carr's Plains to entice the people, especially the children, to remove themselves to the mission. This diary entry from 1866 demonstrates that the practice of enticing children from the Carr's Plains occurred before Green's suggestion. In September 1866, William Dennis, who was the Central Board's honorary correspondent, stated that there were two boys, four girls, ten women and eight men. A year later, HH Wetterhall, the man who had replaced Dennis, reported that there were only nine Aboriginal people, of which three were children. One of these, Billy Denis, 12, was taken by William Dennis to the lower station at Mortlake. See: *Sixth BPA Report*, 9–10, 32.
754 Polkemmet Station in the West Wimmera leased by R Calder. See: *The Squatters' Directory*, 26.
755 Victorian town, some 400 kilometres west of Melbourne, 390 kilometres south-east of Adelaide, 95 kilometres south-west of Horsham.
756 Marie Hartmann was sent with her husband, John Gottlieb, to Suriname as a missionary in 1826. There they worked in Paramaribo and Charlottenburg among the so-called 'Bush negro'. John Hartmann died in 1844. Marie stayed in Suriname working as a single female missionary at Berg-en-dal on the Upper Suriname. She is considered a martyr in the Moravian historiography. See, for example: Hamilton, *A History of the Church Known as the Moravian Church*, 421–23.
757 Née Lobach.
758 Turnow in Lower Lusatia, Germany.
759 Paramaribo, Suriname, is the capital of and largest city in Suriname. Settled by the Dutch in 1580, from 1667 Suriname was continuously a Dutch colony. In 1954, it was a constituent country of the Kingdom of the Netherlands, and gained independence in 1975. In 1765, the Moravians established a mission there at the request of the Dutch Government.
760 Ordination certificate dated 10 December 1863, copy of which is in MAB, PP HJAH, 14. At the bottom of the certificate noted: 'This certificate was examined with a copy recorded Examined and copy vended for the purpose of registering V. Revd. J.A. J. Hartmann under 28 Victoria No. 268 Melbourne 18 May 1867 W. H. Aller Registrar General of Victoria'.

11 December 1864

[Sun] S[pieseke] went to Locheal to see the Blacks who had gathered there, a good number of them; they had a corroborie that night & even asked S. for leave to have it

11 December 1865

[Mon] At 3 ½ a.m. I got up & sent off Phillip in our spring cart to fetch M{is} Kelly who was staying about 6 miles beyond ~~Harry~~ Henry Ellerman's._ Phillip came back about 4 p.m. so Bobby the good old Horse made about 42 miles._ Felt quite unfit to do any work & stopped almost all the day with Polly._

11 December 1866

[Tue] Stayed all day at Mr Calder. Very ~~plas~~ pleasant; had a little bit of a musical evening;_ Miss Youngman governess._

11 December 1869*

[Sat] Started for Apsley,[761] but not having received proper directions went 8 miles out of our way on the road to Eldersely, called at Mr Laidlours & got a boy to put us right again. Stopped at Apsley to bait the horse, & get a cup of tea, then on to Mr M{c} Leod's, a long drive. horse nearly knocked up, thought of camping out, then saw the house. Were kindly received. Plenty of company, very fashionable, quite drawingroom people.

12 December 1864

[Mon] At last I seem to succeed ~~with~~ in getting a proper background for taking likenesses. First of all I made one of calico when I took in the open air but it would not answer; then I made a gallery & at the sitters end I made a strong frame work, stretched some sacking over it covered the same with paper & coulo{u}red it with indian ink but I could not get it to be even, & then the sun shining against the background made the paper burst, I tore the paper of then & tried to to cover the sacking with a thick layer of grey clay dissolved in glue water._ It would not do._ So I took one of our sheets & covered it with fine white paper & coulo{u}red it again with indian ink but the paper not sticking every where to the calico it was full of light spots._

---

761 A town 10 kilometres east of the South Australian border.

I then made a mixture of lampblack, lime & glue but this also would not produce an even ground._ Well I was thinking hard what to do. I then painted it over with white lead mixed with black to produce the desired colour & I put some spirits into the paint_ The result was a beautiful even background cheers! cheers!

M̱ͬ Dobbinson the new presbyterian minister on trial, on his way to Antwerp stopped a few hours with us; ~~whe~~ we had kangaroo tail soup._

12 December 1865

[Tue] S̱ᵖ[ieseke] went off this morning in our little buggy to try to get Martha[762] back again who was said to be somewhere about Niel._ Commenced to day the ~~ex~~ covering of the roof of James's house, putting on the battens for the bark to rest upon.

12 December 1866

[Wed] Left Calder's for Longernong._ Stopped at Horsham, at Bowden's for dinner._ Got Bobby shod at Camerons._

12 December 1869*

[Sun] M̱ͬ M̱ͨ Leod † read Church service & Adolf preached from Matt. XV.[763] After dinner, we visited the blacks, & Adolf addressed them. They talk of coming after Christmas to our place.

13 December 1864

[Wed] ~~All day~~ In my darkroom getting things ready, washing glasses & bottles etc._ S[pieseke]: with some Blacks ~~ab~~ carting lime stone for the garden walks._ Our turkey hen is sitting on her eggs in a corner of our garden_

13 December 1866

[Thu] Left Longernong[764] for M̱ͬ W[illiam]. Dennis'_ A long drive of 23 miles & part of it rather rough country. Passing M̱ͬ Nichols' station about 3 miles from M̱ͬ D's we took a ~~rot~~ wrong turn of the road, but finding

---

762 Martha ran away from the mission with Jerry. Ref. 24 November 1865.
763 KJV. Matthew 15 has 28 verses many of which focus on the primacy of the heart for Christian religiosity, rather than outward appearances or rituals.
764 Longerenong.

out our mistake we had to go accross the plain & get through 2 log fences to rectify the mistake. M:r Dennis did not seem to like the idea of the Blacks leaving his place. He seemed especially to dislike M:r Greens visit._ We felt somewhat discouraged._

13 December 1869*

[Mon] It being very hot, we started late, 2 p.m. It had been arranged for Nancy & her nephew Henry to go with us. M:r M:c Leod lent us a horse, & Billy Officer accompanied us to bring it back. We went that evening to M:r James Hamilton. His wife being very peculiar, not right_ we did not exactly enjoy our visit.

14 December 1865

[Thu] At ¼ to 3 a.m. Polly was delivered of a healthy girl after 3 days labour.[765] The Lord is very gracious upon us._ Dear P. feels well & strong._

14 December 1866

[Fri] Polly & I went early to the camp to see the Bl[acks]:_ Found about 24 of them_ Spoke to them & invited them to come to our place for more we could not do as M:r D[ennis] did not use his influence to induce any of them to come with us there & then. Indeed M:r D changed some what in the course of the morning saying he would not mind if they came to our place._ The Blacks seemed to be M:r D's pets; are well cared for as regards temporals but negleg:c:ted as regards their spiritual improvement. Left at about 11 a.m. & went back to Longernong.

14 December 1868

[Mon] A rather disturbed day_ Ida & Amelia[766] bolted this morning early with Dicky and Peter._ The former deceived us very much. It seems to have been a matter go prepared for some time._ The key for the room they slept in Ida had been carrying about with her all the time, denying that she knew anything about it._ A good may of our people have gone after them, they went Scott's way, to try to get set at least Amelia back, Lake Billy had been made guardian of Amelia by Dick a Dicks

---

765 Eleanor Mary, known as Nelly.
766 Formerly known as Kitty, married to Dick a Dick (later Paul). Prev. Ref: 4 December 1867.

14 December 1869*

[Tue] Left early & called at Maryvale for dinner. M⁽ʳˢ⁾ Johnson very cordial, & interested about our work. Reached M⁽ʳ⁾ Philip's in good time. A pleasant evening.

15 December 1863

Went to Pendelton[767] with Polly to see her cousin Eliza daughter of uncle Mark.[768] We had a little shopping before we got there, & spent a few hours there chiefly at the piano, had a very nice walk back to the town, got to Fairfield rather late for the party at Miss Jackson's sister's labouress' ((got there the finest cup of coffee I ever draund in England.))_

15 December 1865

[Fri] M⁽ʳˢ⁾ Kelly went off to the Lake again. A very nice woman she is, so quiet & gentle & manages so well. We gave her £2 and some other little things._ We agreed to call our little Pet Mary Eleanor.[769] Godmothers were to to be, Miss Eleanor Shaw, & cousin Jane. Godfathers uncle Charles ᵃⁿᵈ ʰⁱˢ ʷⁱᶠᵉ & our brother Dan._ M⁽ʳˢ⁾ Ellerman & children came to see us._

15 December 1866

[Sat] Left Longernong for North Brighton, M⁽ʳ⁾ Jervis[770]- M⁽ʳ⁾ S. Wilson gave me a box of plants, a good many fruittrees & also flowers & ornamental trees._ M⁽ʳ⁾ Jervis an amateur in photography, very kind gentleman

15 December 1869*

[Wed] M⁽ʳˢ⁾ Spieseke got another little boy. We were on our journey westward when it happened.__ having reached M⁽ʳ⁾ Philip's. It was a fearfully hot day, & we stayed till 4.p.m. when we started for St. Mary's Lake: arrived late. pleasant drive; got cool.

---

767 Pendleton is a small village in the county of Lancashire, England.
768 Polly's uncle, Mark Hines, her father's brother, died 1865, aged 52 in Manchester, Ref: 5 January 1865.
769 In other reports, Eleanor Mary. See: *Periodical Accounts* 26 (1866), 31.
770 Possible Jervis of the Carfrae and Jervis squatting runs of Wordigworm in the West Wimmera. See: *The Squatters' Directory*, 28. See also the Correction and Errata page, which notes that John Holt held Lochiel.

16 December 1865

[Sat] Made a little horse for drying babies' clothes; a substantial one.

Rather cold weather so much so that we must have a little fire in our bedroom._

16 December 1866

[Sun] Stayed at M[r] Jervis'. A hot wind all day cooled a little towards evening._

16 December 1867

[Mon] Felt a sickness coming on, & could not tell what it was, & I went to bed.

16 December 1869*

Left St. Mary's Lake at 7 a.m. reached Vectis at 10 a.m Left Macdora[771] behind, & went on with Max to M[r] Calder's. Arrived there to dinner. M[rs] & Miss Langlands were there. Miss Gregory governess. Had some music.

17 December 1863

Fr :) Went again to Manchester[772] with M[ary]: & this time to see cousin Christie it turned out to be a beautiful day rather cold; I bought some nightshirts, I ordered an alpacka[773] & 2 linen suits; bought a box of steel pens; bought a good pair of brazers & a pair of good glovers._ Spent a nice afternoon at cousin Christie's._

17 December 1866

[Mon] Left M[r] Jervis for M[r] Edol's going the direct road across the plains. Before going we I got our likenesses taken, they were not excellent by any means something like mine, & they have the same trouble as I have in intensifying._

---

771 Macdora, the horse.
772 Manchester, UK, is about seven kilometres from the Moravian settlement of Fairfield, where Adolf was working as a teacher in the Moravian boys school.
773 Alpaca. The German word is *Alpaka*.

18 December 1864

[Sun] Timothy without our knowing shot a wild young bull to-night S[pieseke]. & I being carried by the excitement of the moment went across to see see it & spoke about taking some of the meat, but thinking about the matter when comming back we found that we were wrong in having done so, & that alltogether it was not right to shoot the bullock on the Sunday & that we would not take any of the meat, & that we would speak to the Blacks about it._

18 December 1866

[Tue] Back again to our old dear place; found them all well._ Hepenny[774] had suddenly died yesterday. Got some of plants planted out to day.

18 December 1867

[Wed] We found out that my sickness must be the inflammation of the liver I felt very weak, great difficulty in breathing & great pain in the liver, & no appetite whatever. The medecines we used were Merc vivus.[775] Belladonna[776] & Lacteres. My Saviour was gracious unto me & made me to feel his presence._

18 December 1869

[Sat] Returned from our journey westward as far as Mr Hugh Mc Leod. We brought with us the halfcaste boy Henry & his aunt Nancy._

19 December 1864

[Mon] S[pieseke]. spoke to the Blacks this morning about the Bull shot yesterday, & as much as we could notice not one of them touched the meat_

19 December 1865

[Tue] S who had gone yesterday to Mr Edol's in our buggy with March in it, met with an accident as he came to Edol's._ March got frightened by the dogs & bolted; the buggy went against a stump & so M^r Sp & Helene were

---

774 Only other mention of this person is the burial on Ref: 19 December 1866.
775 Homeopathic remedy made from elemental mercury, used often for skin disorders and eye infections.
776 Belladonna is a homeopathic medicine commonly used for headaches, sore throats, tonsillitis, coughs, earaches and fever. Ref: 11 September 1865.

thrown off, happily, without being hurt; the shaft of the cart broke & so March got off & run a good way towards Loyd's._ Still cold weather_ Some showers during the day._

Martha went off again, & we do not know where to; may the Lord be gracious unto her._

19 December 1866

[Wed] Hepenny was buried this afternoon S: addressed the people of whom there were presented a good few._ Planted out the remaining plants I got from Longernong, 4 blue gums, 1 white cedar, & a few more things._ Got the home letters; all well._

19 December 1867

[Thu] There was a great stirr about the 2 women Kitty & Diana.[777] The people in the camp had agreed among themselves that Paddy should have Kitty & Old Frank, Diana; of course Sp: kept a tremendous meeting, & of course the whole thing was brought to nought.[778]_

20 December 1863

Sunday// Preached in Fairfield about the text. "Remember Lot's wife."[779]_

20 December 1864

[Tue] We got a very mild summer: the continual change from heat to cold & the other way makes one feel very weak, Rheumatism etc being the consequences.

---

[777] Spieseke brought these women back to the mission from a trip west in November–December 1867. Ref: 4 December 1867.
[778] By 1869, Kitty (Amelia) was married to Dick a Dick (later Paul, baptised 30 July 1870), and Diana was with Henry. Ref: 9 November 1869.
[779] KJV. Luke 17:32, 'Remember Lot's wife', referencing Genesis 19:26: 'But his wife looked back from behind him, and she became a pillar of salt.' This Bible verse is often interpreted as warning against becoming too attached to the world and worldly things.

21 December 1864

[Tue] B^r Walder arrived here just before dinner ^(with Mr Edolls)._ I was just then engaged mending the lime kiln near the river wh^ch had been destroyed by the water coming in. I built up with the help of 4 Blacks an entirely new fire hole. S[pieseke]. being busy laying down the sleepers for the floor at Phillips house._

21 December 1867

[Sat] I am now convalescent; a few days ago slimy expectoration with now & then reddish matter in it ~~brought~~ made me feel more comfortable. Thanks to my Saviour who spared me so that I am able to go on in my work._ In the evening James came with the spring cart from Aphlex's on Ross' & brought the sick boy George; poor fellow he has been sick a long time, & it does not look likely as if he were to recover._

22 December 1864

[Thu] B^r Meissel arrived to day with Matthew who had gone down to fetch him in our spring cart (ein Schwederlein[780] I cut ~~of~~ a hard piece of white gum some legs for Phillips bedstead table etc_ Daniel is trying to make brick and succeeds pretty well if he only sticks to it, it will be all right._

22 December 1865

[Fri] Polly got up to-day for the first time.[781]_

23 December

24 December 1863

[Thu] Christmas eve_ father Hines[782] & I went to Guide Bridge to meet Dan[783] & John[784] who arrived at the said station ~~at a~~ at 11. p.m._ had a nice walk home._

---

780 This term 'ein Schwederlein' refers to the type of spring cart.
781 After giving birth Ref: 14 December 1865.
782 John Hines, father of Polly.
783 First Ref. Daniel Hines, brother of Polly.
784 First Ref. John Hines, brother of Polly.

24 December 1864

[Sat] A very close day._ In the afternoon there came a heavy thunderstorm w^h cooled the air considerably

24 December 1866

[Mon] Had the Xmas tree in the evening; a very large one it was this time, for we had to hang on it all the presents for the people we got sent from England in our box._ We told the people that there could not be always a Xmas tree, & that they sh^ld look out for their own in time to come. It was a very pleasant evening._

24 December 1867

[Tue] We had then our own little Xmas tree & none of the people came to it except the girls in our house & Kitty & Diana.[785] I was so far recovered from my sickness that I could enjoy it pretty well._

25 December 1864

[Sun] <u>Christmas day</u> We intended to have the Lord's Supper to-night & admit to the same Phillip & his wife[786] & Daniel; but, about 10 a.m. Phillip Mr H. Ellerman's overseer came on horseback saying that a man, Mr Coppick,[787] on his way from the Lake to Antwerp had been lost & that it was now the 3 ^day. Well off went, Phillip, Lake Jack & Brown & Timothy in search of the poor man._ I walked over to Antwerp & kept the morning worship there._

This belongs to the preceding day_

// In the evening we had our Xtree to the delight of the Black people who all came into our dining room. There were a good many presents for the women chiefly who had been useful to us in helping us. //_

25 December 1865

[Mon] Had the Xmas tree in the evening, & ~~als~~ as usual some presents for our people especially for the woman._

---

785 Kitty and Diana being the two women whom Spieseke had brought back with him on a tour of the west. Ref: 4 December 1867.
786 Phillip's wife was Rebecca (formerly Jessie). They married on Ref: 8 May 1864.
787 He was subsequently found by Phillip and others on Ref: 26 December 1864.

25 December 1866

[Tue] Off with Polly to M͏ʳ Edol's following an invitation to join in the Xmas dinner We did not care for the latter but went there for friendships sake._

25 December 1867

[Wed] We had again an invitation to spend Xmas at M͏ʳ Edol's but my sickness of course prevented accepting such a thing._

In the evening George very suddenly died,[788] in the little room on the east end of the house._ We have some hope though that he died in the Lord. Our Xmas tree was quite a private affair, very pleasant though._ I put up the box again for watering & it seems to answer well now._

26 December 1864

[Mon] We gave a X dinner to our people, of course there were a good ma^{n}y who would have liked to come, but we had to refuse them; Somehow xxxxxxxx I did not much approve of the dinner & so did Polly, we would rather have had presents given to all those who were worthy of it._ S[pieseke] & the 2 brethren off to Antwerp after dinner for to see the Xtree._

Well our Blacks found M͏ʳ Coppick, they were not in search for him very long when they found his track, & other indications that he was not very fatherr of either; written on the ground Coppicks lost here" They followed up the track sharply so much so that they hurried past the place where the old man was. A little past him they came to a stick with a piece of paper on it, so they stopped again, & looking round Phillip from our Station spied the old man at a distance making exertions to cry out; so they saved the mans life which most likely would have been extinct the next day as he was very weak already._ They brought the man to M͏ʳ Hnry Ellerman at the Lake, & each of our Blacks that had been after him got £1. much too little for saving a man's life._

26 December 1867

[Thu] Made a dozen of bolts for B͏ʳ Spieseke who lately made half a dozen of stretchers for the boys sleeping room._ 3 of the people have undertaken to top the fence on the other side, as usual very slow work, alltogether there is not much done considering such a number of working men. We had a talk

---

788 George was brought, sickly, to the station by James. Ref: 21 December 1867.

with them in the schoolroom, putting it very plainly to them whether they really want to be helped in getting up a station or whether they preferred the old beggarly way of getting on. Poor poor people!! if only these talkings have the effect to stirr them up to more activity it will do for the present._

27 December 1864

[Tue] In consequence of the dinnerparty given to some of our people, those not invited took great offence at it; they moved their camp a little further off & talked of leaving the place._ S[pieseke]. went down to them in the morning & got them round reasoning with them about it; then he engaged 3 of them to make our fence a little higher to prevent Ellerman's horses from coming in._ They made it by sticking some forks up & laying logs on them._ They were promised £3 from the river to the mallée._ We had the Lords supper in the evening Phillip, Rebecca & Daniel, partook of it for the first time_ I kept it._

27 December 1865

[Wed] Mr Ellerman & family came in the morning & stayed with us all day. Very hot day._ We think of having a love feast, before M^r E[llerman] leaves leaves Antwerp; the time not fixed._

27 December 1866

[Thu] Came back from Mr Edol's where, following an invitation we had spent Christmas day & the day following._ On [Wed] I had a ride with Mr E. into his backcountry to see his dams & very fine they one of 380 yards long._ The Xmas day was a very hot day (hot wind) but it cooled down & the next was very pleasant._

27 December 1867

[Fri] Commenced riveting the iron oven together._ There came a tremendous blast of wind just about dinner time_ The wings of the mill bent so much that they beat against the posts & another lath was knocked off. Everything else stood the blast well, & we had it pumping well in the afternoon._ George was buried[789] in the evening behind the chapel; I kept the burial & spoke upon "Jesus is our highest good he hath saved us by his blood" etc

---

789 George died suddenly Ref. 25 December 1867.

28 December 1864

[Wed] Finished my table for Phillip, a strong substantial table; alltogether there is much done for P. & his wife S[pieseke]. & Walder flooring the house e.t.c.

28 December 1865

[Thu] M[r] Flemming paid us his first visit & stayed tea with us. He also made some arrangements with S[pieseke]. for cutting down trees in the Durrock paddock, as he is putting up a log fence. He pays £10 per mile for that fence. A very hot day.

28 December 1866

[Fri] Last night, ~~the~~ some dogs got among the sheep in the cultivation paddock & bit them frightfully, about 17 as much as we can make out got bitten six of them died & so were given to the people for meat._ About 4 or 5 dogs were killed in the course of the day & very stringent measures will be adopted in future, any dog running about will be killed._ ~~Began~~ Painted 2 of the hoses over again & then made a screw maker from M[r] Edol's xxx[790]

28 December 1867

[Sat] A day in the garden; getting my flower garden into some trim, cutting the thyme border & watering it._ In the evening spoke to Lina[791] & Toney[792] preparatory to their baptism w[h] is to take place to-morrow D. V._ The people as usual went out a hunting they cant be got to give up & take to regular work._ S[pieseke]. & I dug up our potatoes a splendid crop._ I weighed some of the heaviest there was one weighing a pound less an ounze._ We got 2 bags full._

---

790 Word is illegible.
791 First Ref. The only other mention of Lina (also spelt Linna) was her baptism, Ref: 29 December 1867, on which date her husband Toney (baptised name Joshua) was also baptised. Lina was the mother of Philip (previously Charley Charley) and Nathaniel (previously Pepper). She attended the mission school. In 1866, she was reputedly 45 years old. She died November 1870. She retained her name at her baptism. See: *Periodical Accounts* 26 (1866), 420; *Periodical Accounts* 27 (1868), 514. See also: *Further Facts, Fifth Paper*, 5.
792 Toney (later, Joshua) was mentioned frequently before his baptism (Ref: 29 December 1867), but not after. He was an older man who had frequented the school already in 1864, and was the father of Philip and Nathaniel, and the husband of Lina (also spelt Linna, and Lena, Ref: 6 July 1864). See: *Periodical Accounts* 26 (1866), 420.

Our Wedding-day

29 December 1863

Tuesday._ In the morning at 10 oc. we were joined together in holy matrimony I, John, Adolphus, Jerome Hartmann & Mary Hines, by B⁰ Bennet Harvey in the chapel at Fairfield._ My groomsman was B⁰ Fred LaTrobe,[793] Polly's bride's maid was Mary Ann Harvey ^{& cousin Jane Horn}._ The ceremony went off all right, except that B⁰ Harvey made the mistake to call me twice Augustus._ The wedding-breakfast was at B⁰ Harvey's & there were present B⁰ & Sis: Harvey_ B⁰ & Sis: Moore_ ~~My~~ Our parents [&] ~~my~~ brothers Daniell & John_ cousin Jane_ B⁰ Fred Latrobe_ Sis. Mary Ann Harvey Constantine Rückert_ Sis: labouress Sis Jackson_ M⁰ Craig._ Aunty Betsy uncle George's wife._ _ _ _ It was a quiet & blessed opportunity, I made a speech speaking out my heart, but I was so moved that I could hardly get through._ In the evening after having spent a pleasant afternoon in the little cot I set off with Polly to Salem,[794] ~~where we~~ to spent a few days.

29 December 1864

[Thu] Both Polly & I walked over to Antwerp & spent the day there.

29 December 1867

[Sun] In the evening there was the baptism of Toney & Lina, the former got the name Joshua the latter kept her old xx name Lina. I baptized them._ A very windy & cold day, altogether a very cool summer._

30 December 1863

At Salem_ Cousin Henry's birthday & so we had a visit from father, mother ~~& fet~~ aunt Betsy, cousin Jane, and also Daniell & John ~~who~~ set off for London that evening._

30 December 1865

[Sat] Finished the rocking-chair I commenced a few days ago, made of native wood (white gum)

---

793 Ref: 19 September 1863.
794 A township in greater Manchester, England.

30 December 1867

[Mon] Polly, Nelly & I went on a short visit to M͟r Edols as we could not follow the invitation to spend Christmas with them._ We took Max & the buggy & had a beautiful quick drive to the 9 creeks._ We did some shopping at Lloyd's._ M͟r Edols had me about his place telling me all about his new plans of making a new sheepwash, & the garden he intends laying out, & about the steam engine & pump_ Certainly he has great things in view if he can carry out._ There was Miss White & John Ellerman staying there.

31 December 1863

New year's eve at Salem._ _

31 December 1864

[Sat] New year's eve at Ebenezer, Wimmera District, Australia._ How very different a feeling one has here, it being so hot just about this time._ There were present also Walder & Meissel, who are to go to Cooper's Creek, by in some time._ I kept the evening meeting, a kind of Memorabilia._ A hot day 95 degrees[795] in the shade._ I made 2 little flat pieces of wood with handle to it for making butter._ And then as I wanted to season the boªrds for Phillip's door, w͟h I had prepared, before I put them together, I commenced getting my own tools in order w͟h things should have been done long ago._

31 December 1867

[Tue] Back again from Edol's to our place to spend new years eve in our Mission circle._ On returning I found M͟r Sp[ieseke] having finished the flooring of the boys sleeping room._

---

795 This is 35 degrees Celsius.

Selected bibliography

Archives

Dimboola and District Historical Society Archive, Victoria, Australia [DDHS]

The Lorquon Diary of Hugh Campbell, 19 October 1863 to 27 February 1864, copy of the diary supplied by Mr MDN Campbell, a descendant of Hugh Campbell.

Moravian Archives Bethlehem, Pennsylvania, USA [MAB]

Personal Papers [PP], John Adolphus Hieronymus Hartmann [HJAH]. www.moravianchurcharchives.findbuch.net/php/main.php?ar_id=3687#505020484a4148

1. Letterbook, containing copies of letters written by Adolf Hartmann mostly to Australian officials (1868–1871), A. Hartmann to Central Board for the Protection of the Aborigines, 5 October 1869

2. Letterbook, containing copies of letters written by Adolf Hartmann to family members (1864–1871)

3. Letters, written by Adolph and Mary Hartmann to their parents and siblings (1864–1871)

8. Letters, written by Moravian officials to the Hartmanns (1863–1873)

9. Diary, written by Adolph Hartmann (1863–1873)

10. Diary, written by Adolph Hartmann including diary of voyage to Australia (1864–1870)

14. Ordination certificate of Adolph Hartmann (1863)

21. Personal notebook of Adolf Hartmann (1872)

EBENEZER MISSION STATION, 1863-1873

National Library of Australia, Canberra, Australia

Letterbooks of F.A. Hagenauer, 1865–1885. Manuscript. National Library of Australia: NLA MS 3343

Unitätsarchiv, Herrnhut, Germany [UA]

Unity Elders Conference [UEC] Minutes
Protocol der Missionsdepartment [PMD]

Newspapers

The Age (Melbourne)
The Argus (Melbourne)
Hamilton Spectator (Hamilton)
The Leader (Melbourne)
Mount Alexander Mail (Castlemaine)
The Musical World (London)

Periodicals

Missions-Blatt aus der Brüdergemeine (hereafter *Missionsblatt*) (1864)

Missionsblatt (1871)

The *Periodical Accounts relating to the Missions of the Church of the United Brethren Established among the Heathen*, referred to here and in the footnotes as the *Periodical Accounts*, are freely available via the Memorial University of Newfoundland Digital Archives Initiative: collections.mun.ca/cdm/search/collection/cns_permorv. Most volumes cover multiple years: for example, volume 25 covers the years 1863–1866. In the footnotes, the first year is given, not the full timeframe—for example, *Periodical Accounts* 25 (1863).

Periodical Accounts 21 (1853)
Periodical Accounts 22 (1856–1858)
Periodical Accounts 23 (1858–1861)
Periodical Accounts 25 (1863–1866)
Periodical Accounts 26 (1866–1868)
Periodical Accounts 27 (1868–1871)
Periodical Accounts 28 (1871–1873)
Periodical Accounts 29 (1873–1876)
Periodical Accounts 30 (1876–1878)

Periodical Accounts 31 (1878–1881)
Periodical Accounts 34 (1887–1889)

Literature

Anonymous. *The Squatters' Directory, Road Guide, and Key to the Squatting Map of Victoria*. Blundell & Ford: Melbourne, 1865. trove.nla.gov.au/version/ 264832355.

Arnold, David, and Robert Bickers. 'Introduction'. In *Missionary Encounters: Sources and Issues*, edited by Robert A Bickers and Rosemary Seton, 1–10. Surry: Curzon Press, 1996.

Attwood, Bain. 'Cameron, Elizabeth (Bessy) (c. 1851–1895)'. In *Australian Dictionary of Biography*, National Centre of Biography, The Australian National University. Accessed 16 July 2020, adb.anu.edu.au/biography/ Cameron-elizabeth-bessy-12834/text23167.

Attwood, Bain. '"In the Name of All My Coloured Brethren and Sisters": A Biography of Bessy Cameron'. *Hecate: A Women's Interdisciplinary Journal* 12, no. 1-2 (1986): 9–53.

Attwood, Bain. *The Making of the Aborigines*. Sydney: Allen & Unwin, 1989.

Ballantyne, Tony. 'The Changing Shape of the Modern British Empire and its Historiography'. *The Historical Journal* 53, no. 2 (2010): 429–52. doi.org/ 10.1017/S0018246X10000117.

Barry, Amanda, Joanna Cruickshank and Andrew Brown-May (eds). *Evangelists of Empire? Missionaries in Colonial History*. Melbourne: University of Melbourne eScholarship Research Centre, 2008.

Barwick, Diane. *Rebellion at Coranderrk*. Aboriginal History Monograph 5. Canberra: Aboriginal History Inc., 1998.

Beck, Hartmut. *Brüder in Vielen Völkern: 250 Jahre Mission der Brüdergemeine*. Erlangen: Verlag der Ev. -Luth. Mission, 1981.

Blake, Leslie J. 'Langlands, George (1803–1861)'. In *Australian Dictionary of Biography*, National Centre of Biography, The Australian National University. First published 1974. Accessed 30 August 2021, adb.anu.edu.au/biography/ langlands-george-3988/text6305.

Blake, Leslie J. *Vision and Realisation: A Centenary History of State Education in Victoria*, vol. 2. Melbourne: Education Department Victoria, 1973.

Boucher, Leigh. 'The 1869 *Aborigines Protection Act*: Vernacular Ethnography and the Governance of Aboriginal Subjects'. In *Settler Colonial Governance in Nineteenth-Century Victoria*, edited by Leigh Boucher and Lynette Russell, 63–94. Canberra: ANU Press, 2015. doi.org/10.22459/SCGNCV.04.2015.03.

Brock, Peggy (ed.). *Indigenous Peoples and Religious Change*. Leiden: Brill, 2005. doi.org/10.1163/9789047405559.

Brock, Peggy. *Outback Ghettos: A History of Aboriginal Institutionalisation and Survival*. Cambridge: Cambridge University Press, 1993.

Broome, Richard. *Aboriginal Victorians: A History Since 1800*. Crows Nest: Allen & Unwin, 2005.

Byrne, Catherine. '"Free, Compulsory and (Not) Secular": The Failed Idea in Australian Education'. *Journal of Religious History* 37, no. 1 (2013): 20–38. doi.org/10.1111/j.1467-9809.2011.01163.x.

Carey, Hilary M. 'Companions in the Wilderness? Missionary Wives in Colonial Australia, 1788–1900'. *Journal of Religious History* 19, no. 2 (1995): 227–48. doi.org/10.1111/j.1467-9809.1995.tb00257.x.

Choo, Christine. *Mission Girls: Aboriginal Women on Catholic Missions in the Kimberley, Western Australia, 1900–1950*. Perth: University of Western Australia Press, 2001.

Clark, Ian D. *'That's My Country Belonging to Me': Aboriginal Land Tenure and Dispossession in Nineteenth Century Western Victoria*. Melbourne: Heritage Matters, 1998.

Cröger, Ernst Wilhelm. *Geschichte der erneuerten Brüderkirche*. Gnadau: Buchhandlung der evangelischen Brüder-Unität, 1853.

Cruickshank, Joanna. '"A Most Lowering Thing for a Lady": Aspiring to Respectable Whiteness on Ramahyuck Mission'. In *Creating White Australia*, edited by Claire McLisky and Jane Carey, 65–78. Sydney: Sydney University Press, 2009. doi.org/10.30722/sup.9781920899424.

Cruickshank, Joanna, and Patricia Grimshaw. *White Women, Aboriginal Missions and Australian Settler Governments: Maternal Contradictions*. Leiden: Brill, 2019. doi.org/10.1163/9789004397019.

De Araugo, Tess. 'Pepper, Nathaniel (1841–1877)'. In *Australian Dictionary of Biography*, National Centre of Biography, The Australian National University. Accessed 22 April 2020, adb.anu.edu.au/biography/pepper-nathaniel-13148/text23799.

Dougan, Alan. 'Mackie, George (1823–1871)'. In *Australian Dictionary of Biography*, National Centre of Biography, The Australian National University. First published 1974. Accessed 27 October 2020, adb.anu.edu.au/biography/mackie-george-4110/text6571.

Dow, Gwyneth. 'Higinbotham, George (1826–1892)'. In *Australian Dictionary of Biography*, National Centre of Biography, The Australian National University. First published 1972. Accessed 15 March 2022, adb.anu.edu.au/biography/higinbotham-george-3766/text5939.

Edmonds, Penelope. '"We Think That This Subject of the Native Races Should Be Thoroughly Gone Into at the Forthcoming Exhibition": The 1866–67 Intercolonial Exhibition'. In *Seize the Day: Exhibitions, Australia and the World*, edited by Kate Darian-Smith, Richard Gillespie, Caroline Jordan and Elizabeth Willis, 4.1–4.16. Melbourne: Monash University ePress, 2008.

Edwards, Bill. 'The Fate of an Aboriginal Cricketer: When and Where Did Dick-a-Dick Die?'. *Australian Aboriginal Studies* 2 (Fall 1999): 59–61.

Etherington, Norman. 'Missions and Empire'. In *Oxford History of the British Empire. Vol. V: Historiography*, edited by R Winks, 303–14. Oxford: Oxford University Press, 1999. doi.org/10.1093/acprof:oso/9780198205661.003.0019.

Ganter, Regina. *The Contest for Aboriginal Souls: European Missionary Agendas in Australia*. Canberra: ANU Press, 2018. doi.org/10.22459/CAS.05.2018.

Ganter, Regina. 'Letters from Mapoon: Colonising Aboriginal Gender'. *Australian Historical Studies* 30, no. 113 (1999): 267–85. doi.org/10.1080/10314619908596102.

Ganter, Regina, and Patricia Grimshaw. 'Introduction: Reading the Lives of White Mission Women'. *Journal of Australian Studies* 39, no. 1 (2015): 1–6. doi.org/10.1080/14443058.2014.1001308.

Giese, Jill. 'Yanggendyinanyuk (c. 1834–1886)'. In *Australian Dictionary of Biography*, National Centre of Biography, The Australian National University. Published online 2020. Accessed 16 March 2022, adb.anu.edu.au/biography/yanggendyinanyuk-30059/text37299.

Grant, James. 'Stretch, Theodore Carlos Benoni (1817–1899)'. In *Australian Dictionary of Biography*, National Centre of Biography, The Australian National University. Accessed 16 July 2020, adb.anu.edu.au/biography/stretch-theodore-carlos-benoni-4655/text7691.

Grimshaw, Patricia. 'Rethinking Approaches to Women in Missions: The Case of Colonial Australia'. *History Australia* 8, no. 3 (2011): 7–24. doi.org/10.1080/14490854.2011.11668386.

Grimshaw, Patricia, and Elizabeth Nelson, 'Empire, "the Civilising Mission" and Indigenous Christian Women in Colonial Victoria'. *Australian Feminist Studies* 16, no. 36 (2001): 295–309. doi.org/10.1080/08164640120097534.

Gullestad, Marianne. *Picturing Pity: Pitfalls and Pleasures in a Cross-Cultural Communication; Image and Word in a North Cameroon Mission*. New York: Berghahn Books, 2007.

Habermas, Rebekka. 'Mission im 19. Jahrhundert. Globale Netze des Religiösen'. *Historische Zeitschrift* 287, no. 3 (2008): 629–79. doi.org/10.1524/hzhz.2008.0056.

Hamilton, J Taylor. *A History of the Church Known as the Moravian Church, or the Unitas Fratrum, or the Unity of the Brethren, during the Eighteenth and Nineteenth Centuries*. Bethlehem, Pennsylvania: Times Publishing Company, 1900.

Hamilton, J Taylor. *A History of the Missions of the Moravian Church during the Eighteenth and Nineteenth Centuries*. Bethlehem, Pennsylvania: Times Publishing Company, 1901.

Harris, John. *One Blood. 200 Years of Aboriginal Encounter with Christianity: A Story of Hope*. Sutherland: Albatross, 1990.

Hassam, Andrew. *Sailing to Australia: Shipboard Diaries by Nineteenth-Century British Emigrants*. Melbourne: Melbourne University Press, 1994.

Healy, Chris. 'Chained to their Signs: Remembering Breastplates'. In *Body Trade: Captivity, Cannibalism and Colonialism in the Pacific*, edited by B Creed and J Hoorn, 24–35. Annandale, New South Wales: Pluto Press, 2001. hdl.handle.net/11343/35023.

Howitt, AW. *The Native Tribes of South-East Australia*. London: Macmillan, 1904.

Hutton, JE. *History of the Moravian Church*. Second edition, revised and enlarged. London: Moravian Publication Office, 1909.

Intercolonial Exhibition 1866: Official Catalogue: Victoria, New South Wales, Queensland, South Australia, Tasmania, New Zealand, Western Australia, Mauritius, New Caledonia, Batavia. Melbourne: Printed for the Commissioners by Blundell and Ford, [1866?]. viewer.slv.vic.gov.au/?entity=IE4531816&mode=browse.

Jensz, Felicity. 'Controlling Marriages: Friedrich Hagenauer and the Betrothal of Indigenous Western Australian Women in Colonial Victoria'. *Aboriginal History*, no. 34 (2010): 35–54. doi.org/10.22459/AH.34.2011.02.

Jensz, Felicity. *German Moravian Missionaries in the British Colony of Victoria, Australia, 1848–1908: Influential Strangers.* Leiden: Brill, 2010. doi.org/ 10.1163/ej.9789004179219.i-274.

Jensz, Felicity. 'Miscarriage and Coping in the Mid-Nineteenth Century: Private Notes from Distant Places'. *Gender & History* 32, no. 3 (2020): 270–85. doi.org/ 10.1111/1468-0424.12478.

Jensz, Felicity. 'Religious Migration and Political Upheaval: German Moravians at Bethel in South Australia, 1851–1907'. *Australian Journal of Politics & History* 56, no. 3 (2010): 351–65. doi.org/10.1111/j.1467-8497.2010.01558.x.

Jensz, Felicity. 'Writing the Lake Boga Failure'. *Traffic: An Interdisciplinary Postgraduate Journal*, no. 3 (2003): 147–61.

Kenny, Robert. *The Lamb Enters the Dreaming: Nathanael Pepper and the Ruptured World.* Melbourne: Scribe, 2007.

Konrad, Dagmar. *Missionsbräute: Pietistinnen des 19. Jahrhunderts in der Basler Mission.* Münster/New York/München/Berlin: Waxmann, 2001.

Kröger, Rüdiger. *Bilder aus der Herrnhuter Mission. Fotografien des 19. Jahrhunderts aus den Sammlungen des Unitätsarchivs.* Herrnhut: Comenius-Buchhandlung GmbH, 2008.

Longmire, Anne. *Nine Creeks to Albacutya: A History of the Shire of Dimboola.* North Melbourne: Hargreen Publishing Company, 1985.

Lydon, Jane. *Fantastic Dreaming: The Archaeology of an Aboriginal Mission.* Lanham, Maryland: Altamira Press, 2009.

Mallett, Ashley Alexander. *The Black Lords of Summer: The Story of the 1868 Aboriginal Tour of England and Beyond.* St Lucia: University of Queensland Press, 2002.

Mason, JCS. *The Moravian Church and the Missionary Awakening in England, 1760–1800.* Suffolk: The Boydell Press for The Royal Historical Society, 2001.

Mason, John, and Lucy Torode. *Three Generations of the La Trobe Family in the Moravian Church.* Newtownabbey: Moravian History Magazine, 1997.

McLisky, Claire, Lynette Russell and Leigh Boucher. 'Managing Mission Life, 1869–1886'. In *Settler Colonial Governance in Nineteenth-Century Victoria*, edited by Leigh Boucher and Lynette Russell, 117–38. Canberra: ANU Press, 2015. doi.org/10.22459/SCGNCV.04.2015.05.

McQuilton, John. 'Morgan, Daniel (Dan) (1830–1865)'. In *Australian Dictionary of Biography*, National Centre of Biography, The Australian National University. First published 2005. Accessed May 2021, adb.anu.edu.au/biography/morgan-daniel-dan-13109/text23717.

Mettele, Gisela. *Weltbürgertum oder Gottesreich: Die Herrnhuter Brüdergemeine als globale Gemeinschaft 1727–1857*. Göttingen: Vandenhoeck & Ruprecht, 2009.

Nelson, Elizabeth, Sandra Smith and Patricia Grimshaw (eds). *Letters from Aboriginal Women of Victoria, 1867–1926*. Melbourne: The University of Melbourne, History Department, 2002.

Pepper, Phillip, and Tess De Araugo. *You Are What You Make Yourself to Be: The Story of a Victorian Aboriginal Family 1842–1980*. Melbourne: Hyland House, 1980.

Pietsch, Tamson. 'Bodies at Sea: Travelling to Australia in the Age of Sail'. *Journal of Global History* 11, no. 2 (2016): 209–28. doi.org/10.1017/S1740022816 000061.

Podmore, Colin. *The Moravian Church in England 1728–1760*. Oxford: Clarendon Press, 1998. doi.org/10.1093/acprof:oso/9780198207252.001.0001.

Podmore, Colin. 'Zinzendorf and the English Moravians'. *Journal of Moravian History* 3 (Fall 2007): 31–50. doi.org/10.2307/41179832.

Rademaker, Laura. *Found in Translation: Many Meanings on a North Australian Mission*. Honolulu: University of Hawai'i Press, 2018. doi.org/10.1515/9780 824873585.

Reilly, Dianne. 'Charles Joseph La Trobe: An Appreciation'. *The La Trobe Journal* 71 (Autumn 2003), 5–15.

Schneider, HG. *Missionsarbeit der Brüdergemeine in Australien*. Gnadau: Verlag der Unitäts-Buchhandlung, 1882.

Schutt, Amy C. *Peoples of the River Valleys: The Odyssey of the Delaware Indians*. Philadelphia: University of Pennsylvania Press, 2007. doi.org/10.9783/97808 12203790.

Seelinger, Frank. *Maria Elisabeth Heyde – Versuch einer biographischen Annäherung auf Grundlage der Tagebuchnotizen für die Jahre 1862 bis 1870, inklusiv Transkription*. Ulm: Technische Hochschule Wildau, 2005. opus4.kobv.de/opus4-th-wildau/frontdoor/index/index/docId/18 (accessed 3 February 2021).

Serle, Geoffrey. 'Westgarth, William (1815–1889)'. In *Australian Dictionary of Biography*, National Centre of Biography, The Australian National University. First published 1976. Accessed 10 April 2020, adb.anu.edu.au/biography/westgarth-william-4830/text8057.

Sherlock, Peter. 'Missions, Colonialism and the Politics of Agency'. In *Evangelists of Empire? Missionaries in Colonial History*, edited by Amanda Barry, Joanna Cruickshank and Andrew Brown-May, 12–20. Melbourne: University of Melbourne eScholarship Research Centre, 2008.

Smyth, Robert Brough. *The Aborigines of Victoria: With Notes relating to the Habits of the Natives of Other Parts of Australia and Tasmania. Compiled from Various Sources for the Government of Victoria, vol. II*. Melbourne: John Ferres, Government Printer, 1878.

Swain, Tony, and Deborah Bird Rose. *Aboriginal Australians and Christian Missions: Ethnographic and Historical Studies*. Adelaide: Australian Association for the Study of Religions, 1988.

Tarnay, SM. 'Goethe, Matthias (1827–1876)'. In *Australian Dictionary of Biography*, National Centre of Biography, The Australian National University. First published 1972. Accessed 7 May 2021, adb.anu.edu.au/biography/goethe-matthias-3625/text5633.

Taylor, Phil. *Karkarooc: Mallee Shire History, 1896–1995*. Yarriambiack Shire Council: Warracknabeal, 1996.

Vogt, Peter. '"Everywhere at Home": The Eighteenth-Century Moravian Movement as a Transatlantic Religious Community'. *Journal of Moravian History*, no. 1 (2006): 7–29.

Waugh, T. *A History of Fulneck School*. Leeds: Richard Jackson, 1909.

Westwood, JJ. *The Journal of J.J. Westwood (Evangelist), or, An Account of Eight Years' Itineracy to the Townships and Squatting Stations of Victoria, New South Wales, South Australia, and Tasmania*. Melbourne: Clarson, Shallard & Co. 1865.

Williams, John. *A Narrative of Missionary Enterprises in the South Sea Islands: With Remarks Upon the Natural History of the Islands, Origin, Languages, Traditions, and Usages of the Inhabitants*. London: William Clowes and Sons, 1837.

EBENEZER MISSION STATION, 1863–1873

Reports

Governmental

Central Board Appointed to Watch Over the Interests of the Aborigines in the Colony of Victoria / Board for the Protection of the Aborigines in the Colony of Victoria

Referred to in the footnotes as BPA reports.

First Report of the Central Board Appointed to Watch Over the Interests of the Aborigines in the Colony of Victoria, no. 39. Melbourne: John Ferres, Government Printer, 1861.

Fourth Report of the Central Board Appointed to Watch Over the Interests of the Aborigines in the Colony of Victoria, no. 19. Melbourne: John Ferres, Government Printer, 1864.

Fifth Report of the Central Board Appointed to Watch Over the Interests of the Aborigines in the Colony of Victoria, no. 13. Melbourne: John Ferres, Government Printer, 1866.

Sixth Report of the Central Board Appointed to Watch Over the Interests of the Aborigines in the Colony of Victoria, no. 47. Melbourne: John Ferres, Government Printer, 1869.

Seventh Report of the Board for the Protection of the Aborigines in the Colony of Victoria, no. 41. Melbourne: John Ferres, Government Printer, 1871.

Eighth Annual Report of the Board for the Protection of the Aborigines in the Colony of Victoria, no. 60. Melbourne: John Ferres, Government Printer, 1872.

Royal Commissions and Government Inquiries

Report of the Royal Commission Appointed by His Excellency to Enquire into and Report upon the Operation of the System of Public Education; Together with Minutes of Evidence and Appendices. Melbourne: John Ferres, Government Printer, 1867. www.parliament.vic.gov.au/papers/govpub/VPARL1867No27.pdf.

State Parliament of Victoria, second session, *The Report and Proceedings of the Board Lately Appointed to Inquire into the Charges Brought against Mr. Cobham, Superintendent of Police of the Wimmera District*, 16 December 1870, www.parliament.vic.gov.au/papers/govpub/VPARL1870_2ndSessionNoC3.pdf.

Government Acts

The Land Act, 1862 and the Amending Land Act, 1865: Together with the Regulations and Forms under the Act. Melbourne: George Robertson. nla.gov.au/nla.obj-71931024.

Non-Governmental

Melbourne Association in Aid of the Moravian Mission

Referred to in the footnotes as *Facts, First Paper* and for subsequent reports, *Further Facts*, with the paper number.

Facts relating to the Moravian Mission, First Paper. Melbourne: WM Goodhugh & Co, 1860.

Further Facts relating to the Moravian Mission Read with the Report of the Committee at the First Annual Meeting of the Melbourne Association in Aid of the Moravian Mission, Second Paper. Melbourne: WM Goodhugh & Co, 1861.

Further Facts relating to the Moravian Mission Read in Connection with the Report of the Committee at the Annual Meeting of the Melbourne Association in Aid of the Moravian Mission, Third Paper. Melbourne: WM Goodhugh & Co, 1862.

Further Facts relating to the Moravian Mission Read in Connection with the Report of the Committee at the Annual Meeting of the Melbourne Association in Aid of the Moravian Mission, Fourth Paper. Melbourne: WM Goodhugh & Co, 1863.

Further Facts relating to the Moravian Mission Read in Connection with the Report of the Committee at the Annual Meeting of the Victorian Association in Aid of the Moravian Mission, Fifth Paper. Melbourne: Fergusson & Moore, 1866.

Further Facts relating to the Moravian Mission Read in Connection with the Report of the Committee at the Annual Meeting of the Victorian Association in Aid of the Moravian Mission, Sixth Paper. Melbourne: Fergusson & Moore, 1867.

Theses

Longworth, Alison. '"Was It Worthwhile?" An Historical Analysis of Five Women Missionaries and Their Encounters with the Nyungar People of South-West Australia'. PhD thesis, Murdoch University, 2005.

Index

A

Albert	9 July 1864; 11 July 1864; 14 July 1864; 2 September 1864; 18 October 1864; 9 March 1865; 11 April 1865; 21 August 1865; 23 August 1865; 11 September 1865; 22 September 1865; 12 April 1866; 3 May 1866; 25 May 1866; 15 June 1866; 6 August 1866; 17 January 1867; 3 August 1868; 2 September 1868; 22 November 1869
Amelia (*see* Kitty, previous name)	24 November 1864; 9 January 1865; 22 January 1865; 9 February 1865; 18 February 1865; 21 August 1865; 12 January 1866; 4 December 1867; 19 December 1867; 24 December 1867; 22 March 1868; 27 July 1868; 14 December 1868; 26 July 1869; 9 November 1869
Amos	5 August 1866; 4 May 1867; 30 October 1869
Archie	21 October 1864; 23 August 1865; 24 March 1866; 6 August 1866
Augusta (Margaret's daughter)	17 August 1868; 23 August 1869

B

Bandel (*see* Peter)	
Barber	1 October 1868
Betsy	17 April 1869; 1 May 1869
Betsy, death of	3 October 1866
'Blacks'	
Longernong	25 August 1864; 29 March 1866; 27 November 1866
Morton Plains	9 January 1868

	Scott's [Lake Hindmarsh]	8 February 1865; 9 February 1865; 13 February 1865; 18 February 1865; 29 August 1866; 19 March 1867; 3 June 1867; 14 December 1868
	Tatiara/Tatta Yarra	13 February 1865; 14 February 1865; 19 February 1865; 26 February 1865; 27 February 1865; 3 October 1865; 23 August 1866
	Vectis people	5 December 1866
Bob		9 January 1868
Bobby (brother of Lizzie)		26 March 1867; 22 August 1867; 5 September 1867; 2 January 1868
Boney		17 September 1864; 14 February 1865; 31 August 1866; 17 January 1867
Boopboop/Booppoop/Boop-poop/Bopoop/Bubbub/Bupbup (*see* George)		
Brown (*see also* baptismal name Samuel)		25 December 1864; 3 January 1865; 9 January 1865; 21 August 1865; 19 October 1865; 13 August 1866; 27 August 1866

C

Camerons	12 December 1866
Charles Arthur (son of Margaret)	7 August 1870
Charley (baptismal name Walter)	31 July 1870
Charley Charley (*see* Philipp/Phillip/Philip)	
Charley, Old (*see* Old Charley)	
Charlotte, wife of Little	27 July 1867
Cogle	6 November 1868; 1 May 1869
Commodore	28 November 1864
Corney/Corny	13 June 1864; 5 January 1865; 31 January 1865; 29 August 1865; 31 August 1866; 25 February 1867; 27 November 1867

INDEX

D

Daniel	22 May 1864; 23 May 1864; 26 May 1864; 10 July 1864; 18 July 1864; 19 July 1864;; 1 October 1864; 5 October 1864; 7 October 1864; 22 December 1864; 25 December 1864; 27 December 1864; 5 January 1865; 17 January 1865; 1 April 1865; 6 July 1865; 4 October 1865
his father and mother	1 April 1865
David, Elizabeth's husband	25 April 1866; 19 May 1866; 30 June 1866; 26 January 1867; 15 March 1867; 7 May 1867; 12 June 1867; 24 June 1867
Davy	16 November 1865
Diana	4 December 1867; 19 December 1867; 24 December 1867; 9 November 1869
Dick a Dick (*see* Paul)	
Dick a Dick (Yanggendyinanyuk)	12 March 1869
Dicky (Lily's husband)	18 May 1865; 21 August 1865; 23 August 1865; 11 September 1865; 22 September 1865; 19 October 1865; 12 November 1865; 2 May 1866; 13 June 1866; 14 June 1866; 6 August 1866; 13 February 1867; 7 May 1867; 26 May 1867; 22 August 1867; 2 September 1868; 3 December 1866; 14 December 1868
Doctor Charley	31 January 1865
Donald	14 September 1867; 20 March 1868

E

Edward (*see* James)	
his wife	29 January 1865
Elizabeth (formerly Mary, David's wife)	28 May 1864; 29 May 1864; 10 June 1864; 17 July 1864; 4 January 1865; 27 July 1865 (baptism); 3 February 1866; 21 February 1866; 25 February 1866; 3 December 1866; 7 May 1867; 24 June 1867
Emma (young girl)	14 June 1864; 23 January 1865; 21 February 1865; 13 June 1866; 14 June 1866; 1 March 1867; 26 March 1867; 2 January 1868

her parents (Paddy and ?)	14 June 1864; 23 January 1865
Esther	7 July 1869; 25 July 1869

F

Fanny (Sandy's wife)	28 August 1866; 27 November 1866; 5 December 1866; 27 May 1867
her two daughters	28 August 1866; 5 December 1866
Flower, Bessy	20 March 1868

Frank (Mary's husband) (*see* Old Boney)

G

George (Boopboop/ Booppoop/Boop-poop/ Bopoop/Bubbub/ Bupbup, Judy's son)	22 May 1864; 29 May 1864; 9 July 1864; 11 July 1864; 14 July 1864; 2 September 1864; 18 October 1864; 19 February 1865; 26 February 1865; 27 February 1865; 21 December 1867; 25 December 1867; 27 December 1867
George (from Longernong)	25 August 1864
Guary	27 July 1867

H

Harry	18 September 1864; 5 September 1867; 9 January 1868
Hearty/Harty	10 June 1864; 31 January 1865; 28 February 1865; 18 July 1866; 10 November 1866
Henry, Nancy's nephew	13 December 1869; 18 December 1869
Hepenny	18 December 1866; 19 December 1866

I

Ida	17 August 1868; 22 August 1869; 14 December 1868

J

Jack, Old Man	9 February 1865; 18 February 1865
Jacky (Stephen) (Lily's (Lydia's) husband)	23 May 1864; 5 December 1864; 3 November 1865; 7 June 1866; 13 August 1866; 31 August 1866; 19 September 1866; 29 October 1866; 10 November 1866; 15 March 1867; 17 June 1867; 6 July 1867; 7 July 1867; 11 September 1867; 11 October 1867; 12 October 1867; 1 October 1868; 3 October 1868

INDEX

Jacky Lake/Lake Jack	25 December 1864; 29 January 1865; 28 February 1865
James (formerly Edward, Ruth's husband)	17 September 1864; 23 September 1864; 22 Ocotber 1864; 24 October 1864; 26 October 1864; 4 January 1865; 7 January 1865; 9 January 1865; 29 Janurary 1865; 3 February 1865; 13 February 1865; 6 April 1865; 7 April 1865; 19 April 1865; 30 May 1865; 23 June 1865; 28 June 1865; 11 July 1865; 25 July 1865; 26 July 1865; 13 October 1865;19 October 1865; 24 October 1865; 27 November 1865; 20 November 1865; 12 December 1865; 21 February 1866; 23 February 1866; 25 February 1866; 2 May 1866; 5 May 1866; 7 May 1866; 8 May 1866; 11 May 1866; 28 May 1866; 13 June 1866; 15 June 1866; 16 June 1866; 5 August 1866; 27 September 1866; 29 October 1866; 15 March 1867; 17 June 1867; 24 June 1867; 26 August 1867; 21 December 1867; 4 November 1868; 5 November 1868; 6 November 1868
Janet (Maggie)	31 July 1870
Jemmy	9 December 1869
Jenny (*see* Old Jenny)	
Jerry (Martha's husband)	19 October 1865; 27 October 1865; 24 November 1865; 7 May 1866; 10 November 1866; 2 January 1867; 17 January 1867
Jerry (from Tatta Yarra)	30 January 1865
Jessie (*see* baptismal name Rebecca)	
Jimmy	24 August 1867
John, King of the Wimmera Blacks	25 August 1864; 22 February 1865; 5 September 1867
Jonathan (Mary's husband)	31 August 1866; 29 September 1866; 10 October 1866; 11 October 1866; 12 October 1866
Joseph (Matthew and Margaret's son)	8 February 1866; 24 February 1866; 10 November 1867
Joshua (*see* baptismal name Tony/Toney)	
Judy (George's mother, wife of Little)	19 February 1865; 26 February 1865; 11 October 1866;2 January 1867; 27 July 1867

K

King Barney	20 February 1865
King Cole	26 August 1864; 9 October 1864; 30 January 1865
and Lady	26 August 1864; 9 October 1864
King John (*see* Johnny)	
King Peter	10 July 1864; 8 October 1864; 23 April 1865
Kitty (*see* Amelia)	
Kitty, Granny	5 September 1867

L

Lake Billy	14 December 1868
Lanke/Lanky	22 October 1864; 24 November 1864; 24 January 1865; 11 May 1865; 12 May 1865; 24 May 1865; 29 July 1865; 14 August 1865; 15 August 1865; 17 August 1865
Lena (Nathanael's mother)	6 July 1864
Liberty (*see* Matthew)	
Lily/Lilly	18 October 1864
Lily (Dicky's wife, mother of Rosa)	28 November 1864; 13 February 1867; 26 May 1867; 28 May 1867; 3 December 1866
Lilly (Richard's wife)	5 December 1864
Lily/Lilly (Jack's wife, *see* Lydia)	
Lilly (Makenzie's wife)	2 September 1864
Lina	28 December 1867; 29 December 1867
Little (husband of Judy and Charlotte)	27 February 1865; 2 January 1867; 27 July 1867; 1 August 1867; 27 July 1868
Lizzie/Lizzy (Mark's wife)	20 February 1867; 15 March 1867; 19 March 1867; 26 March 1867; 2 June 1867; 3 June 1867; 4 June 1867; 6 July 1867; 7 July 1867; 15 August 1868
Long Charley	30 July 1864
Lydia (formerly Lily/Lilly)	5 December 1864; 22 January 1865; 21 August 1865; 13 August 1866; 29 September 1866; 15 March 1867; 6 July 1867; 7 July 1867

M

Magdalene	14 July 1866; 18 July 1866; 5 August 1866; 22 August 1866; 23 August 1866; 3 September 1866; 23 September [1866]; 29 September 1866; 4 May 1867; 27 October 1867; 22 July 1869; 23 July 1869; (29 July 1869)
Maggy/Maggie (Lizzie's sister)	18 May 1865; 26 March 1867; 26 August 1867; 5 September 1867
Maggie (*see* Janet)	
Margaret (Matthew's wife)	25 June 1864; 6 August 1864; 17 August 1864; 10 August 1864; 11 August 1864; 12 August 1864; 13 August 1864; 15 August 1864; 16 August 1864; 22 August 1864; 18 September 1864; 4 February 1865; 24 February 1865; 4 April 1865; 27 April 1865; 6 June 1865; 7 June 1865; 17 July 1865; 28 July 1865; 13 January 1866; 6 February 1866; 8 February 1866; 22 August 1866; 4 May 1867; 5 November 1867; 17 August 1868; 25 July 1870; 7 August 1870
her son (Charles Arthur)	25 July 1870
her son (Joseph)	8 February 1866; 24 February 1866; 10 November 1867
her son (Robert)	
Mark (Thomas Marks, Lizzie's husband)	22 May 1864; 20 March 1865; 21 April 1865; 23 April 1865; 1 May 1865; 5 May 1865; 12 May 1865; 4 July 1865; 18 July 1865; 21 August 1865; 3 October 1865; 11 November 1865; 12 January 1866; 13 January 1866; 20 February 1867; 4 March 1867; 15 March 1867; 19 March 1867; 3 June 1867; 4 June 1867; 6 July 1867; 7 July 1867; 8 July 1867; 12 July 1867; 1 February 1868
Martha (Jerry's wife)	24 November 1865; 12 December 1865; 19 December 1865; 7 May 1866; 6 October 1866; 1 November 1866; 10 November 1866; 17 January 1867
Mary (*see* Elizabeth)	
Mary Ann (Teddy's wife)	22 June 1865; 23 June 1865; 25 June 1865; 27 June 1865
Mary (Frank's wife)	31 August 1866; 12 July 1867

Mary (Joe's wife)	24 May 1864; 30 May 1864; 31 May 1864; 13 June 1864; 10 July 1864; 9 August 1864; 9 January 1868
Mary (Jonathan's wife)	11 October 1866
Mary (Old Boney's wife, Young Boney/Timothy's mother)	17 September 1864; 1 April 1865; 22 May 1865
Mary (daughter of Old Jenny's)	9 August 1864
Matthew (surname Elliott, formerly Liberty, Margaret's husband)	8 May 1864; 22 May 1864; 27 May 1864; 28 May 1864; 10 June 1864; 25 June 1864; 26 June 1864; 29 June 1867; 30 June 1864; 4 July 1864; 6 July 1864; 7 July 1864; 8 July 1864; 9 July 1864; 10 July 1864; 20 July 1864; 24 July 1864; 25 July 1864; 17 July 1864; 6 August 1864; 8 August 1864; 11 August 1864; 13 August 1864; 15 August 1864; 16 August 1864; 22 August 1864; 18 September 1864; 8 October 1864; 23 October 1864; 24 October 1864; 27 October 1864; 24 November 1864; 22 December 1864; 4 February 1865; 20 February 1865; 21 February 1865; 22 February 1865; 23 February 1865; 24 February 1865; 27 February 1865; 9 March 1865; 18 March 1865; 26 March 1865; 4 April 1865; 10 April 1865; 11 April 1865; 18 April 1865; 22 April 1865; 23 April 1865; 27 April 1865; 8 May 1865; 23 May 1865; 30 May 1865; 6 June 1865; 8 June 1865; 17 July 1865; 28 July 1865; 11 August 1865; 29 August 1865; 7 September 1865; 2 October 1865; 16 October 1865; 4 November 1865; 20 November 1865; 13 January 1866; 24 January 1866; 6 February 1866; 24 May 1866; 22 August 1866; 27 August 1866; 29 August 1866; 31 August 1866; 12 November 1866; 15 March 1867; 4 May 1867; 17 July 1867; 2 January 1868; 1 February 1868; 22 November 1869
Minnie	26 March 1867; 22 August 1867; 26 August 1867; 5 September 1867; 2 January 1868

N

Nahri	31 January 1868
Nancy (Matthew's sister)	27 February 1865; 15 August 1866
Nancy (Henry's aunt)	13 October 1866; 13 December 1869; 18 December 1869

Napier	7 May 1867
Napoleon	23 January 1865; 9 March 1865; 21 August 1865; 23 August 1865; 11 September 1865; 22 September 1865; 5 December 1865; 12 April 1866; 25 May 1866; 13 June 1866; 14 June 1866; 25 August 1866; 31 August 1866
Nathanael/Nathaniel (Pepper)	19 May 1864; 22 May 1864; 23 May 1864; 29 May 1864; 30 May 1864; 1 June 1864; 3 June 1864; 6 June 1864; 10 June 1864; 29 June 1864; 2 July 1864; 6 July 1864; 7 July 1864; 12 July 1864; 15 July 1864; 19 July 1864; 20 July 1864; 1 August 1864; 2 August 1864; 10 August 1864; 23 August 1864; 5 October 1864; 12 October 1864; 21 October 1864; 22 October 1864; 23 October 1864; 24 October 1864; 27 October 1864; 28 October 1864; 17 November 1864; 4 January 1865; 21 January 1865; 19 February 1865; 27 February 1865; 9 March 1865; 18 March 1865; 8 April 1865; 22 April 1865; 24 April 1865; 27 April 1865; 4 May 1865; 5 May 1865; 11 May 1865; 20 May 1865; 23 May 1865; 6 June 1865; 3 October 1865; 20 November 1865; 16 March 1866; 7 June 1866; 18 July 1866; 24 July 1866; 30 July 1866; 27 August 1866; 29 August 1866; 12 November 1866; 27 November 1866; 28 November 1866; 4 March 1867; 15 March 1867; 24 June 1867; 12 July 1867; 27 October 1867; 1 February 1868; 3 May 1869
his child (deceased)	19 May 1864
Neddy	14 October 1864; 15 October 1864
Neptune	3 May 1866; 18 May 1866

O

Old Boney (Frank, Mary's husband)	17 September 1864; 14 February 1865; 22 May 1865; 31 August 1866; 17 January 1867; 12 July 1867
Old Charlie/Charley	23 January 1865; 4 July 1865; 17 July 1865; 31 August 1866; 23 September 1866; 24 September 1866; 26 September 1866
Old Frank	25 February 1867; 5 September 1867; 19 December 1867

Old Jenny	24 May 1864; 8 July 1864; 10 July 1864; 9 August 1864; 23 January 1865; 18 May 1865
Old Joe (Mary's husband)	24 May 1864; 30 May 1864; 31 May 1864; 13 June 1864; 5 July 1864; 6 July 1864; 9 July 1864; 10 July 1864; 9 August 1864; 26 June 1867; 9 January 1868
Old John	23 November 1867
Old Man Billy	30 October 1864; 31 October 1864; 1 November 1864
Old Man Jack	9 February 1865; 18 February 1865
Old Peter	7 January 1868
Old Sam	9 July 1864; 12 July 1864

P

Paddy	14 June 1864; 6 September 1865; 21 February 1866; 25 February 1866; 3 March 1866; 14 June 1866; 25 August 1866; 19 March 1867; 24 August 1867; 19 December 1867
Paul (Dick a Dick)	14 December 1868; 12 March 1869; 26 July 1869; 9 November 1869; 30 July 1870; 3 September 1870
Pearce	27 October 1866; 18 March 1867; 1 February 1868
Peilan	10 January 1869
Pelham [Cameron] (Donald's brother)	20 March 1868
Peter (Young Peter?)	3 April 1865; 27 April 1865; 6 February 1866; 14 December 1868
Peter (Bandel)	6 June 1865; 8 June 1865; 26 August 1867; 9 January 1868

INDEX

Phillip/Philip/Philipp (formerly Charley Charley, Rebecca's husband, Nathaniel's brother)	8 May 1864; 19 May 1864; 12 June 1864; 27 June 1864; 4 July 1864; 16 July 1864; 18 July 1864; 19 July 1864; 24 July 1864; 25 July 1864; 30 July 1864; 1 August 1864; 9 August 1864; 16 August 1864; 25 August 1864; 26 October 1864; 3 November 1864; 24 November 1864; 21 December 1864; 22 December 1864; 25 December 1864; 26 December 1864; 27 December 1864; 28 December 1864; 31 December 1864; 3 January 1865; 4 January 1865; 7 January 1865; 10 January 1865; 11 January 1865; 17 January 1865; 22 January 1865; 24 January 1865; 11 February 1865; 13 February 1865; 19 February 1865; 25 February 1865; 28 February 1865; 15 March 1865; 18 March 1865; 26 March 1865; 6 April 1865; 7 April 1865; 19 April 1865; 20 April 1865; 1 May 1865; 4 May 1865; 22 May 1865; 30 May 1865; 18 July 1865; 26 July 1865; 27 July 1865; 21 August 1865; 6 October 1865; 27 October 1865; 27 November 1865; 11 December 1865; 24 February 1866; 7 May 1866; 19 May 1866; 7 June 1866; 7 July 1866; 30 July 1866; 27 August 1866; 29 August 1866; 11 September 1866; 19 September 1866; 13 October 1866; 5 December 1866; 14 March 1867; 7 May 1867; 4 June 1867; 13 June 1867; 8 July 1867; 10 July 1867; 7 August 1867; 11 September 1867; 8 January 1868; 6 December 1868; 26 July 1869; 22 August 1869; 26 August 1869; 22 November 1869; 6 January 1870
Prince Albert (*see* Albert)	
Prince Peter	3 August 1868

R

Rachel	19 May 1864; 2 June 1864; 6 June 1864; 9 June 1864; 11 July 1864; 16 August 1864; 17 January 1865; 16 March 1866; 26 March 1866; 15 June 1867; 23 March 1869; 3 April 1869

EBENEZER MISSION STATION, 1863–1873

Rebecca (formerly Jessy, wife of Phillip)	8 May 1864; 2 June 1864; 13 June 1864; 8 July 1864; 11 July 1864; 12 July 1864; 17 July 1864; 30 July 1864; 27 December 1864; 10 January 1865; 17 January 1865; 24 January 1865; 24 February 1866; 30 July 1866; 28 August 1866; 13 October 1866; 14 March 1867; 30 July 1867; 4 October 1867; 14 June 1869; 26 July 1869
Richard	2 June 1864; 28 November 1864; 5 December 1864; 4 June 1865; 8 July 1865; 6 August 1865; 21 August 1865; 13 October 1865; 10 November 1865; 7 June 1866
Robert (Margaret's son)	5 November 1867
Robroy	9 January 1868
Rosa (daughter of Lily and Dicky)	28 November 1864; 5 December 1864; 13 February 1867; 3 December 1866; 26 May 1867; 28 May 1867
Ruth (James' wife)	16 June 1866; 5 August 1866; 7 August 1867; 12 August 1867; 15 November 1867; 17 November 1867; 5 November 1868

S

Samuel (formerly Brown)	25 December 1864; 9 January 1865; 21 August 1865; 19 October 1865; 13 August 1866; 27 August 1866; 15 March 1867; 4 June 1867; 1 February 1868
Sandy (Fanny's husband) (Vectis)	28 August 1866; 27 May 1867; 24 August 1867; 26 March 1869
and his two children	26 March 1869
Sarah (Martha)	24 January 1865; 11 July 1865; 27 July 1865; 24 November 1865; 12 December 1865; 19 December 1865; 7 May 1866; 6 October 1866; 1 November 1866; 10 November 1866; 17 January 1867; 28 March 1870
Sem-down	6 June 1866
Sintax	2 June 1864; 9 January 1868
Sissy	17 April 1869; 3 May 1869
Stephen/Steven (Jacky)	13 August 1866; 31 August 1866; 11 September 1866; 19 September 1866; 29 October 1866; 10 November 1866; 15 March 1867; 17 June 1867; 6 July 1867; 7 July 1867; 11 October 1867; 12 October 1867; 1 October 1868; 3 October 1868

Steward/Stuart, Wirremande/Werimanda	1 February 1868; 9 March 1870
Susan (first wife of Timothy)	28 May 1864; 8 July 1864; 10 July 1864; 9 August 1864; 2 September 1864; 18 October 1864; 29 January 1865; 31 January 1865; 21 August 1865; 12 February 1866

T

Talliho (Tallyho, *see* Timothy)	
Tarpot	2 January 1868
Teddy (Mary Ann's husband)	2 June 1864; 22 May 1865; 31 January 1865; 22 February 1866; 18 July 1866; 8 January 1868; 9 January 1868
Timothy (formerly Talliho/Tallyho, Susan's and Tobsy's husband)	28 May 1864; 13 June 1864; 8 July 1864; 10 July 1864; 17 July 1864; 24 October 1864; 26 October 1864; 18 December 1864; 25 December 1864; 29 January 1865; 18 April 1865; 22 April 1865; 1 May 1865; 5 May 1865; 30 May 1865; 23 June 1865; 28 June 1865; 11 April 1865; 27 July 1865; 3 August 1865; 16 October 1865; 20 November 1865; 13 January 1866; 21 February 1866; 22 February 1866; 24 February 1866; 7 May 1866; 28 May 1866; 15 June 1866; 3 July 1866; 3 September 1866; 29 September 1866; 28 November 1866; 8 December 1866; 8 January 1867; 15 March 1867; 5 April 1867; 15 April 1867; 4 June 1867; 10 June 1867; 12 June 1867; 6 July 1867; 7 July 1867; 7 August 1867; 5 January 1868
Timpo/Timpi	25 February 1865; 27 February 1865
Tobsy/Topsy (Timothy's second wife)	5 December 1865; 13 January 1866; 30 January 1866; 3 February 1866; 6 June 1866; 5 April 1867; 15 April 1867; 6 July 1867; 7 July 1867; 5 January 1868; 10 January 1868; 23 February 1869; 28 March 1870
and her son	5 January 1868; 10 January 1868
Tony/Toney (Joshua)	19 May 1864; 8 July 1864, 12 July 1864; 19 July 1864; 22 July 1864; 26 October 1864; 10 April 1865; 21 April 1865; 24 April 1865; 10 June 1867; 28 December 1867; 29 December 1867

EBENEZER MISSION STATION, 1863–1873

W

Waape	28 October 1864
Wimmera Charley	9 August 1864

www.ingramcontent.com/pod-product-compliance
Lightning Source LLC
Chambersburg PA
CBHW042042240426
43667CB00048B/2959